CSS3

JASON CRANFORD TEAGUE

Peachpit Press

Visual QuickStart Guide

CSS3

Jason Cranford Teague

Peachpit Press
1249 Eighth Street
Berkeley, CA 94710
510/524-2178
510/524-2221 (fax)

Find us on the Web at www.peachpit.com
To report errors, please send a note to errata@peachpit.com
Peachpit Press is a division of Pearson Education

Project Editor: Nancy Peterson
Development Editor: Bob Lindstrom
Copyeditors: Anne Marie Walker, Liz Merfeld
Technical Editor: Chris Mills
Production Editor: Cory Borman
Compositor: Danielle Foster
Indexer: Jack Lewis
Cover design: Peachpit Press

ISBN 13: 978-0-321-71963-8

ISBN 0-321-71963-8

9 8 7 6 5 4 3 2 1

Printed and bound in the United States of America

Dedication

For Jocelyn and Dashiel, the two most dynamic forces in my life.

Special Thanks to:

Tara, my soul mate and best critic.

Dad and **Nancy** who made me who I am.

Uncle Johnny, for his unwavering support.

Pat and **Red**, my two biggest fans.

Nancy P., who kept the project going.

Bob and **Anne Marie**, who dotted my i's and made sure that everything made sense.

Chris, who held my feet to the fire on every line of code.

Danielle and **Cory**, who put the book together with great patience and made it look pretty.

Thomas, who was always there when I needed help.

Heather, who gave me a chance when I needed it most.

Judy, Boyd, Dr. G and teachers everywhere who care. Keep up the good work.

Charles Dodgson (aka Lewis Carroll), for writing *Alice's Adventures in Wonderland*.

John Tenniel, for his incredible illustrations of *Alice's Adventures in Wonderland*.

Douglas Adams, **Neil Gaiman**, **Philip K. Dick**, and **Carl Sagan** whose writings inspire me every day.

BBC 6 Music, The Craig Charles Funk and Soul Show, Rasputina, Stricken City, Groove Armada, Electrocute, Twisted Tongue, Bat for Lashes, Cake, Client, Jonathan Coulton, Cracker, Nine Inch Nails, 8mm, KMFDM, Nizlopi, the Pogues, Ramones, New Model Army, Cocteau Twins, the Sisters of Mercy, the Smiths, Mojo Nixon, Bauhaus, Lady Tron, David Bowie, Falco, T. R ex, Bad Religion, The National, Dr. Rubberfunk, Smoove and Turell, JET, Depechee Mode, Ian Dury, The Kinks, This Mortal Coil, Rancid, Monty Python, the Dead Milkmen, New Order, Regina Spektor, The Sex Pistols, Dead Can Dance, Beethoven, Bach, Brahms, Handel, Mozart, Liszt, Vivaldi, Holst, Synergy, and **Garrison Keillor** (for the *Writer's Almanac*) whose noise helped keep me from going insane while writing this book.

Contents at a Glance

Table of Contents

Introduction

These days, everyone is a Web designer. Whether you are adding a comment to a Facebook page, creating your own blog, or building a Fortune 50 Web site, you are involved in Web design.

As the Web expands, everyone from PTA presidents to presidents of multinational corporations is using this medium to get messages out to the world because the Web is the most effective way to communicate your message to the people around you and around the world.

Knowing how to design for the Web isn't always about designing complete Web sites. Many people are creating simple Web pages for auction sites, their own photo albums, or their blogs. So, whether you are planning to redesign your corporate Web site or place your kid's graduation pictures online, learning Cascading Style Sheets (CSS) is your next step into the larger world of Web design.

What Is This Book About?

HTML is how Web pages are structured. CSS is how Web pages are designed. This book deals primarily with how to use CSS to add a visual layer to the HTML structure of your Web pages.

CSS is a style sheet language; that is, it is *not* a programming language. Instead, it's code that tells a device (usually a Web browser) how the content in a file should be displayed. CSS is meant to be easily understood by anyone, not just "computer people." Its syntax is straightforward, basically consisting of rules that tell an element on the screen how it should appear.

This book also includes the most recent additions to the CSS language, commonly referred to as CSS3 (or CSS Level 3). CSS3 builds on and extends the previous version of CSS. For the time being, it's important to understand what is new in CSS3 because some browsers (most notably Internet Explorer) have incomplete support or no support for these new features.

CSS3 Visual QuickStart Guide has three parts:

- **CSS Introduction and Syntax (Chapters 1–4)**—This section lays the foundation you require to understand how to assemble basic style sheets and apply them to a Web page. It also gives you a crash course in HTML5.

- **CSS Properties (Chapters 5–12)**—This section contains all the styles and values that can be applied to the elements that make up your Web pages.

- **Working with CSS. (Chapters 13–15)**—This section gives advice and explains best practices for creating Web pages and Web sites using CSS.

Who is this book for?

To understand this book, you need to be familiar with HTML (Hypertext Markup Language). You don't have to be an expert, but you should know the difference between a `<p>` element and a `<br>` tag. That said, the more knowledge of HTML you bring to this book, the more you'll get out of it.

Chapter 2 deals briefly with HTML5, bringing you up to date on the latest changes. If you are already familiar with HTML, this chapter has everything you will need to get going.

What tools do you need for this book?

The great thing about CSS and DHTML is that, like HTML, they don't require any special or expensive software. Their code is just text, and you can edit it with programs as simple as TextEdit (Mac OS) or NotePad (Windows).

Why Standards (Still) Matter

The idea of a standard way to communicate over the Internet was the principle behind the creation of the World Wide Web: You should be able to transmit information to any computer anywhere in the world and display it in the way the author intended. In the beginning, only one form of HTML existed, and everyone on the Web used it. This situation didn't present any real problem because almost everyone used Mosaic, the first popular graphics-based browser, and Mosaic was the standard. That, as they say, was then.

Along came Netscape Navigator and the first HTML extensions were born. These extensions worked only in Netscape, however, and anyone who didn't use that browser was out of luck. Although the Netscape extensions defied the standards of the World Wide Web Consortium (W3C), most of them—or at least some version of them—eventually became part of those very standards. According to some people, the Web has gone downhill ever since.

The Web is a very public form of discourse, the likes of which has not existed since people lived in villages and sat around the campfire telling stories every night. The problem is that without standards, not everyone in the global village can make it to the Web campfire. You can use as many bleeding-edge techniques as you like. You can include Flash, JavaScript, QuickTime video, Ajax, HTML5, or CSS3 but if only a fraction of browsers can see your work, you're keeping a lot of fellow villagers out in the cold.

When coding for this book, I spent 35 to 45 percent of my time trying to get the code to run as smoothly as possible in Internet Explorer, Firefox (and related Mozilla browsers), Opera, Safari, and Chrome. This timeframe holds true for most of my Web projects; much of the coding time is spent on cross-browser inconsistencies. If the browsers stuck to the standards, this time would be reduced to almost nothing. Your safest bet as a designer, then, is to know the standards of the Web, try to use them as much as possible, and demand that the browser manufacturers use them as well.

Values and Units Used in This Book

Throughout this book, you'll need to enter various values to define properties. These values take various forms, depending on the needs of the property. Some values are straightforward—a number is a number—but others have special units associated with them.

Values in angle brackets (< >) represent one type of value (**Table i.1**) that you will need to choose, such as <length> (a length value like **12px**) or <color> (a color value). Words that appear in code font are literal values and should be typed exactly as shown, such as **normal**, **italic**, or **bold**.

Length values

Length values come in two varieties:

- **Relative values**, which vary depending on the computer being used (**Table i.2**).

- **Absolute values**, which remain constant regardless of the hardware and software being used (**Table i.3**).

I generally recommend using ems to describe font sizes for the greatest stability between operating systems and browsers.

TABLE I.1 Value Types

Value Type	What It Is	Example
<number>	A number	1, 2, 3
<length>	A measurement of distance or size	1in
<color>	A chromatic expression	red
<percentage>	A proportion	35%
<URL>	The absolute or relative path to a file on the Internet	http://www.mySite.net/images/01.jpg

TABLE I.2 Relative Length Values

Unit	Name	What It Is	Example
em	Em	Relative to the current font size (similar to percentage)	3em
ex	x-height	Relative to the height of lowercase letters in the font	5ex
px	Pixel	Relative to the monitor's resolution	125px

TABLE I.3 Absolute Length Values

Unit	Name	What It Is	Example
pt	Point	72pt = 1inch	12pt
pc	Picas	1pc = 12pt	3pc
mm	Millimeters	1mm = .24pc	25mm
cm	Centimeters	1cm = 10mm	5.1cm
in	Inches	1in = 2.54cm	8.25in

Color values

You can describe color on the screen in a variety of ways, but most of these descriptions are just different ways of telling the computer how much red, green, and blue are in a particular color.

Chapter 7 provides an extensive explanation of color values.

Browser-safe Colors?

Certain colors always display properly on any monitor. These colors are called browser-safe colors. You'll find them fairly easy to remember because their values stay consistent. In hexadecimal values, you can use any combination of 00, 33, 66, 99, CC, and FF. In numeric values, use 0, 51, 102, 153, 204, or 255. In percentages, use 0, 20, 40, 60, 80, or 100.

Percentages

Many of the properties in this book have a percentage as their values. The behavior of each percentage value depends on the property in use.

URLs

A Uniform Resource Locator (URL) is the unique address of something on the Web. This resource could be an HTML document, a graphic, a CSS file, a JavaScript file, a sound or video file, a CGI script, or any of a variety of other file types. URLs can be local—describing the location of the resource relative to the current document—or global—describing the absolute location of the resource on the Web and beginning with *http://*.

Reading This Book

For the most part, the text, tables, figures, code, and examples should be self-explanatory. But you need to know a few things in advance to understand this book.

CSS value tables

Each section that explains a CSS property includes a quick-reference table of the values that the property can use, as well as the browsers and CSS levels compatible with those values **Ⓐ**. The Compatibility column displays the first browser version that supported the value type. **Table i.4** lists the browser abbreviations used in this book. Keep in mind, though, that even if the value is available in a particular version of the browser, it may not be available for all operating systems.

TABLE I.4 Browser Abbreviations

Abbreviation	Browser
IE	Microsoft Internet Explorer
FF*	Mozilla Firefox
O	Opera
S	Apple Safari
C	Google Chrome

* Includes other Mozilla-based browsers: Camino and Flock

Cursor Values

Value	Compatibility
<cursor name>	IE4, N6, CSS2
<URL>	CSS2
auto	IE4, N6, CSS2

Values supported by this property

Version of CSS where this value was introduced

Earliest version of the browser in which this value is supported

Ⓐ The property tables in Part 1 of this book show you the values available with a property, the earliest browser version in which the value is available, and with which version of CSS the value was introduced.

The Code

For clarity and precision, this book uses several layout techniques to help you see the difference between the text of the book and the code.

Code looks like this:

```
<style>
p { font-size: 12pt; }
</style>
```

All code in this book is presented in lowercase. In addition, quotes in the code always appear as straight quotes (" or '), not curly quotes (" or '). There is a good reason for this distinction. Curly quotes (also called smart quotes) will cause the code to fail.

When you type a line of code, the computer can run the line as long as needed; but in this book, lines of code have to be broken to make them fit on the page. When that happens, you'll see a gray arrow →, indicating that the line of code is continued from above, like this:

```
.title { font: bold 28pt/26pt times,
 ›serif; color: #FFF; background
 ›color: #000; background-image:
→url(bg_ title.gif); }
```

A numbered step often includes a line of code in red from the main code block:

```
p { color: red; }
```

This is a reference to help you pinpoint where that step applies in the larger code block that accompanies the task. This code will then be highlighted in red in the code listing to help you more easily identify it.

Web Site for This Book

I hope you'll be using a lot of the code from this book in your Web pages, and you are free to use any code in this book without asking my permission (although a mention about the book is always appreciated). However, be careful—retyping information can lead to errors. Some books include a CD-ROM containing all the code from the book, and you can copy it from that disc. But guess who pays for that CD? You do. And CDs aren't cheap.

But if you bought this book, you already have access to the largest resource of knowledge that ever existed: the Web. And that's exactly where you can find the code from this book.

My support site for this Visual QuickStart Guide is at www.speaking-in-styles.com/css3vqs.

This site includes all the code you see in the book, as well as quick-reference charts. You can download the code and any important updates and corrections from this site.

Understanding CSS3

Cascading Style Sheets, or CSS, is a language used to specify the visual appearance of a Web page—in contrast to HTML (HyperText Markup Language), which is a markup language that defines the structure of a document for distribution on the Web. HTML tells a Web browser how the content is organized on the page, whereas CSS tells the browser how it should look.

CSS3, an abbreviation for CSS Level 3, is the next generation of this style language that adds several new capabilities. It may still be under development by the W3C (World Wide Web Consortium), but CSS3 has already taken its place alongside HTML5 at the forefront of all cutting-edge Web design.

What Is a Style?

Word processors allow writers to change text appearance word by word or paragraph by paragraph, as well as in an entire document by means of *styles*.

Styles combine multiple properties—such as weight, font family, italicization, color, and size— that you want to apply to similar text types—titles, headers, captions, and so on—and group these properties under a common name.

Suppose you want all the section titles in your document to be bold, Georgia font, italic, red, and 16 point. You could assign all those attributes to a style called Chapter Title 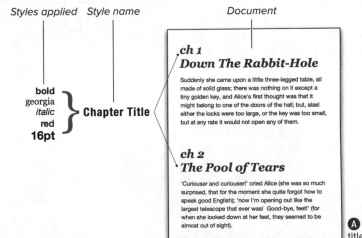.

Whenever you type a chapter title, you only need to use the Chapter Title style, and all those attributes are applied to the text in one fell swoop. Even better, if you later decide that you really want all of those titles to be 18 point instead of 14 point, you can just change the definition of Section Title. The word processor automatically changes the appearance of all the text marked with that style throughout the document.

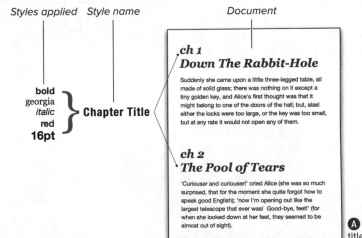

Styles applied　*Style name*　　　　*Document*

bold
georgia
italic
red
16pt
} **Chapter Title**

ch 1
Down The Rabbit-Hole

Suddenly she came upon a little three-legged table, all made of solid glass; there was nothing on it except a tiny golden key, and Alice's first thought was that it might belong to one of the doors of the hall; but, alas! either the locks were too large, or the key was too small, but at any rate it would not open any of them.

ch 2
The Pool of Tears

'Curiouser and curiouser!' cried Alice (she was so much surprised, that for the moment she quite forgot how to speak good English); 'now I'm opening out like the largest telescope that ever was! Good-bye, feet!' (for when she looked down at her feet, they seemed to be almost out of sight).

Ⓐ Styles being applied to section titles in a word-processing page.

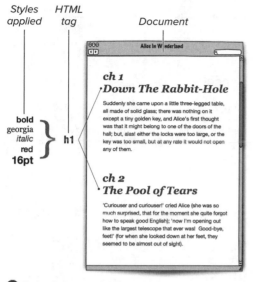

Styles applied — HTML tag — Document

bold
georgia
italic
red
16pt
} h1

A Styles being applied to an HTML tag.

What Are Cascading Style Sheets?

Cascading Style Sheets bring the same style-setting convenience to the Web that you have in most word processors. You can set the CSS in one central location to affect the appearance of specific HTML tags, on a single Web page, or across an entire Web site.

Although CSS works with HTML, it is not HTML. Rather, CSS is a separate *stylesheet language* that enhances the abilities of HTML (a *mark-up language*) by allowing you to redefine the way that existing tags display their content.

For example, the level 1 header tag container, `<h1>...</h1>`, allows you to apply styles to a section of HTML text and turn it into a header. But the exact display of the header is determined by the viewer's browser, not by the HTML code.

Using CSS, you can change the nature of the header tag so that it will be displayed how you want it to look—for example, bold, Times font, italic, red and 14 points **A**. As with word processor styles, you could choose to change the styling of the `<h1>` tag (for example, change the text size to 18pt) which would automatically change the text size of all h1 elements on the affected Web page.

Table 1.1 shows some of the things you can do with CSS and where to find more information in this book.

How does CSS work?

When a visitor loads one of your Web pages, by either typing in the address or clicking a link, the server (the computer that stores the Web page) sends the HTML file to the visitor's computer along with any files linked to or embedded in the HTML file. Regardless of where the CSS code is, the visitor's browser will interpret it and apply it to the HTML to render the Web page using that browser's particular *rendering engine* that is then displayed in the browser window **B**.

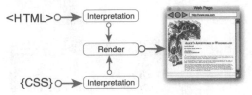

B The code used to create the Web page is downloaded, interpreted, and then rendered by the browser to create the final display.

TABLE 1.1 CSS Properties

Property	What You Control	For More Info, See:
Background	Color or image behind the page or behind a single element on the page	Chapter 7
Box	Margins, padding, outline, borders, width, height	Chapter 10
Color	Text color	Chapter 7
Font	Letter form, size, boldface, italic	Chapter 5
Generated Content	Counting and quotes	Chapter 9
Lists	Bullets and numbering	Chapter 8
Table	Table borders, margins, captions	Chapter 8
Text	Kerning, leading, alignment, case	Chapter 6
Transformations	Moving, rotating, skewing	Chapter 12
Transitions	Changing styles over time	Chapter 12
UI	Cursor	Chapter 9
Visual effect	visibility, visible area, opacity	Chapter 11
Visual formatting	Position and placement	Chapter 11

C An HTML page using CSS to add an image in the background. Position the content down and to the right, and format the text.

D The same code displayed without the benefit of CSS. The page still displays but without the formatting of **C**.

The interpretation by the browser's rendering engine is where your headaches begin. The W3C has gone to great lengths to create specifications by which browser developers should render the Web code. Nonetheless, bugs, omissions, and misinterpretations still creep in, meaning that no two browsers will render a Web page in exactly the same way. For the most part, these differences go unnoticed by most users, but occasionally the differences are glaring and require that you do some extra work to get the page to look right with the broadest spectrum of browsers.

TIP You always face the possibility that your page will be rendered *without* the CSS because of an error or because the device in use does not accommodate CSS, such as with many mobile phone browsers. You should always consider how your page will look without the CSS styles, and make sure that, structurally, the page will still make sense, as shown in **C** and **D**.

The Evolution of CSS

Over the years, CSS has evolved under the guidance of the W3C into its current form, but the process has often been slow. Although CSS is a standard—created by the W3C's CSS Working Group—it is up to each browser to interpret and implement that standard. This has led to uneven implementation, with some browsers way ahead of others 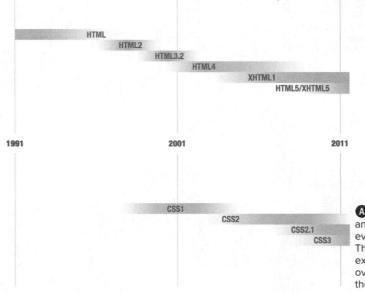.

Even more troublesome is that, although the standard strives to be as clear and specific as possible, different browsers will implement the specifications with slightly different quirks.

All modern browsers (Internet Explorer, Firefox, Safari, Opera) support CSS2 (which includes CSS1 and CSS-Positioning). However, after years of development, CSS3 remains a work in progress, supported by some browsers (Firefox, Safari, and Opera) but still under development in others (Internet Explorer).

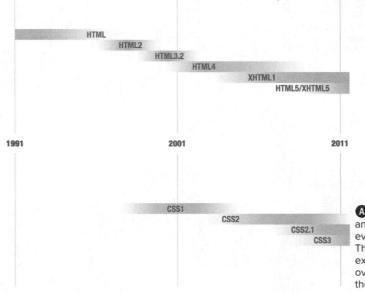

Ⓐ The evolutionary paths of HTML and CSS have not been particularly even or steady over the years. This timeline is not meant to be an exact chart, but provides a general overview of when each version of the standard was in its prime.

CSS Level 1 (CSS1)

The W3C released the first official version of CSS in 1996. This early version included the core capabilities associated with CSS, such as the ability to format text, set fonts, and set margins. Netscape 4 and Internet Explorer 3 and 4 support Level 1.

Web designers needed a way to position elements on the screen precisely. CSS1 was already released, and CSS Level 2 was still in the future, so the W3C released a stopgap solution: CSS-Positioning. This standard proposed that the parties concerned could debate for awhile before the CSS-P standard became official. Netscape and Microsoft jumped on these proposals, however, and included the preliminary ideas in version 4 of their browsers.

CSS Level 2 (CSS2)

The CSS2 spec came out in 1998 and is the most widely adopted by browser makers. Level 2 includes all the attributes of the previous two versions, plus an increased emphasis on international accessibility and the capability to specify media-specific CSS.

In 2006, the W3C published an updated version: CSS Level 2.1, which corrected some errors, clarified a few issues, and included specifications for features that had already been implemented in some browsers. CSS2.1 has effectively replaced CSS2.

CSS Level 3 (CSS3)

Unlike CSS1 and 2, a single, comprehensive CSS3 does not exist. Instead, rather than trying to release the entire specification at once, the CSS Working Group has split the spec into a series of modules; each of which has its own developmental timeline.

http://www.w3.org/Style/CSS/current-work

TIP While knowing the differences between the CSS versions may be interesting, it isn't necessary for using styles on the Web. What you do need to know is which styles are supported by the browsers you're designing for. Although all modern browsers support most of the CSS Level 2 specification, older browsers support combinations of older versions of CSS. Appendix A details which CSS properties each browser supports.

CSS and HTML

When HTML was first created, style properties were defined directly in the code. However, rather than just adding more and more tags to HTML, the W3C (see the sidebar "What is the World Wide Web Consortium?") introduced Cascading Style Sheets to fill the design void in straight HTML, allowing the Web to become semantic in structure.

Take the **<strong>** tag, for example. In HTML, this common tag does one thing and one thing only: It makes text "stronger," usually by making it bolder. However, using CSS, you can "redefine" the **<strong>** tag so that it not only makes text bolder, but also displays text in all caps and in a particular font to add more emphasis. You could even make the **<strong>** tag *not* make text bold.

Although both HTML and CSS have evolved over the years, they have rarely evolved in tandem. Instead, each standard has pretty much followed its own path. However, both CSS3 and HTML5 will be hitting primetime over the next few years, creating the new foundation and framework for modern Web sites.

The power of CSS comes from its ability to mix and match rules from different sources to tailor your Web pages' layout to your exact needs. In some ways, it resembles computer programming—which is not too surprising, because a lot of this stuff was created by programmers instead of designers. But once you get the hang of it, "speaking" CSS will become as natural as putting together a sentence Ⓐ.

Ⓐ The three core Web technologies (HTML, CSS, and JavaScript) work in ways that are similar to parts of speech. HTML provides the nouns, CSS the adjectives and adverbs, and JavaScript adds the verbs.

Types of CSS Rules

The best thing about cascading style sheets is that they are amazingly simple to set up. They don't require plug-ins or fancy software—just text files with rules in them. A CSS rule defines what the HTML should look like and how it should behave in the browser window.

CSS rules come in three types, each with specific uses:

- **HTML selector.** The text portion of an HTML tag is called the *selector*. For example, **h1** is the selector for the **<h1>** tag. The HTML selector is used in a CSS rule to redefine how the tag displays. (See "(re)Defining an HTML Tag" in Chapter 3). For example:

  `h1 { color: red; }`

  will style:

  `<h1>...</h1>`

- **Class.** A *class* is a "free agent" rule that can be applied to any HTML tag at your discretion. You can name the class almost anything you want. Because a class can be applied to multiple HTML tags, it is the most versatile type of selector. (See "Defining Reusable Classes" in Chapter 3). For example:

  `.myClass { font: bold 1.25em`
  `→ times; }`

  will style:

  `<h1 class="myClass">...</h1>`

continues on next page

- **ID.** Much like class selectors, *ID rules* can be applied to any HTML tag. *ID selectors,* however, should be applied only once to a particular HTML tag on a given page to create an object for use with a JavaScript function. For example:

```
#myObject1 { position: absolute;
→ top: '10px; }
```

will style:

```
<h1 id="myObject1">...</h1>
```

What Is the World Wide Web Consortium?

The World Wide Web Consortium (www.w3.org) is an organization that sets many of the standards that browser developers eventually use to create their products, including HTML and CSS, with the notable exception of JavaScript.

Created in 1994, the W3C's mission is "to lead the World Wide Web to its full potential by developing common protocols that promote its evolution and ensure its interoperability."

The W3C comprises more than 400 member organizations around the world. These organizations include vendors of technology products and services, content providers, corporate users, research laboratories, standards bodies, and governments.

According to its Web site, the W3C has four goals:

- **Web for Everyone.** To make the Web accessible to all people by promoting technologies that take into account the vast differences in culture, education, ability, material resources, and physical limitations of users on all continents.

- **Web on Everything.** To allow all devices easy access to the Web. Although most access is still through desktop or laptop computers, an increasing array of devices can access the Web.

- **Knowledge Base.** To develop an environment that permits each user to make the best use of the resources available on the Web.

- **Trust and Confidence.** To guide the Web's development with careful consideration for the novel legal, commercial, and social issues raised by this technology.

```
  HTML, Class,
    or ID                 Declaration
┌─────┴─────┐   ┌──────────┴──────────┐
selector { property: value; }
└────────────────────┬────────────────────┘
                   Rule
```

A The basic syntax of a CSS rule. This starts with a selector (HTML, Class, or ID). Then add a property, a value for that property, and a semicolon, which together are called a definition. You can add as many definitions as you need as long as they are separated by a semicolon.

The Parts of a CSS Rule

All rules, regardless of their locations or types, have the following structural elements:

- **Selectors** are the alphanumeric characters that identify a rule. A selector can be an HTML tag selector, a class selector, an ID selector, a universal selector (discussed in Chapter 3) or a combination of those basic selectors to create context-based styles (discussed in Chapter 4).

- **Properties** identify what is being defined. Several dozen properties are available; each is responsible for an aspect of the page content's behavior and appearance.

- **Values** are assigned to a property to define its nature. A value can be a keyword such as "red," a number, or a percentage. The type of value used depends solely on the property to which it is assigned.

After the selector **A**, a CSS rule consists of properties and their values, which together are referred to as a *declaration*. A single CSS rule can have multiple declarations separated by a semicolon (;).

Browser CSS extensions

In addition to supporting the specified CSS properties set by the W3C, a browser developer will occasionally introduce browser-specific properties. This is often done for one of two reasons:

- A spec is still under development by the W3C but the browser developer wants to start using the style now.

- The browser developer wants to try a new idea but doesn't want to wait for the W3C to accept it and begin work on it, which can take years.

Sometimes the exact syntax of the official CSS specification will be slightly different from the "sand-box" version created for a specific browser.

To avoid confusion and ensure forward compatibility of CSS code, each rendering engine has adapted its own prefix to use with CSS properties that are extensions unique to that browser. The prefixes for each browser are shown in **Table 1.2**.

These CSS extensions sometimes overlap and conflict when different browsers promote their own solutions. The good news is that due to the nature of CSS, you can include versions of each of the properties for individual browsers, so that the browser will use whichever version suits it **B**. Throughout the book, I include browser CSS extensions, when appropriate, so that you can ensure the widest interoperability of your styles.

TIP Although you don't have to include a semicolon with the last definition in a list, experience shows that adding this semicolon can prevent future headaches. For example, if you later decide to add a new definition to the rule and forget to put in the required semicolon before the addition, you may cause the rule to fail completely. What's worse, not only will that one definition will fail, but all the definitions in the rule won't be used.

```
selector { -moz-property: value;
           -webkit-property: value;
           -o-property: value;
           -ms-property: value;
           property: value;  }
```

B The browser CSS extensions can all be included as available to ensure that the style is applied if available to a particular browser.

TIP Most browser manufacturers will drop an extension version of a style within two releases after they adopt the official version. This practice allows designers to catch up before their style sheets stop working.

TIP Don't confuse the selector of an HTML tag with its attributes. In the following tag, for example, `img` is the selector, and `src` is an attribute:

```
<img src="picture.gif">
```

TABLE 1.2 CSS Browser Extensions

Extension	Rendering Engine	Browser(s)	Example
-moz-	Mozilla	Firefox, Camino	-moz-border-radius
-ms-	Trident	Internet Explorer	-ms-layout-grid
-o-	Presto	Opera	-o-border-radius
-webkit-	Webkit	Chrome, Safari	-webkit-border-radius

A The "New in CSS3" mark.

New in CSS3

This is a particularly exciting time to be a Web designer, because we are about to get an entirely new palette of tools. A lot of new capabilities in CSS3 are ready for prime time (or will be soon) that will explode your creativity.

This slim volume covers the breadth of CSS3, much of which remains unchanged since CSS2/2.1. If you are an old hand at CSS, look for the "New in CSS3" mark A which will help you quickly find the good stuff.

Here's a brief peak at what's new:

- **Borders**—Multiple border colors on a side, border images, and rounded corners

- **Backgrounds**—Multiple backgrounds can be added to a single element, backgrounds can be more precisely positioned, backgrounds can be extended and clipped to the inside or outside of a border, and backgrounds can be resized.

- **Color**—Color opacity settings, gradients in backgrounds, and HSL color values

- **Text**—Text shadows, text overflow, and word wrapping

- **Transformations**—Scale, skew, move, and rotate an element in 2D or 3D space.

- **Transitions**—Simple dynamic style transitions

- **Box**—Add Drop shadows, place user-resizable boxes, set overflow separately in horizontal and vertical directions, use outline offset to set space between the outline and the border, apply box model specifications to set how width and height are applied to a box.

continues on next page

- **Content**—Styles can add content to an element.

- **Opacity**—Elements can be transparent.

- **Media**—Style pages based on the viewport size, color, aspect ratio, resolution and other important design considerations.

- **Web fonts**—Updates and extends the ability to link to fonts for use in a design.

Not everything in the CSS3 specification is ready to be used, though (see "CSS3 and the Promise of Internet Explorer 9"). When it would be jumping the gun to start using new features right now, I've added a section near the end of some chapters called "Coming Soon!" with quick overviews of what to expect in the future.

CSS3 and the Promise of Internet Explorer 9

Currently Internet Explorer accounts for around 70 percent of browser usage. Most of this represents IE8 users; slightly fewer IE7 users; and a small but still significant number of IE6 users.

None of these browsers support CSS3.

You can use some workarounds. Occasionally, an IE-specific code performs a similar function to the CSS3 code, and in a few (rare) cases a CSS3 property that's been around for awhile has made it into IE8. For the most part, however, the segment of your audience that uses Internet Explorer will be left out in the cold if you use CSS3.

But hark, what's this appearing on the horizon? It's IE9, which Microsoft has double-secret-pinky sworn will completely and fully support every last detail in the CSS3 specification, or at least the important ones. This is great news, but as of this writing, IE9 is still in Beta, with no clear release date. And even after its release it will be sometime before IE6, 7, and 8 disappear.

For now, I suggest that you use CSS3 only as a *design enhancement*, unless you *know* your audience will not be using Internet Explorer—for example, if you are developing iPhone apps. The design enhancement a concept is explained in more detail in Chapter 12.

HTML5 Primer

HTML5 is the next big thing for frontend Web development. Although it's still under development and yet to be implemented in some browsers (most notably Internet Explorer) you can use some simple work-arounds and HTML5 has gone to great lengths to maintain backward compatibility. With only a few tricks, you can implement HTML5 today while making sure it works with older browsers.

Let's take a look at what markup languages are and how HTML5 fits into the new world order.

What Is HTML?

The HyperText Markup Language is simply a system of *tags* that define *elements* on the page, which create the *structure* of a document for use on the Web. For example, you take a block of text **A** and add HTML tags, as follows: **B**

```
<h1>Alice In Wonderland</h1>
```

Here, you've used the **<h1>** tag to create a header element which is the most important header for the page: the level 1 header. Different tags are used to tag different kinds of elements, and tags can be placed within other tags. For example:

```
<p>I wonder if I shall fall right
⟶ <em>through</em> the earth!</p>
```

These tags tell the browser that the text is a paragraph, and the word "through" should be presented with emphasis, probably by displaying it in italics.

Alice in Wonderland

I wonder if I shall fall right through the earth!

A Plain text without any markup.

B The same text content with HTML tags applied.

Basic HTML Document Structure

All HTML documents have similar basic structure, which includes the following elements:

- **Doctype (`<!DOCTYPE>`)** sets the type of markup language the document is using (**Table 2.4**). This is important to include so that the browser can quickly and accurately interpret the HTML code.

- **Head (`<head>`)** includes information *about* the page, such as the title and meta tags. You should also place links to external CSS and JavaScript files in this area. The head should not be confused with a page *header*. Nothing in the head of the page will be directly displayed in the body.

- **Body (`<body>`)** contains the elements you actually see in the Web browser window, such as navigation, headers, paragraphs, list, table, images, and much more.

HTML Properties

HTML elements can be modified by placing HTML *properties* within the tag. Some properties are optional, some improve the performance of the element, and some are needed for an element to work properly. For example, the anchor tag (`<a>`) uses the **href** property to define where a link is pointing:

```
<a href="http://www.jasonspeaking.com">
   Jason
</a>
```

Properties are also used to connect an HTML element to styles using the style, class, or id properties:

```
<p style="color: red;">Alice</a>
<p class="hilight char names">Alice
→ </a>
<p id="name01">Alice</a>
```

Every tag has one or more properties that can be applied to them. These become especially important when we start using CSS to style tags based on property values, as explained in Chapter 4.

HTML and CSS

Most HTML tags have *browser inherited styles* associated with them. These default styles are actually defined by the Web browser developer. Because the browser developer has added them, you need to remember that they are there and will affect your design. For example, the **<em>** tag will italicize text on most browsers. No cosmic constant dictates that emphasized text is italicized; it's just that the guys and gals programming the browser software decided to do it that way. The good news is that you can use CSS to override the browser styles.

For the most part, default styles are consistent from browser to browser, although some noticeable differences exist, especially with margins and font size. Many designers will start "from scratch" by resetting as many of the defaults as possible using a CSS reset (see Chapter 14).

What Is SVG?

The Scalable Vector Graphics (SVG) format is a method for creating vector graphics on the Web (see w3.org/Graphics/SVG/). Like Flash, instead of plotting each point in a graphic, SVG data describes two points and then plots the path between them as a straight line or curve.

Although it still lags behind Flash in browser penetration, SVG is natively supported in Firefox, Safari, and Chrome. The holdout is Microsoft's Internet Explorer, which will not have SVG support until version 9. (Adobe does provide an IE plug-in at www.adobe.com/svg.)

Unlike Flash, which uses an editor to create files and hides much of its graphics code, SVG is a mark-up language that can be freely read.

element	element	element

A Inline elements flow horizontally using a soft line break when reaching the edge of its parent element.

Types of HTML Elements

HTML includes a large number of elements, each with its own specific tag and use for structuring documents. Elements can generally be sorted into two categories:

- **Inline elements** have no line breaks associated with the element **A**. **Table 2.1** lists the inline-tag selectors that CSS can use.

continues on next page

TABLE 2.1 HTML Selectors for Inline Elements

Selector	HTML Use	Selector	HTML Use
a	Anchored link	label	Label for form element
abbr	Abbreviation	legend	Title in fieldset
address	A physical address	link	Resource reference
area	Area in image map	mark*	Marked text
audio*	Sound content	meter*	Measurement range
bm	Bold text	nav*	Navigation links
cite	Short citation	optgroup	Group of form options
code	Code text	option	An option in a drop-down list
del	Deleted text	q	Short quote
details*	Details of an element	small	Small print
dfn	Defined term	select	Selectable list
command*	Command button	source*	Media resource
datalist*	Drop-down list	span	Localized style formatting
em	Emphasis	strong	Strong emphasis
font	Font appearance	sub	Subscript
i	Italic	summary*	Details header
iframe	Inline sub-window	sup	Superscript
img	Image embedding	tbody	Table body
input	Input field	td	Table data
ins	Inserted text	time*	Date/time
keygen*	Generated key in form	var	Variable
kbd	Keyboard text		

* New in HTML5

- **Block-level elements** place a line break before and after the element **B**. **Table 2.2** lists the block-level element selectors that CSS can use.

element
element
element

B Block-level elements stack vertically on top of each other.

TABLE 2.2 HTML Selectors for Block-level Elements

Selector	HTML Use	Selector	HTML Use
article*	Article content	header*	Section or page header
aside*	Aside content	hgroup*	Groups header information
blockquote	Long quotation	hr	Horizontal rule
body	Page body	li	List item
br	Line break	map	Image map
button	Push button	object	Object embedding
canvas*	Draw area	ol	Ordered list
caption	Table caption	output*	Form output
col	Table column	p	Paragraph
colgroup	Group of table columns	pre	Preformatted text
dd	Definition description	progress*	Displays progress of time consuming task
div	Division	section*	Section in Web page
dl	Definition list	table	Table
dt	Definition term	tbody	Table body
embed	External content	textarea	Form text input area
fieldset	Fieldset label	tfoot	Table footer
figcaption*	Figure Caption	th	Table header
figure*	Groups media content and caption	thead	Table header
footer*	Section or page footer	tr	Table row
form	Input form	ul	Unordered list
h1–6	Heading levels 1–6	video*	video player
head	Information about the page		

* New in HTML5

Not all CSS definitions can be applied to all HTML elements. Whether a particular CSS property can be applied (or not) depends on the nature of the element. For the most part, it's fairly obvious when a property can be applied.

For example, you wouldn't expect the text-indent property, which indents the first line of a paragraph, to apply to an inline tag such as **<b>;** in fact, it can't be applied. When you do need help in this area, see Appendix A to determine the CSS properties that can be applied to specific HTML elements.

The Evolution of HTML5

HTML5 is the next step in Web markup and will take over from XHTML. Although XHTML2 was in development for almost eight years, it was laid to rest in 2009 in favor of HTML5.

To understand how this happened, let's take a little trip back to the halcyon days of the Web at the end of the twentieth century—1997, to be precise. It was still a Web 1.0 world, although we didn't yet know to call it that. The dotcom bubble was just starting to inflate, and everyone was surfing the Web with Netscape Navigator. Into that landscape the World Wide Web Consortium (W3C) introduced HTML 4.0 (HTML4).

HTML4 was a vast improvement, because for the first time it was created by a standards body that gave everyone a seat at the table and believed that Web pages should display the same across all available browsers.

And then came XHTML

XHTML 1 (released in 2001) is a rewriting of the HTML 4.01 standard using XML, and was intended to bring the power of XML to Web page development. XHTML uses the XML Doctype. XHTML employs all the same tags as HTML, but the code will still work with a browser that does not understand XML.

Although XHTML 2 was primarily meant to be a transitional technology to a brave new Web technology, from its very beginning, something went horribly wrong.

The problem with XHTML2

It was quickly realized that even XHTML 1 was not enough to evolve the Web from its relatively static "page" nature into a truly interactive and universal environment of applications. XHTML2 was meant to change all of that. Starting in August 2002, the authors of the XHTML standard began crafting a new language that they hoped would completely retool Web markup for the twenty-first century, bringing about a golden age of semantic Web pages, interactivity, internationalization, device independence, and tapioca pudding for everyone! But they forgot one thing: XHTML2 was not written to be backward compatible with older Web markup languages. Existing browsers would not be able to run this whiz-bang new markup language. Web developers would have to develop one version of their site for older browsers and another for the XHTML2 standard.

And then there was HTML5

In June 2003, HTML5 started life as Web Applications 1.0 and was created by the Web HyperText Application Technology Working Group (WHATWG), an organization that was not associated with the W3C. Instead, this independent group, frustrated with the slow pace and errant direction that XHTML2 was taking, began working on an alternative standard that would be backward compatible, more suitable for writing applications *and* pages, and would also address many practical issues that Web developers faced.

For several years, both languages were developed simultaneously. But in 2007, seeing that Web Applications 1.0 was further along than XHTML2, the W3C adapted it as the starting point for a new HTML5 standard, publishing the "First Public Working Draft" of the specification on January 22, 2008. To focus attention on HTML5, the W3C did not renew the XHTML Working Group's charter and XHTML2 was no more.

Is it HTML5 or XHTML5?

Although XHTML2 has disappeared, the need to unify XML and HTML has not. Therefore, a parallel initiative exists to create XHTML5. To be clear, this is *not* a new or different markup language; it is simply HTML5 written using XML rules and is similar to XHTML.

If you know XHTML, then learning XHTML5 should not be difficult. They differ primarily in the ways they treat tags. Some of the most important differences are listed in **Table 2.3**.

Whether you use HTML5 or XHTML5 is your call. But, honestly, I'm enjoying the more forgiving nature of HTML5, and it's what I'm using for the code in this book.

TABLE 2.3 HTML5 vs. XHTML5

	XHTML5	HTML5
Tag case	lowercase	upper or lowercase
Closing tags	required	optional
Self closing tags	required	optional
MIME type	application/xml *or* application/xhtml+xml	text/html
Well-formedness errors	fatal	not fatal

What's Not in HTML5?

HTML5 includes several changes. But if you want to start using it today, you also need to know what is *not* available anymore. The frame tags—frameset, frame, noframes—have been eliminated, but the iframe is still available. Most presentation tags have been eliminated—such as basefont, big, center, font, s, strike, tt, u—and although b (bold) and I (italic) are still included, some debate continues over that decision.

Also, unlike XHTML, stand-alone tags such as `<img>` and `<br>` will not have to be self-closing. So, rather than using `<br />`, it's back to just `<br>`. But really, isn't that a lot simpler?

What's New in HTML5?

HTML5 makes important structural changes to Web pages. For example, you can specify common elements such as headers, footers, articles, and asides. In addition, HTML5 introduces many features natively (that is, features built into the browser) that used to require plug-ins and/or scripting in the form of new elements and APIs:

- **The Canvas element** allows scriptable bitmap editing.

- **Document editing** permits users to edit content directly in Web pages.

- **Web forms** self validate and include more input types.

- **Drag-and-drop** allows the manipulation of elements without scripting.

- **Audio and Video Timed media playback** enables native control of media files without plug-ins.

- **New structural elements** remove the burden of using `<div>` tags with classes and IDs to create common elements such as headers and footers.

HTML5 is where Web design and development is headed. Many browsers have already started supporting some of its features, even though it's not yet a complete standard, yet. That said, one notable (and frequent) support curmudgeon is Internet Explorer. However, Microsoft has pledged to introduce HTML5 support in IE version 9.

How Does HTML5 Structure Work?

I'll let you in on a little secret: You can start using the HTML5 syntax today to structure your Web pages and use it with CSS3 (or older versions of CSS). To understand how, let's take a look at how HTML5 works.

One of the most significant changes in HTML5 is the addition of structural elements that will greatly enhance the semantic philosophy behind Web markup 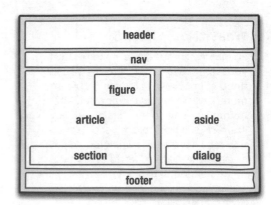. Most of the new structural tags are self-explanatory, but a few require some elaboration:

- **<header>** can be used for page headers, section headers, article headers, or an aside header.

- **<nav>** can be included independently or as part of the header and/or footer.

- **<section>** defines the main parts of a page, generally one that includes articles.

- **<article>** is an individual blog entry or blog entry abstract.

- **<figure>** is used to contain images, audio, and video that are embedded in the page.

- **<dialog>** replaces the **<dl>** element to contain conversation transcripts.

- **<aside>** is used for support content on a page, such as related links, secondary navigation, and of course, ads.

- **<footer>** is similar to the header and can be placed at the bottom of other elements.

Unfortunately, not all browsers are equipped to understand HTML5 without a little help.

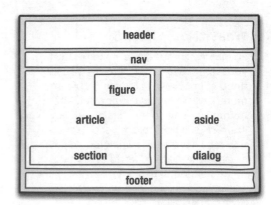

Ⓐ The wireframe of a typical HTML5 document.

Code 2.1 *HTML5page.html*—This shows a typical HTML5 page that is structured to use a header, navigation, article, aside, and footer for the layout grid.

```
<!DOCTYPE html>
<html dir="ltr" lang="en-US">
  <head>
    <meta charset="utf-8">
    <title>HTML5</title>
  </head>
  <body>
    <header>
      <nav></nav>
    </header>
    <section>
      <article>
        <header></header>
          <figure></figure>
        <footer></footer>
      </article>
        <dialog><dialog>
    </section>
    <aside></aside>
    <footer></footer>
  </body>
</html>
```

Using HTML5 Structure Now

HTML5 is not implemented on most current browsers (and it may be some time before it is), but you can follow some steps now to prepare for the future.

Although CSS can be applied to any version of HTML in use today—including XHTML 1 and HTML 4.01—I'll be using HTML5 throughout this book. This book is by no means an exhaustive resource of HTML5. However, I want to show you how to set up the basic Web document that I'll reference in future chapters.

Setting up a basic HTML5 document:

1. Add the HTML5 doctype (**Table 2.4**). Notice that the new !DOCTYPE for HTML5 is much simpler than the complex and hard-to-decipher HTML and XHTML doctypes in use today (**Code 2.1**). It simply tells the browser to use HTML.

   <!DOCTYPE html>

continues on next page

TABLE 2.4 Doctypes

Markup Language	Doctype Code
HTML 4.01 Loose	<!DOCTYPE HTML PUBLIC "-//W3C//DTD HTML 4.01 Transitional//EN" "http://www.w3.org/TR/html4/loose.dtd">
HTML 4.01 Strict	<!DOCTYPE HTML PUBLIC "-//W3C//DTD HTML 4.01//EN" "http://www.w3.org/TR/html4/strict.dtd">
HTML 4.01 Frameset	<!DOCTYPE HTML PUBLIC "-//W3C//DTD HTML 4.01 Frameset//EN" "http://www.w3.org/TR/html4/frameset.dtd">
XHTML1 Transitional	<!DOCTYPE html PUBLIC "-//W3C//DTD XHTML 1.0 Transitional//EN" "http://www.w3.org/TR/xhtml1/DTD/xhtml1-transitional.dtd">
XHTML1 Strict	<!DOCTYPE html PUBLIC "-//W3C//DTD XHTML 1.0 Strict//EN" "http://www.w3.org/TR/xhtml1/DTD/xhtml1-strict.dtd">
XHTML1 Frameset	<!DOCTYPE html PUBLIC "-//W3C//DTD XHTML 1.0 Frameset//EN" "http://www.w3.org/TR/xhtml1/DTD/xhtml1-frameset.dtd">
HTML5/XHTML5	<!DOCTYPE html>

2. Add the HTML tag, including the intended language and the language direction (generally **ltr** for left-to-right text).

```
<html dir="ltr" lang="en-US">...
→ </html>
```

3. Add the head to your document, which is where you will specify information about this document, including the title and the character set used by the text. I recommend using UTF-8 for best results.

```
<head>...</head>
```

4. Add the body to your document. This is where all the content to be displayed is added. I recommend giving every body element in your site at least one unique class name and others to identify its location in the site. By doing so, you can add styles on a per-page and per-section basis without including multiple CSS files.

```
<body class="section Name
→ pageName">...</body>
```

5. Add the header tag for your page. This is *not* the same as the head tag in step 3. This is where you put all the content that is displayed in your Web pages header. You can also include the navigation here or include it separately, depending on your design needs.

```
<header>...</header>
```

6. Add the navigation tag, and include links to the top-level pages in your site.

```
<nav>...</nav>
```

7. Add one or more article tags, which will contain the important content on this page. Many Web browsers and RSS newsreaders will now allow the user to focus on the articles to get to the main content of the page. Figures and sections fit well here.

   `<article>...</article>`

8. Add the aside tag, which is where supplemental content to the article is placed. This is also sometimes called a sidebar or rail, depending on who you talk to. It can include anything you want, but I like putting comments and dialog over here.

   `<aside>...</aside>`

9. Finally, add a footer tag at the bottom of the page. This generally includes redundant top-level navigation, copyrights, and other small print.

   `<footer>...</footer>`

And that's it. You are ready to start using HTML5 tags. Go crazy. Oh, wait, that's right: it works in everything *but* Internet Explorer, which just happens to make up the majority of browsers in use today. So, what do you do?

Making HTML5 work in Internet Explorer

Although Internet Explorer does not know HTML5 tags, there is a partial fix (or kludge) that involves using JavaScript to create the HTML5 elements:

document.createElement('header');

Referred to as the "HTML5 Shiv," this will "teach" Internet Explorer 6 (and later versions) that these elements exist, and that they should be treated as HTML tags. You can add one of these lines of JavaScript for each of the HTML5 elements you need.

To make it simple to add these new tags, create an external JavaScript file (**Code 2.2**) and link to it from your HTML document using the IE conditional (**Code2.3**), which you'll explore in greater detail in Chapter 13.

Code 2.2 *HTML5forIE.js*—This adds a blank HTML tag for each of the HTML5 tags that Internet Explorer is missing.

```
/*** CSS VQS - Chapter 2 - HTML5forIE.js ***/
document.createElement('abbr');
document.createElement('article');
document.createElement('aside');
document.createElement('audio');
document.createElement('bb');
document.createElement('canvas');
document.createElement('datagrid');
document.createElement('datalist');
document.createElement('details');
document.createElement('dialog');
document.createElement('eventsource');
document.createElement('figure');
document.createElement('footer');
document.createElement('header');
document.createElement('hgroup');
document.createElement('mark');
document.createElement('menu');
document.createElement('meter');
document.createElement('nav');
document.createElement('output');
document.createElement('progress');
document.createElement('section');
document.createElement('time');
document.createElement('video');
```

Why Use a Doctype?

If you do not use a doctype, modern browsers are forced into Quirks mode. That's a bad situation if you are creating new Web pages because it leaves the interpretation of the code solely to the discretion of the browsers, which can translate into a lot of display inconsistencies.

If you do not include the doctype in your Web page, newer browsers may not recognize all of your code.

Code 2.3 *HTML5page.html*—This includes a link to the JavaScript in Code 2.2.

```html
<!DOCTYPE html>
<html dir="ltr" lang="en-US">
  <head>
    <meta charset="utf-8">
    <title>HTML5</title>

  <!--[if IE ]>
    <script src="script/HTML5forIE.js"
    → type="text/javascript"></script>
  <![endif]-->

  </head>
  <body class="pageName">
    <header></header>
    <nav></nav>
    <article>
      <figure></figure>
      <section></section>
    </article>
    <aside>
      <dialog></dialog>
    </aside>
    <footer></footer>
  </body>
</html>
```

Code 2.4 *HTML5forIE.js*—This does the same job as Code 2.2 but uses a JavaScript loop, making the code more compact.

```javascript
/*** CSS VQS - Chapter 2 - HTML5forIE.js ***/
(function(){if(!/*@cc_on!@*/0)return;var e =
→ "abbr,article,aside,audio,bb,canvas,
→ datagrid,datalist,details,dialog,
→ eventsource,figure,footer,header,hgroup,
→ mark,menu,meter,nav,output,progress,
→ section,time,video".split(',');
→ for(var i=0;i<e.length;i++)
→ {document.createElement(e[i])}})()
```

TIP If you want to get fancy, replace Code 2.2 with the JavaScript loop shown in **Code 2.4**. This has the same effect but is more compact.

TIP The document in this example has been structured to address my needs, but you needn't follow hard and fast rules for tag placement and nesting. You can place the navigation in the header, the footer, the article, or aside. Similarly, figures can go in the aside or the head. The preceding example is just a basic common Web page structure.

Putting It All Together

1. **Create a new HTML file.** I recommend using TextEdit on Mac or SimpleText on Windows. I do *not* recommend Microsoft Word because it can add invisible code that creates problems.

2. **Add a doctype.** For our purposes, the HTML5 doctype is the one to use.

3. **Add the <html>…</html> tag.** Optionally, you can also add the language and direction properties.

4. **Add the <head>…</head> tag.** The head is where all of the information *about* the page goes.

5. **Add the <title>…</title> tag.** This is where you want to place the title of your Web page that will appear in the Windows title bar.

6. **Place any <meta> tags you need into the head.** Meta tags provide the information about the page, such as author, language, and copyright.

7. **Add a link to the IE JavaScript HTML5 shiv.** You will need to create that as an external file and then link to it here. If you need the code, grab it from www.speaking-in-styles.com/ie5shiv.

8. **Add the <body>…</body> tag.** The body is where everything that appears in the Web page will be placed. In later chapters you will also learn to add a class and/or ID to this tag to help differentiate it from other pages in the site.

9. **Save this as index.html.** You now have an empty HTML5 Web document, ready for your CSS3.

CSS Basics

CSS lets you control all the elements of your document's appearance—fonts, text, colors, backgrounds, sizes, borders, spacing, positioning, visual effects, tables, and lists. However, the real power of using CSS for styles is that you can change the appearance of every page on your Web site by changing only a few lines of CSS code.

With savvy use of CSS, you can start with a plain page of text, and by adding visual design and interaction, turn it into a webbed environment.

The Basic CSS Selectors

CSS works by defining the styles of the elements on a Web page using *CSS rules*. Rules are applied using *selectors*, which come in three basic varieties: HTML selectors are used to reference a specific tag; class selectors, which are applied individually to elements; or an ID selector that is applied to a single element on the page (**Table 3.1**). You will use these three basic selectors constantly, and they are the best place to start. In Chapter 4, you will learn about using other selectors for creating more selective styling.

TABLE 3.1 Basic Selectors

Format	Selector Name	What Elements Are Styled	Compatibility
a	HTML	All specified HTML tags	IE4, FF1, S1, C1, O3.5, CSS1
.myClass	Class	Any HTML tag where class is applied	IE4, FF1, S1, C1, O3.5, CSS1
a.myClass	Dependent Class	Specified HTML tag where class is applied	IE4, FF1, S1, C1, O3.5, CSS1
#myID	ID	Any HTML tag where ID applied	IE4, FF1, S1, C1, O3.5, CSS1
a#myID	Dependent ID	Specified HTML tag where ID is applied	IE4, FF1, S1, C1, O3.5, CSS1
*	Universal	All HTML tags	IE7, FF1, S1, C1, O3.5, CSS2

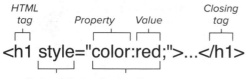

HTML tag · Property · Value · Closing tag

`<h1 style="color:red;">...</h1>`

Style attribute · Declaration

A The general syntax for defining styles directly in an HTML tag.

Inline: Adding Styles to an HTML Tag

Although using CSS means you do not have to set the appearance of each tag individually, you still have the freedom to set a style within an individual tag, which is referred to as an *inline* style **A**.

This is useful when you've set styles for the page in the head or in an external style sheet, and you need to override those styles on a case-by-case basis. However, you should only do this as a last resort. Because inline styles have the highest priority in the cascade order, they are virtually impossible to override.

To set the style properties of individual HTML tags:

1. **Add the style property to the HTML tag.** Type `style=` in the HTML tag to which you want to apply styles (**Code 3.1**)

   `<h1 style=`

2. **Add your CSS declarations in a comma-separated list.** In quotes, type your style declarations in the format `property: value`, using a semicolon (;) and separating individual declarations. Be sure to close the declaration list with quotation marks.

   ```
   font:italic bold small-caps
   →3em/.9 Constantia, Georgia,
   →Times, 'Times New Roman',
   →Serif; color:red"
   ```

3. **Finish your HTML tag and add content.** After closing the tag, add the content to be styled. Then close the tag pair with the corresponding end tag.

   ```
   >Alice&#8217;s Adventures In
   →Wonderland</h1>
   ```

Code 3.1 An inline style is applied to the **h1** tag to define the font properties and color **Ⓑ**.

```html
<!-- HTML5 -->
<!DOCTYPE html>
<html lang="en">
<head>
<meta http-equiv="Content-Type" content="text/html; charset=UTF-8">
<title>Alice's Adventures in Wonderland</title>
</head>
<body>
<h1 style="font:italic bold small-caps 3em/.9 Constantia, Georgia, Times, 'Times New Roman', Serif;
→ color:red">Alice&#8217;s Adventures In Wonderland</h1>
<p class="byline">by <span class="author">Lewis Carroll</span></p>
<article>
<header>
<h2><strong>Chapter I.</strong> Down the Rabbit-Hole</h2>
</header>
<p>Alice was beginning to get very tired of sitting by her sister on the
bank,...</p>
</article>
</body>
</html>
```

ALICE'S ADVENTURES IN WONDERLAND

by Lewis Carroll

Chapter I. Down the Rabbit-Hole

Alice was beginning to get very tired of sitting by her sister on the bank, and of having nothing to do: once or twice she had peeped into the book her sister was reading, but it had no pictures or conversations in it, 'and what is the use of a book,' thought Alice 'without pictures or conversation?'

So she was considering in her own mind (as well as she could, for the hot day made her feel very sleepy and stupid), whether the pleasure of making a daisy-chain would be worth the trouble of getting up and picking the daisies, when suddenly a White Rabbit with pink eyes ran close by her.

There was nothing so **very** remarkable in that; nor did Alice think it so **very** much out of the way to hear the Rabbit say to itself, 'Oh dear! Oh dear! I shall be late!' (when she thought it over afterwards, it occurred to her that she ought to have wondered at this, but at the time it all seemed quite natural); but when the Rabbit actually **took a watch out of its waistcoat-pocket**, and looked at it, and then hurried on, Alice started to her feet, for it flashed across her mind that she had never before seen a rabbit with either a waistcoat-pocket, or a watch to take out of it, and burning with curiosity, she ran across the field after it, and fortunately was just in time to see it pop down a large rabbit-hole under the hedge.

Ⓑ The results of Code 3.1. The header level 1 has been set to red using a bold, italic, small-caps version of the Constantia font at three times its original size (3em).

TIP You should *never* use inline styles in your final Web site. See the sidebar, "Why You Should Never Use Inline Styles in Your Final Web Site."

TIP So as not to confuse the browser, it is best to use double quotation marks ("...") around the declaration list and single quotation marks ('...') around any values in the declaration list, such as font names with spaces.

TIP Font names made up of more than two words are placed in single quotes ('Font Name') when used with a style.

TIP When you are copying and pasting code from an application such as Microsoft Word into a Web-editing application such as Adobe Dreamweaver, make sure that you convert all smart quotes ("...") to straight quotes ("...").

TIP A common mistake is to confuse the equals sign (=) with the colon (:). Although the style attribute in the tag uses an equals sign, remember that CSS declarations always use a colon.

Why You Should Never Use Inline Styles in Your Final Web Site

Because inline styles are the last line of styling, you cannot override them using embedded or external style sheets. As a result, you are either stuck with this style permanently or you have to change it manually, which may not always be possible. If you are working on a large scale Web site, the HTML code is often set independently of the styles, and designers may not be able to access that code or easily change it.

I once spent three days trying to restyle a widget for a major Internet company, only to realize that the link style wouldn't change because the developer had used an inline style. Because I couldn't edit the HTML code, I was stuck.

Inline styles can be useful for quickly testing styles. But to retain maximum flexibility, I recommend always placing your final styles into external style sheets, as discussed later in this chapter.

That said, it is likely that you will encounter places where a developer added inline styles to ensure design control. This is especially common in a content management system (CMS) such as Wordpress or Drupal.

Embedded: Adding Styles to a Web Page

To add styles that apply to a single Web page—rather than just a single element (inline) or an entire Web site (external)—you *embed* the style rules in the Web page using the **<style>** tag, which in turn will hold all your style rules 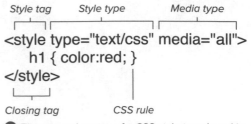.

Adding styles in this manner can look identical to adding styles directly to an HTML tag (as seen in the previous section). However, when you place styles in a common location—preferably in the **<head>** of the document—you can easily change all the styles in a document. For example, rather than specifying the style of a single **<h1>** tag, you can specify the style of *all* the <h1> tags on the entire page, and then change the rule in one place to change the appearance of all level 1 headers on that page.

Style tag   *Style type*   *Media type*

```
<style type="text/css" media="all">
   h1 { color:red; }
</style>
```

Closing tag   *CSS rule*

Ⓐ The general syntax of a CSS style tag placed in an HTML document.

To set the style for tags in an HTML document:

1. Type the opening **style** tag in the head of your document (Code 3.2). Define the **type** attribute as **"text/css"**, which defines the styles that follow as CSS, not just any style. Also, define the **media** type using a value of **all**, which will apply the style sheet to the page regardless of the type of machine used to output it. Then close the **style** tag.

   ```
   <style type="text/css"
   →media="all">...</style>
   ```

2. **Add your CSS rules.** Within the **style** container from step 1, start a new rule by typing the selector to which you want to add styles, followed by opening and closing curly brackets (**{}**).

(Basic selectors—HTML, class, IDs, and universal—are explained earlier in this chapter, and contextual selectors are explained in Chapter 4.)

h1 {...}

Within the brackets of your rule, type the declarations to be assigned to this rule—formatted as **property: value**—using a semicolon (**;**) and separating individual declarations in the list.

3. **Add all the CSS rules you want to define.** Rules obey the cascade order (explained in detail in Chapter 5). But generally, you can overrule a style by rewriting it lower in the list.

h2 {...}

TIP To make a rule more easily readable, you can also add one or more line breaks, spaces, or tabs after a declaration without interfering with the code.

TIP Although you can place embedded styles anywhere in your HTML document, I highly recommend placing them at the top of your documents in the <head>; otherwise, the page will display *without* the styles at first and then blink as the page redisplays with the styles.

TIP However, I do not recommend placing embedded styles in your final Web page at all. Although they aren't as difficult to override as inline styles, embedded styles can confound you later when trying to redesign a page. It's always best to put all your styles in an external style sheet (explained in the next section) where site-wide changes are easy to make.

Code 3.2 Style rules are added within the `<style>` tag. A rule is added for the level 1 header to set its color, but it has no effect **B**, because the inline style in the `<h1>` tag overrides it. That's why you should never use inline styles in your final code.

```
<!-- HTML5 -->
<!DOCTYPE html>
<html lang="en">
<head>
<meta http-equiv="Content-Type" content="text/html; charset=UTF-8">
<title>Alice's Adventures in Wonderland</title>
<style type="text/css" media="all">
  h1 {
    color: gray; }
  h2 {
    font-size: normal lighter small-caps 2em;
    color: darkred; }
</style>
</head>
<body>
<h1 style="font:italic bold small-caps 3em/.9 Constantia, Georgia, Times, 'Times New Roman', Serif;
→ color:red">Alice&#8217;s Adventures In Wonderland</h1>
<p class="byline">by <span class="author">Lewis Carroll</span></p>
<article>
<header>
<h2><strong>Chapter I.</strong> Down the Rabbit-Hole</h2>
</header>
<p>Alice was beginning to get very tired of sitting by her sister on the
bank,...
</p>
</article>
</body>
</html>
```

ALICE'S ADVENTURES IN WONDERLAND

by Lewis Carroll

Chapter I. Down the Rabbit-Hole

Alice was beginning to get very tired of sitting by her sister on the bank, and of having nothing to do: once or twice she had peeped into the book her sister was reading, but it had no pictures or conversations in it, 'and what is the use of a book,' thought Alice 'without pictures or conversation?'

So she was considering in her own mind (as well as she could, for the hot day made her feel very sleepy and stupid), whether the pleasure of making a daisy-chain would be worth the trouble of getting up and picking the daisies, when suddenly a White Rabbit with pink eyes ran close by her.

There was nothing so very remarkable in that; nor did Alice think it so very much out of the way to hear the Rabbit say to itself, 'Oh dear! Oh dear! I shall be late!' (when she thought it over afterwards, it occurred to her that she ought to have wondered at this, but at the time it all seemed quite natural); but when the Rabbit actually **took a watch out of its waistcoat-pocket**, and looked at it, and then hurried on, Alice started to her feet, for it flashed across her mind that she had never before seen a rabbit with either a waistcoat-pocket, or a watch to take out of it, and burning with curiosity, she ran

B The results of Code 3.2. Although the color for the `<h1>` tag is set to gray in the `<style>` tag, the inline style overrides it. Only the style for the `<h2>` tag hits its mark, coloring the chapter title a dark red.

External: Adding Styles to a Web Site

A major benefit of CSS is that you can create a style sheet once and use it either in a single Web page or throughout your entire Web site. To do this, you create an *external* CSS file separate from the HTML document that contains only CSS code—no HTML, JavaScript, or any other code.

Establishing an external CSS file is a two-step process. First, you set up the CSS rules in a text file. Second, you link or import this file into an HTML document using the **<link>** tag or the **@import** rule **A**.

Creating an external style sheet

The first step in using an external style sheet globally on a Web site is to create the external file that contains all the CSS code. However, unlike adding embedded styles, you do *not* use **<style>** tags in an external CSS file. In fact, doing so would cause the external style sheet to fail.

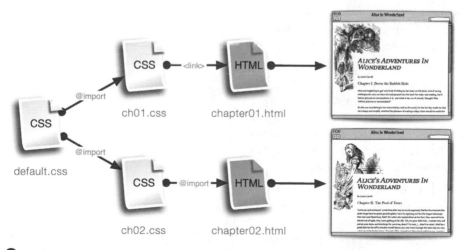

A External CSS files can be used to style HTML pages directly by linking or importing them. External CSS files also can be imported into each other to combine styles and then brought into an HTML document.

In this example, I set up three CSS files: *default.css*, *ch01.css*, and *ch02.css*.

To set up an external CSS file:

1. **Create a new text file.** You can use a text editor or Web-editing software. Save the file using the .css extension. For example, **default.css**.

   Notepad or SimpleText will do, but you may want to use a specialized code editing software programs such as Coda or BBedit.

   Do *not* use Microsoft Word. It adds its own markup code that will interfere with your CSS code.

2. **Import CSS files.** This is optional, but you can create as many external style sheets as you want and import style sheets into each other to combine their styles (**Code 3.4** and **Code 3.5**). However, if an import rule is included in an external style sheet, it must be placed before all other CSS code. See "Importing a style sheet" in this chapter for more information.

   ```
   @import{default.css}
   ```

3. **Add your CSS rules to the text file (Code 3.3).** Do *not* include any other code types—no HTML or JavaScript.

   Start a new rule by typing the selector to which you want to add styles, followed by opening and closing curly brackets ({}). (Basic selectors—HTML, class, IDs, and universal—are explained in this chapter, and contextual selectors are explained in Chapter 4.)

   ```
   body { padding: 200px 0 0 175px; }
   ```

   In the brackets of your rule, type the declarations to be assigned to this rule—formatted as **property: value**—using a semicolon (**;**) and separating individual declarations in the list. (You can also add comments as explained later in this chapter.)

You can now connect this file to your Web pages using one of the following two methods:

- **Link.** Use the **<link>** tag to connect external CSS files to an HTML file.

- **Import.** Use **@import** to connect external CSS files to an HTML file.

TIP Although the external CSS file can have any name, it's a good idea to use a name that will remind you of the purpose of these styles. The name "navigation.css," for example, is probably a more helpful name than "657nm87gp.css."

TIP A CSS file should not contain any HTML tags (especially not the **<style>** tag) or other content, with the exception of CSS comments and imported styles.

Code 3.3 *default.css*—All the basic styles for the Web site are contained in the default external style sheet.

```
body {
  padding: 200px 0 0 175px; }
h1 {
  color: black; }
h2 {
  color: gray; }
p {
  font: normal 100%/1.5 Corbel, Helvetica, Arial, Sans-serif;
  color: red; }
```

Code 3.4 *ch01.css*—Imports the default styles from default.css and then adds specific styles for Chapter 1.

```
@import url('default.css');
body {
  background: white url('../_images/AAIW-illos/alice23a.gif') no-repeat 0 0; }
```

Code 3.5 *ch02.css*—Imports the default styles from default.css and then adds specific styles for Chapter 2.

```
@import url('default.css');
body {
  background: white url('../_images/AAIW-illos/alice40b.gif') no-repeat 0 0; }
```

Linking to a style sheet

External style sheet files can be applied to any HTML file using the `<link>` tag **B**. Linking a CSS file affects the document in the same way as if the styles had been embedded directly in the head of the document; but, by placing it in a separate file, the code can be reused across multiple Web pages and changes made in the one central file will affect all of those pages.

To link to an external CSS file:

1. **Add a link tag to your HTML document.** Within the `<head>...</head>` of your HTML document (**Code 3.6**), open your `<link>` tag and type a space.

   `<link`

2. **Specify the link's relation to the document as a stylesheet.** This is important, since the link tag can be used to add other file types. Leaving this out will cause many browsers to not load the code.

   `rel="stylesheet"`

3. **Specify the location of the CSS file to be used, either global or local.** For example, *ch01.css*. This is the full path and name (including extension) of the external CSS document. In Chapter 15, you'll explore style sheet strategies for locating external style sheets in relation to your HTML Documents.

   `href="ch01.css"`

4. **Specify the type of information that is being linked.** In this example, it's a text file containing CSS.

   `type="text/css"`

5. **Specify the media type to which this style sheet should be applied.** For more details, see "Quarrying the Media" in Chapter 4.

   `media="all">`

Link tag   Link relationship

```
<link
    rel="stylesheet"
    href="filename.css"—  URL for
                           linked file
    type="text/css"——     Type of
                           linked file
    media="all"
                 —————     Media type
/>
```

B The general syntax for the link tag.

TIP You can use the `<link>` tag to add as many style sheets to a page as you want.

TIP Keep in mind that the more style sheets you link to, the more server calls your Web page makes, and the slower it loads. Link as needed, but try to minimize links by combining files where possible.

Code 3.6 *chapter01.html*—Links to the external style sheet ch01.css (Code 3.4), which also includes the styles in default.css (Code 3.3) .

```
<!-- HTML5 -->
<!DOCTYPE html>
<html lang="en">
<head>
<meta http-equiv="Content-Type" content="text/html; charset=UTF-8">
<title>Alice's Adventures in Wonderland</title>
<link href="ch01.css" type="text/css" rel="stylesheet" media="all">
<style type="text/css" media="all">
  h1 {
    color: gray; }
  h2 {
    font-size: normal lighter small-caps 2em;
    color: darkred; }
</style>
</head>
<body>
<h1 style="font:italic bold small-caps 3em/.9 Constantia, Georgia, Times, 'Times New Roman', Serif;
→ color:red">Alice&#8217;s Adventures In Wonderland</h1>
<p class="byline">by <span class="author">Lewis Carroll</span></p>
<article>
<header>
<h2><strong>Chapter I.</strong> Down the Rabbit-Hole</h2>
</header>
<p>Alice was beginning to get very tired of sitting by her sister on the
bank,...</p>
</article>
</body>
</html>
```

ALICE'S ADVENTURES IN WONDERLAND

by Lewis Carroll

Chapter I. Down the Rabbit-Hole

Alice was beginning to get very tired of sitting by her sister on the bank, and of having nothing to do: once or twice she had peeped into the book her sister was reading, but it

C The results of Code 3.6. Our page with all the default and Chapter 1 specific styles applied.

Importing a style sheet

Another way to bring external style sheets into a document is to use the **@import** rule **D**. The advantage of importing is that it can be used not only to put an external CSS file in an HTML document file, but also to import one external CSS file into another.

To import an external CSS file:

1. Within the head of your HTML document, add a **style** element (Code 3.7). This is the same as discussed earlier in this chapter.

   ```
   <style type="text/css"
   → media="all">...</style>
   ```

2. Add your @import rule. In the **<style>** tag, before any other CSS code you want to include, type **@import()**, and between the parentheses include the URL of the CSS document to be imported. The URL can be global, in which case it would start with **http://**, or it could be a local path pointing to another file in the same domain.

   ```
   @import url(ch02.css);
   ```

   You can include as many imports as you want, but all of them must be placed before any embedded CSS code in that **<style>** tag.

3. Add the rest of your embedded CSS. You can include additional embedded CSS rules here, if necessary. (See "Embedded: Adding Styles to a Web Page" in this chapter.)

TIP You can also place **@import** directly into another external style sheet. This will import the CSS code from one style sheet to the other so that when the second style sheet is linked or imported into an HTML file, the styles from the first style sheet are also included.

rule name   *URL for external file*

@import url(filename.css);

D The general syntax for the @import rule.

Code 3.7 *chapter02.html*—Links to the external style sheet ch02.css (Code 3.5), which also includes the styles in default.css (Code 3.3)  ⓔ.

```
<!-- HTML5 -->
<!DOCTYPE html>
<html lang="en">
<head>
<meta http-equiv="Content-Type" content="text/html; charset=UTF-8">
<title>Alice's Adventures in Wonderland</title>
<style type="text/css" media="all">
  @import url('ch02.css');
  h1 {
    color: gray; }
  h2 {
    font-size: normal lighter small-caps 2em;
    color: darkred; }
</style>
</head>
<body>
<h1 style="font:italic bold small-caps 3em/.9 Constantia, Georgia, Times, 'Times New Roman', Serif;
→ color:red">Alice&#8217;s Adventures In Wonderland</h1>
<p class="byline">by <span class="author">Lewis Carroll</span></p>
<article>
<header>
<h2><strong>Chapter II.</strong> The Pool of Tears</h2>
</header>
<p>'Curiouser and curiouser!' cried Alice,</p>
</article>
</body>
</html>
```

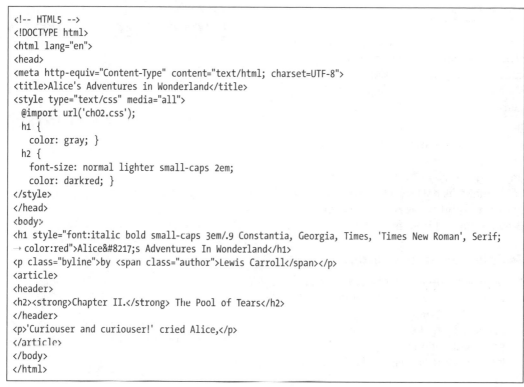

ⓔ The results of Code 3.7. The page with all of the default and Chapter 2 specific styles applied.

(Re)Defining HTML Tags

Almost all HTML tags have default browser styles associated with them. Take the `<strong>` tag, for example: Its inherent style declaration is the equivalent of `font-weight: bold.`

By adding new CSS declarations to the **strong** HTML selector, you can change any element tagged as **strong** to look like anything you want 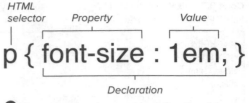. For example, you could make all italicized text bold or even set `font-weight: normal`, which would prevent the text from being bold.

A The general syntax used to define the styles for an HTML tag.

To define an HTML selector:

1. **Start with the HTML selector whose properties you want to define.** Add a curly bracket (**{**) to open your rule (**Code 3.8**). Make sure you always close your declaration list with a curly bracket (**}**). If you forget this, it will ruin your day!

   `strong {...}`

   CSS rules can be defined in the head of your document within the `<style>` tags or in an external CSS file that is imported or linked to the HTML document. (See "Embedded: Adding Styles to a Web Site.")

   continues on page 50

Code 3.8 *Chapter01.html*—Adds a new style for the **`<strong>`** tag to make it gray, a bit smaller, not bold. This is also styled as a block level element so that whatever appears after it starts on a new line **B**.

```html
<!-- HTML5 -->
<!DOCTYPE html>
<html lang="en">
<head>
<meta http-equiv="Content-Type" content="text/html; charset=UTF-8">
<title>Alice's Adventures in Wonderland</title>
<style type="text/css" media="all">
  @import url('ch01.css');
  h1 {
    color: gray; }
  h2 {
    font-size: normal lighter small-caps 2em;
    color: darkred; }
  strong {
    color: gray;
    font-size: .75em;
    font-weight: normal;
    display: block; }
</style>
</head>
<body>
<h1 style="font:italic bold small-caps 3em/.9 Constantia, Georgia, Times, 'Times New Roman', Serif;
→ color:red">Alice&#8217;s Adventures In Wonderland</h1>
<p class="byline">by <span class="author">Lewis Carroll</span></p>
<article>
<header>
<h2><strong>Chapter I.</strong> Down the Rabbit-Hole</h2>
</header>
<p>Alice was beginning to get very tired of sitting by her sister on the
bank,...</p>
</article>
</body>
</html>
```

B The results of Code 3.8. The chapter number is now styled separately from the rest of the chapter title.

2. **Add declarations for styles.** Within the brackets, type the style declarations to be assigned to this HTML tag—formatted as **`property: value`**—using a semicolon (**`;`**) and separating individual declarations in the list. You can also add one or more line breaks, spaces, or tabs after a declaration without interfering with the code to make it more readable.

   `color: gray;`

   Add as many declarations as you want, but be sure that the properties will work with the HTML tag in question. For example, you cannot use the **`text-indent`** property (which works only on block elements) to define the bold tag (which is an inline element). See Appendix A to verify the properties that can be assigned to specific selectors.

   TIP Redefining a tag does not implicitly override that tag's preexisting properties. Thus, the **`<strong>`** tag still makes text bold unless you explicitly tell it not to with **`font-weight: normal`**.

   TIP Although the body tag can also be redefined, it acts like a block-level tag. (See "Types of HTML Tags" in Chapter 2.) Any inherited properties will affect everything on the page. You can actually use this to your advantage to set default page styles, as explained in Chapter 4, "Inheriting Properties from Parents."

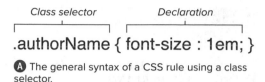

.authorName { font-size : 1em; }

A The general syntax of a CSS rule using a class selector.

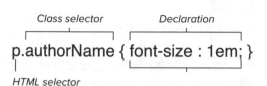

p.authorName { font-size : 1em; }

B The general syntax of a dependent class selector rule.

Defining Reusable Classes

A *class* selector allows you to set up an independent style that you can apply to any HTML tag **A**. Unlike an HTML selector, which automatically targets a specific tag, a class selector is given a unique name that is then specified using the **style** attribute in the HTML tag or in any tags you want to use it. However, you can also specify styles to apply using a class applied to a specific HTML tag, making it a *dependent class* **B**.

To define a class selector:

1. **Give your class a name.** Type a period (**.**) and a class name you give it; then open and close your declaration block with curly brackets (**{}**) (**Code 3.9**).

   `.author {...}`

   CSS classes can be defined in the head of your document within the **style** tags or in an external CSS file that is imported or linked to the HTML document.

   continues on next page

The class name can be anything you choose, with the following caveats:

▸ Use only letters and numbers. You can use hyphens and underscores, but not at the beginning of the name.

▸ The first character cannot be a number, underscore, or hyphen.

▸ Don't use spaces.

author is an independent class, so you can use it with any HTML tag you want, with one stipulation: The properties set for the class must work with the type of tag you use it on.

2. **Add declarations to the rule.** Within the brackets, type the declarations to be assigned to this class—formatted as **property: value**—using a semicolon (**;**) and separating individual declarations in the list. You can also add one or more line breaks, spaces, or tabs after a declaration without interfering with the code to make it more readable.

font-size: 1.25em;

3. **Add dependent classes to your CSS.** You create dependent classes, which tie the declarations of the class to a particular HTML tag by placing an HTML selector in front of the class.

p.byline {...}

byline is a dependent class and will be applied only to **<p>** tags using **class="byline"**.

In the same document, you can create different versions of the dependent class (using the same name) for different tags and also have an independent class (applied to all tags with the class), as shown in step 1.

continues on page 54

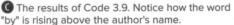

C The results of Code 3.9. Notice how the word "by" is rising above the author's name.

Code 3.9 *chapter01.html*—Adds classes to style both the byline (if it's in a paragraph) and the author's name **C**.

```
<!-- HTML5 -->
<!DOCTYPE html>
<html lang="en">
<head>
<meta http-equiv="Content-Type" content="text/html; charset=UTF-8">
<title>Alice's Adventures in Wonderland</title>
<style type="text/css" media="all">
  @import url('ch01.css');
  h1 {
    color: gray; }
  h2 {
    font-size: normal lighter small-caps 2em;
    color: darkred; }
  strong {
    font-weight: normal;
    color: black; }
  p.byline {
    font-size: 1.25em;
    font-style: normal;
    font-weight: bold;
    word-spacing: -.3em;
    text-align: right;
    color: rgba(255, 0, 0,.75); }
  .author {
    font-size: 1.25em;
    font-style: normal;
    font-weight: bold;
    color: rgba(255, 0, 0,1);
    word-spacing: 0em;
    text-transform: uppercase;
    vertical-align: -.6em; }
</style>
</head>
<body>
<h1 style="font:italic bold small-caps 3em/.9 Constantia, Georgia, Times, 'Times New Roman', Serif;
→ color:red">Alice&#8217;s Adventures In Wonderland</h1>
<p class="byline">by <span class="author">Lewis Carroll</span></p>
<article>
<header>
<h2><strong>Chapter I.</strong> Down the Rabbit-Hole</h2>
</header>
<figure id="gallery">
<img src="../_images/AAIW-illos/alice26a.png" alt="alice15a">
<figcaption>
"Twinkle, twinkle, little bat!<br/>
How I wonder what you're at!"
</figcaption>
</figure>
<p>
Alice was beginning to get very tired of sitting by her sister on the
bank,...</p>
</article>
</body>
</html>
```

4. Add the class attribute to the HTML tag to which you want to apply it.

```
<p class="byline"><span
→ class="author">...</span></p>
```

You can apply multiple classes to a single HTML tag by adding additional class names in a space separated list:

```
class="name1 name2 name3"
```

Notice that when you defined the class in the **CSS**, it began with a period (**.**). However, you do *not* use the period when referencing the class name in an HTML tag. Using a period here will cause the class to fail.

TIP You can mix a class with ID and/or inline rules within an HTML tag (See "Inline: Adding Styles to an HTML Tag" and "Defining Unique IDs" in this chapter.)

TIP Because the `<div>` and `<span>` tags have no preexisting properties, you can use them to effectively create your own HTML tags by adding classes. However, use these sparingly because once they are associated, you are locked into using those specific classes with those specific locations.

ID selector   *Declaration*

#content { position : relative; }

A The general syntax for an ID selector rule.

ID selector   *Declaration*

div#content { position : relative; }

HTML selector

B The general syntax for the dependent ID selector rule.

Defining Unique IDs

Like the class selector, the ID selector can be used to create unique styles that are independent of any particular HTML tag **A**. Thus, they can be assigned to any HTML tag. IDs are used in HTML to help establish the structure of your page layout, identifying unique elements in the code, singling them out for special treatment, either for positioning with CSS or JavaScript.

To define an ID selector:

1. **Add the ID selector to your CSS.** ID rules always start with a number sign (#) followed by the name of the ID (**Code 3.10**).

   ```
   #gallery {...}
   ```

   The name can be a word or any set of letters or numbers you choose, with the following caveats:

   ▸ Use only letters and numbers. You can use hyphens and underscores, but do so with caution. Some earlier browsers reject them.

   ▸ The first character cannot be a number, hyphen, or underscore.

   ▸ Don't use spaces.

   CSS rules can be defined in the head of your document within the **<style>** tags or in an external CSS file that is imported or linked to the HTML document.

   continues on next page

2. **Add declarations to your ID.** Within the curly brackets, type the style declarations to be assigned to this ID—formatted as **property: value**—using a semicolon (**;**) and separating individual declarations in the list. You can also add one or more line breaks, spaces, or tabs after a declaration without interfering with the code to make it more readable.

   `position:relative;`

3. Add the `id` attribute to the HTML tag of your choice, with the name of the ID as its value.

   `<figure id="gallery">...</figure>`

   Notice that although the number sign (**#**) is used to define an ID selector, it is *not* included for referencing the ID in the HTML tag. If you add it, the rule will fail.

   TIP You can also create dependent IDs **B**, which use the declarations of the ID only when applied to a particular HTML tag. However, I never have a use for these because the point of IDs is that you use them only once per page.

   TIP Although you can use the same name for both a class and ID, you should try to avoid this because it will inevitably lead to confusion.

   TIP You can mix an ID with a class and/or inline rules within an HTML tag.

   TIP IDs can give each screen element a unique name and identity. This is why an ID is used only once, for one element in a document, to make it an object that can be manipulated with JavaScript.

Code 3.10 *chapter01.html*—The gallery ID is added to allow special positioning of the image block containing a figure **C**.

```
<!-- HTML5 -->
<!DOCTYPE html>
<html lang="en">
<head>
<meta http-equiv="Content-Type" content="text/html; charset=UTF-8">
<title>Alice's Adventures in Wonderland</title>
<style type="text/css" media="all">
  @import url('ch01.css');
  h1 {
    color: gray; }
  h2 {
    font-size: normal lighter small-caps 2em;
    color: darkred; }
  strong {
    font-weight: normal;
    color: black; }
  p.byline {
    font-size: 1.25em;
    font-style: normal;
    font-weight: bold;
    word-spacing: -.3em;
    text-align: right;
    color: rgba(255, 0, 0,.75); }
  .author {
    font-size: 1.25em;
    font-style: normal;
    font-weight: bold;
    color: rgba(255, 0, 0,1);
    word-spacing: 0em;
    text-transform: uppercase;
    vertical-align: -.6em; }
  #gallery {
    position: relative;
    bottom: 10px;
    right: 10px;
    display: block;
    font-style: italic;
    width: 300px;
    float: left;
    margin: 0 20px 20px 0;
    border: 6px double rgba(142, 137, 129,.5); }
</style>
</head>
<body>
<h1 style="font:italic bold small-caps 3em/.9 Constantia, Georgia, Times, 'Times New Roman', Serif;
→ color:red">Alice&#8217;s Adventures In Wonderland</h1>
<p class="byline">by <span class="author">Lewis Carroll</span></p>
```

code continues on next page

```
<article>
<header>
<h2><strong>Chapter I.</strong> Down the Rabbit-Hole</h2>
</header>
<figure id="gallery">
<img src="../_images/AAIW-illos/alice26a.png" alt="alice15a">
<figcaption>
"Twinkle, twinkle, little bat!<br/>
How I wonder what you're at!"
</figcaption>
</figure>
<p>
Alice was beginning to get very tired of sitting by her sister on the
bank,...</p>
</article>
</body>
</html>
```

C The results of Code 3.10. The Gallery figure has been floated into the page and then slightly offset.

Asterisk

$*$ { margin: 0; }

Declaration

A The general syntax for the universal selector rule.

Defining Universal Styles

The universal selector is a wildcard character that works as a stand-in to represent any HTML type selector that can appear in that position in a contextual list **A**.

Keep in mind, though, that the universal selector can be used in place of any HTML selector in any configuration, not just as a stand alone selector as shown in this section. The usefulness of this will become apparent in the next chapter when you use contextual styles.

To use the universal selector:

1. **Add the universal selector.** Type an asterisk (*) and then the open curly bracket (**Code 3.11**). This selector is then a wildcard that can be any HTML tag.

   `* {...}`

2. **Add declarations to your universal selector rule.** Within the curly brackets, type the style declarations to be assigned to this ID—formatted as **property: value**—using a semicolon (**;**) and separating individual declarations in the list. You can also add one or more line breaks, spaces, or tabs after a declaration without interfering with the code to make it more readable.

   `margin: 0;`

In this format, the styles are applied to *every* element on the page.

TIP Universal selectors provide an easy way to create a CSS reset, explained in chapter 13.

TIP Universal selectors do *not* work in IE6.

TIP Although you can also apply styles to the html or body element to have them cascade to their child elements, not all styles will be inherited by their children. Using the universal selector applies the styles directly to every element.

Code 3.11 *chapter01.html*—The universal selector is used to reset the margin and padding of all elements to 0, overriding any browser default styles **B**.

```
<!-- HTML5 -->
<!DOCTYPE html>
<html lang="en">
<head>
<meta http-equiv="Content-Type" content="text/html; charset=UTF-8">
<title>Alice's Adventures in Wonderland</title>
<style type="text/css" media="all">
 @import url('ch01.css');
 * {
   margin: 0;
   padding: 0; }
 h1 {
   color: gray; }
 h2 {
   font-size: normal lighter small-caps 2em;
   color: darkred; }
 strong {
   font-weight: normal;
   color: black; }
 p.byline {
   font-size: 1.25em;
   font-style: normal;
   font-weight: bold;
   word-spacing: -.3em;
   text-align: right;
   color: rgba(255, 0, 0,.75); }
 .author {
   font-size: 1.25em;
   font-style: normal;
   font-weight: bold;
   color: rgba(255, 0, 0,1);
   word-spacing: 0em;
   text-transform: uppercase;
   vertical-align: -.6em; }
 #gallery {
   position: relative;
   bottom: 10px;
   right: 10px;
   display: block;
   font-style: italic;
   width: 300px;
   float: left;
   margin: 0 20px 20px 0;
   border: 6px double rgba(142, 137, 129,.5); }
</style>
</head>
<body>
```

code continues on next page

```
<h1 style="font:italic bold small-caps 3em/.9 Constantia, Georgia, Times, 'Times New Roman', Serif;
→ color:red">Alice&#8217;s Adventures In Wonderland</h1>
<p class="byline">by <span class="author">Lewis Carroll</span></p>
<article>
<header>
<h2><strong>Chapter I.</strong> Down the Rabbit-Hole</h2>
</header>
<figure id="gallery">
<img src="../_images/AAIW-illos/alice26a.png" alt="alice15a">
<figcaption>
"Twinkle, twinkle, little bat!<br/>
How I wonder what you're at!"
</figcaption>
</figure>
<p>
Alice was beginning to get very tired of sitting by her sister on the
bank,...</p>
</article>
</body>
</html>
```

B The results of Code 3.11. All the margins are 0, giving you a clean slate for your designs.

Grouping: Defining Elements Using the Same Styles

If you want two or more selectors to have the same declarations, group the selectors in a list separated by commas **A**. You can define common attributes in the declaration block and then add rules for each selector individually to refine them, if you like.

To group selectors:

1. **Add a grouping of selectors, separated by commas.** Type the list of selectors (HTML, class, or ID) separated by commas (**Code 3.12**). You can also add one or more line breaks, spaces, or tabs after a comma without interfering with the code to make it more readable.

   `h1, h2, .byline, #gallery {...}`

   These selectors all receive the same declarations. CSS rules can be defined within the **style** tags in the head of your document or in an external CSS file that is imported or linked to the HTML document.

Comma-separated list of selectors   *Declaration*

`h1,h2,.copy,#head { font-size : 1em; }`

A The general syntax for a list of selectors, all receiving the same declaration block.

2. **Add common declarations for the selector grouping.** Within the curly brackets, type the style declarations to be assigned to all of the listed selectors—formatted as **property: value**—using a semicolon (**;**) and separating individual declarations in the list. You can also add one or more line breaks, spaces, or tabs after a declaration without interfering with the code to make it more readable.

```
font-family: Constantia, Georgia,
→Times, "Times New Roman", Serif;
```

3. **Add refinements as needed.** You can then individually add or change declarations for each selector to tailor it to your needs. If you are overriding a declaration set in the group rule, make sure that this rule is placed after the group rule in your CSS. (See "Determining the Cascade Order" in Chapter 4.)

```
h1 {...}
```

TIP Grouping selectors like this can save a lot of time and repetition. But be careful. By changing the value of any of the properties in the combined declaration, you change that value for every selector in the list.

TIP Grouping selectors does not directly affect their cascade order (explained in Chapter 4); rather, the grouping is treated as if each selector had this rule assigned to it in the order the selectors are listed.

Code 3.12 *chapter01.html*—Common styles for the level 1 and level 2 headers, byline class, and gallery ID are defined **B**.

```html
<!-- HTML5 -->
<!DOCTYPE html>
<html lang="en">
<head>
<meta http-equiv="Content-Type" content="text/html; charset=UTF-8">
<title>Alice's Adventures in Wonderland</title>
<style type="text/css" media="all">
 @import url('ch01.css');
 * {
   margin: 0;
   padding: 0;
 }
 h1, h2, .byline, #gallery {
   font-family: Constantia, Georgia, Times, "Times New Roman", Serif;
 }
 h1 {
   color: gray; }
 h2 {
   font-size: normal lighter small-caps 2em;
   color: darkred;
 }
 strong {
   font-weight: normal;
   color: black;
 }
 p.byline {
   font-size: 1.25em;
   font-style: normal;
   font-weight: bold;
   word-spacing: -.3em;
   text-align: right;
   color: rgba(255, 0, 0,.75);
 }
 .author {
   font-size: 1.25em;
   font-style: normal;
   font-weight: bold;
   color: rgba(255, 0, 0,1);
   word-spacing: 0em;
   text-transform: uppercase;
   vertical-align: -.6em;
 }
 #gallery {
   position: relative;
   bottom: 10px;
   right: 10px;
   display: block;
```

code continues on next page

```
    font-style: italic;
    width: 300px;
    float: left;
    margin: 0 20px 20px 0;
    border: 6px double rgba(142, 137, 129,.5);
  }
</style>
</head>
<body>
<h1 style="font:italic bold small-caps 3em/.9 Constantia, Georgia, Times, 'Times New Roman', Serif;
→ color:red">Alice&#8217;s Adventures In Wonderland</h1>
<p class="byline">by <span class="author">Lewis Carroll</span></p>
<article>
<header>
<h2><strong>Chapter I.</strong> Down the Rabbit-Hole</h2>
</header>
<figure id="gallery">
<img src="../_images/AAIW-illos/alice26a.png" alt="alice15a">
<figcaption>
"Twinkle, twinkle, little bat!<br/>
How I wonder what you're at!"
</figcaption>
</figure>
<p>
Alice was beginning to get very tired of sitting by her sister on the
bank,...</p>
</article>
</body>
</html>
```

B The results of Code 3.12. The font family Constantia is applied to all of the common elements.

Adding Comments to CSS

Comments allow you to add important notes to your code, as a reminder to yourself or others. A comment does not affect code; comments only add notes or give guidance to those viewing your code. You can include comments in `<style>` tags or in an external CSS file.

To include comments in a style sheet:

1. **Add an opening comment mark.** To open a comment area in a style sheet (**Code 3.13**), type a slash (/) and an asterisk (*).

    /*

Code 3.13 Comments in the CSS code have no effect on the final product. They are just there to add notes.

```
/*** CSS3 VQS | Chapter 3 | cssbasics-01.css ***/

body {
  background: white url(../_images/AAIW-illos/alice23a.gif) no-repeat 0 0;
  padding: 200px 0 0 175px; }
h1 {
  color: black; }
h2 {
  color: gray; }
p {
  font: normal 100%/1.5 Corbel, Helvetica, Arial, Sans-serif;
  color: red; }
```

2. **Type your comments.** You can use any letters, numbers, symbols, or even line breaks by pressing the Return or Enter key.

```
CSS3 VQS | Chapter 3 |
→ cssbasics-01.css
```

3. **Add a closing comment mark.** Close your comment by typing an asterisk (*) and a slash (/).

```
*/
```

TIP Within the slash asterisk, you can add whatever text you want.

TIP You cannot nest comments.

TIP Comments are a great way to organize your code, allowing you to add "headers" that separate different parts of the code.

TIP I recommend placing constant values—like color values—at the top of your CSS code in comments for quick reference.

Putting It All Together

1. **Add content to your HTML file.** Using the HTML file you created in chapter 2, add text and image content. I tend to use *Alice's Adventures in Wonderland*, but anything will do. A great source for text is Project Guttenberg (*www.gutenberg.org*).

2. **Mark up your content.** All styles require markup in the Web page to give them something to be applied to. Make sure to tag headers and paragraphs.

3. **Add classes and IDs to your markup.** Classes give you a "hook" to apply specific styles to specific elements. Don't go overboard, though. Only add classes where it useful to differentiate kinds of elements and IDs to differentiate a specific element in the design.

4. **Add your HTML, class, and ID declarations to the head of your document** in a `<style>` tag. You can style these however you see fit, based on the styles presented in chapters 5-12.

5. **Add comments to your CSS code.** The note can include information about the code, or contact information about the creator (you) and how to contact them with questions.

6. **Move your embedded styles from step 4 into an external file.** Create the text file and then copy and past *just* the CSS code (everything between but not including the `<style>` tags) into the text file. Make sure to save the file with a *.css* extension.

7. **Add a `<link>` from the external style sheet.** When you test your Web page in a browser, it should look just like it did on Step 4, but no the CSS is accessible to all of your Web pages.

Selective Styling

It's not enough to style a Web page element. The art of CSS—and thus the art of Web design—is the ability to style elements based on their context. You must consider where an element is in the document; which elements surround it; its attributes, content, and dynamic state; and even the platform displaying the element (screen, handheld device, TV, and so on).

Selective styling is the closest that CSS gets to traditional computer programming, allowing you to style elements *if* they meet certain criteria. This level of styling can get increasingly complex, so it's important, at least in this chapter, to start out as simply as possible and build a firm foundation of understanding.

In This Chapter

The Element Family Tree

When a tag is surrounded by another tag—one inside another—the tags are *nested*.

```
<h2><strong>Chapter 2</strong> The
Pool of Tears<h2>
```

In a nested set, the outer element in this example (`<h2>`) is called the *parent*, and the inner element (`<strong>`) is the *child*. The child tag and any children of that child tag are the parents' *descendents*. Two tags in the same parent are called *siblings*, and two tags immediately next to each other are *adjacent siblings* Ⓐ.

- **Parent elements** contain other elements (children). Child elements will often inherit styles from a parent element.

- **Descendent elements** are any elements within another element.

- **Child elements** are first generation descendent elements in relation to the parent. Second generation and higher elements are sometimes referred to as *grandchildren*.

- **Adjacent** or **preceding sibling elements** are child elements of the same generation that are immediately next to each other in the HTML code.

In Chapter 3, you learned ways to specify the styles of an individual element regardless of where it is placed in the HTML code. However, CSS also lets you specify the element's style depending on its context. Using *contextual selectors*, you can specify styles based on a tag's relationship to other tags, classes, or IDs on the page.

Parent   Descendent child
```
 ┌ <article class="copy">
 │    <p>
 │              <em>Alice's Adventures</em>
 │              <strong>In Wonderland</strong>
 │    </p>
 └  </article>
```
Preceding sibling   Adjacent sibling

Ⓐ The article element is the parent to the elements created by the paragraph, strong, and emphasis tags, which are its descendents. Only the paragraph tag is a direct child. The elements created by the emphasis and strong tags are the children of the paragraph tag, and each other's siblings.

Space-separated
list of selectors   Declaration List

.copy h1 em { color: red; }

A The general syntax for the descendent selector.

Space seperated
list of selectors   Declaration list

.copy * em { color: red; }

Universal selector

B The general syntax for the descendent selector using the universal selector.

Defining Styles Based on Context

Contextual styles allow you to specify how a particular element should appear based on its parents and siblings. For example, you may want an emphasis tag to appear one way when it's in the main header of the page and differently when it appears in the sub-header. You may want still another appearance in a paragraph of text. These *combinatory* selectors (**Table 4.1**) are among the most used and useful CSS.

Styling descendents

You can style individual descendent elements depending on their parent selector or selectors in a space-separated list. The last selector will receive the style if and only if it is the descendent of the preceding selectors **A**.

When you want to indicate that the exact selector does not matter at any given level, you can use the universal selector (*) described in Chapter 3 **B**.

TABLE 4.1 Combinator Selectors

Format	Selector Name	Elements Are Styled If...	Compatibility
a b c	Descendent	**c** descendent of **b** descendent of **a**	IE4, FF1, O3.5, S1, C1, CSS1
a * b	Universal	**b** within **a** regardless of **b**'s parents	IE7, FF1, O4, S1, C1, CSS2
a > b	Direct Child	**b** direct child of **a**	IE7 FF1, O3.5, S1, C1, CSS1
a + b	Adjacent Sibling	sibling **b** immediately after **a**	IE7, FF1, O5, S1, C1, CSS2
a ~ b	General Sibling	sibling **b** anywhere after **a**	IE8, FF1, O5, S1, C1, CSS2

To style descendent elements:

1. **Set up a list of descendent selectors.** Type the HTML selector of the parent tag, followed by a space, and then the final child or another parent (**Code 4.1**).

   ```
   article.copy h1 em {...}
   ```

   You can type as many HTML selectors as you want for as many parents as the nested tag will have, *but the last selector in the list is the one that receives all the styles in the rule.*

2. **Styles will be used if the pattern is matched.**

   ```
   <article class="copy">
   → <h1><em>...</em></h1></article>
   ```

   The style will be applied if and only if the final selector occurs as a descendent nested within the previous selectors.

Alice's Adventures in *Wonderland*

Chapter 2. The Pool of Tears

'Curiouser and curiouser!' *cried* Alice...

And she went on *planning*...

Poor *Alice!*

    ALICE'S RIGHT FOOT, *ESQ.*

Oh dear, what *nonsense* I'm talking!'...

C The results of Code 4.1. The only text that meets the selective criteria is in red, which is only the emphasis tag in the h1, in this example.

Code 4.1 The style is set for the emphasis tag if its parents are the **h1** tag and the article tag using the copy class **C**.

```
<!-- HTML5 -->
<!DOCTYPE html>
<html lang="en">
<head>
<meta http-equiv="Content-Type" content="text/html; charset=UTF-8" />
<title>Alice's Adventures in Wonderland</title>
<style type="text/css" media="all">
  article.copy h1 em {
    color: red;
    font-weight: bold;
    font-style: italic; }
</style>
</head>
<body>
<article class="copy">
  <h1>Alice's Adventures in <em>Wonderland</em></h1>
  <h2><em>Chapter 2.</em> The Pool of Tears</h2>
  <p>'Curiouser and curiouser!' <em>cried</em> Alice,...</p>
  <p>And she went on <em>planning</em>,...</p>
  <p>Poor <em>Alice!</em></p>
  <blockquote>ALICE'S RIGHT FOOT, <em>ESQ.</em></blockquote>
  <p>Oh dear, what <em>nonsense</em> I'm talking!',...</p>
</article>
</body>
</html>
```

Alice's Adventures in *Wonderland*

Chapter 2. The Pool of Tears

'Curiouser and curiouser!' *cried* Alice...

And she went on *planning*...

Poor *Alice!*

    ALICE'S RIGHT FOOT, *ESQ.*

Oh dear, what *nonsense* I'm talking!'...

D The results of Code 4.2. The text in red matches the selective criteria with the universal selector. In this case, all emphasis tags match.

TIP Like grouped selectors, contextual selectors can include class selectors (dependent or independent), ID selectors in the list, and HTML selectors.

To style descendents universally:

1. **Set up a list of descendent selectors including a universal selector.** Type the HTML selector of the parent tag, followed by a space, and then an asterisk (*) or other selectors (**Code 4.2**).

   ```
   article.copy * {...}
   ```

2. **Styles will be used if the pattern is matched.** Generally, the universal selector is used at the end of a list of selectors so that the style is applied to all of a parent's children.

   ```
   <article class="copy">
   → <h1>Alice's Adventures in
   → <em>Wonderland</em></h1>
   → <h2><em>Chapter 2.</em> The Pool
   → of Tears</h2>
   → <p>...<em>...</em>...</p>
   → </article>
   ```

Code 4.2 The style is set for the emphasis tag with *any* parent that's in an article tag using the copy class **D**.

```
<!-- HTML5 -->
<!DOCTYPE html>
<html lang="en">
<head>
<meta http-equiv="Content-Type" content="text/html; charset=UTF-8" />
<title>Alice's Adventures in Wonderland</title>
<style type="text/css" media="all">
  article.copy * em {
    color: red;
    font-weight: bold; }
</style>
</head>
<body>
<article class="copy">
  <h1>Alice's Adventures in <em>Wonderland</em></h1>
  <h2><em>Chapter 2.</em> The Pool of Tears</h2>
  <p>'Curiouser and curiouser!' <em>cried</em> Alice,...</p>
  <p>And she went on <em>planning</em>,...</p>
  <p>Poor <em>Alice!</em></p>
  <blockquote>ALICE'S RIGHT FOOT, <em>ESQ.</em></blockquote>
  <p>Oh dear, what <em>nonsense</em> I'm talking!',...</p>
</article>
</body>
</html>
```

Styling only the children

If you want to style only a parent's child elements (not a grandchild descendent), you must specify the parent selector and child selector, separated by a close angle bracket (>) 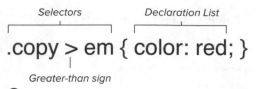.

Selectors   *Declaration List*

.copy > em { color: red; }

Greater-than sign

E The general syntax of the direct child selector.

To define child selectors:

1. **Set up a list of direct child selectors.**
    Type the selector for the parent element (HTML, class, or ID), followed by a right angle bracket (>) and the child selector (HTML, class, or ID).

    ```
    article.copy > p > em {...}
    ```

    You can repeat this as many times as you want with the final selector being the target to which you apply the styles (**Code 4.3**). You can have *one* space between the selector and the greater-than sign or no spaces.

2. **Styles will be used if the pattern is matched.**

    ```
    <article class="copy"><p>...
    → <em>...</em>...</p></article>
    ```

    The styles from step 1 are applied if and only if the final selector is an immediate child element nested in the preceding element. Placing the tag within any other HTML tags will disrupt the pattern.

Code 4.3 The style is applied to the emphasis tag only if it is a child of a paragraph that is in turn the child of an article tag using the copy class **F**.

```html
<!-- HTML5 -->
<!DOCTYPE html>
<html lang="en">
<head>
<meta http-equiv="Content-Type" content="text/html; charset=UTF-8" />
<title>Alice's Adventures in Wonderland</title>
<style type="text/css" media="all">
  article.copy > p > em {
    color: red;
    font-weight: bold; }
</style>
</head>
<body>
<article class="copy">
  <h1>Alice's Adventures in <em>Wonderland</em></h1>
  <h2><em>Chapter 2.</em> The Pool of Tears</h2>
  <p>'Curiouser and curiouser!' <em>cried</em> Alice,...</p>
  <p>And she went on <em>planning</em>,...</p>
  <p>Poor <em>Alice!</em></p>
  <blockquote>ALICE'S RIGHT FOOT, <em>ESQ.</em></blockquote>
  <p>Oh dear, what <em>nonsense</em> I'm talking!',...</p>
</article>
</body>
</html>
```

Alice's Adventures in *Wonderland*

Chapter 2. The Pool of Tears

'Curiouser and curiouser!' *cried* Alice...

And she went on *planning*...

Poor *Alice!*

    ALICE'S RIGHT FOOT, *ESQ.*

Oh dear, what *nonsense* I'm talking!'...

F The results of Code 4.3. The text in red matches the direct child criteria. In this case the emphasis tags match within the paragraphs but not within the headers.

Styling siblings

Siblings are elements that have the same parent. You can style a sibling that is immediately adjacent to another or occurs anywhere after that sibling Ⓗ.

To define adjacent sibling selectors:

1. **Set up a list of adjacent sibling selectors.** Type the selector for the first element (HTML, class, or ID), a plus sign (+), and then the selector (HTML, class, or ID) for the adjacent element to which you want the style applied (**Code 4.4**).

   p + p {...}

2. **Styles will be used if the pattern is matched.**

   <p>...</p><p>...</p><p>...</p>

   The styles will be applied to any sibling that occurs immediately after the preceding selector with no other selectors in the way. Placing any element between them (even a break tag) will disrupt the pattern.

Selectors   *Declaration List*

p + p { color: red; }

Plus sign

Ⓖ The general syntax for the adjacent sibling selector.

Selectors   *Declaration List*

p ~ p { color: red; }

Tilde

Ⓗ The general syntax for the general sibling selector.

Code 4.4 The style is applied to the emphasis tag only if it is in a paragraph that is immediately after another paragraph **❶**.

```
<!-- HTML5  >
<!DOCTYPE html>
<html lang="en">
<head>
<meta http-equiv="Content-Type" content="text/html; charset=UTF-8" />
<title>Alice's Adventures in Wonderland</title>
<style type="text/css" media="all">
  p + p em {
    color: red;
    font-weight: bold; }
</style>
</head>
<body>
<article class="copy">
  <h1>Alice's Adventures in <em>Wonderland</em></h1>
  <h2><em>Chapter 2.</em> The Pool of Tears</h2>
  <p>'Curiouser and curiouser!' <em>cried</em> Alice,...</p>
  <p>And she went on <em>planning</em>,...</p>
  <p>Poor <em>Alice!</em></p>
  <blockquote>ALICE'S RIGHT FOOT, <em>ESQ.</em></blockquote>
  <p>Oh dear, what <em>nonsense</em> I'm talking!',...</p>
</article>
</body>
</html>
```

Alice's Adventures in *Wonderland*

Chapter 2. **The Pool of Tears**

'Curiouser and curiouser!' *cried* Alice...

And she went on ***planning***...

Poor *Alice!*

    ALICE'S RIGHT FOOT, *ESQ.*

Oh dear, what *nonsense* I'm talking!'...

❶ The results of Code 4.4. The text in red matches the adjacent sibling criteria—the emphasis tags within the second and third paragraphs in this case—but does not match the fourth paragraph because a block quote is in the way.

To define general sibling selectors:

1. Set up a list of general sibling selectors. Type the selector for the first sibling element (HTML, class, or ID), a tilde sign (~), and then another selector (HTML, class, or ID) (**Code 4.5**).

   `p ~ p {...}`

   You can repeat this as many times as necessary, but the last selector in the list is the one you are targeting to be styled.

2. Styles will be used if the pattern is matched.

   ```
   <p>...</p><p>...</p><p>...</p>
   → <blockquote>...</blockquote>
   → <p>...</p>
   ```

TIP The styles will be applied to *any* siblings that occur after the first sibling selector, not just the first one, but any siblings of the same type until another type of element is encountered. Child siblings are not supported in IE6, so you will need to style these separately. See Chapter 13 for more information on adding styles specifically for Internet Explorer.

TIP Although the universal selector shown in this section is used with the combinatory selectors, it can be used with any selector type. Table 4.2 shows how you can apply it.

TABLE 4.2 Universal Selector Examples

Format	Elements Are Styled If...
a * b	**b** within **a** regardless of **b**'s parents
a > * > b	**b** is the direct child of any element that is the direct child of **a**
a + * + b	sibling **b** immediately after any element that is immediately after **a**
*:hover	mouse pointer over any element
*:disabled	any element that is disabled
*:first-child	first child of any element
*:lang()	any element using specified language code
*:not(s)	any element that is not the using indicated selectors
*::first-letter	any element's first letter

Code 4.5 The style is applied to the emphasis tag if it is in a paragraph with any preceding sibling that is a paragraph **J**.

```
<!-- HTML5 -->
<!DOCTYPE html>
<html lang="en">
<head>
<meta http-equiv="Content-Type" content="text/html; charset=UTF-8" />
<title>Alice's Adventures in Wonderland</title>
<style type="text/css" media="all">
  p ~ p em {
    color: red;
    font-weight: bold; }
</style>
</head>
<body>
<article class="copy">
   <h1>Alice's Adventures in <em>Wonderland</em></h1>
   <h2><em>Chapter 2.</em> The Pool of Tears</h2>
   <p>'Curiouser and curiouser!' <em>cried</em> Alice,...</p>
   <p>And she went on <em>planning</em>,...</p>
   <p>Poor <em>Alice!</em></p>
   <blockquote>ALICE'S RIGHT FOOT, <em>ESQ.</em></blockquote>
   <p>Oh dear, what <em>nonsense</em> I'm talking!',...</p>
</article>
</body>
</html>
```

Alice's Adventures in *Wonderland*

Chapter 2. **The Pool of Tears**

'Curiouser and curiouser!' *cried* Alice...

And she went on *planning*...

Poor *Alice!*

    ALICE'S RIGHT FOOT, *ESQ*.

Oh dear, what *nonsense* I'm talking!'...

J **The results of Code 4.5.** The text in red matches the general sibling criteria—in this case the emphasis tags within the second, third, *and* fourth paragraphs.

Working with Pseudo-classes

Many HTML elements have special states or uses associated with them that can be styled independently. One prime example of this is the link tag, `<a>`, which has link (its normal state), a visited state (when the visitor has already been to the page represented by the link), hover (when the visitor has their mouse over the link), and active (when the visitor clicks the link). All four of these states can be styled separately.

A *pseudo-class* is a predefined state or use of an element that can be styled independently of the default state of the element **A**.

- **Links (Table 4.3)**—Pseudo-classes are used to style not only the initial appearance of the anchor tag, but also how it appears after it has been visited, while the visitor hovers their mouse over it, and when visitors are clicking it.

- **Dynamic** (Table 4.3)—Pseudo-classes can be applied to any element to define how it is styled when the user hovers over it, clicks it, or selects it.

- **Structural (Table 4.4)**—Pseudo-classes are similar to the sibling combinatory selectors but allow you to specifically style elements based on an exact or computed numeric position.

- **Other** (Table 4.4)—Pseudo-classes are available to style elements based on language or based on what tag they are *not*.

SelectorColon   *Declaration List*

a:link { color: red; }

colon   *Pseudo-class*

A General syntax of a pseudo-class.

TABLE 4.3 Link and Dynamic Pseudo-Classes

Format	Name	Elements Are Styled If...	Compatibility
`:link`	Link	the value of href is not in history	IE4, FF1, O3.5, S1, CSS1
`:visited`	Visited Link	the value of href is in history	IE4, FF1, O3.5, S1, CSS1
`:target`	Targeted Link	a targeted anchor link	FF1.3, S1.3, C1, O9.5 CSS3
`:active`	Active	the element is clicked	IE7, FF1, O3.5, S1, CSS1
`:hover`	Hover	the pointer is over the element	IE4*, FF1, O3.5, S1, CSS2
`:focus`	Focus	the element has screen focus	IE7, FF1, O7, S1, CSS2

* Only available for anchor tags until IE7

TABLE 4.4 Structural/Other Pseudo-Classes

Format	Name	Elements Are Styled If...	Compatibility
`:root`	Root	is the top level element in a document	FF1.5, O9.5, S3.1, C3, CSS3
`:empty`	Empty	has no children	FF1.5, O9.5, S3.1, C3, CSS3
`:only-child`	Only Child	has no siblings	FF1.5, O9.5, S3.1, C3, CSS3
`:only-of-type`	Only of Type	has its unique selector among its siblings	FF1.5, O9.5, S3.1, C3, CSS3
`:first-child`	First-Child	is the first child of another element	FF1.5, O9.5, S3.1, C3, CSS2
`:nth-of-type(n)`	Nth of Type	is the nth element with that selector	FF1.5, O9.5, S3.1, C3, CSS3
`:nth-last-of-type(n)`	Nth From Last of Type	is the nth element with that selector from the last element with that selector	FF1.5, O9.5, S3.1, C3, CSS3
`:last-child`	Last Child	is the last child in the parent element	FF1.5, O9.5, S3.1, C3, CSS3
`:first-of-type`	First of Type	is the first of its selector type in the parent element	FF1.5, O9.5, S3.1, C3, CSS3
`:last-of-type`	Last of Type	is the last of its selector type in the parent element	FF1.5, O9.5, S3.1, C3, CSS3
`:lang()`	Language	has a specified language code defined	IE8, FF1.5, O9.5, S3.1, C3, CSS2.1
`:not(s)`	Negation	is not using specific selectors	FF1.5, O9.5, S3.1, C3, CSS3

Styling links

Although a link is a tag, its individual states are not. To set properties for these states, you must use the pseudo-classes associated with each state that a link can have (in this order):

- **:link** lets you declare the appearance of hypertext links that have not yet been selected.

- **:visited** lets you set the appearance of links that the visitor selected previously—that is, the URL of the **href** attribute in the tag is part of the browser's history.

- **:hover** lets you set the appearance of the element when the visitor's pointer is over it.

- **:active** sets the style of the element when it is clicked or selected by the visitor.

For ideas on which styles to use with links, see the sidebar "Picking Link Styles."

To set contrasting link appearances:

1. Style the anchor tag.

   ```
   a {...}
   ```

   Although not required, it's best to first define the general anchor style (**Code 4.6**). This differs from setting the **:link** pseudo-class in that these styles are applied to all the link pseudo-classes. So, you want to declare any styles that will remain constant or are changed in only one of the states.

continues on page 84

Chapter 1.

Down The Rabbit-Hole

Chapter 2. The Pool of Tears —— Link

Chapter 3. A Caucus-Race —— Visited
and a Long Tale

Chapter 4. The Rabbit Sends —— Hover
in a Little Bill

Chapter 5. Advice from a —— Active
Caterpillar

Chapter 6. Pig and Pepper

Chapter 7. A Mad Tea-Party

Chapter 8. The Queen's
Croquet-Ground

Chapter 9. The Mock
Turtle's Story

Chapter 10. The Lobster
Quadrille

Chapter 11. Who Stole The
Tarts?

Chapter 12. Alice's Evidence

B The results of Code 4.6 show the links styled for each state to help the user understand what's going on.

Code 4.6 The link styles are set for the default and then all four link states, creating color differentiation **B**. Notice also that I've turned off underlining with text decoration but added an underline effect using border bottom.

```
<!-- HTML5 -->
<!DOCTYPE html>
<html lang="en">
<head>
<meta http-equiv="Content-Type" content="text/html; charset=UTF-8" />
<title>Alice's Adventures in Wonderland</title>
<style type="text/css" media="all">
  a {
    display: block;
    text-decoration: none;
    padding: 5px;
    width: 200px; }
  a:link {
    color: rgb(255,102,102);
    border-bottom: 1px dotted rgb(255,51,5,51); }
  a:visited {
    color: rgb(255,153,153);
    border-bottom: 1px dotted rgb(255,235,235); }
  a:hover {
    color: rgb(255,0,0);
    border-bottom: 1px solid rgb(255,0,0); }
  a:active {
    color: rgb(0,0,255);
    border-bottom: 1px dotted rgb(102,102,102); }
</style>
</head>
<body>
<navigation>
  <a href=""><strong>Chapter 1. </strong>Down The Rabbit-Hole</a>
  <a href=""><strong>Chapter 2. </strong>The Pool of Tears</a>
  <a href=""><strong>Chapter 3. </strong>A Caucus-Race and a Long Tale</a>
  <a href=""><strong>Chapter 4. </strong>The Rabbit Sends in a Little Bill</a>
  <a href=""><strong>Chapter 5. </strong>Advice from a Caterpillar</a>
  <a href=""><strong>Chapter 6. </strong>Pig and Pepper</a>
  <a href=""><strong>Chapter 7. </strong>A Mad Tea-Party</a>
  <a href=""><strong>Chapter 8. </strong>The Queen's Croquet-Ground</a>
  <a href=""><strong>Chapter 9. </strong>The Mock Turtle's Story</a>
  <a href=""><strong>Chapter 10. </strong>The Lobster Quadrille</a>
  <a href=""><strong>Chapter 11. </strong>Who Stole The Tarts?</a>
  <a href=""><strong>Chapter 12. </strong>Alice's Evidence</a>
</navigation>
</body>
</html>
```

2. **Style the *default* link state.** Type the selector (anchor tag, class, or ID) of the element you want to style, followed by a colon (:), and then `link`.

   `a:link {...}`

   You can override styles set for the anchor tag, but this rule should always come before the `:visited` pseudo-class.

3. **Style the *visited* link style.** Type the selector (anchor, class, or ID) of the element you want to style, followed by a colon (:), and then `visited`.

   `a:visited {...}`

4. **Style the *hover* link state.** Type the selector (anchor, class, or ID) of the element you want to style, followed by a colon (:), and then `hover`.

   `a:hover {...}`

5. **Style the *active* link state.** Type the selector (anchor, class, or ID) of the element you want to style, followed by a colon (:), and then `active`.

   `a:active {...}`

6. **Style is applied to the link state as needed.**

   `<a href="chapater01.html">...</a>`

   All links on the page will obey the rules you lay down here when styling the various link states. You can—and should—use selective styling to differentiate link types.

Picking Link Styles

Most browsers default to blue for unvisited links and red or purple for visited links. The problem with using two different colors for visited and unvisited links is that visitors may not remember which color applies to which type of link. The colors you choose must distinguish links from other text on the screen and distinguish among the states (link, visited, hover, and active) without dominating the screen and becoming distracting.

I recommend using a color for unvisited links that contrasts with both the page's background color and the text color. Then, for visited links, use a darker or lighter version of the same color that contrasts with the background but is dimmer than the unvisited link color. Brighter unfollowed links will then stand out dramatically from the dimmer followed links.

For example, on a page with a white background and black text, I might use bright red for links (rgb(255,0,0)) and pale red (rgb(255,153,153)) for visited links. The brighter version stands out; the paler version is less distinctive, but still obviously a link.

TIP In this example, the pseudo-classes are applied directly to the anchor tag, but any class or ID could have been used as long as it was then applied to an anchor tag.

TIP You can apply the dynamic pseudo-classes :hover, :active, and :focus to any element, not just links.

TIP The general anchor link styles will be inherited by the different states and between states. The font you set for the :link appearance, for example, will be inherited by the :active, :visited, and :hover states.

TIP The Web is a hypertext medium, so it is important that users be able to distinguish among text, links, and visited links. Because users don't always have their Underline Links option turned on, it's a good idea to set the link appearance for every document.

TIP If you use too many colors, your visitors may not be able to tell which words are links and which are not.

TIP The link styles are set for the entire page in this example, but links can be used for a variety of purposes. For example, links might be used for global navigation, in a list of article titles, or even as a dynamic control. To that end, it's a good idea to style links depending on their usage:

```
nav a {...}
nav a:link {...}
nav a:visited {...}
```

The preceding styles would be applied only to links in the navigation element.

Styling for interaction

Once loaded, Web pages are far from static. Users will start interacting with the page right away, moving their pointers across the screen and clicking hither and yon. The dynamic pseudo-classes allow you to style elements as the user interacts with them, providing visual feedback:

- **:hover**—Same as for links, but sets the appearance of the element when the pointer is hovering over it.

- **:focus**—Applied to elements that can receive focus, such as form text fields.

- **:active**—Same as for links, but sets the style of the element when it is clicked or selected.

To define a dynamic pseudo-class:

1. Style the *default* element.

   `input {...}`

   Although optional, it's generally a good idea to set the default, nondynamic style for the elements receiving dynamic styles (**Code 4.7**).

2. Style the *hover* state of the element. Type the selector (HTML, class, or ID), a colon (**:**), and then **hover**.

   `input:hover {...}`

   As soon as the pointer enters the element's box (see Chapter 10 for details about the box model), the style change will occur.

Code 4.7 The input elements are set to change style when the user interacts with them by hovering, selecting (focus), or clicking (active) **C**.

```
<!-- HTML5 -->
<!DOCTYPE html>
<html lang="en">
<head>
<meta http-equiv="Content-Type"
→ content="text/html; charset=UTF-8" />
<title>Alice's Adventures in Wonderland
→ </title>
<style type="text/css" media="all">
  input {
    border: 3px solid rgb(153,153,153);
    background-color: rgb(204,204,204);
    color: rgb(153,153,153);
    padding: 0 5px;
    font-size: 2em; }
  input:hover {
    border-color: rgb(204,153,153);
    color: rgb(102,102,102); }
  input:focus {
    border-color: rgb(255,0,0);
    background-color: rgb(255,255,255);
    color: rgb(0,0,0);
    outline: none; }
  input:active {
    color: rgb(255,0,0);
    border-color: rgb(255,0,0);
    background-color: rgb(0,0,0); }
</style>
</head>
<body>
<form>
  <input type="text" value="First Name">
  <input type="text" class="hover" value="Last
Name">
  <input type="text" class="focus"
  → value="eMail">
  <input type="button" class="active"
  → value="Search">
</form>
</body>
</html>
```

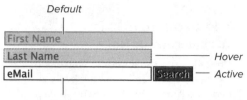

Default

First Name

Last Name ———— *Hover*

eMail   Search — *Active*

Focus

C **The results of Code 4.7.** This shows a simple form field in the four dynamic states. Providing this visual feedback can help users know which form field is ready for use or that they have clicked a button.

TIP I recommend caution when changing some attributes for :hover. Changing typeface, font size, weight, and other properties may make the text grow larger or smaller than the space reserved for it in the layout and force the whole page to reflow its content, which can really annoy visitors.

TIP In this example, input is used to show the dynamic states. The input has one styling drawback in that all input types use the same tag. Later in this chapter, you will see how to use tag attributes to set styles, which will allow you to set different styles for text fields and buttons.

3. **Style the *focus* state of the element.**
   Type the selector (HTML, class, or ID), a colon (:), and then **focus**.

   `input:focus {...}`

   As soon as the element receives focus (is clicked or tabbed to), the style change occurs and then reverts to the hover or default style when the element loses focus (called *blur*).

4. **Style the *active* state of the element.**
   Type the selector (HTML, class, or ID), a colon (:), and then **active**.

   `input:active {...}`

   As soon as the user clicks within the element's box (explained in Chapter 10), the style change will occur and then revert to either the hover or default style when released.

5. **The styles are applied to the elements' states as necessary in reaction to the user.**

   ```
   <input type="button"
   →value="Search">
   ```

   All the tags using the specific selector will have their states styled.

TIP The order in which you define your link and dynamic pseudo-classes makes a difference. For example, placing the :hover pseudo-class before the :visited pseudo-class keeps :hover from working after a link has been visited. For best results, define your styles in this order: link, visited, hover, focus, and active.

TIP One way to remember the pseudo-element order is the meme LoVe HAte: Link Visited Hover Active.

TIP You will want to always set :focus if you're setting :hover. Why? Hover is applied only to nonkeyboard (mouse) interactions with the element. For keyboard-only Web users, :focus will apply.

NEW IN CSS3: Styling specific children with pseudo-classes ★

Designers often want to apply a style to an element that is the first element to appear within another element, such as a parent's first child.

The first-child pseudo-element has been available since CSS2; however, CSS3 offers an assortment of new structural pseudo-elements for styling an element's child element exactly (Table 4.4):

- `:first-child`—Sets the appearance of the first instance of a selector type if it is the first child of its parent.

- `:first-of-type`—Sets the appearance of an element the first time its selector type appears within the parent.

- `:nth-child(#)`—Sets the appearance of the specific occurrence of the specified child element. For example, the third child element of a paragraph would be `p:nth-child(3)`.

- `:nth-of-type(#)`—Sets the appearance of the specific occurrence of a selector type within the parent. For example, the seventh paragraph would be `p:nth-of-type(7)`.

- `:nth-last-of-type(#)`—Sets the appearance of the specific occurrence of a selector type within the parent, but from the bottom. For example, the third paragraph from the bottom would be `p:nth-last=of-type(3)`.

- `:last-child`—Sets the appearance of the element of the indicated selector type if it is the last child of the parent.

- `:last-of-type`—Sets the appearance of the last instance of a particular selector type within its parent.

Text Decoration: To Underline or Not

Underlining is the standard way of indicating a hypertext link on the Web. However, the presence of many underlined links turns a page into an impenetrable mass of lines, and the text becomes difficult to read. In addition, if visitors have underlining turned off, they cannot see the links, especially if the link and text colors are the same.

CSS allows you to turn off underlining for links, overriding the visitor's preference. I recommend this practice and prefer to rely on clear color choices to highlight hypertext links or to rely on the alternative underlining method of border-bottom, which allows you better control over the style of the underline. See Chapter 14 for more information.

Code 4.8 The list has styles set for it based on location within the list **D**.

```
<!-- HTML5 -->
<!DOCTYPE html>
<html lang="en">
<head>
<meta http-equiv="Content-Type"
→ content="text/html; charset=UTF-8" />
<title>Alice's Adventures in Wonderland
→ </title>
<style type="text/css" media="all">
  li:first-child { font-size: .875em; }
  li:first-of-type { color: red; }
  li:nth-of-type(3) { font-size: 1.5em }
  li:nth-last-of-type(2)  { font-size: 2em; }
  li:last-of-type { color: red; }
  li:last-child { font-size: 2.5em; }
</style>
</head>
<body>
<ol>
  <li>Alice</li>
  <li>The White Rabbit</li>
  <li>The Mad Hatter</li>
  <li>The Queen of Hearts</li>
  <li>The Door Mouse</li>
</ol>
</body>
</html>
```

1. Alice
2. The White Rabbit
3. The Mad Hatter
4. The Queen of Hearts
5. The Door Mouse

D The results of Code 4.8 show the items in the list styled separately. In this case, the first child and first of type are the same element as the last element and last of type.

To style the children of an element:

1. **Style the children based on their positions in the parent.** Type the selector (HTML, class, or ID) of the element you want to style, a colon (:), and one of the structural pseudo-elements from Table 4.4 (**Code 4.8**).

   `li:first-child {...}`

   `li:first-of-type {...}`

   `li:nth-of-type(3) {...}`

   `li:nth-last-of-type(2) {...}`

   `li:last-child {...}`

   `li:last-of-type {...}`

2. **Elements will be styled if they match the pattern.**

   `<li>...</li>`

   Set up your HTML with the selectors from step 1 in mind.

Styling for a particular language

The World Wide Web is just that, all around the world, which means that anyone, anywhere can see your pages. It also means that Web pages are created in many languages.

The :lang() pseudo-class lets you specify styles that depend on the language specified by the language property.

To set a style for a specific language:

1. **Style an element based on its language code.** Type the selector (HTML, class, or ID) of the element you want to style, a colon (:), `lang`, and enter the letter code for the language you are defining within parentheses (**Code 4.9**).

   `p:lang(fr) {...}`

2. **The element is styled if it has a matching language code.** Set up your tag in the HTML with the language attributes as necessary.

   `<p lang="fr">...</p>`

   If the indicated selector has its language attribute equal to the same value that you indicated in parentheses in step 1, the style is applied.

> **TIP** You can use any string as the language letter code, as long as it matches the value in the HTML. However, the W3C recommends using the codes from RFC 3066 or its successor. For more on language tags, visit www.w3.org/International/articles/language-tags.

> **TIP** Language styles can go far beyond simple colors and fonts. Many languages have specific symbols for quotes and punctuation, which CSS can add. In Chapter 9, you will find information on how to style quotes for a particular language.

Code 4.9 Styles are set to turn paragraphs red if they are in French (fr) **E**.

```
<!-- HTML5 -->
<!DOCTYPE html>
<html lang="en">
<head>
<meta http-equiv="Content-Type"
→ content="text/html; charset=UTF-8" />
<title>Alice's Adventure's in Wonderland
→ </title>
<style type="text/css" media="all">
  p:lang(fr) {
    color: red;
    font-style: italic; }
</style>
</head>
<body>
  <p>It sounded an excellent plan,...</p>
  <p lang="fr">On aurait dit un excellent
  → plan,...</p>
</body>
</html>
```

It sounded an excellent plan, no doubt, and very neatly and simply arranged; the only difficulty was, that she had not the smallest idea how to set about it; and while she was peering about anxiously among the trees, a little sharp bark just over her head made her look up in a great hurry.

On aurait dit un excellent plan, sans doute, et fort proprement et simplement disposés, la seule difficulté, c'est qu'elle n'avait pas la moindre idée de comment s'y prendre, et tandis qu'elle regardait avec anxiété à propos parmi les arbres, une petite barque forte juste sur sa tête la faisait paraître en toute hâte.

E The results of Code 4.9 show the paragraph in French rendered in red (with my apologies to French speakers).

Code 4.10 If the element is a paragraph that does *not* use the dialog class, it will be displayed in red and italics **F**.

```
<!-- HTML5 -->
<!DOCTYPE html>
<html lang="en">
<head>
<meta http-equiv="Content-Type"
→ content="text/html; charset=UTF-8" />
<title>Alice's Adventures in Wonderland</
→ </title>
<style type="text/css" media="all">
  p:not(.dialog) {
    color: red;
    font-style: italic; }
</style>
</head>
<body>
<p class='dialog'>"Why?" said the
→ Caterpillar.</p>

<p>Here was another puzzling question,...</p>

<p class='dialog'>"Come back!" the
→ Caterpillar,..."</p>
</body>
</html>
```

NEW IN CSS3: *Not* styling an element ★

So far you've looked at ways to style a tag if it *is* something. The negation selector, **:not,** allows you to *not* style something for a particular selector.

To not set a style for a particular element:

1. **Style elements to exclude certain selectors.** Type the selector (HTML, class, or ID) of the element you want to style, a colon (**:**), **not**, and enter the selectors you want excluded from this rule in parentheses (**Code 4.10**).

   ```
   p:not(.dialog) {...}
   ```

2. **The element is not styled if it contains the indicated selector.**

   ```
   <p class='dialog'>...</p>
   → <p>...</p>
   ```

   The styles are applied to elements that match the initial selector but *not* the selector in parentheses.

"Why?" said the Caterpillar.

Here was another puzzling question; and as Alice could not think of any good reason, and as the Caterpillar seemed to be in a VERY unpleasant state of mind, she turned away.

"Come back!" the Caterpillar called after her. "I've something important to say!"

F **The results of Code 4.10.** This shows that the paragraph that does use the dialog class does not receive the style.

Working with Pseudo-elements

A *pseudo-element* is a specific, unique part of an element—such as the first letter or first line of a paragraph—that can be styled independently of the rest of the element. (For a list of other pseudo-elements, see **Table 4.5**.)

Working with first letters and lines

You can access the first letter of any block of text directly using the `:first-letter` pseudo-element. The first line of any block of text can be isolated for style treatment using the `:first-line` pseudo-element.

To highlight the beginning of an article:

1. **Style the default version of the element.**

   ```
   article p {...}
   ```

   Although not required, it's generally a good idea to set the default style of the selector for which you will be styling the :**first-letter** pseudo-element (**Code 4.11**).

Selectors

| *Colon* | *Pseudo-element* | *Declaration List* |

p:first-letter { color: red; }

p::first-letter { color: red; }

Colon×2

Ⓐ The general syntax for pseudo-elements. Pseudo-elements can have either a single or double colon, but use a single colon at present for increased browser compatibility.

TABLE 4.5 Pseudo-Elements

Format	Name	Elements Are Styled If...	Compatibility
`:first-letter`, `::first-letter`	the first Letter	first letter in text	IE5.5, FF1, O3.5, S1, CSS1
`:first-line`, `::first-line`	the first line of text	they are the first line of text	IE5.5, FF1, O3.5, S1, CSS1
`:after`, `::after`	After	space immediately before element	IE8, FF1, O5, S1, CSS2
`:before`, `::before`	Before	space immediately after element	IE8, FF1, O5, S1, CSS2

Code 4.11 Styles are set for the first letter and first line of the first paragraph in an article **B**.

```
<!-- HTML5 -->
<!DOCTYPE html>
<html lang="en">
<head>
<meta http-equiv="Content-Type"
→ content="text/html; charset=UTF-8" />
<title>...</title>
<style type="text/css" media="all">
  article p {
    font-size: 16px;
    line-height: 24px;
    color: rgb(102,102,102) }
  article p:first-of-type:first-letter {
    color: red;
    font-size: 3em;
    float: left;
    margin-right: 5px; }
  article p:first-of-type:first-line {
    font-size: 1.25em;
    font-weight: bold;
    color: rgb(0,0,0); }
</style>
</head>
<body>
<article>
<h1>Alice's Adventures in Wonderland</h1>
  <p>The moment Alice appeared,...</p>
  <p>The executioner's argument was,...</p>
  <p>The King's argument was,...</p>
</article>
</body>
</html>
```

Alice's Adventures in Wonderland

The moment Alice appeared, she was appealed to by all three to settle the question, and they repeated their arguments to her, though, as they all spoke at once, she found it very hard indeed to make out exactly what they said.

The executioner's argument was, that you couldn't cut off a head unless there was a body to cut it off from: that he had never had to do such a thing before, and he wasn't going to begin at HIS time of life.

The King's argument was, that anything that had a head could be beheaded, and that you weren't to talk nonsense.

B The results of Code 4.11. A common typographic trick to draw the reader's eye to the beginning of a paragraph is to use a drop cap and to bold the first line of text, as shown here.

2. **Style the first letter of the element if it is the first of its type.** Type the selector you want to style the first letter of (**article p**), a colon (:), and then **first-letter**.

   **article p:first-of-type:
   → first-letter {...}**

   To affect only the first paragraph in an article, you can add the **:first-of-type** pseudo-class, as in this example.

3. **Style the first line of the element's text if it is the first of its type.** Type the selector (**article p**) for which you want to style the first letter, a colon (:), and then **first-line**.

   **article p:first-of-type:
   → first-line {...}**

   In this example, the **first-of-type** pseudo-class is added so that only the first paragraph in an article is styled.

4. **The element's first letter and first line of text is styled if it is the first of its type in the parent element.** Add the class attribute to the relevant HTML tag.

   <p>...</p>

   Although you do not have to use a class, you generally will want to selectively style the first letter of elements rather than styling them all universally.

TIP Drop cap styled letters are a time-honored way to start a new section or chapter by making the first letter of a paragraph larger than subsequent letters and moving several lines of text to accommodate the larger letter. Medieval monks used drop caps with illuminated manuscripts. Now you can use them on the Web.

Setting content before and after an element

The `:before` and `:after` pseudo-elements can be used to generate content that appears above or below a selector. Generally, these pseudo-classes are used with the **content** property. (See "Adding Content Using CSS" in Chapter 9.) The pseudo-elements let you add and style repetitive content to the page in a consistent way.

To set content before and after an element:

1. **Style the element.**

   h1 {...}

   Although not required, it's generally a good idea to set the default style of the selector for which you will be styling the `:before` and `:after` pseudo-elements. (See **Code 4.12**.)

2. **Add content before the element.** Type the selector (HTML, class, or ID) you want to add content before, a colon (:), and then the keyword **before**.

   h1:before { content:... }

   Next, declare the **content** property and define what generated content goes before the element and how it should be styled.

3. **Add content after the element.** Type the selector (HTML, class, or ID) you want to add content after, a colon (:), and then the keyword **after**.

   h1:after { content:... }

   Next, declare the **content** property and define what generated content goes after the element and how it should be styled.

Code 4.12 Before and after pseudo-elements are used to add content—images **C**, in this case—to the page header **D**.

```
<!-- HTML5 -->
<!DOCTYPE html>
<html lang="en">
<head>
<meta http-equiv="Content-Type"
→ content="text/html; charset=UTF-8" />
<title>...</title>
<style type="text/css" media="all">
  h1 {
    font-size: 2em;
    color: red;
    font-style: italic; }
  h1:before {
    content:  url('../_images/bullet-01.png'); }
  h1:after {
    content: url('../_images/bullet-02.png'); }
</style>
</head>
<body>
<h1>Alice's Adventures in Wonderland</h1>
  <p>The moment Alice appeared,...</p>
  <p>The executioner's argument was,...</p>
  <p>The King's argument was,...</p>
</article>had a head could be beheaded,
→ and that you weren't to talk nonsense.</p>
</article>
</body>
</html>
```

C bullet-01.png & bullet-02.png will be used as flourishes around titles.

◆▶ Alice's Adventures in Wonderland ◀◆

The moment Alice appeared, she was appealed to by all three to settle the question, and they repeated their arguments to her, though, as they all spoke at once, she found it very hard indeed to make out exactly what they said.

The executioner's argument was, that you couldn't cut off a head unless there was a body to cut it off from: that he had never had to do such a thing before, and he wasn't going to begin at HIS time of life.

The King's argument was, that anything that had a head could be beheaded, and that you weren't to talk nonsense.

D The header now has a bit of flourish added before and after by the CSS. These images take up space as if they were in an image tag, but do not show up in the HTML code.

Coming Soon!
Styling the Selection

Although not implemented in enough (or any) browsers to make it worth even thinking about yet, a great new pseudo-element is coming to CSS3, `::selection`, which will style any element selected by the user.

TIP The pseudo-elements syntax in CSS3 has undergone a slight change from the CSS2 syntax (which is rare). Pseudo-elements now have a double colon to distinguish them from pseudo-classes. Existing pseudo-elements can use either single or double colons. New and future pseudo-elements should use double colons, but will work with a single colon.

TIP Since IE8 does not support double colon syntax for CSS2 pseudo-elements, it's a good idea to use single colon syntax for now until all browsers have adopted the syntax.

TIP Be careful when using before and after to add content to your page. This content will not appear to search engines or screen readers, so do not rely on it for anything vital.

Defining Styles Based on Tag Attributes

Although style attributes should all be handled by CSS, many HTML tags still have attributes that define how they behave. For example, the image tag, **img,** always includes the **src** attribute to define the source for the image file to be loaded.

Styles can be assigned to an HTML element based on an attribute or an attribute value, allowing you to set styles if the attribute has been set, is or is not a specific value, or contains a specific value (**Table 4.6**).

To set styles based on an element's attributes:

1. **Set styles if the element has a specific property**. To set styles based on the existence of an attribute, type the selector you want to style (HTML, class, or ID), a left bracket ([), the name of the attribute you want to check for, and a right bracket (]) (**Code 4.13**) **Ⓐ**.

   a[title] {...}

Selector

Attribute　　　*Declaration*

a[title] { color: red; }

Square brackets

Ⓐ The general syntax of an attribute selector.

TABLE 4.6 Attribute Selectors

Format	Name	Elements Are Styled If That Element:	Compatibility
[attr]	Attribute	has specified attribute	IE7, FF1.5, O5, S2, CSS2
[attr="value"]	Exact value	has specified attribute equal to exact value	IE7, FF1.5, O5, S2, CSS2
[attr~="value"]	Spaced List	has specified attribute equal to exact value within space-separated list	IE7, FF1.5, O5, S2, CSS2
[attrl="value"]	Hyphenated List	has specified attribute equal to exact value within hyphen-separated list	IE7, FF1.5, O5, S2, CSS2
[attr^="value"]	Begins with	has specified attribute equal to exact value at beginning	CSS3
[attr$="value"]	Ends With	has specified attribute equal to exact value at end	CSS3
[attr*="value"]	Contains	has specified attribute equal to exact value anywhere	CSS3

Code 4.13 HTML tags can have different attributes, and you can add styles to an element based on its attributes **B**.

```
<!-- HTML5 -->
<!DOCTYPE html>
<html lang="en">
<head>
<meta http-equiv="Content-Type"
→ content="text/html; charset=UTF-8" />
<title>Alice's Adventures in Wonderland</
→ title>
<style type="text/css" media="all">
  a[title] { display: block; color: rgb(0,0,0);
  → font-size: .8em; }
  a[title="Home"] {color: rgb(51,0,0);
  → font-size: 1em;}
  a[title~="email"] { color:rgb(102,0,0);
  → font-size: 1.2em; }
  a[title|="resume"] { color: rgb(153,0,0);
  → font-size: 1.4em;}
  a[href^="http://"] {color: rgb(204,0,0);
  vfont-size: 1.6em;}
  a[href$=".info"] {color: rgb(235,0,0);
  → font-size: 1.8em;}
  a[href*="speakinginstyles"]
  → {color: rgb(255,0,0); font-size: 2em;}
</style>
</head>
<body>
<navigation>
  <h2>About the Author</h2>
  <a href="" title="Portfolio">Portfolio</a>
  <a href="index.html" title="Home">Home
  → Page</a>
  <a href="" title="contact email
  → link">Email</a>
  <a href="" title="resume-link">R√©sum√©</a>
  <a href="http://www.jasonspeaking.com"
  → title="blog">JasonSpeaking</a>
  <a href="http://www.fluidwebtype.info"
  → title="book">Fluid Web Typography</a>
  <a href="http://www.speakinginstyles.com"
  → title="book">Speaking In Styles</a>
</navigation>
</body>
</html>
```

This will assign the styles you declare only if the tag has this attribute assigned to it regardless of the value.

2. **Set styles if a string exactly matches the property's value.** To set styles based on an attribute's exact value, type the selector you want to style (HTML, class, or ID), a left bracket ([), the name of the attribute you want to check for, an equals sign (=), the value you are testing for in quotes ('...'), and a right bracket (]). The value is case sensitive.

   `a[title='home'] {...}`

   This will assign the styles you declare only if the tag has this attribute assigned to it with the exact assigned value.

continues on next page

B The results of Code 4.13. This shows how styles are applied to elements based on their properties.

3. **Set styles if a string is in a space-separated list of values**. To set styles based on an attribute's value that is within a list of space-separated values (for example, a particular word in a sentence), type the selector you want to style (HTML, class, or ID), a left bracket ([), the name of the attribute you want to check for, a tilde (~), an equals sign (=), the value you are testing for in quotes ('...'), and a right bracket (]).

`a[title~="email"] {...}`

This will assign the styles you declare only if the tag has the attribute assigned to it with a value that contains the string as part of a space-separated list. Generally, this means that it is a word in a sentence. Partial words do not count. So in this example, testing for `'mail'` would not work.

4. **Sets the style if the string is in a hyphenated list of values assigned to the property.** To set styles based on an attribute's value being the first in a list separated by hyphens, type the selector you want to style (HTML, class, or ID), a left bracket ([), the name of the attribute you want to check for, a bar (|), an equals sign (=), the value you are testing for in quotes ('...'), and a right bracket (]).

`a[title|="resume"]`

This will assign the styles you declare only if the tag has this attribute assigned to it with a value that contains the string at the beginning of a hyphen-separated list. Generally, this is used for styling languages as an alternative to using the language pseudo-class.

5. **NEW IN CSS3 ★: Set styles if a string is the value's prefix.** To set styles based on the value at the beginning of an attribute, type the selector you want to style (HTML, class, or ID), a left bracket ([), the name of the attribute you want to check for, a carat (^), an equals sign (=), the value you are testing for in quotes ('...'), and a right bracket (]).

```
a[href^="http://"]
```

This will assign the styles you declare only if the value string occurs exactly as it is in the quotes at the beginning of the attribute value.

6. **NEW IN CSS3 ★: Set styles if a string is the property value's suffix.** To set styles based on an attribute's value being the first in a hyphen-separated list, type the selector you want to style (HTML, class, or ID), a left bracket ([), the name of the attribute you want to check for, a dollar sign ($), an equals sign (=), the value you are testing for in quotes ('...'), and a right bracket (]).

```
a[href$=".info"]
```

This will assign the styles you declare only if the value occurs at the end of the attribute's value.

7. **Set styles if a string is anywhere in the property value.** To set styles based on an attribute's value being the first in a hyphen-separated list, type the selector you want to style (HTML, class, or ID), a left bracket ([), the name of the attribute you want to check for, an asterisk (*), an equals sign (=), the value you are testing for in quotes ('...'), and a right bracket (]).

```
a[href*="speakinginstyles"]
```

This will assign the styles you declare if the value occurs anywhere in the attribute's value.

TIP Values are case sensitive. In other words, 'Alice' and 'alice' are two different values.

NEW IN CSS3: Querying the Media ★

In Chapter 3 you learned how to specify style sheets for a particular media type, allowing you to set styles depending on whether the HTML is output to a screen, print, TV, or a handheld or other device (**Table 4.7**). CSS3 adds an important new capability that allows you to set styles based on common interface properties such as width, height, aspect ratio, and number of available colors.

Media queries and the **@media** rule can be used to tailor your page, not just to a general device type but to the specific device your site visitor is using. This includes sizing for print, for mobile devices, or to best fit the size of the open browser window.

Media queries

If you want to know the current size of the browser window, why not just ask the browser? JavaScript gives you the ability to do this, but it's a cumbersome way to get some basic facts about the Webbed environment your design is trying to fit into.

Media queries provide you with several common media properties that you can test **A** and then delivers the style sheet that best suits the environment.

Although media queries have many properties (**Table 4.8**), they come in five basic flavors:

- **Aspect-ratio** looks for the relative dimensions of the device expressed as a ratio: 16:9, for example.

- **Width** and **height** looks for the dimensions of the display area. These can also be expressed as maximum and minimum values.

continues on page 102

TABLE 4.7 Media Values

Value	Intended for
screen	Computer displays
tty	Teletypes, computer terminals, and older portable devices
tv	Television displays
projection	Projectors
handheld	Portable phones and PDAs
print	Paper
braille	Braille tactile readers
speech	Speech synthesizers
all	All devices

```
media="
    screen
    and (min-width: 600px)
    and (max-width: 980px)"
```

A The general syntax for media queries.

TABLE 4.8 Media Query Properties

Property	Value	Compatibility
aspect-ratio	<ratio>	FF3.5, S1, C1, O9.5, CSS3
max-aspect-ratio	<ratio>	FF3.5, S1, C1, O9.5, CSS3
min-aspect-ratio	<ratio>	FF3.5, S1, C1, O9.5, CSS3
device-aspect-ratio	<ratio>	FF3.5, S1, C1, O9.5, CSS3
max-device-aspect-ratio	<ratio>	FF3.5, S1, C1, O9.5, CSS3
min-device-aspect-ratio	<ratio>	FF3.5, S1, C1, O9.5, CSS3
color	<integer>	FF3.5, S1, C1, O10, CSS3
max-color	<integer>	FF3.5, S1, C1, O10, CSS3
min-color	<integer>	FF3.5, S1, C1, O10, CSS3
color-index	<integer>	FF3.5, S1, C1, O10, CSS3
max-color-index	<integer>	FF3.5, S1, C1, O10, CSS3
min-color-index	<integer>	FF3.5, S1, C1, O10, CSS3
device-height	<length>	FF3.5, S1, C1, O9.5, CSS3
max-device-height	<length>	FF3.5, S1, C1, O9.5, CSS3
min-device-height	<length>	FF3.5, S1, C1, O9.5, CSS3
device-width	<length>	FF3.5, S1, C1, O9.5, CSS3
max-device-width	<length>	FF3.5, S1, C1, O9.5, CSS3
min-device-width	<length>	FF3.5, S1, C1, O9.5, CSS3
height	<length>	FF3.5, S1, C1, O9.5, CSS3
max-height	<length>	FF3.5, S1, C1, O9.5, CSS3
min-height	<length>	FF3.5, S1, C1, O9.5, CSS3
monochrome	<integer>	FF3.5, S1, C1, O10, CSS3
max-monochrome	<integer>	FF3.5, S1, C1, O10, CSS3
min-monochrome	<integer>	FF3.5, S1, C1, O10, CSS3
orientation	portrait, landscape	FF3.5, S1, C1, CSS3
resolution	<resolution>	FF3.5, S1, C1, O10, CSS3
max-resolution	<resolution>	FF3.5, S1, C1, O10, CSS3
min-resolution	<resolution>	FF3.5, S1, C1, O10, CSS3
scan	progressive, interlaced	FF3.5, S1, C1, O10, CSS3
width	<length>	FF3.5, S1, C1, O9.5, CSS3
max-width	<length>	FF3.5, S1, C1, O9.5, CSS3
min-width	<length>	FF3.5, S1, C1, O9.5, CSS3

- **Orientation** looks for *landscape* (height greater than width) or *portrait* (width greater than height) layout. This allows you to tailor designs for devices that can flip.

- **Color**, **Color-index**, and **monochrome** finds the number of colors or bits per color. These allow you to tailor your design for black and white mobile devices.

- **Resolution** looks at the density of pixels in the output. This is especially useful when you want to take advantage of display devices that have a higher resolution than 72 dpi.

By default, media queries are for the viewport (see Chapter 11 for details on the viewport) with the exception of those that specify *device*, in which case they are for the entire screen or output area. For example, width is the width of the visible browser viewport within the screen, whereas device-width is the width of the entire screen.

Code 4.14 *default.css*—These styles are applied regardless of the media type and include sans-serif fonts, a dark background, and light text.

```
/*** Default Styles ***/

body {
  background: black url('../_images/AAIW-illos/
  → alice23b.gif') no-repeat 0 0;
  margin: 0 0;
  padding: 200px 0 0 175px; }
h1 {
  color: white;
  font-style: italic; }
h2 {
  color: rgb(153,153,153); }
p {
  font: normal 100%/1.5 Corbel, Helvetica,
  → Arial, Sans-serif;
  color: rgb(204,204,204); }
```

Code 4.15 *print.css*—These styles are tailored for the printed page, changing the background to white (assuming white paper), serif fonts, black text, and a different background image to match.

```
/*** For Print ***/

body {
  background: white url('../_images/AAIW-illos/
  → alice23a.gif') no-repeat 0 0;
  padding: 200px 0 0 175px;
  }
h1 {
  color: black; }
p {
  font: normal 12pt/2 Constantia, palatino,
  → times, "times new roman", serif;
  color: rgb(0,0,0); }
```

Using media queries to specify styles:

1. **Create your style sheets**. Create a default media style sheet that captures all the general styles for your design and save it. I like to call mine **default. css** (Code 4.14).

   Create style sheets for the various media or specific devices for which you will be designing. Print is generally good to include (**Code 4.15**). You can call the sheet **print.css**, but you might also want to create style sheets specifically for popular mobile devices such as the iPhone (**Code 4.16**), which you could name **iphone.css**.

continues on next page

Code 4.16 *iphone.css*—These styles are specific for use on an iPhone and are loosely based on that mobile device's look and feel.

```
/*** iPhone Styles ***/

body {
  -webkit-text-size-adjust:none;
  background: rgb(102,102,102) url('../ images/
  → AAIW-illos/alice23c.gif') no-repeat
  → center 0;
  padding: 120px 20px 20px 20px; }
h1 { color: rgb(153,125,125);
  text-shadow: 0 0 5px rgb(0,0,0); }
p {
  font: normal 1em/1.25em "helvetica neue",
  → Helvetica, Arial, Sans-serif;
  color: rgb(255,255,255); }
```

2. **Add the viewport meta tag.** In the head of your HTML document (**Code 4.17**), add a meta tag with a name equal to viewport and content, as shown.

```
<meta name="viewport"
→content="width=device-width;
→initial-scale=1.0;
→maximum-scale=1.0;
→user-scalable=0;">
```

This will prevent devices with smaller screens, most notably the iPhone, from resizing the page, overriding your styles to be set in step 5.

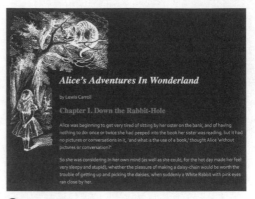

B Code 4.17 output to a computer screen. This version uses a dark background and an inverted version of the *Alice's Adventures in Wonderland* illustration. On an LCD screen, the lightly colored text will look fine.

Code 4.17 The HTML code links to all three of the style sheets, which are displayed in default **B**, Print **C**, and in the iPhone **D**. The iPhone style sheet uses media queries to set a device's width range in keeping with the iPhone. Notice that I used screen for the media type because the iPhone indentifies itself as a screen, not a handheld device.

```
<!-- HTML5 -->
<!DOCTYPE html>
<html lang="en">
<head>
<meta http-equiv="Content-Type" content="text/html; charset=UTF-8">
<meta name="viewport" content="width=device-width; initial-scale=1.0; maximum-scale=1.0;
→user-scalable=0;">
<title>Alice's Adventure's In Wonderland</title>
<link rel="stylesheet" media="all" href="default.css" >
<link rel="stylesheet" media="print" href="print.css">
<link rel="stylesheet" media="screen and (max-device-width: 480px) and (min-device-width: 320px)"
→href="iphone.css" >
</head>
<body>
<h1>Alice&#8217;s Adventures In Wonderland</h1>
<p class="byline">by <span class="author">Lewis Carroll</span></p>
<article><!-- Article -->
<header>
<h2><strong>Chapter I.</strong> Down the Rabbit-Hole</h2>
</header>
<p>
Alice was beginning to get very tired of sitting by her sister,...</p>
</article>
</body>
</html>
```

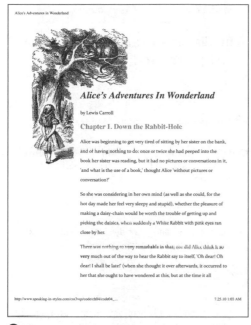

C Code 4.17 output to a printer. The background is white, and the background image is no longer inverted. This works better in print.

D Code 4.17 on an iPhone. A specially tailored version to fit the width of an iPhone uses a custom header of the Cheshire cat.

3. **Link to your *default* style sheet.** In the head of your HTML document, type a `<link>` tag that references the default version of the CSS and define **media** as **all**.

```
<link rel="stylesheet"
→ media="all" href="default.css" >
```

4. **Link to your *print* style sheet.** Immediately after the `<link>` tag, add another `<link>` tag that references the print version of the CSS and define **media** as **print**.

```
<link rel="stylesheet"
→ media="print" href="print.css">
```

5. **Use a media query to link to a style sheet.** Immediately after the previous `<link>` tag, add another `<link>` tag that references the style sheet for a specific media type and then add media queries (Table 4.8) in parentheses connecting multiple queries with **and**.

```
<link rel="stylesheet"
→ media="screen and
→ (max-device-width: 480px)
→ and (min-device-width: 320px)"
→ href="iphone.css" >
```

TIP Before media queries were introduced, Web developers used JavaScript to detect browser dimensions and colors. Media queries render those techniques obsolete, at least for styling purposes.

TIP In this example, media queries are applied to the media property value of the `<link>` tag, but you can just as easily apply them to the media property of the `<style>` tag.

Using the @media rule

Media queries allow you specify styles in the media property of `<link>` and `<style>` tags, but the **@media** rule  allows you to embed media queries directly into a style sheet.

Using @media to specify styles:

1. **Create your style sheets.** Create an external style sheet or embed a style sheet in the body of your document (**Code 4.18**).

2. **Use the @media rule to specify styles with media queries.** In the head of your HTML document, type @ and media. Then specify the media type (Table 4.7) and any media queries (Table 4.8) for the styles.

   ```
   @media screen and
   → (max-device-width: 480px) and
   → (min-device-width: 320px) {...}
   ```

   For example, you might specify that these styles are for screens with a width between 320px and 480px. Finish with curly brackets. Add any media-specific styles between the curly brackets.

3. **Add other styles as necessary.**

   ```
   h2 strong {...}
   ```

   You can add more **@media** rules or other nonmedia-specific rules. However, all CSS rules that are not in @rules (**@media**, **@font-face**, **@import**, and so on) must come after the @rules.

4. **Link to the style sheet from your HTML document.** Place a link tag to add the external CSS file (**Code 4.19**).

   TIP Remember that @media rules can go in external or embedded style sheets.

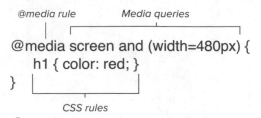

```
@media screen and (width=480px) {
   h1 { color: red; }
}
```

 The general syntax of the **@media** rule.

Code 4.18 *screen.css*—The iPhone code from Code 4.15 has been combined with more generic screen CSS.

```
/*** Screen Styles ***/

@media screen and (max-device-width: 480px)
→ and (min-device-width: 320px) {

  /*** iPhone Styles ***/

  body {
    -webkit-text-size-adjust:none; color: red;
    background: rgb(102,102,102) url('../_images/
  → AAIW-illos/alice23c.gif') no-repeat
  → center 0;
      padding: 120px 20px 20px 20px; }
  h1 {
    color: rgb(153,125,125);
    text-shadow: 0 0 5px rgb(0,0,0); }
  p {
    font: normal 1em/1.25em "helvetica neue",
Helvetica, Arial, Sans-serif;
    color: rgb(255,255,255); }
}

h2 strong {
  display: block;
  color: red;
  font-size: .75em;
  font-style: italic; }
```

Code 4.19 The HTML code links to the various style sheets for different media types. The big difference between this version and Code 4.16 is that the iPhone-specific code is now embedded in *screen.css*, so I'm not including media queries 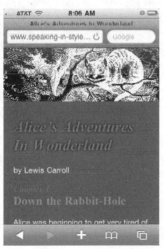.

```
<!-- HTML5 -->
<!DOCTYPE html>
<html lang="en">
<head>
<meta http-equiv="Content-Type" content="text/html; charset=UTF-8">
<meta name="viewport" content="width=device-width; initial-scale=1.0; maximum-scale=1.0;
→ user-scalable=0;">
<title>Alice's Adventures In Wonderland</title>
<link rel="stylesheet" media="all" href="default.css" >
<link rel="stylesheet" media="print" href="print.css">
<link rel="stylesheet" media="screen" href="screen.css">
</head>
<body>
<h1>Alice&#8217;s Adventures In Wonderland</h1>
<p class="byline">by <span class="author">Lewis Carroll</span></p>
<article><!-- Article -->
<header>
<h2><strong>Chapter I.</strong> Down the Rabbit-Hole</h2>
</header>
<p>
Alice was beginning to get very tired of sitting by her sister,...</p>
</article>
</body>
</html>
```

F Code 4.18 on an iPhone. This looks the same as **D**, but the code is now in an **@media** rule.

Styling for Print

With the advent of laser and inkjet printers, we seem to be buried under mounds of perfectly printed paper. Even the Web seems to have *increased* the amount of paper we use. If an article on the Web is longer than a couple of scrolls, many people print it.

But the Web was created to display information on the screen, not on paper. Web graphics look blocky when printed, and straight HTML lacks much in the way of layout controls. That said, you can take steps to improve the appearance of printed Web pages. Looking good in print and on the Web may take a little extra effort, but your audience will thank you in the long run.

Here are six simple things you can do to improve the appearance of your Web page when it is printed:

- **Use page breaks before page headers** to keep them with their text.

- **Separate content from navigation.** Try to keep the main content—the part your audience is interested in reading—in a separate area of the design from the site navigation. You can then use CSS to hide navigation in the printed version with a

  `nav { display: none }`

  included in the print style sheet.

- **Avoid using transparent colors in graphics.** This is especially true if the graphic is on a background color or a graphic other than white. The transparent area of a GIF image usually prints as white regardless of the color behind it in the window. This situation is not a problem if the graphic is on a white background to begin with, but the result is messy if the graphic is supposed to be on a dark background.

- **Avoid using text in graphics.** The irony of printing content from the Web is that text in graphics, which may look smooth in the window can look blocky when printed; but regular HTML text, which may look blocky on some PC screens, can print smoothly on any decent printer. Try to stick with HTML text as much as possible.

- **Avoid dark-colored backgrounds and light-colored text.** Generally you want to keep white as your background color for most of the printed page, and black or dark gray for the text.

- **Do not rely on color to convey your message when printed.** Although color printers are quite common these days, many people are still printing with black-and-white printers or printing in black and white on color printers to save money.

Inheriting Properties from a Parent

No, this book hasn't suddenly become the *Visual QuickStart Guide to Real Estate*. Child and descendent HTML tags generally assume the styles of their parents—*inherit* them—whether the style is set using CSS or is inherited from a browser style. This is called *inheritance of styles*.

For example, if you set an ID called *copy* and give it a font-family value of Times, all of its descendents would inherit the Times font style. If you set a **bold** tag to red with CSS, all of its descendents will inherit both the applied red and the inherent bold style Ⓐ.

CSS
b { color : red; }
.copy { font-family: times; }

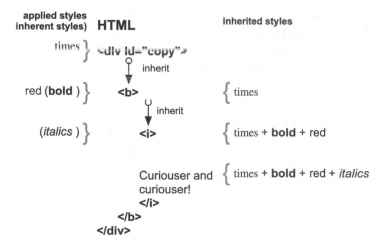

RESULT

Curiouser and curiouser!

Ⓐ The final result of the styles applied and inherited is bold, red, and italicized text in Times font.

In some cases, a style property is not inherited from its parent—obvious properties such as margins, width, and borders. You will probably have no trouble figuring out which properties are inherited and which are not. For example, if you set a padding of four pixels for the paragraph tag, you would not expect bold tags within the paragraph to also add a padding of four pixels. If you have any doubts, see Appendix A, which lists all of the CSS properties and how they are inherited.

If you did want to force an element to inherit a property of its parent, many CSS properties include the `inherit` value. So, in the previous example, to force all the bold tags in a paragraph to take on the 4px padding, you could set their `padding` value to `inherit`.

Managing existing or inherited property values

When defining the styles for a selector, you do not cause it to lose any of its inherited or inherent attributes unless you specifically override those styles. All those properties are displayed unless you change the specific existing properties that make up its appearance.

In addition to overriding the relevant property with another value, many CSS properties have values that allow you to override inheritance:

- **inherit**—Forces a property to be inherited that would normally not be inherited, or overrides other applied style values and inherits the parent's value.

- **none**—Hides a border, image, or other visual element.

- **normal**—Forces no style to be applied.

- **auto**—Allows the browser to determine how the element should be displayed based on context.

```
h1 { color: red !important; }
```

Selector   Declaration   !important

A The general syntax for **!important**.

Code 4.20 The **!important** value has been added to the color property in the first **h1**, but not in the second **B**. Typically, the second **h1** would override the first, but not in this case.

```
<!-- HTML5 -->
<!DOCTYPE html>
<html lang="en">
<head>
<meta http-equiv="Content-Type"
→ content="text/html; charset=UTF-8" />
<title>Alice's Adventures in Wonderland
→ </title>
<style type="text/css" media="all">
  h1 {
    color: red !important;
    font-size: 3em; }...
  h1 {
    color: black;
    font-size: 2em; }
</style>
</head>
<body>
<article>
  <h1>Alice's Adventures in
  → <em>Wonderland</em></h1>
</article>
</body>
</html>
```

Alice's Adventures in *Wonderland*

B The result of Code 4.20. The style that is most important wins the day, so the text is red rather than black.

Making a Declaration !important

You can add the **!important** declaration to a property-value declaration to give it the maximum weight when determining the cascade order **A**. Doing so ensures that a declaration is applied regardless of the other rules in play. (See "Determining the Cascade Order" in this chapter.)

To force use of a declaration:

1. **Add your CSS rule (Code 4.20).**

   h1 {...}

   You can use an HTML, class, or ID selector. CSS rules can be defined within the **<style>** tags in the head of your document (see "Embedded: Adding Styles to a Web Page" in Chapter 3) or in an external CSS file that is then imported or linked to the HTML document (see "External: Adding Styles to a Web Site" in Chapter 3).

2. **Make it important.** Type a style declaration, a space, **!important**, and a semicolon (;) to close the declaration.

   color: red !important;

3. **Add other styles.**

   font-size: 1em;

   Add any other declarations you wish for this rule, making them **!important** or not, as you desire.

   !important is a powerful tool, second only to inline styles for determining style cascade. **!important** is great for debugging your CSS; but, because it can interfere with making changes later, it should never be used in the final Web site code.

TIP Setting a shorthand property to
!important (background, for example) is the
same as setting each sub-property (such as
background-color) to be !important.

TIP A common mistake is to locate !impor-
tant after the semicolon in the declaration.
This causes the browser to ignore the declaration and, possibly, the entire rule.

TIP If you are debugging your style sheet
and can't get a particular style to work, try
adding !important to it. If it still doesn't
work, the problem is most likely a typo rather
than another overriding style.

TIP Many browsers allow users to define
their own style sheets for use by the browser.
Most browsers follow the CSS 4.1 specification
in which a user-defined style sheet overrides
an author-defined style sheet.

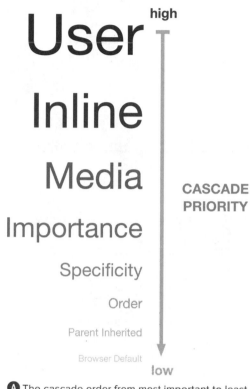

User

Inline

Media

CASCADE
PRIORITY

Importance

Specificity

Order

Parent Inherited

Browser Default

low

A The cascade order from most important to least important.

Determining the Cascade Order

Within a single Web page, style sheets may be linked, imported, or embedded. Styles may also be declared inline in the HTML.

In addition, many browsers allow visitors to have their own style sheets that can override yours. It's guaranteed, of course, that simultaneous style sheets from two or more sources will have conflicting declarations. Who comes out on top?

The cascade order refers to the way styles begin at the top of the page and, as they cascade down, collect and replace each other as they are inherited. The general rule of thumb is that the last style defined is the one that is used.

However, at times, two or more styles will conflict. Use the following procedure to determine which style will come out on top and be applied to a given element.

To determine the cascade-order value for an element:

Collect all styles that will be applied to the element. Find all the inherent, applied, and inherited styles that will be applied to the element, and then use the following criteria to determine which styles are applied in the cascade order, with the criteria at the top being most important **A**.

1. **User styles**

   Most Web browsers allow users to specify their own default style sheet. In principle, these always have precedence over other styles.

   continues on next page

2. **Inline styles**

   If the style is inline (see Chapter 3), it is always applied regardless of all other factors. That's why you should *never* use them in your final HTML code.

3. **Media type**

   Obviously, if the media type is set for a style and element that is not being displayed in that media type, the style will not be used.

4. **Importance**

   Including **!important** with a declaration gives it top billing when displayed. (See "Making a Declaration **!important**" in this chapter.)

   Many browsers let users define their own style sheets for use by the browser. If both the page author and the visitor have included **!important** in their declarations, the user's declaration wins.

   In theory, an author's style sheets override a visitor's style sheets unless the visitor uses the **!important** value. In practice, however, most browsers favor a user's style sheet when determining which declarations are used for a tag.

5. **Specificity**

   The more contextually specific a rule is, the higher its cascade priority. So the more HTML, class, and ID selectors a particular rule has, the more important it is. In determining this priority, ID selectors count as 100, classes count as 10, and HTML selectors are worth only 1. Thus,

   `#copy p b { color: red; }`

   is worth 102, whereas

   `b { color : lime; }`

   is only worth 1. So, the first rule would have higher specificity and the color would be red.

   This priority setting may seem a bit silly at first, but it allows context-sensitive and ID rules to carry more weight, ensuring that they will be used.

6. **Order**

   If the conflicting declarations applied to an element are equal at this point, CSS gives priority to the last rule listed, in order. Remember that inline styles always win.

7. **Parent inherited styles**

   These styles are inherited from the parent.

8. **Browser default styles**

   These styles are applied by the browser and are the least important.

Putting It All Together

1. **Using the HTML code you created in Chapter 3, style all descendents of the paragraph tag to bold.** This requires using the universal selector.

2. **Style all paragraph siblings.** Turn all paragraphs that follow another paragraph to gray.

3. **Add hypertext links to your page, and then use the link pseudo-classes to style them.** Remember to style all four link states.

4. **Style the first letter and first line of text of the first paragraph in your page.** Start by styling the first line of all paragraphs and then use pseudo-classes to focus on the first paragraph.

5. **Style images with an alt tag value with a black rule and images that do not have a value with a red rule.** This is useful for highlighting images you need to add alt values to.

6. **Style your page for print by hiding navigation and using a white background and dark text.** You want to consider media other than screen for your designs.

7. **Play around with adding more styles and then changing the order to see how the order affects which styles are applied.** Pay careful attention to the cascade order and how specificity affects that.

8. **Play around with adding !important to different styles to see how it affects which styles are applied.** Remember, the **!important** property is very powerful and should only be used to help you style your page while working. The final design should be able to work without it.

5

Font Properties

Typography is one of your most power-ful tools for presenting organized, clean-looking documents. It's also the best tool for presenting chaotic, grungy-looking documents.

The fonts you use go a long way toward getting your message across in just the way you want—whether that message is classical, grunge, or anything in between. I often say that fonts are to type what voice is to speech. Typeface, font weight, italic, and other typographic effects not only help designers to guide a visitor's eye around the page, but they also add a layer of meaning.

CSS gives you the ability to control the appearance of fonts, also known as *let-terforms*, in your Web pages. You can set the font family, boldface, and italic attri-butes, and the limited font sizes available with HTML tags. CSS3 refines the ability to download font files (called *Webfonts*) from your server and apply them to the text in your Web page, giving you the power to use virtually any font you want in your designs.

Code 5.1 The HTML code for this chapter is simply a few headlines and a few paragraphs of text, importing the *font-properties.css* style sheet. You'll be adding CSS code to this external style sheet throughout the chapter to build the final CSS file Ⓐ.

```
<!-- HTML5 -->
<!DOCTYPE html>
<html lang="en">
<head>
<meta charset="utf-8">
<title>Alice's Adventure's In Wonderland | Chapter I</title>
<link href="../_css/font-properties.css" type="text/css" rel="stylesheet">
</head>
<body id="chapter1" class="book aaiw chapter">
<h1>Alice&#8217;s Adventures In Wonderland</h1>
<p class="byline">by <span class="author">Lewis Carroll</span></p>
<article><!-- Article -->
<header>
<h2><strong>Chapter I.</strong> Down the Rabbit-Hole</h2>
</header>
<p>
Alice was beginning to get very tired of sitting by her sister on the
bank, and of having nothing to do: once or twice she had peeped into the
book her sister was reading, but it had no pictures or conversations in
it, 'and what is the use of a book,' thought Alice 'without pictures or
conversation?'
</p>
</article>
</body>
</html>
```

Alice's Adventures In Wonderland

by Lewis Carroll

Chapter I. Down the Rabbit-Hole

Alice was beginning to get very tired of sitting by her sister on the bank, and of having nothing to do: once or twice she had peeped into the book her sister was reading, but it had no pictures or conversations in it, 'and what is the use of a book,' thought Alice 'without pictures or conversation?'

So she was considering in her own mind (as well as she could, for the hot day made her feel very sleepy and stupid), whether the pleasure of making a daisy-chain would be worth the trouble of getting up and picking the daisies, when suddenly a White Rabbit with pink eyes ran close by her.

There was nothing so **very** remarkable in that; nor did Alice think it so **very** much out of the way to hear the Rabbit say to itself, 'Oh dear! Oh dear! I shall be late!' (when she thought it over afterwards, it occurred to her that she ought to have wondered at this, but at the time it all seemed quite natural); but when the Rabbit actually **took a watch out of its waistcoat-pocket**, and looked at it, and then hurried on, Alice started to her feet, for it flashed across her mind that she had never before seen a rabbit with either a waistcoat-pocket, or a watch to take out of it, and burning with curiosity, she ran across the field after it, and fortunately was just in time to see it pop down a large rabbit-hole under the hedge.

Ⓐ This is what your Web page (Code 5.1) looks like before any CSS is applied to it. In this chapter you will be adding font stylings.

Understanding Typography on the Web

A *type family* (commonly referred to in Web design as a *font family*) is a category of typefaces that have similar characteristics. Each character within a font is referred to as a *glyph*. The advantages of HTML text compared to text in Flash or in graphics are that it is easy to edit if changes are required, and it can adjust to the width of the screen on which it is viewed. In addition, content is often stored within databases and then output as HTML text.

However, HTML text has some severe design limitations. By and large, most of the textual control is left up to the visitor's browser, and you cannot currently do some things, such as run text vertically rather than horizontally, without using CSS Transitions (Chapter 12) which are not cross-browser yet.

What seems more stifling is that you are limited to the fonts available on the visitor's machine. However, recent browser developments are quickly changing this perception. As CSS3 grows in popularity, so do a wider range of typeface possibilities as Webfonts become available.

Specifying the character set

In the previous chapter, you found that when you create an HTML5 document, you need to specify the character set in use by your page. A character set is simply a list or *repertoire* of characters with a unique code or name that the browser will recognize to display the text.

You specify the character set in the head of your HTML page using a meta tag. The most popular international character set is the UTF-8 (8-bit Unicode Transformation Format) character set:

```
<meta charset="utf-8">
```

Alternatively, if you are writing only in English, another common character set is the ISO 8859-1 character set:

```
<meta http-equiv="Content-
Type" content="text/html;
charset=ISO-8859-1" />
```

Both UTF-8 and ISO 8859-1 work about the same for English, but UTF-8 supports other alphabets. I highly recommend sticking with UTF-8. Web sites (even your local newspaper) are often translated on the fly into different languages.

One other important point: if you specify a character in your HTML that doesn't exist in the specified character set, the browser generally will display an error marker in place of the character .

 **A** This glyph, or one like it, will appear in place of any characters that the browser does not recognize as a part of the character set.

TABLE 5.1 Generic Font Families

Name	Example
Serif	Times New Roman
Sans-serif	Helvetica and Arial
Monospace	Courier New
Cursive	Brush Script MT
Fantasy	Papyrus

Generic font families

CSS defines five generic font families into which most fonts can be categorized (Table 5.1).

- **Serif**—A *serif* is the small ornamentation at the end of a letter that gives it a distinguishing quality. Serifs are holdovers from the days of stonecutting and pen strokes. Serifs often improve legibility by making individual letters stand out from their neighbors.

  Serif fonts are generally best suited for the display of larger text onscreen (14px or larger) or for smaller printed text. They are not so good for smaller text on a screen, because the serifs often obscure the letter. Serif fonts often portray a more conservative feel.

- **Sans-serif**—As you might guess, *sans-serif* fonts are those fonts without serifs.

  Although the characters are less distinctive, sans-serif fonts work better for smaller text on a screen. Sans-serif fonts often portray a more modern and often casual feel.

- **Monospace**—Although *monospace* fonts can have serifs or not, their distinguishing feature is that each letter occupies the same amount of space. The lowercase letter *l*, for example, is much thinner than the uppercase letter *M*. In non-monospace fonts, the letter *l* occupies less space than the *M*, but a monospace font adds extra space around the *l* so that it occupies the same amount of space as the *M*.

  Monospace fonts work best for text that has to be exactly (but not necessarily quickly) read, such as programming code, in which typos can spell disaster. Although easier to scan, monospace fonts can become monotonous for reading large amounts of text. Monospace fonts often give a technical or typewritten feel to text.

- **Cursive**—*Cursive* fonts attempt to mimic cursive or calligraphic handwriting, usually in a highly stylized manner with the letters generally appearing partially or completely connected.

  Cursive fonts are best reserved for decoration and large headlines; they are not as readable in large chunks of text. Cursive fonts give an energetic and expressive feel to text.

continues on next page

- **Fantasy**—Decorative fonts that don't fit into any of the preceding categories are referred to as *fantasy* fonts. These fonts usually are extremely ornamental but are still letters, so exclude dingbats or picture fonts, illustrations, or icons.

  Like cursive fonts, fantasy fonts are best reserved for decoration. You should use fantasy fonts sparingly and choose them carefully to reinforce the look and feel of your Web site, since each fantasy font invariably has a strong personality.

B Examples of Dingbats. These are drawn from the dingbat font, Webdings.

Dingbats

Although it does not have an official CSS designation, there is another important category of fonts to consider. *Dingbats*, also called *symbol* or *picture* fonts, do not represent numbers or letters, but are instead a collection of icons or pictograms each corresponding to a letter on the keyboard. The most common example of this font type is Webdings, which is installed on most computers. Webdings is a collection of common international symbols **B**. Although these glyphs can be used in place of a graphic version of the icon, there is no guarantee that the font will be installed.

However, if you use dingbats as Webfonts, as described later in this chapter, you can be relatively sure that you will get what you want, replacing some graphic icons with dingbat icons.

& © ® ™
½ ¼ ¾
« » ± ¤ ÷
∞ ≈ ≤ ⊇
⊕ ⇐ ↔ ⇔

C Examples of a few common character entities. These can be coded into HTML to ensure that they are represented accurately in the final output.

What Are Webfonts?

Webfonts are a recent development in Web design that allow you to include fonts in your Web designs by linking to a font file on your server. Although this seems simple (and it is), this ability has been a long time in coming and will revolutionize Web typography.

HTML character entities

A more reliable alternative to dingbat fonts are HTML *character entities* **C**. These are a collection of specialized glyphs that, instead of being represented by a single letter, are represented by code that begins with an ampersand (&) and ends with a semicolon (;). For example, the ampersand is represented in the code as:

&

For many characters (such as the ampersand), this is the only way to display them consistently across browsers and operating systems.

Setting a Font-Stack

The **font-family** property lets you determine the visual effect of your message by choosing the font for displaying your text (**Table 5.2**). The typeface you use to display your text can make a powerful difference in how readers perceive your message Ⓐ. Whether you use a serif, sans-serif, monospace, cursive, or fantasy typeface can speak volumes before your visitor even reads the first line of text.

To define the font family for an element:

1. Add the **font-family** property to your CSS rule. Type the property name **font-family**, followed by a colon. In this example, **font-family** is applied to the body tag, which will set the font for the entire page (**Code 5.2**).

   ```
   font-family:
   ```

2. Define the name of the *primary font* you want to use, followed by a comma. This name is not case sensitive. Fonts that contain a space in their names must be enclosed in quotation marks, either single or double (**"Times New Roman"** or **'times new roman'** will both work).

   ```
   Helvetica,
   ```

Times
Arial
Courier
Brush Script
Papyrus

Ⓐ Examples of different typefaces. What voice do you hear?

TABLE 5.2 Font-Family Values

Value	Compatibility
<family-name>	IE3, FF1, S1, C1, O5.5, CSS1
serif	IE3, FF1, S1, C1, O5.5, CSS1
sans-serif	IE4/3, FF1, S1, C1, O5.5, CSS1
cursive	IE4, FF1, S1, C1, O5.5, CSS1
fantasy	IE4, FF1, S1, C1, O5.5, CSS1
monospace	IE4, FF1, S1, C1, O5.5, CSS1

Alice's Adventures In Wonderland
by Lewis Carroll

Chapter I. Down the Rabbit-Hole

Alice was beginning to get very tired of sitting by her sister on the bank, and of having nothing to do: once or twice she had peeped into the book her sister was reading, but it had no pictures or conversations in it, 'and what is the use of a book,' thought Alice 'without pictures or conversation?'

So she was considering in her own mind (as well as she could, for the hot day made her feel very sleepy and stupid), whether the pleasure of making a daisy-chain would be worth the trouble of getting up and picking the daisies, when suddenly a White Rabbit with pink eyes ran close by her.

There was nothing so very remarkable in that; nor did Alice think it so very much out of the way to hear the Rabbit say to itself, 'Oh dear! Oh dear! I shall be late!' (when she thought it over afterwards, it occurred to her that she ought to have wondered at this, but at the time it all seemed quite natural); but when the Rabbit actually **took a watch out of its waistcoat-pocket**, and looked at it, and then hurried on, Alice started to her feet, for it flashed across her mind that she had never before seen a rabbit with either a waistcoat-pocket, or a watch to take out of it, and burning with curiosity, she ran across the field after it, and fortunately was just in time to see it pop down a large rabbit-hole under the hedge.

Ⓑ The body copy is displayed in Helvetica, Arial, or Trebuchet MS, depending on which is available on the visitor's computer. However, headers are displayed in Georgia, Times, or Times New Roman, again, depending on availability.

Code 5.2 *font-properties.css*—Two separate typefaces are applied to the page Ⓑ. The first affects the appearance of all text on the page; the second affects only headers and the **.byline** class.

```
/*** CSS VQS - Chapter 5 - fontproperties.css ***/

body {
  font-family: Helvetica, Arial, Sans-serif; }

h1, h2, h3, h4, h5, h6, .byline {
  font-family: Georgia, Times, "Times New Roman", Serif; }
```

Font or Font Family?

Keep in mind the difference between a font and a font family. A font family is a series of fonts with similar appearance—such as Times—whereas a font refers to a specific version—such as Times normal, Times bold, Times italic, Times bold italic, and so on.

Why Include Understudy Fonts and Generic Font Families?

When you provide a list of fonts, the browser tries to use the first font on that list. If it isn't available, the browser continues through the list until it finds a font that is installed on the visitor's computer. If no match is found, the browser displays the text in the visitor's default font. The advantage of specifying a generic font is that the browser tries to display the text in the same style of font, even if the specific fonts on the list are not available.

As a last resort, you can include the generic font family so that a browser can make an intelligent decision on the closest matching font.

The advantage of using understudy and generic font families is that, even if a desired font is not available, you can still control which font is used in its place or, at least, get a close match.

TIP Try to choose fonts with a similar size. Different fonts will have different relative sizes even if set to the same font size.

TIP Some typefaces are easiest to read on a screen; others look better when printed. Always consider the destination when choosing your fonts.

3. **Define a list of alternative fonts, called** *understudy fonts,* **separated by commas.** You can include as many as you want. These fonts will be used (in the order specified) if the previous font in the list is not available on the visitor's computer. See "Why Include Understudy Fonts" in this chapter for more details.

```
Arial,
```

4. **Define the generic font family.** After the last understudy font, type the name of the generic font family for the particular style of font you're using. **Table 5.1** lists generic values for font families. Although including this value is optional, doing so is a good idea.

```
Sans-serif;
```

5. **Add typeface overrides.** After a font is set for the body of the page, it will be used in all text throughout the entire Web page, with the exception of text in forms. You need to add another font-family declaration to your CSS only if you want to change the font for a particular element. This is due to the fact that properties cascade to their child elements, as described in chapter 4.

The exception to the cascade rule are form elements such as input, text, area, button, etc., which require their fonts to be set in the form element to cascade down.

```
font-family: Georgia, Times,
→'Times New Roman', Serif;
```

TIP If you will be using bold, italic/oblique, and/or bold italic/oblique versions of the font, be sure that the font family supports all of these typefaces. If not, the text will not display properly or, worse, the browser will try to synthesize these versions. Either way, the results will not look professional.

Finding Fonts

Look around the Web, and what do you see? You usually see five fonts: Arial, Georgia, Verdana, Trebuchet MS, and Times New Roman. This situation came about for one simple reason: Arial, Georgia, Verdana, Trebuchet MS, and Times New Roman are preinstalled on virtually every Mac and PC.

I am sick of them.

Don't get me wrong—these are great fonts, easy to read at many sizes. But as I said earlier, typography adds a language to text that goes far beyond the written word.

Web-based typography is mired in using Times for serif fonts and Helvetica/Arial for sans-serif fonts. This arrangement mutes the power of typography, and all Web pages begin to look the same.

But there is new hope. Two factors are changing the way designers think about their typefaces. The first is that dozens of fonts are commonly preinstalled on Macs and PCs. The second, and most profound change, is that all the major browsers now support the use of downloadable Webfonts.

Web-safe fonts

What are the alternatives to the "fatal five"? That depends on the computer the person visiting your site is using. Mac and Windows computers have certain standard fonts that should always be installed. In addition, Internet Explorer (which comes installed on most computers these days) installs several additional fonts.

Of course, there's no guarantee that these fonts will be installed, but because they came with the operating system and unless they have been removed, they are just as likely to be available as Times, Helvetica, or Arial.

A The list of Web-safe fonts on www.fluidwebtype .info/websafefonts includes a visual example of each typeface. You can sort the list by name, available weights and styles, operating system availability, and rank.

TABLE 5.3 Font-Family Values

Browser	OTF/TTF	EOT	SVG	WOFF
Internet Explorer		IE4		Coming
Firefox	FF3.5			FF3.6
Safari	S3.1*		S3.1	
Chrome	C4.0		C4.0	Coming
Opera	O10		O10	Coming

* Not available on Safari Mobile. SVG can be used.

You can find a list of Web-safe fonts on my Web site, *www.fluidwebtype.info/web-safefonts*. It lists these fonts, and includes examples of what they should look like and which similar-looking fonts can be used as replacements **A**.

Downloadable Webfonts

For years it has been technically feasible to download a font just as you would an image and use it in your design. However, the browser developers have only recently added this feature. The good news is that you can now download fonts (called Webfonts) to the vast majority of Web users. The bad news is that different browsers use different file formats (**Table 5.3**).

Here is a list of the file formats:

- **TTF/OTF.** TrueType and OpenType fonts are the type you are most likely to have on your computer. They are commonly used today and represent the majority of fonts sold. That said, they have no built-in security to prevent their unlicensed use.

- **EOT.** Embedded OpenType is a format developed by Microsoft in the late 1990s to allow secure downloadable fonts for the Web. However, because the technology was proprietary for many years and EOT fonts were hard to create, the format didn't catch on. Because it is the only format supported by IE and has been supported since IE4, it has gained new life for implanting Webfonts for IE.

continues on next page

- **SVG.** A separate W3C standard from CSS, Scalable Vector Graphics can include font information. Some browsers, such as Safari mobile, support only this format.

- **WOFF.** Web Open Font Format may be the new kid on the block, developed in mid-2009, but it is already becoming the frontrunner as the default Webfont file format. This format includes some protection for the font—such as licensing—but is not nearly as cumbersome as EOT.

To deploy Webfonts in your design, the trick is to include links to multiple font files; the browser will then use the format that works for it. The good news is that, with a bit of clever coding, this can easily be accomplished (see "Setting a Better Font-stack," next.) To learn how to download or convert fonts to these multiple font file formats (see "Using Font Squirrel to Convert Font Files" in this chapter).

Setting a better font stack

Let's look again at the font stack and how to leverage Web-safe fonts and Webfonts to create a design that rises above the visual monotony that you commonly see on the Web.

To define a Web-safe font or Webfont for an element:

1. **Add the font face rule to your CSS.** Begin by typing the **@font-face** rule, where you will define the name and location of the font file you want to use in your designs (**Code 5.3**).

   @font-face {

Code 5.3 *font-properties.css*—I've added the Web-safe fonts Corbel and Constantia to the body and header texts, respectively, and then downloaded the Webfont "Little Trouble Girl" for use in the **h1** page title **B**.

```
/*** CSS VQS - Chapter 5 - fontproperties.
→ css ***/

@font-face {
  font-family: 'Title Font';
  src: url('../_fonts/Little-Trouble-Girl/
  → littletroublegirl-webfont.eot');
  src: local('☺'), url('../_fonts/Little-
  → Trouble-Girl/littletroublegirl-webfont.
  → woff') format('woff'), url('../_fonts/
  → Little-Trouble-Girl/littletrouble
  → girl-webfont.ttf') format('truetype'),
  → url('../_fonts/Little-Trouble-Girl/
  → littletroublegirl-webfont.svg#webfont')
  → format('svg');
  font-weight: normal;
  font-style: normal;
  font-variant: normal; }

body {
  font-family: Corbel, Helvetica, Arial,
  → Sans-serif; }

h1, h2, h3, h4, h5, h6, .byline {
  font-family: Constantia, Georgia, Times,
  → "Times New Roman", Serif; }

h1 {
  font-family: 'Title Font', Constantia,
  → Georgia, Times, "Times New Roman",
  → Serif; }
```

Alice's Adventures In Wonderland

by Lewis Carroll

Chapter I. Down the Rabbit-Hole

Alice was beginning to get very tired of sitting by her sister on the bank, and of having nothing to do: once or twice she had peeped into the book her sister was reading, but it had no pictures or conversations in it, 'and what is the use of a book,' thought Alice 'without pictures or conversation?'

So she was considering in her own mind (as well as she could, for the hot day made her feel very sleepy and stupid), whether the pleasure of making a daisy-chain would be worth the trouble of getting up and picking the daisies, when suddenly a White Rabbit with pink eyes ran close by her.

There was nothing so **very** remarkable in that; nor did Alice think it so **very** much out of the way to hear the Rabbit say to itself, 'Oh dear! Oh dear! I shall be late!' (when she thought it over afterwards, it occurred to her that she ought to have wondered at this, but at the time it all seemed quite natural); but when the Rabbit actually **took a watch out of its waistcoat-pocket**, and looked at it, and then hurried on, Alice started to her feet, for it flashed across her mind that she had never before seen a rabbit with either a waistcoat-pocket, or a watch to take out of it, and burning with curiosity, she ran across the field after it, and fortunately was just in time to see it pop down a large rabbit-hole under the hedge.

B The page is now looking a bit more distinctive typographically by including fonts that are not often seen on the Web.

2. **Define the name of your font family.** Type the name of the font family you want to import. This can actually be anything you choose, as long as you reference it consistently in your font stack.

   `font-family: 'Title Font';`

   Many developers choose to use just the name of the font, but I recommend creating a name that indicates how the font is used in the design. Then, if the typeface is changed, you don't have to change the font name everywhere it is referenced.

   Remember: if you want to use a font name with two or more words separated by a space, put the whole name in quotes.

3. **Define the source of the EOT format of the font file.** Add your font file sources. Always begin with the EOT file for use in Internet Explorer, but *do not* add a format attribute.

   `src: url('Little-Trouble-Girl/`
   `littletroublegirl-webfont.eot');`

4. **Add a local source decoy.** Now for a little trick. Because Internet Explorer ignores the local source attribute, you can place it before your other font file sources, and IE will just skip this code, which would otherwise cause an error. You can insert anything you want for the name of the font. But because some browsers will trigger an alert if your CSS tries to access a local font file, it's best to just use a random character (such as a smiley face).

   `src: local('☺'),`

continues on next page

5. **Define the source of the WOFF, TrueType or OpenType, and SVG format of the font file.** Now add the location of your WOFF, TTF/OTF, or SVG font files. Each browser will use the one best suited for it.

```
url('Little-Trouble-Girl/
⇥ littletroublegirl-webfont.woff')
⇥ format('woff'),
```

```
url('Little-Trouble-Girl/
⇥ littletroublegirl-webfont.ttf')
⇥ format('truetype'),
```

```
url('Little-Trouble-Girl/
⇥ littletroublegirl-webfont.
⇥ svg#webfont') format('svg');
```

6. *Optionally* **add weight, style, and variants associated with this font.** This will mean the font is only used if these properties are also applied with the specific value. These are still buggy in many browsers, so I would avoid them for now.

```
font-weight: normal;
font-style: normal;
font-variant: normal }
```

7. **Add the *Web-safe font* name to your font stack.** To leverage one of the Web-safe fonts, place it as the first typeface in your font stack.

```
font-family: Corbel, Helvetica,
⇥ Arial, Sans-serif;
```

8. **Add the *Webfont* name to your font stack.** To leverage a downloaded Webfont and trigger its download, place the name you gave it at as the first value of the font stack.

```
font-family: 'Title Font',
⇥ Constantia, Georgia, Times,
⇥ "Times New Roman", Serif;
```

TIP The "Smiley Face" Bullet Proof @font-face technique was originally developed by Paul Irish (www.paulirish.com).

TIP For more information on Mac fonts, see developer.apple.com/textfonts/.

TIP For more information on Windows fonts, see www.microsoft.com/typography/fonts/. For a more detailed examination of Webfonts and Web typography in general, check out my book *Fluid Web Typography* (fluidwebtype.info).

Using Font Squirrel to Convert Font Files

Although you are now free to start downloading Webfonts for use in your designs, you still face two major hurdles:

1. **Legal.** While you might assume that you can use a purchased font as a Webfont, that is rarely the case. Most fonts have usage restrictions outlined in their End User License Agreements (EULA). If the EULA does not specifically state that you can use a font for **@font-face** linking, you can't do so legally. To be sure, check with the font vendor before proceeding.

2. **Technical.** How do you get all of those different font formats? Currently, even if licensed to do so, most font foundries or resellers do not provide these formats.

What to do?

One great resource I use regularly is the Font Squirrel Web site (www.fontsquirrel.com), which provides an index to over 500 freely licensed, downloadable Webfonts. Each is complete with all the font formats as well as sample CSS code **C**.

As if that were not great enough, the site also provides an insanely useful tool—the @font-face Kit Generator **D**—that can convert any OTF or TTF file into EOT, SVG, and WOFF formats (www. fontsquirrel.com/fontface/generator). It's easy to use and fast. Just make sure that your EULA is in order before using it.

C Font Squirrel (www.fontsquirrel.com) offers over 500 free fonts that are ready for use in your Web site.

D Use the @font-face Kit Generator (www.fontsquirrel.com/fontface/generator) to convert any licensed fonts for use on the Web.

Webfont Service Bureaus

Another up-and-coming option for adding specific fonts to a Web design is Webfont service bureaus, which provide licensed fonts for your use (generally at a cost) but retain the actual files on their own servers while allowing you to reference them in your code. Some enable this with a straightforward CSS link; others use their own proprietary methods, generally incorporating JavaScript.

The advantages to using Webfont service bureaus include:

- Fonts are licensed, so you don't have to worry about violating a EULA and getting sued.
- Fonts are hosted on the bureaus' servers, which means you are taking up less bandwidth on your own servers.
- Browser support is handled by the bureau, as are potential updates and upgrades.

However, there are disadvantages as well:

- Since the fonts are on a third-party server, you are depending on someone else's system to always be fast and reliable.
- If you do not have a copy of the font on your own computer, you will not be able to create graphical comps to show clients.
- Price scales vary from service to service. Some charge a one-time fee; others require a yearly subscription. If you forget to pay, your font goes bye-bye.

New Webfont service bureaus are coming online all the time, but the top ones currently include:

- **Typekit** (*www.typekit.com*)
- **Kernest** (*www.kernest.com*)
- **Typotheque** (*www.typotheque.com*)
- **Ascender** (*www.ascender.com*)
- **Fontdeck** (*www.fontdeck.com*)
- **Google Font API** (*code.google.com/apis/webfonts/*)

A The height (size) of a font is measured from the descender to the ascender (usually the cap height). The x-height is the height of lowercase letters.

TABLE 5.4 Font-Size Values

Value	Compatibility
<length>	IE3, FF1, S1, C1, O5.5, CSS1
<percentage>	IE3, FF1, S1, C1, O5.5, CSS1
smaller	IE4, FF1, S1, C1, O5.5, CSS1
larger	IE4, FF1, S1, C1, O5.5, CSS1
xx-small	IE3, FF1, S1, C1, O5.5, CSS1
x-small	IE3, FF1, S1, C1, O5.5, CSS1
small	IE3, FF1, S1, C1, O5.5, CSS1
medium	IE3, FF1, S1, C1, O5.5, CSS1
large	IE3, FF1, S1, C1, O5.5, CSS1
x-large	IE3, FF1, S1, C1, O5.5, CSS1
xx-large	IE3, FF1, S1, C1, O5.5, CSS1

Setting the Font Size

With CSS, you can specify the size of the text on the screen using several notations or methods **A**, including the traditional print-based point-size notation, percentage, absolute size, and even a size relative to the surrounding text (**Table 5.4**).

Fonts can be set as either absolute sizes, which define the size based against a standard length measurement, or relative sizes, which are in relation to defaults set for the browser.

To define the font size for an element:

1. Add the font size property to your CSS. Type the property name **font-size**, followed by a colon (**Code 5.4**).

   font-size:

2. Define the font size.

   100%;

   Type a value for the fontsize, which could be any of the following options:

   ▸ A relative or absolute length unit (often, the font size in pixels or ems). See "Values and Units Used in This Book" in the Introduction for more detail.

   ▸ An absolute size keyword relative to the default page size: **xx-small**, **x-small**, **small**, **medium**, **large**, **x-large**, and **xx-large**

   ▸ A relative size keyword of **smaller** or **larger** to describe the font size in relation to its parent element

continues on page 135

Code 5.4 *font-properties.css*—I've defined the default size of text on the page as 100% (the default size the user has set) and then set other font sizes on the page relative to that font size **B**.

```css
/*** CSS VQS - Chapter 5 - fontproperties.css ***/

@font-face {
  font-family: 'Title Font';
  src: url('../_fonts/Little-Trouble-Girl/littletroublegirl-webfont.eot');
  src: local('☺'), url('../_fonts/Little-Trouble-Girl/littletroublegirl-webfont.woff') format('woff'),
  → url('../_fonts/Little-Trouble-Girl/littletroublegirl-webfont.ttf') format('truetype'),
  → url('../_fonts/Little-Trouble-Girl/littletroublegirl-webfont.svg#webfont') format('svg');
  font-weight: normal;
  font-style: normal;
  font-variant: normal; }

body {
  font-family: Corbel, Helvetica, Arial, Sans-serif;
  font-size: 100%; }

h1, h2, h3, h4, h5, h6, .byline {
  font-family: Constantia, Georgia, Times, "Times New Roman", Serif; }

h1 {
  font-family: 'Title Font', Constantia, Georgia, Times, "Times New Roman", Serif;
  font-size: 3em; }

h2 {
  font-size: 2em; }

h2 strong {
  font-size: .5em; }

p {
  font-size: .875em; }

strong {
  font-size: 1.25em; }

.byline {
  font-size: 1em; }

.byline .author {
  font-size: 1.25em; }
```

Alice's Adventures In Wonderland

by Lewis Carroll

Chapter 1. **Down the Rabbit-Hole**

Alice was beginning to get very tired of sitting by her sister on the bank, and of having nothing to do: once or twice she had peeped into the book her sister was reading, but it had no pictures or conversations in it, 'and what is the use of a book,' thought Alice 'without pictures or conversation?'

So she was considering in her own mind (as well as she could, for the hot day made her feel very sleepy and stupid), whether the pleasure of making a daisy-chain would be worth the trouble of getting up and picking the daisies, when suddenly a White Rabbit with pink eyes ran close by her.

There was nothing so **very** remarkable in that; nor did Alice think it so **very** much out of the way to hear the Rabbit say to itself, 'Oh dear! Oh dear! I shall be late!' (when she thought it over afterwards, it occurred to her that she ought to have wondered at this, but at the time it all seemed quite natural); but when the Rabbit actually **took a watch out of its waistcoat-pocket,** and looked at it, and then hurried on, Alice started to her feet, for it flashed across her mind that she had never before seen a rabbit with either a waistcoat-pocket, or a watch to take out of it, and burning with curiosity, she ran across the field after it, and fortunately was just in

B The font size helps determine its legibility on the page. Titles are usually larger than body copy; but some text, such as the `<strong>` and `<em>` tags, may need a little more attention.

▸ A percentage representing how much larger (values over 100%) or smaller (values less than 100%) the text is relative to the size of its parent element

The value you use will depend on your need; however, it is generally recommended to set relative font sizes to allow visitors final control of how large they are displayed.

3. **Add font size overrides as needed.**

`h1 { font-size: 3em; }`

The only reason you would need to reset the font-size is if you need to increase or decrease it compared to the size set in the body. If you are using ems to set size, which I recommend, then remember that this is relative to the size of the parent. So a size of 2em would be twice as large as the parent, whereas a size of .5em would be half the size.

TIP Avoid defining screen media font sizes using points or other absolute font sizes because these tend to render inconsistently across platforms. However, they're fine to use for print style sheets.

TIP When setting font sizes, your best strategy is to set a relative-length size for the `<body>` tag (such as 100%), and then use absolute font sizes (such as *small*) or relative font sizes (such as *larger*) to adjust the size. Doing so ensures the most consistent and versatile page viewing regardless of the actual media used (computer screen, printed page, handheld, and so on.)

NEW IN CSS3: Adjusting Font Size for Understudy Fonts ★

Font sizes are measured based on the height of capital letters, but it is the lowercase letters that often vary the most from font to font. If you are relying on understudy fonts, your font sizes might look very different, even though the same physical size is set **Ⓐ**. To help alleviate this, CSS3 introduces the **font-size-adjust** property, which allows you to set the font size relative to lowercase letters rather than uppercase.

To do this, you specify a numeric value that lowercase fonts should be sized to as a multiple of the font size (**Table 5.5**). For example, if the font size is 18 pixels and you set a font-size-adjust of .5, lowercase letters will be sized at 9 pixels. As a result, all the fonts will have the same apparent size relative to each other, even if their x-heights vary greatly.

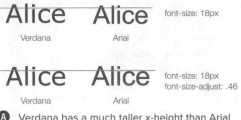

Ⓐ Verdana has a much taller x-height than Arial (top), but using font-size-adjust, you can set the lowercase letters to use the same height, ensuring greater consistency regardless of which font the browser uses.

TABLE 5.5 Font-Size-Adjust Values

Value	Compatibility
<number>	FF3*, CSS3
none	FF3*, CSS3

*FF1 for Windows

To adjust the font size for an element:

1. **Add the font size adjust property to your CSS.** Type the property name **font-size-adjust**, followed by a colon (**Code 5.5**).

   font-size-adjust:

2. **Define a size value.**

   .5;

   Type a value to adjust the font size by:

   ▸ A numeric value of 0 or greater as a multiplier for the current font-size to adjust the text size based on the x-height,

   ▸ **none**, to leave the font-size unadjusted

TIP You can calculate these values by dividing the set font-size by the font's x-height, or you can just "eyeball" it until the value for the font-size adjust appears to have no effect on the font size of the primary font.

TIP Font-size-adjust will adjust the size of all your glyphs (capitals as well lower case), but does so relative to the lower case letters rather than upper case.

Code 5.5 *font-properties.css*—The font size has been adjusted so that lowercase letters are half the size of uppercase letters **B**. An exception is with the header font, where the size is set at .46 **C**.

```css
/*** CSS VQS - Chapter 5 - fontproperties.css ***/

@font-face {
  font-family: 'Title Font';
  src: url('../_fonts/Little-Trouble-Girl/littletroublegirl-webfont.eot');
  src: local('☺'), url('../_fonts/Little-Trouble-Girl/littletroublegirl-webfont.woff') format('woff'),
  → url('../_fonts/Little-Trouble-Girl/littletroublegirl-webfont.ttf') format('truetype'),
  → url('../_fonts/Little-Trouble-Girl/littletroublegirl-webfont.svg#webfont') format('svg');
  font-weight: normal;
  font-style: italic;
  font-variant: normal; }

body {
  font-family: Helvetica, Arial, Sans-serif;
  font-size: 100%;
  font-size-adjust: .5; }

h1, h2, h3, h4, h5, h6, .byline {
  font-family: Georgia, Times, "Times New Roman", Serif;
  font-size-adjust: .46; }

h1 {
  font-family: Constantia, Georgia, Times, "Times New Roman", Serif;
  font-size: 3em; }

h2 {
  font-size: 2em; }

h2 strong {
  font-size: .5em; }

p {
  font-size: .875em; }

strong {
  font-size: 1.25em; }

.byline {
  font-size: 1.25em; }

.byline .author { }
```

Alice's Adventures In Wonderland

by Lewis Carroll

Chapter I. Down the Rabbit-Hole

Alice was beginning to get very tired of sitting by her sister on the bank, and of having nothing to do: once or twice she had peeped into the book her sister was reading, but it had no pictures or conversations in it, 'and what is the use of a book,' thought Alice 'without pictures or conversation?'

So she was considering in her own mind (as well as she could, for the hot day made her feel very sleepy and stupid), whether the pleasure of making a daisy-chain would be worth the trouble of getting up and picking the daisies, when suddenly a White Rabbit with pink eyes ran close by her.

There was nothing so **very** remarkable in that; nor did Alice think it so **very** much out of the way to hear the Rabbit say to itself, 'Oh dear! Oh dear! I shall be late!' (when she thought it over afterwards, it occurred to her that she ought to have wondered at this, but at the time it all seemed quite natural); but when the Rabbit actually **took a watch out of its waistcoat-pocket**, and looked at it, and then hurried on, Alice started to her feet, for it flashed across her mind that she had never before seen a rabbit with either a waistcoat-pocket, or a watch to take out of it, and burning with curiosity, she ran across the field after it, and fortunately was just in time to see it pop down a large rabbit-hole under the hedge.

B Shows the page using the secondary fonts without font-size-adjust applied.

Alice's Adventures In Wonderland

by Lewis Carroll

Chapter I. Down the Rabbit-Hole

Alice was beginning to get very tired of sitting by her sister on the bank, and of having nothing to do: once or twice she had peeped into the book her sister was reading, but it had no pictures or conversations in it, 'and what is the use of a book,' thought Alice 'without pictures or conversation?'

So she was considering in her own mind (as well as she could, for the hot day made her feel very sleepy and stupid), whether the pleasure of making a daisy-chain would be worth the trouble of getting up and picking the daisies, when suddenly a White Rabbit with pink eyes ran close by her.

There was nothing so **very** remarkable in that; nor did Alice think it so **very** much out of the way to hear the Rabbit say to itself, 'Oh dear! Oh dear! I shall be late!' (when she thought it over afterwards, it occurred to her that she ought to have wondered at this, but at the time it all seemed quite natural); but when the Rabbit actually **took a watch out of its waistcoat-pocket**, and looked at it, and then hurried on, Alice started to her feet, for it flashed across her mind that she had never before seen a rabbit with either a waistcoat-pocket, or a watch to take out of it, and burning with curiosity, she ran across the field after it, and fortunately was just in time to see it pop down a large rabbit-hole under the hedge.

C Shows the fonts adjusted. The change is slight but improves the overall readability.

normal *italic oblique*

TABLE 5.6 Font-Style Values

Value	Compatibility
normal	IE3, FF1, S1, C1, O5.5, CSS1
italic	IE3, FF1, S1, C1, O5.5, CSS1
oblique	IE4, FF1, S1, C1, O5.5, CSS1

COMING SOON: Font-stretch

Although not currently implemented in any browser, CSS3 includes the new property, **font-stretch**. The command

font-stretch: condensed;

allows you to reference particular font widths, such as expanded and condensed Ⓑ. Some fonts include font widths that stretch or compress the font and are different from bold, which simply makes the letterform consistently thicker. Most fonts will not have these properties, but for those that do, using **font-stretch** will be the best way to access them.

Ⓑ Normal, extended, and condensed versions of Univers LT Std, which can be referenced by the **font-stretch** property when it becomes available.

Making Text Italic

Two kinds of styled text that are often confused are *italic* and *oblique*. An italic font is a special version of a particular font, redesigned with more pronounced serifs and usually a slight slant to the right. An oblique font, on the other hand, is simply a font that is slanted to the right but otherwise identical to the normal version.

Using the **font-style** property (**Table 5.6**), you can define a font as italic, oblique, or normal. When a font is set to italic but does not have an explicit italic version, the font defaults to oblique Ⓐ.

To set font-style for an element:

1. **Add the font style property to your CSS.** Type the property name **font-style** (**Code 5.6**), followed by a colon (:).

    font-style:

2. **italic;**

    Define a style value. Type a value for the **font-style**. Your options are:

    ▸ **italic**, which displays the type in an italic version of the font

    ▸ **oblique**, which slants the text to the right

    ▸ **normal**, which overrides any other styles set

3. **h2 strong { font-style: normal; }**

    Add style overrides as needed. You can override italics or oblique by setting the font style for a child element to **normal**.

Code 5.6 *font-properties.css*—The **h1** and **h2** tags both have italic set for them with this being overridden in the **strong** tag within an **h2** Ⓒ. We also need to change the font-style in the @font-face rule. This does not actually italicize the downloaded font, it just tells the browser to use this in place of an italicized version.

```
/*** CSS VQS - Chapter 5 - fontproperties.css ***/

@font-face {
  font-family: 'Title Font';
  src: url('../_fonts/Little-Trouble-Girl/littletroublegirl-webfont.eot');
  src: local('☺'), url('../_fonts/Little-Trouble-Girl/littletroublegirl-webfont.woff') format('woff'),
  → url('../_fonts/Little-Trouble-Girl/littletroublegirl-webfont.ttf') format('truetype'),
  → url('../_fonts/Little-Trouble-Girl/littletroublegirl-webfont.svg#webfont') format('svg');
  font-weight: normal;
  font-style: italic;
  font-variant: normal; }

body {
  font-family: Corbel, Helvetica, Arial, Sans-serif;
  font-size: 100%;
  font-size-adjust: .5; }

h1, h2, h3, h4, h5, h6, .byline {
  font-family: Constantia, Georgia, Times, "Times New Roman", Serif;
  font-size-adjust: .46; }

h1 {
  font-family: 'Title Font', Constantia, Georgia, Times, "Times New Roman", Serif;
  font-size: 3em;
  font-style: italic; }

h2 {
  font-size: 2em;
  font-style: normal; }

h2 strong {
  font-size: .5em;
  font-style: italic; }

p {
  font-size: .875em; }

strong {
  font-size: 1.25em; }

.byline {
  font-size: 1.25em;
  font-style: italic; }

.byline .author {
  font-style: normal; }
```

TIP Many browsers do not differentiate between italic and oblique but will simply use the fonts italic version (if available), even when they are set to oblique.

TIP If an italicized or oblique version of the typeface does not exist, many browsers will attempt to synthesize one by slanting the normal version of the font to the right. This rarely looks good and should be avoided.

TIP Many Web designers underline words to draw visual attention to them. I recommend using italic or oblique text instead. Underlining often causes the page to look cluttered. More important, underlined text might be confused with hypertext links.

TIP Italicized text generally fits into a more compact space than non-italic text (called roman in traditional typesetting terms) and could be used to save screen space. But be careful—at small point sizes, italic can be difficult to read on the screen.

Alice's Adventures In Wonderland

by Lewis Carroll

Chapter I. Down the Rabbit-Hole

Alice was beginning to get very tired of sitting by her sister on the bank, and of having nothing to do: once or twice she had peeped into the book her sister was reading, but it had no pictures or conversations in it, 'and what is the use of a book,' thought Alice 'without pictures or conversation?'

So she was considering in her own mind (as well as she could, for the hot day made her feel very sleepy and stupid), whether the pleasure of making a daisy-chain would be worth the trouble of getting up and picking the daisies, when suddenly a White Rabbit with pink eyes ran close by her.

There was nothing so **very** remarkable in that; nor did Alice think it so **very** much out of the way to hear the Rabbit say to itself, 'Oh dear! Oh dear! I shall be late!' (when she thought it over afterwards, it occurred to her that she ought to have wondered at this, but at the time it all seemed quite natural); but when the Rabbit actually **took a watch out of its waistcoat-pocket**, and looked at it, and then hurried on, Alice started to her feet, for it flashed across her mind that she

---

C Italics are often used to help set off text, such as with the word "by," or to add emphasis, as with the chapter title.

Setting Bold, Bolder, Boldest

CSS provides several options that allow you to set different levels of boldness for text. Many fonts have various weights associated with them; these weights have the effect of making the text look more or less bold (**Table 5.7**). CSS can take advantage of this feature **A**.

To define bold text in a CSS rule:

1. Add the font weight property to your CSS. Type the property name **font-weight** (**Code 5.7**), followed by a colon (**:**).

   `font-weight:`

2. Define the weight.

   `bold;`

   Type the value for the **font-weight** property, using one of the following options:

   ▸ **bold**, which sets the font to boldface

   ▸ **bolder** or **lighter**, which sets the font's weight to be bolder or lighter relative to its parent element's weight

   ▸ A value from **100** to **900**, in increments of 100, which increases the weight, based on alternative versions of the font that are available

   ▸ **normal**, which overrides other weight specifications

TIP Use font-weight to add emphasis to text, but use it sparingly. If everything is bold, nothing stands out.

TIP In reality, most fonts support only **normal** and **bold**, so relative values have an absolute effect

normal   **bold**

A The difference between normal and bold text is evident here.

TABLE 5.7 Font-Weight Values

Value	Compatibility
normal	IE3, FF1, S1, C1, O5.5, CSS1
bold	IE3, FF1, S1, C1, O5.5, CSS1
lighter	IE4, FF1, S1, C1, O5.5, CSS1
bolder	IE4, FF1, S1, C1, O5.5, CSS1
100-900*	IE4, FF1, S1, C1, O5.5, CSS1

* Depending on available font weights

Alice's Adventures In Wonderland

by Lewis Carroll

Chapter I. Down the Rabbit-Hole

Alice was beginning to get very tired of sitting by her sister on the bank, and of having nothing to do: once or twice she had peeped into the book her sister was reading, but it had no pictures or conversations in it, 'and what is the use of a book,' thought Alice 'without pictures or conversation?'

So she was considering in her own mind (as well as she could, for the hot day made her feel very sleepy and stupid), whether the pleasure of making a daisy-chain would be worth the trouble of getting up and picking the daisies, when suddenly a White Rabbit with pink eyes ran close by her.

There was nothing so very remarkable in that; nor did Alice think it so very much out of the way to hear the Rabbit say to itself, 'Oh dear! Oh dear! I shall be late!' (when she thought it over afterwards, it occurred to her that she ought to have wondered at this, but at the time it all seemed quite natural); but when the Rabbit actually took a watch out of its waistcoat-pocket, and looked at it, and then hurried on, Alice started to her feet, for it flashed across her mind that she

B The author's name and the chapter title are made to stand out. Notice that the text in strong tags is no longer bold. You can make text "strong" in many ways, including making it bold or bigger.

Font-Weight Numbers

Most fonts do not have nine weights, so if you specify a **font-weight** value that is not available, another weight is used, based on the following system:

- **100** to **300** use the next lighter weight, if available, or the next darker weight.

- **400** and **500** may be used interchangeably.

- **600** to **900** use the next darker weight, if available, or the next lighter weight.

Code 5.7 *font-properties.css*—The **h1** tag is set to be bold (which it would normally be), but the **h2** tag is set to be lighter, which has the effect of using the normal font. You can even make strong text not bold by setting its weight to normal **B**.

```css
/*** CSS VQS - Chapter 5 - fontproperties.css ***/

@font-face {
  font-family: 'Title Font';
  src: url('../_fonts/Little-Trouble-Girl/littletroublegirl-webfont.eot');
  src: local('☺'), url('../_fonts/Little-Trouble-Girl/littletroublegirl-webfont.woff') format('woff'),
  → url('../_fonts/Little-Trouble-Girl/littletroublegirl-webfont.ttf') format('truetype'),
  → url('../_fonts/Little-Trouble-Girl/littletroublegirl-webfont.svg#webfont') format('svg');
  font-weight: bold;
  font-style: italic;
  font-variant: normal; }

body {
  font-family: Corbel, Helvetica, Arial, Sans-serif;
  font-size: 100%;
  font-size-adjust: .5; }

h1, h2, h3, h4, h5, h6, .byline {
  font-family: Constantia, Georgia, Times, "Times New Roman", Serif;
  font-size-adjust: .46; }

h1 {
  font-family: 'Title Font', Constantia, Georgia, Times, "Times New Roman", Serif;
  font-size: 3em;
  font-style: italic;
  font-weight: bold; }

h2 {
  font-size: 2em;
  font-style: normal;
  font-weight: lighter; }

h2 strong {
  font-size: .5em;
  font-style: italic; }


p {
  font-size: .875em; }

strong {
  font-size: 1.25em;
  font-weight: normal; }

.byline {
  font-size: 1em;
  font-style: italic; }

.byline .author {
  font-size: 1.25em;
  font-style: normal;
  font-weight: bold; }
```

Creating Small Caps

Small caps (sometimes referred to as *mini-caps*) are useful for emphasizing titles (**Table 5.8**). With small caps, lowercase letters are converted to uppercase but in a slightly smaller size than regular uppercase letters Ⓐ.

To set small caps for an element:

1. **Add the font variant property to your CSS.** Type the property name **font-variant** (**Code 5.8**), followed by a colon (:).

   font-variant:

2. **Define a value for the variant.**

   small-caps;

   Type the value of the **font-variant** property, using one of the following options:

   ▸ **small-caps**, which sets lowercase letters as smaller versions of true uppercase letters

   ▸ **normal**, which overrides other font-variant values that might be inherited

TIP Small caps are best reserved for titles or other special text; they can be hard to read at smaller sizes.

Normal   SMALLCAPS

Ⓐ With small caps, all the letters are uppercase, but the first letter is larger than the others.

TABLE 5.8 Font-Variant Values

Value	Compatibility
normal	IE4, FF1, S1, C1, O3.5, CSS1
small-caps	IE4, FF1, S1, C1, O3.5, CSS1

ALICE'S ADVENTURES IN WONDERLAND

by **Lewis Carroll**

Chapter I. DOWN THE RABBIT-HOLE

Alice was beginning to get very tired of sitting by her sister on the bank, and of having nothing to do: once or twice she had peeped into the book her sister was reading, but it had no pictures or conversations in it, 'and what is the use of a book,' thought Alice 'without pictures or conversation?'

So she was considering in her own mind (as well as she could, for the hot day made her feel very sleepy and stupid), whether the pleasure of making a daisy-chain would be worth the trouble of getting up and picking the daisies, when suddenly a White Rabbit with pink eyes ran close by her.

There was nothing so **very** remarkable in that; nor did Alice think it so **very** much out of the way to hear the Rabbit say to itself, 'Oh dear! Oh dear! I shall be late!' (when she thought it over afterwards, it occurred to her that she ought to have wondered at this, but at the time it all seemed quite natural); but when the Rabbit actually **took a watch out of its waistcoat-pocket**, and looked at it, and then hurried on, Alice started to her feet, for it flashed across her mind that she

Ⓑ Using small caps for the title is an elegant way to set it off from the rest of the text.

Code 5.8 *font-properties.css*—Small caps are applied to both header 1 and header 2, but disabled in the strong element within the **h2**. Note that the font-variant declaration was changed in the @font-face to small-caps rule so that the downloaded font will display in the **h1** Ⓑ.

```css
/*** CSS VQS - Chapter 5 - fontproperties.css ***/

@font-face {
  font-family: 'Title Font';
  src: url('../_fonts/Little-Trouble-Girl/littletroublegirl-webfont.eot');
  src: local('☺'), url('../_fonts/Little-Trouble-Girl/littletroublegirl-webfont.woff') format('woff'),
  → url('../_fonts/Little-Trouble-Girl/littletroublegirl-webfont.ttf') format('truetype'),
  → url('../_fonts/Little-Trouble-Girl/littletroublegirl-webfont.svg#webfont') format('svg');
  font-weight: bold;
  font-style: italic;
  font-variant: small-caps; }

body {
  font-family: Corbel, Helvetica, Arial, Sans-serif;
  font-size: 100%;
  font-size-adjust: .5; }

h1, h2, h3, h4, h5, h6, .byline {
  font-family: Constantia, Georgia, Times, "Times New Roman", Serif;
  font-size-adjust: .46; }

h1 {
  font-family: 'Title Font', Constantia, Georgia, Times, "Times New Roman", Serif;
  font-size: 3em;
  font-style: italic;
  font-weight: bold;
  font-variant: small-caps; }

h2 {
  font-size: 2em;
  font-style: normal;
  font weight: lighter;
  font-variant: small-caps; }

h2 strong {
  font-size: .5em;
  font-style: italic;
  font-variant: normal; }

p {
  font-size: .875em; }

strong {
  font-size: 1.25em; }

.byline {
  font-size: 1em;
  font-style: italic; }

.byline .author {
  font-size: 1.25em;
  font-style: normal;
  font-weight: bold; }
```

Setting Multiple Font Values

Although you can set font properties independently, it is often useful, not to mention more concise, to put all font elements in a single declaration (**Table 5.9**). To do this, you use the shorthand **font** property.

To define several font attributes simultaneously in a rule:

1. **Add the font property to your CSS.** Type the property name **font** (**Code 5.9**), followed by a colon (**:**). Then type the values in the same order that they are typed in the remaining steps of this exercise.

   ```
   font:
   ```

2. *Optional,* **Define a style value.** Type a **font-style** value, followed by a space. (See "Making Text Italic" in this chapter.)

   ```
   italic
   ```

3. *Optional,* **Define a weight value.** Type a **font-weight** value, followed by a space. (See "Setting Bold, Bolder, Boldest" in this chapter.)

   ```
   bold
   ```

4. *Optional,* **Define a variant value.** Type a **font-variant** value, followed by a space. (See "Creating Small Caps" in this chapter.)

   ```
   small-caps
   ```

TABLE 5.9 Font Values

Value	Compatibility
<font-style>	IE3, FF1, S1, C1, O3.5, CSS1
<font-variant>	IE3, FF1, S1, C1, O3.5, CSS1
<font-weight>	IE3, FF1, S1, C1, O3.5, CSS1
<font-size>	IE3, FF1, S1, C1, O3.5, CSS1
<line-height>	IE3, FF1, S1, C1, O3.5, CSS1
<font-family>	IE3, FF1, S1, C1, O3.5, CSS1
visitor styles	IE4, FF1, S2, C1, O6, CSS2

5. **Define a size value.** Type a `font-size` value. (See "Setting the Font Size" in this chapter.)

   100%

6. *Optional,* **Define a line height value.** Type a forward slash (/), a `line-height` value, and a space. (See "Adjusting Text Spacing" in Chapter 6).

   /.9

7. **Define a font family value.** Type a `font-family` value and closing semi-colon. (See "Setting a Font Stack" in this chapter.)

   ```
   'Title Font', Constantia, Georgia,
   →Times, "Times New Roman", Serif;
   ```

TIP The font shorthand property is a real time-saver, and I try to use it as often as possible. It not only takes less time to type and edit, but can reduce the size of your code and speed up your load time.

TIP Code editing software, such as Coda and Dreamweaver, tend to default to the individual properties rather than the shorthand.

TIP If you don't want to set a particular style, variant, or weight value in the list, just leave it out. The browser will use its default value instead. However, you do have to include at least one value, even if it's just `normal`.

TIP If you need to override a value set by the `font` shorthand property, it's generally best to use the full property (such as `font-style`, `font-variant`, `font-weight`, and `font-family`).

Code 5.9 *font-properties.css*—Wherever possible, the font properties have been combined into the shorthand **font** property. This requires that the size, font family, and at least one of the other font properties are defined Ⓐ.

```
/*** CSS VQS - Chapter 5 - fontproperties.css ***/

@font-face {
  font-family: 'Title Font';
  src: url('../_fonts/Little-Trouble-Girl/littletroublegirl-webfont.eot');
  src: local('☺'), url('../_fonts/Little-Trouble-Girl/littletroublegirl-webfont.woff') format('woff'),
  → url('../_fonts/Little-Trouble-Girl/littletroublegirl-webfont.ttf') format('truetype'),
  → url('../_fonts/Little-Trouble-Girl/littletroublegirl-webfont.svg#webfont') format('svg');
  font-weight: bold;
  font-style: italic;
  font-variant: small-caps; }

body {
  font: normal 100%/1.5 Corbel, Helvetica, Arial, Sans-serif;
  font-size-adjust: .5; }

h1, h2, h3, h4, h5, h6, .byline {
  font-family: Constantia, Georgia, Times, "Times New Roman", Serif;
  font-size-adjust: .46; }

h1 {
  font: italic bold small-caps 3em/.9 'Title Font', Constantia, Georgia, Times, "Times New Roman",
  → Serif;
  }

h2 {
  font-size: 2em;
  font-style: normal;
  font-weight: lighter;
  font-variant: small-caps; }

h2 strong {
  font-size: .5em;
  font-style: italic;
  font-variant: normal; }

p {
  font-size: .875em; }

strong {
  font-size: 1.25em; }

.byline {
  font-size: 1em;
  font-style: italic; }

.byline .author {
  font-size: 1.25em;
  font-style: normal;
  font-weight: bold; }
```

Alice's Adventures In Wonderland

by **Lewis Carroll**

Chapter I. Down the Rabbit-Hole

Alice was beginning to get very tired of sitting by her sister on the bank, and of having nothing to do: once or twice she had peeped into the book her sister was reading, but it had no pictures or conversations in it, 'and what is the use of a book,' thought Alice 'without pictures or conversation?'

So she was considering in her own mind (as well as she could, for the hot day made her feel very sleepy and stupid), whether the pleasure of making a daisy-chain would be worth the trouble of getting up and picking the daisies, when suddenly a White Rabbit with pink eyes ran close by her.

There was nothing so **very** remarkable in that; nor did Alice think it so **very** much out of the way to hear the Rabbit say to itself, 'Oh dear! Oh dear! I shall be late!' (when she thought it over afterwards, it occurred to her that she ought to have wondered at this, but at the time it all seemed quite natural); but when the Rabbit actually **took a watch out of its**

Ⓐ This version should look similar to the previous section except for the space between lines of text.

Mimicking the Visitor's Styles

Wouldn't it be nice if you could match your visitor's system font styles? You can do this by simply declaring the font style to be one of the following keywords (for example, **font: icon;**):

- **caption**: the font style being used by controls, such as buttons
- **icon**: the font style being used to label icons
- **menu**: the font style being used in drop-down menus and menu lists
- **message-box**: the font style being used in dialog boxes
- **small-caption**: the font style being used for labeling small controls
- **status-bar**: the font style being used in the window's status bar at the top of the window

Putting It All Together

1. **Add a CSS rule for the body element, defining the font stack.** Use the HTML from chapter 4, and in the `<style>` tag, add a **body{...}** rule and a declaration for the font family (the font stack). Try out different fonts and see how they work in your system.

2. **Use Webfonts with the header.** Place an **@font-face{...}** rule at the top of your CSS code, pointing to a Webfont file (it can be on your local system), and add a rule for the page headers (**h1**, **h2**, **h3**, etc...) with the Webfont the first listed in the font stack.

3. **Specify the size of fonts in the body.** Add a **font-size** declaration in your body rule. Play around with different values and units to see how this affects your page.

4. **Specify a font adjustment.** Add **font-adjustment** to the body rule, and then change your font stack around to see how this affects different fonts' sizes.

5. **Specify the font weight for headers.** Browser default styles generally make headers bold, so play around with what they look like in normal (roman) style.

6. **Style headers with small-caps.** Add **font-variant** to the header rules.

7. **Combine style rules using the font shorthand.** Use the **font** property to combine as many of the independent font properties into a single declaration.

6

Text Properties

Text is everywhere and is used for everything from the ingredients in breakfast cereal to an ode to a Grecian urn. It is the best system that humans have ever devised for recording complex thoughts. Many people think of text as simply a way to record words, but typography adds a voice to the meaning of the words. Typography affects how text appears by controlling not only the shapes and sizes of the letters used (the font), but also the spaces between letters, words, lines, and paragraphs.

Unfortunately, many of the challenges of typography on the Web have come about as a result of a need to circumvent the limitations of the medium. The challenge of Web typography is to improve screen text legibility, as well as to guide the viewer's attention to important content. It's a difficult balancing act, but this chapter will prepare you with the right tools.

In This Chapter

Code 6.1 The HTML5 code used for the examples in this chapter. This code links to the final CSS code from Chapter 5 and also links a new file—*text-properties.css*—that we will be building in this chapter.

```
<!-- HTML5 -->
<!DOCTYPE html>
<html lang="en">
<head>
<meta charset="utf-8">
<title>Alice's Adventure's In Wonderland | Chapter II</title>
<link href="../_css/font-properties.css" type="text/css" rel="stylesheet">
<link href="../_css/text-properties.css" type="text/css" rel="stylesheet">
<!--[if IE ]>
  <style>@import url(_css/ie.css);</style>
  <script src="_script/HTML5forIE.js" type="text/javascript"></script>
<![endif]-->
</head>
<body id="chapter2" class="book aaiw chapter">
<header>
<h1>Alice&#8217;s Adventures In Wonderland</h1>
<p class="byline">by <span class="author">Lewis Carroll</span></p>
/header
<article>
<header><h2><strong>CHAPTER II.</strong> The Pool of Tears</h2></header>
<p>'Curiouser and curiouser!' cried Alice <span class="strike">(she was so much surprised, that
for the moment she quite forgot how to speak good English);</span> 'now I'm
opening out like the largest telescope that ever was! Good-bye, feet!'
(for when she looked down at her feet, they seemed to be almost out of
sight, they were getting so far off). 'Oh, my poor little feet, I wonder
who will put on your shoes and stockings for you now, dears? I'm sure
<em>I</em> shan't be able!...</p>
<p>And she went on planning to herself how she would manage it. 'They must
go by the carrier,' she thought; 'and how funny it'll seem, sending
presents to one's own feet! And how odd the directions will look!</p>
<div class="asis">
    Alice's Right Foot ESQ.
        Hearthrug,
            Near the fender,
                (with Alice's love).
</div>
</article>
<footer>
  <ul>
    <li><a href="" target="_self">Table of Contents</a></li>
    <li><a href="" target="_self">About the Author</a></li>
    <li><a href="" target="_self">About the Books</a></li>
    <li><a href="" target="_self">About the Site</a></li>
  </ul>
</footer>
</body>
</html>
```

TABLE 6.1 Letter-Spacing Values

Value	Compatibility
normal	IE4, FF1, S1, C1, O3.5, CSS1
<length>	IE4, FF1, S1, C1, O3.5, CSS1

Code 6.2 *text-properties.css*—space has been compressed in the level 1 heading (the book title) to create a cramped effect Ⓐ. The chapter name has been spaced out; however, the spacing was overridden in the chapter number ("Chapter II."), so it appears normal. I've also closed up the spacing after the first letter in the first paragraph, which is being set as a drop cap.

```
/*** CSS3 VQS | Chapter 6 | text-properties.
→ css ***/

h1 {
  letter-spacing: -.05em; }

h2 {
  letter-spacing: 2px; }

h2 strong {
  letter-spacing: 0; }

header + p:first-letter {
  letter-spacing: -.05em; }
```

ALICE'S ADVENTURES IN WONDERLAND

by **Lewis Carroll**

CHAPTER II. THE POOL OF TEARS

'C uriouser and curiouser!' cried Alice (she was so much surprised, that for the moment she quite forgot how to speak good English), 'now I'm opening out like the largest telescope that ever was! Good-bye, feet!' (for when she looked down at her feet, they seemed to be almost out of sight, they were getting so far off). 'Oh, my poor little feet, I wonder who will put on your shoes and stockings for you now, dears? I'm sure I shan't be able! I shall be a great deal too far off to trouble myself about you: you must manage the best way you can;—but I must be kind to them,' thought Alice, 'or perhaps they won't walk the way I want to go! Let me see: I'll give them a new pair of boots every Christmas.'

And she went on planning to herself how she would manage it. 'They must go by the carrier,' she thought: 'and how funny it'll

Ⓐ **Code 6.2 applied to code 6.1:** By changing its spacing, the book title takes on a slightly more distinctive, logo-like appearance, and spacing out the chapter title makes it stand out slightly.

Adjusting Text Spacing

CSS gives you the ability to easily adjust text spacing, including the space between individual letters (*tracking*), words, and lines of text in a paragraph (*leading*). Of course, you could apply nonbreaking spaces and the line break tag to get a similar effect in straight HTML, but these "kludges" are difficult to implement, control, and change. With CSS, you have exact control over these elements.

Adjusting the space between letters (tracking)

Tracking is the amount of space between letters in a word, which, in CSS, is controlled with the **letter-spacing** property (**Table 6.1**). More space between letters often improves text readability. On the other hand, too much space can hamper reading by making individual words appear less distinct.

To define tracking:

1. Add the letter-spacing property to your CSS rule. Type **letter-spacing** in the CSS declaration list, followed by a colon (:) (**Code 6.2**).

   ```
   letter-spacing:
   ```

2. Specify the amount of space between your letters.

   ```
   -.05em;
   ```

   Type a value for the **letter-spacing** property, using either of the following:

   ▸ A positive or negative length value, such as **-.05em**, which sets the distance between letters. For more information, see "Values and Units Used in This Book" in the Introduction.

   ▸ **normal**, which overrides inherited spacing attributes.

TIP Tracking should not be confused with kerning. Although both can add space between letters to improve legibility, they work in different ways. See the sidebar, "Tracking or Kerning?"

TIP Generally, setting letter spacing in ems is preferred because it spaces the letters based on font size. When the text size is changed, the letter spacing automatically adjusts with it.

TIP A positive value for `letter-spacing` adds space between letters; a negative value closes the space. A value of 0 does not add or subtract space but prevents justification of the text. (See "Aligning Text Horizontally" in this chapter.)

Tracking or Kerning?

Whereas *tracking* refers to the spacing between letters in a word, *kerning* refers to the spacing between individual letter pairs in a proportional font. Is this splitting hairs? There actually is a distinction.

Tracking is applied to a word to equally space all the letters; kerning is applied between each letter to give each space the same visual appearance. However, using tracking may mean that some letters are spaced farther apart than others if it improves the readability. Although you could use CSS letter spacing to manually set the space between each letter, I do not recommend it. True text kerning is generally done using specialized layout software because it's very hard to do just by eyeballing the letters.

Code 6.3 *text-properties.css*—When applied to code 6.1, The words in the level 1 heading are spaced almost on top of each other, but this works because the words are visually separated by the capital letters **B**. The words in the chapter title class are spaced out. The copy (body text) is slightly spaced out, which has the overall effect of lightening the page by creating more white space.

```
/*** CSS3 VQS | Chapter 6 | text-properties.
→ css ***/


h1 {
  letter-spacing: -.05em;
  word-spacing: -.1em; }

h2 {
  letter-spacing: 2px;
  word-spacing: 3px; }

h2 strong {
  letter-spacing: 0; }

p {
  word-spacing: .075em; }

header + p:first-letter {
  letter-spacing: -.05em; }

.byline {
  word-spacing: -.3em; }

.byline .author {
  word-spacing: 0; }
```

ALICE'S ADVENTURES IN WONDERLAND

*by*Lewis Carroll

CHAPTER II. THE POOL OF TEARS

'C uriouser and curiouser!' cried Alice (she was so much surprised, that for the moment she quite forgot how to speak good English); 'now I'm opening out like the largest telescope that ever was! Good-bye, feet!' (for when she looked down at her feet, they seemed to be almost out of sight, they were getting so far off). 'Oh, my poor little feet, I wonder who will put on your shoes and stockings for you now, dears? I'm sure I shan't be able! I shall be a great deal too far off to trouble myself about you: you must manage the best way you can—but I must be kind to them,' thought Alice, 'or perhaps they won't walk the way I want to go! Let me see: I'll give them a new pair of boots every Christmas.'

And she went on planning to herself how she would manage it. 'They must go by the carrier,' she thought; 'and how funny

B Code 6.3 applied to Code 6.1: The space between the words has been changed for effect in the titles and slightly increased to lighten the copy.

Adjusting space between words

Just as tracking and word spacing adjustments can both help and hinder legibility, adding a little space between words on the screen using the **word-spacing** property (Table 6.2) can make your text easier to read. But too much space interrupts the path of the reader's eye across the screen and interferes with reading.

To define word spacing:

1. Add the word-spacing property to your declaration list. Type **word-spacing** in the CSS declaration list, followed by a colon (**:**) (**Code 6.3**).

   word-spacing:

2. Specify the amount of space between words.

   .1em;

   Set the value for **word-spacing**, using one of the following:

   ▸ A positive or negative length value, representing the amount of space between words (**-.1em**, for example). For more information, see "Values and Units Used in This Book" in the Introduction.

   ▸ **normal**, which overrides inherited values.

TIP Like letter spacing, use word spacing very sparingly. Generally, the natural word spacing has been optimized for readability. Changing that spacing often does more harm than good.

TABLE 6.2 Word-Spacing Values

Value	Compatibility
normal	IE6, FF1, S1, C1, O3.5, CSS1
<length>	IE6, FF1, S1, C1, O3.5, CSS1

Adjusting space between lines of text (leading)

Anyone who has typed a term paper knows that they are usually double-spaced to make reading easier and allow space for comments. The leading between lines also can be increased for a dramatic effect by creating negative space between the text. The **line-height** property (**Table 6.3**) adds space between the text *baselines* (the bottoms of most letters).

To define leading:

1. Add the line-height property to your rule. Type **line-height** in the CSS declaration list, followed by a colon (**:**) (**Code 6.4**).

   ```
   line-height:
   ```

2. Specify the space between lines of text.

   ```
   .9;
   ```

   Type a value for **line-height**, using one of the following options:

   - A number to be multiplied by the font size to get the spacing value (**2.0** for double-spacing, for example). Although a value of **2** works, it will not validate properly, so always include the decimal.

TABLE 6.3 Line-Height Values

Value	Compatibility
normal	IE3, FF1, S1, C1, O3.5, CSS1
<number>	IE4, FF1, S1, C1, O3.5, CSS1
<length>	IE3, FF1, S1, C1, O3.5, CSS1
<percentage>	IE3, FF1, S1, C1, O3.5, CSS1

Code 6.4 *text-properties.css*—The default **line-height** has been set in the body to be 1.5 spaces, but paragraph copy has been set to 24px. Assuming that the font size is 12px, that will double-space the text. The book title spacing has been tightened up slightly **C**.

```
/*** CSS3 VQS | Chapter 6 | text-properties.
→ css ***/

body {
  line-height: 1.5; }

h1 {
  letter-spacing: -.05em;
  word-spacing: -.1em;
  line-height: .9; }

h2 {
  letter-spacing: 2px;
  word-spacing: 3px; }

h2 strong {
  letter-spacing: 0; }

p {
  word-spacing: .075em;
  line-height: 24px; }

header + p:first-letter {
  letter-spacing: -.05em;
  line-height: 24px; }

.byline {
  word-spacing: -.3em; }

.byline .author {
  word-spacing: 0; }
```

TIP Adding space between lines of text enhances legibility—especially with large amounts of text. Generally, a line height of 1.5 to 2 times the font size is appropriate.

TIP To double-space text, set the line-height value to 2 or 200%. Likewise, a value of 3 or 300% results in triple-spaced text.

TIP You can use a percentage value lower than 100% or length values smaller than the font size to smash lines together. Although this effect may look neat in moderation, it won't ingratiate you with your readers if they can't actually read the text.

TIP Line height can also be defined at the same time as the font size using the font shorthand property. (See "Setting Multiple Font Values" in Chapter 5.)

▸ A length value, such as **24px**. The space for each line of text is set to this size regardless of the designated font size. So if the font size is set to **12px** and the line height is set to **24px**, the text will be double-spaced. See "Values and Units Used in This Book" in the Introduction.

▸ A percentage, which sets the line height proportionate to the font size used for the text.

▸ **normal**, which overrides inherited spacing values.

ALICE'S ADVENTURES IN WONDERLAND

*by*Lewis Carroll

CHAPTER II. THE POOL OF TEARS

'C uriouser and curiouser!' cried Alice (she was so much surprised, that for the moment she quite forgot how to speak good English); 'now I'm opening out like the largest telescope that ever was! Good-bye, feet!' (for when she looked down at her feet, they seemed to be almost out of sight, they were getting so far off). 'Oh, my poor little feet, I wonder who will put on your shoes and stockings for you now, dears? I'm sure I shan't be able! I shall be a great deal too far off to trouble myself about you: you must manage the best way you can;—but I must be kind to them,' thought Alice, 'or perhaps they won't walk the way I want to go! Let me see: I'll give them a new pair of boots every Christmas.'

And she went on planning to herself how she would manage it. 'They must go by the carrier,' she thought; 'and how funny it'll seem, sending presents to one's own feet! And how odd the directions will look!

Ⓒ Code 6.4 applied to code 6.1: The line height in the paragraphs has been loosened to make it easier to read and scan.

Setting Text Case

When you're dealing with dynamically generated output, such as from a database, you can never be sure whether the text will appear in uppercase, lowercase, or a combination of the two. With the **text-transform** property (**Table 6.4**), you can control the ultimate case of the text no matter how it begins.

To define the text case:

1. **Add the text-transform property to your CSS.** Type **text-transform** in the CSS declaration list, followed by a colon (**:**) (**Code 6.4**).

   text-transform:

2. **Specify the text case.**

   uppercase;

   Type one of the following **text-transform** values to specify how you want the text to be treated:

   ▶ **capitalize** sets the first letter of each word to uppercase.

   ▶ **uppercase** forces all letters to uppercase.

   ▶ **lowercase** forces all letters to lowercase.

   ▶ **none** overrides inherited text-case values and leaves the text unaltered.

TABLE 6.4 Text-Transform Values

Value	Compatibility
capitalize	IE4, FF1, S1, C1, O3.5, CSS1
uppercase	IE4, FF1, S1, C1, O3.5, CSS1
lowercase	IE4, FF1, S1, C1, O3.5, CSS1
none	IE4, FF1, S1, C1, O3.5, CSS1

Code 6.5 *text-properties.css*—The **text-transform** property lets you take control of the text case. The author name is forced to capitalize as is the class **.asis** Ⓐ.

```
/*** CSS3 VQS | Chapter 6 | text-properties.
→ css ***/

body {
  line-height: 1.5; }

h1 {
  letter-spacing: -.05em;
  word-spacing: -.1em;
  line-height: .9em; }

h2 {
  letter-spacing: 2px;
  word-spacing: 3px; }

h2 strong {
  letter-spacing: 0; }

p {
  word-spacing: .075em;
  line-height: 24px; }

header + p:first-letter {
  letter-spacing: -.05em;
  line-height: 24px; }

.byline {
  word-spacing: -.3em; }

.byline .author {
  word-spacing: 0;
  text-transform: uppercase; }

.asis {
  text-transform: uppercase; }
```

TIP The `text-transform` property is best reserved for formatting dynamically generated text. If the names in a database are all uppercase, for example, you can use `text-transform` to make them more legible.

TIP Keep in mind that `capitalize` will capitalize all letters in the text, even word such as "of" and "the" that should remain lowercase. In reality, `capitalize` is primarily useful for names.

TIP DON'T TYPE YOUR TEXT IN ALL CAPS. When HTML text is in caps, it makes it a lot harder to control in CSS. Plus, anyone using an assistive device for reading will hear this as shouting. It's better to use normal text plus text transform to style text as uppercase.

ALICE'S ADVENTURES IN WONDERLAND

*by*LEWIS CARROLL

CHAPTER II. THE POOL OF TEARS

'Curiouser and curiouser!' cried Alice (she was so much surprised, that for the moment she quite forgot how to speak good English); 'now I'm opening out like the largest telescope that ever was! Good-bye, feet!' (for when she looked down at her feet, they seemed to be almost out of sight, they were getting so far off). 'Oh, my poor little feet, I wonder who will put on your shoes and stockings for you now, dears? I'm sure I shan't be able! I shall be a great deal too far off to trouble myself about you: you must manage the best way you can;—but I must be kind to them,' thought Alice, 'or perhaps they won't walk the way I want to go! Let me see: I'll give them a new pair of boots every Christmas.'

And she went on planning to herself how she would manage it. 'They must go by the carrier,' she thought; 'and how funny it'll seem, sending presents to one's own feet! And how odd the directions will look!

A **Code 6.5 applied to Code 6.1:** Lewis Carroll's name under the book title is all in caps (as opposed to small caps, explained in Chapter 5).

NEW IN CSS3: Adding a Text Drop Shadow ★

The drop shadow is a time-honored method for adding depth and texture to two-dimensional designs. Most browsers support the **text-shadow** property, part of CSS3 (**Table 6.5**), which allows you to define the color, offset (x and y), spread, and blur for any text drop shadow. Although this property will not currently work in other browsers, neither will it interfere with them.

To define the text shadow:

1. **Add the text-shadow property to your CSS rule.** Type **text-shadow** in the CSS declaration list, followed by a colon (**:**) (**Code 6.5**).

   text-shadow:

2. **Specify the x, y offset.** Type a space followed by two positive or negative length values separated by a space.

   2px 2px

   The first value is the vertical distance to offset the shadow (positive is down; negative is up). The second value is the horizontal offset (positive is right; negative is left).

3. **Specify the amount of blur.** Type a space and then a positive length value for the amount of blur to apply to the shadow. All negative values will be treated as 0.

   2px

TABLE 6.5 Text-Shadow Values

Value	Compatibility
<color>	FF1.9, S1.1, C2, O10, CSS3
<x-offset>	FF1.9, S1.1, C2, O10, CSS3
<y-offset>	FF1.9, S1.1, C2, O10, CSS3
<blur>	FF1.9, S1.1, C2, O10, CSS3
none	FF1.9, S1.1, C2, O10, CSS3

ALICE'S ADVENTURES IN WONDERLAND

by LEWIS CARROLL

CHAPTER II. THE POOL OF TEARS

'C uriouser and curiouser!' cried Alice (she was so much surprised, that for the moment she quite forgot how to speak good English); 'now I'm opening out like the largest telescope that ever was! Good-bye, feet!' (for when she looked down at her feet, they seemed to be almost out of sight, they were getting so far off). 'Oh, my poor little feet, I wonder who will put on your shoes and stockings for you now, dears? I'm sure I shan't be able! I shall be a great deal too far off to trouble myself about you: you must manage the best way you can;—but I must be kind to them,' thought Alice, 'or perhaps they won't walk the way I want to go! Let me see: I'll give them a new pair of boots every Christmas.'

And she went on planning to herself how she would manage it. 'They must go by the carrier,' she thought, 'and how funny it'll seem, sending presents to one's own feet! And how odd the directions will look!

Ⓐ Code 6.6 applied to code 6.1: Although you may need to compare the altered title with the previous screen captures to notice the difference, the title now looks slightly recessed on the page, as if it were embossed. And the chapter title now really hops off the page.

Code 6.6 *text-properties.css*—The `drop-shadow` property allows you to set the x,y offset and the blur radius. The book title has dual shadows, creating a subtle embossed effect Ⓐ, whereas the chapter title has a strong shadow slightly offset to lift the words off the page.

```
/*** CSS3 VQS | Chapter 6 | text-properties.
→ css ***/

body {
  line-height: 1.5; }

h1 {
  letter-spacing: -.05em;
  word-spacing: -.1em;
  line-height: .9em;
  text-shadow: rgba(51,51,51,.9) -1px -1px 3px,
  → rgba(203,203,203,.9) 1px 1px 3px; }

h2 {
  letter-spacing: 2px;
  word-spacing: 3px;
  line-height: 1em;
  text-shadow: rgba(0,0,0,.5) 2px 2px 2px; }

h2 strong {
  letter-spacing: 0;
  text-shadow: none; }

p {
  word-spacing: .075em;
  line-height: 24px; }

p strong {
  text-transform: uppercase; }

header + p:first-letter {
  letter-spacing: -.05em;
  line-height: 24px;
  text-shadow: rgba(51,51,51,.9) -1px -1px 3px,
  → rgba(203,203,203,.9) 1px 1px 3px; }

.byline {
  word-spacing: -.3em; }

.byline .author {
  word-spacing: 0;
  text-transform: uppercase; }

.asis {
  text-transform: uppercase; }
```

4. **Specify the color.** Type a space and then a color value for the shadow.

   `rgba(0,0,0,.5);`

   For more information on color values, see "Choosing Color Values" in Chapter 7.

5. **Add more shadows.** You can add multiple shadows (as many as you want) to any block of text. To do so, you can add another text-shadow declaration to the rule, or add a comma followed by another definition.

   `text-shadow: rgba(51,51,51,.9)`
   `→ -1px -1px 3px, rgba(203,203,203,.9)`
   `→ 1px 1px 3px;`

   TIP You can set the value to `none` to override a shadow that was previously set in the **CSS**.

   TIP Using RGBA works best for shadows. Anything under that shadow will realistically show through.

   TIP Although this is a "shadow," you can use any color for it. Therefore, if your text is on a dark background, you could use a light color to create a drop "glow."

   TIP In Chapter 11, you'll learn how to set a box-shadow that works a lot like the `text-shadow` property but is applied to the element's box.

   TIP Shadows do not affect the position of the text they are placed behind.

   TIP Text shadows are great way to make links pop off the page when used with the `:hover` pseudo class.

Aligning Text Horizontally

Traditionally, text is aligned at its left margin (left justified) or fully justified, which aligns the text at both the left and right margins (often called *newspaper style*). In addition, for emphasis or special effect, text can be centered on the screen or even right justified. The **text-align** property (**Table 6.6**) gives you control of the text's alignment and justification.

To define text alignment:

1. Add the text-align property to your CSS. Type **text-align** in the CSS declaration list, followed by a colon (**:**) (**Code 6.6**).

   text-align:

2. Specify the horizontal alignment.

   center;

   Set one of the following alignment styles:

   ▸ **left** to align the text on the left margin.

   ▸ **right** to align the text on the right margin.

   ▸ **center** to center the text within its area.

   ▸ **justify** to align the text on both the left and right margins.

   ▸ **inherit** makes the text take its parents' alignment.

   ▸ **auto** uses the default alignment, generally left.

TABLE 6.6 Text-Align Values

Value	Compatibility
left	IE3, FF1, S1, C1, O3.5, CSS1
right	IE3, FF1, S1, C1, O3.5, CSS1
center	IE3, FF1, S1, C1, O3.5, CSS1
justify	IE4, FF1, S1, C1, O3.5, CSS1
inherit	IE4, FF1, S1, C1, O3.5, CSS1
auto	IE4, FF1, S1, C1, O3.5, CSS1

Ⓐ **Code 6.7 applied to code 6.1:** Although it's a bit zig-zaggy with left-, right-, center-, and fully-justified text, we'll be changing the title and byline formatting later in this book when I talk about positioning.

Code 6.7 *text-properties.css*—The **.byline** class has been right justified **Ⓐ**, whereas the chapter title in the level 2 heading has been centered, and the copy has been fully justified.

```css
/*** CSS3 VQS | Chapter 6 | text-properties.
→ css ***/

body {
  line-height: 1.5; }

h1 {
  letter-spacing: -.05em;
  word-spacing: -.1em;
  line-height: .9em;
  text-shadow: rgba(51,51,51,.9) -1px -1px 3px,
  → rgba(203,203,203,.9) 1px 1px 3px; }

h2 {
  letter-spacing: 2px;
  word-spacing: 3px;
  line-height: 1em;
  text-shadow: rgba(0,0,0,.5) 2px 2px 2px;
  text-align: center; }

h2 strong {
  letter-spacing: 0;
  text-shadow: none; }

p {
  word-spacing: .075em;
  line-height: 24px;
  text-align: justify; }

p strong {
  text-transform: uppercase; }

header + p:first-letter {
  letter-spacing: -.05em;
  line-height: 24px;
  text-shadow: rgba(51,51,51,.9) -1px -1px 3px,
  → rgba(203,203,203,.9) 1px 1px 3px; }

.byline {
  word-spacing: -.3em;
  text-align: right; }

.byline .author {
  word-spacing: 0;
  text-transform: uppercase; }

.asis {
  text-transform: uppercase; }
```

TIP Text is left justified by default.

TIP Fully justifying text may produce some strange results on the screen because spaces between words must be added to make each line the same length. In addition, opinions differ as to whether full justification helps or hinders readability.

Aligning Text Vertically

Using the **vertical-align** property, you can specify the vertical position of one inline element relative to the elements above or below it . This means that the **vertical-align** property (**Table 6.7**) can be used only with inline tags and table tags—that is, tags without a break before or after them, such as the anchor (**<a>**), image (**<img>**), emphasized text (**<em>**), strong text (**<strong>**), and table data (**<td>**) tags.

To define vertical alignment:

1. **Add the vertical align property to your rule.** Type **vertical-align** in the declaration list, followed by a colon (**:**) (**Code 6.8**).

   vertical-align:

continues on page 166

A The different alignment types. The lines are shown only as guides.

TABLE 6.7 Vertical-Align Values

Value	Compatibility
super	IE4, FF1, S1, C1, O3.5, CSS1
sub	IE4, FF1, S1, C1, O3.5, CSS1
baseline	IE4, FF1, S1, C1, O3.5, CSS1
<relative>	IE5.5, FF1, S1, C1, O3.5, CSS1
<length>	IE5.5, FF1, S1, C1, O3.5, CSS1
<percentage>	IE7, FF1, S1, C1, O3.5, CSS1

B Code 6.8 applied to code 6.1: The chapter number and "by" in the byline have been moved up relative to the text to which they refer.

Code 6.8 *text-properties.css*—Use **vertical-alignment** with relative or absolute values, depending on the results you desire **B**.

```css
/*** CSS3 VQS | Chapter 6 | text-properties.css ***/

body {
  line-height: 1.5; }

h1 {
  letter-spacing: -.05em;
  word-spacing: -.1em;
  line-height: .9em;
  text-shadow: rgba(51,51,51,.9) -1px -1px 3px, rgba(203,203,203,.9) 1px 1px 3px; }

h2 {
  letter-spacing: 2px;
  word-spacing: 3px;
  line-height: 1em;
  text-shadow: rgba(0,0,0,.5) 2px 2px 2px;
  text-align: center; }

h2 strong {
  letter-spacing: 0;
  text-shadow: none;
  vertical-align: super; }

p {
  word-spacing: .075em;
  line-height: 24px;
  text-align: justify; }

p strong {
  text-transform: uppercase; }

header + p:first-letter {
  letter-spacing: -.05em;
  line-height: 24px;
  text-shadow: rgba(51,51,51,.9) -1px -1px 3px, rgba(203,203,203,.9) 1px 1px 3px; }

.byline {
  text-align: right;
  word-spacing: -.3em; }

.byline .author {
  word-spacing: 0;
  text-transform: uppercase;
  vertical-align: -.6em; }

.asis {
  text-transform: uppercase; }
```

2. Specify the vertical alignment.

```
super;
```

Type a value for the vertical text alignment using one of these options:

- ▸ **super** superscripts the text above the baseline.
- ▸ **sub** subscripts the text below the baseline.
- ▸ **baseline** places the text on the baseline (its default state).
- ▸ A relative value from **Table 6.8** that sets the element's alignment relative to its parent's alignment. To align the top of your text with the top of the parent element's text, for example, you would use **text-top**.
- ▸ A percentage value, which raises or lowers the element's baseline proportionate to the parent element's font size (**25%**, for example).

TIP Superscript is great for footnotes, which can be hyperlinked to notes at the bottom of the current page or to another Web page.

TIP The sup and sub tags can also be used to used superscript and subscript, but should not be used for design (as in this case) but for footnotes or mathematical notation.

TIP If you are creating a multicolumn layout, you might encounter problems with vertical alignment when it doesn't appear where it should be. In those cases, a good fallback is to use relative positioning, as explained in Chapter 10.

TABLE 6.8 Setting an Element's Position Relative to the Parent Element

Type	To align the element
top	Top to highest element in line
middle	Middle to middle of parent
bottom	Bottom to lowest element in line
text-top	Top to top of parent element's text
text-bottom	Bottom to bottom of parent element's text

Math and Science

Superscript and subscript are used for scientific notation. To express the Pythagorean theorem, for example, you would use superscripts:

$a^2 + b^2 = c^2$

A water molecule might be expressed with subscripts as follows:

H_2O

However, keep in mind that neither subscript nor superscript will reduce the text size, so you may also want to include **font-size** in your definition to achieve a true scientific notation style. (See "Setting the Font Size" in Chapter 5).

TABLE 6.9 Text-Indent Values

Value	Compatibility
<length>	IE3, FF1, S1, C1, O3.5, CSS1
<percentage>	IE3, FF1, S1, C1, O3.5, CSS1
inherit	IE3, FF1, S1, C1, O3.5, CSS1

ALICE'S ADVENTURES IN WONDERLAND

*by*LEWIS CARROLL

CHAPTER II. THE POOL OF TEARS

'Curiouser and curiouser!' cried Alice (she was so much surprised, that for the moment she quite forgot how to speak good English); 'now I'm opening out like the largest telescope that ever was! Good-bye, feet!' (for when she looked down at her feet, they seemed to be almost out of sight, they were getting so far off). 'Oh, my poor little feet, I wonder who will put on your shoes and stockings for you now, dears? I'm sure I shan't be able! I shall be a great deal too far off to trouble myself about you: you must manage the best way you can;—but I must be kind to them,' thought Alice, 'or perhaps they won't walk the way I want to go! Let me see: I'll give them a new pair of boots every Christmas.'

And she went on planning to herself how she would manage it. 'They must go by the carrier,' she thought; 'and how funny it'll seem, sending presents to one's own feet! And how odd the directions will look!
ALICE'S RIGHT FOOT ESQ. HEARTHRUG, NEAR THE FENDER, (WITH ALICE'S LOVE).
Oh dear, what nonsense I'm talking!'

Just then her head struck against the roof of the hall: in fact she was now more than nine feet high, and she at once took up the little golden key and hurried off to the garden door.

Poor Alice! It was as much as she could do, lying down on one side, to look through into the garden with one eye; but to get through was more hopeless than ever: she sat down and began to cry again.

'You ought to be ashamed of yourself,' said Alice, 'a great girl like you,' (she might well say this), 'to go on crying in this way! Stop this moment, I tell you!' But she went on all the same, shedding gallons of tears, until there was a large pool all round her, about four inches deep and reaching half down the hall.

After a time she heard a little pattering of feet in the distance, and she hastily dried her eyes to see what was

Ⓐ Code 6.9 applied to code 6.1: All paragraphs except the first paragraph are indented a space that is equivalent to two letters. The indent space will adjust with the font size.

TIP Because indenting is more common in the print world than the online world, you may want to consider using indents for only the printer-friendly versions of your page.

Indenting Paragraphs

Indenting the first word of a paragraph several spaces (five spaces, traditionally) is the time-honored method of introducing a new paragraph.

On the Web, however, indented paragraphs haven't worked because most browsers compress multiple spaces into a single space. Instead, paragraphs have been separated by an extra line break.

Using the **text-indent** property (**Table 6.9**), you can specify extra horizontal space at the beginning of the first line of text in a paragraph and restore the traditional paragraph style.

To define text indentation:

1. **Add the text indent property to your CSS.** Type **text-indent** in the CSS declaration list, followed by a colon (**:**) (Code 6.9).

   `text-indent:`

2. **Specify the amount of indentation.**

   `2em;`

   Type a value for the indent, using one of the following options:

   ▸ A length value such as **2cm** creates a nice, clear indent. (See "Values and Units Used in This Book" in the Introduction.)

   ▸ A percentage value indents the text proportionate to the parent's (paragraph) width (**10%**, for example).

TIP If you are using indentation to indicate paragraphs, you should set the margin and padding of paragraphs to 0 to override the <p> tag's natural tendency to add space between paragraphs. You'll learn more about margins and padding in Chapter 8.

Code 6.9 *text-properties.css*—Although you can indent any block of text, indentation is generally associated with paragraphs, and I've set all of the paragraphs to indent 2em Ⓐ. However, the first paragraph in a section is generally not indented; therefore, I've set the first paragraph after a header to always have an indention of 0. I did cheat a bit for this example, because I've set the margin and padding, which we will not explore until Chapter 8.

```
/*** CSS3 VQS | Chapter 6 | text-properties.css ***/

body {
  line-height: 1.5; }

h1 {
  letter-spacing: -.05em;
  word-spacing: -.1em;
  line-height: .9em;
  text-shadow: rgba(51,51,51,.9) -1px -1px 3px, rgba(203,203,203,.9) 1px 1px 3px; }

h2 {
  letter-spacing: 2px;
  word-spacing: 3px;
  line-height: 1em;
  text-shadow: rgba(0,0,0,.5) 2px 2px 2px;
  text-align: center; }

h2 strong {
  letter-spacing: 0;
  text-shadow: none;
  vertical-align: super; }

p {
  word-spacing: .075em;
  line-height: 24px;
  text-align: justify;
  text-indent: 2em;
  margin: 0;
  padding: 0; }

p strong {
  text-transform: uppercase;
  vertical-align: middle; }

header + p {
  text-indent: 0; }

header + p:first-letter {
  letter-spacing: -.05em;
  line-height: 24px;
  text-shadow: rgba(51,51,51,.9) -1px -1px 3px, rgba(203,203,203,.9) 1px 1px 3px; }

.byline {
  word-spacing: -.3em;
  text-align: right; }

.byline .author {
  word-spacing: 0;
  text-transform: uppercase;
  vertical-align: -.6em; }

.asis {
  text-transform: uppercase; }
```

TABLE 6.10 White-Space Values

Value	Compatibility
normal	IE5.5, FF1, S1, C1, O4, CSS1
pre	IE5.5, FF1, S1, C1, O4, CSS1
nowrap	IE5.5, FF1, S1, C1, O4, CSS1

Controlling White Space

As you've learned, browsers traditionally collapsed multiple spaces into a single space unless a **<pre>** tag was used. CSS lets you allow or disallow that space collapsing, as well as designate whether text can break at a space (similar to the **<nobr>** tag) using the **white-space** property (**Table 6.10**).

An excellent example of this is the mouse tail poem from Chapter 3 of *Alice in Wonderland*. This poem is shaped like a curvy mouse tail . If the **white-space** property value is assigned **pre** for the **poem** class, all those spaces collapse 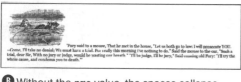. However, if it's assigned a value of **nowrap**, the spaces and line breaks are ignored, and the text stretches as far to the right on the page as necessary .

A The **pre** value keeps all spaces so the poem retains its distinctive mouse tail shape rather than collapsing.

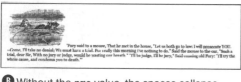

B Without the **pre** value, the spaces collapse along with the mouse tail.

C With the **no-wrap** value, the poem stretches vertically across the window, forcing a horizontal scroll to accommodate its width.

To define white space:

1. Add the white space property to your CSS rule. Type **white-space** in the CSS declaration list, followed by a colon (:) (Code 6.10).

   ```
   white-space:
   ```

2. Specify how you want white space treated.

   ```
   pre;
   ```

   Type one of the following options:

   ▸ **pre** preserves multiple spaces.

   ▸ **nowrap** prevents line wrapping without a **
** tag.

   ▸ **normal** allows the browser to determine how spaces are treated. This setting usually forces multiple spaces to collapse into a single space.

TIP Do not confuse the <nobr> and <pre> tags with the white-space property values of nowrap and pre. Although they basically do the same thing, the no break tag is being phased out (deprecated) and should not be used.

TIP The text content of any tag that receives the nowrap value runs horizontally as far as necessary regardless of the browser window's width. The user may be forced to scroll horizontally to read all the text, so this setting is usually avoided.

TIP nowrap is great for preventing content from wrapping in table data cells.

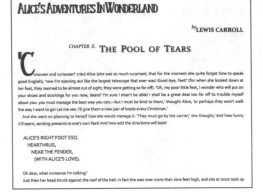

D Code 6.10 applied to code 6.1: The note has been set along a diagonal by adding spaces. These would collapse if not for the **pre** value applied to it.

Code 6.10 *text-properties.css*—The class **.asis** is set up to preserve the HTML text as it appears in the code by setting the **white-space** to **pre**. This is useful for formatting the note that Alice is sending to her foot in the formatting that the author intended **Ⓓ**.

```css
/*** CSS3 VQS | Chapter 6 | text-properties.css ***/

body {
  line-height: 1.5; }

h1 {
  letter-spacing: -.05em;
  word-spacing: -.1em;
  line-height: .9em;
  text-shadow: rgba(51,51,51,.9) -1px -1px 3px, rgba(203,203,203,.9) 1px 1px 3px; }

h2 {
  letter-spacing: 2px;
  word-spacing: 3px;
  line-height: 1em;
  text-shadow: rgba(0,0,0,.5) 2px 2px 2px;
  text-align: center; }

h2 strong {
  letter-spacing: 0;
  text-shadow: none;
  vertical-align: super; }

p {
  line-height: 24px;
  text-align: justify;
  text-indent: 1em;
  margin: 0;
  padding: 0; }

header + p {
  text-indent: 0; }

header + p:first-letter {
  letter-spacing: -.05em;
  line-height: 24px;
  text-shadow: rgba(51,51,51,.9) 1px -1px 3px, rgba(203,203,203,.9) 1px 1px 3px; }

p strong {
  text-transform: uppercase;
  vertical-align: middle; }

.byline {
  word-spacing: -.3em;
  text-align: right; }

.byline .author {
  word-spacing: 0;
  text-transform: uppercase;
  vertical-align: -.6em; }

.asis {
  text-transform: uppercase;
  white-space: pre; }
```

Decorating Text

Using the **text-decoration** property (**Table 6.11**), you can adorn text in one of three ways: underline, overline, or line-through. Used to add emphasis, these decorations attract the reader's eye to important areas or passages on your Web page.

To decorate (or undecorate) text:

1. Add the text decoration property. Type **text-decoration** in the CSS declaration list, followed by a colon (**:**) (**Code 6.11**).

   text-decoration:

2. Specify the text decoration you want (or not).

   none;

   Type a value for the **text-decoration** property. Choose one of the following:

   ▸ **underline** places a line below the text.

   ▸ **overline** places a line above the text.

   ▸ **line-through** places a line through the middle of the text (also called strikethrough).

   ▸ **none** overrides decorations set elsewhere.

TABLE 6.11 Text-Decoration Values

Value	Compatibility
none	IE3, FF1, S1, C1, O3.5, CSS1
underline	IE3, FF1, S1, C1, O3.5, CSS1
overline	IE4, FF1, S1, C1, O3.5, CSS1
line-through	IE3, FF1, S1, C1, O3.5, CSS1

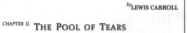

A Code 6.11 applied to code 6.1: A line of text has been struck out.

B Code 6.11 applied to code 6.1: The links in the footer of the page are no longer underlined.

Code 6.11 *text-properties.css*—I use text decoration to set up a class called **.strike** that can be used to strike out unwanted text Ⓐ and to turn off the underline on hypertext links Ⓑ.

```css
/*** CSS3 VQS | Chapter 6 | text-properties.css ***/

body {
  line-height: 1.5; }

h1 {
  letter-spacing: -.05em;
  word-spacing: -.1em;
  line-height: .9em;
  text-shadow: rgba(51,51,51,.9) -1px -1px 3px, rgba(203,203,203,.9) 1px 1px 3px; }

h2 {
  letter-spacing: 2px;
  word-spacing: 3px;
  line-height: 1em;
  text-shadow: rgba(0,0,0,.5) 2px 2px 2px;
  text-align: center; }

h2 strong {
  letter-spacing: 0;
  text-shadow: none;
  vertical-align: super; }

p {
  line-height: 24px;
  text-align: justify;
  text-indent: 1em;
  margin: 0;
  padding: 0; }

p:first-of-type {
  text-indent: 0; }

article p:first-of-type:first-letter {
  letter-spacing: -.05em;
  line-height: 24px;
  text-shadow: rgba(51,51,51,.9) -1px -1px 3px, rgba(203,203,203,.9) 1px 1px 3px; }

p strong {
  text-transform: uppercase;
  vertical-align: middle; }

a {
  text-decoration: none; }

.byline {
  word-spacing: -.3em;
  text-align: right; }

.byline .author {
  word-spacing: 0;
  text-transform: uppercase;
  vertical-align: -.6em; }

.asis {
  text-transform: uppercase;
  white-space: pre; }

.strike {
  text-decoration: line-through; }
```

TIP You can also type a space and add another `text-decoration` value (Table 6.11). As long as the first value is not none, you can use multiple text decorations by adding more values in a list separated by spaces, as follows:

```
overline underline line-through
```

TIP Ding dong, the blink is dead. With CSS3, the `blink` value has been officially removed as a text decoration option, and the `<blink>` HTML tag is long gone. Now if you want to annoy your visitors with blinking text, you'll have to use Adobe Flash.

TIP Text decorations are applied across an entire text block element rather than on a letter-by-letter basis. This means that a child element cannot override the text decoration set by its parent.

TIP Although a child element cannot override its parent's text decoration, child elements can have additional text decoration added to them. In the example, notice that the emphasis tag uses strikethrough, which is added to the underlining already supplied by the paragraph tag.

TIP Striking through text is useful for text that you want to show as deleted. For example, I've used strikethrough in online catalogs that include sale prices. I show the original price in strikethrough with the sale price next to it. That said, using the `<del>` tag is a better option because it communicates deletion.

TIP Honestly, the only time I use text decoration is to turn off hypertext link underlining. Underlining is just too indiscriminate, placing a hard line under the text in the same color as the text. Some work is being done to provide more underline control to set the space, color, and style of the underline.

Underlining Links?

Setting **text-decoration: none**; in the `<a>` tag overrides the underline in hypertext links, even if the visitor's browser is set to underline links. In my experience, many visitors look for underlining to identify links. Although I don't like underlining for links—it clutters the page, and CSS offers many superior alternatives—I receive angry emails from visitors when I turn off underlining.

One alternative to the **text-decoration** property is to use the **border-bottom** property with the link tag to provide faux underlining. This gives you much better control over the underline appearance, and it even allows you to use different colors. For more information, see "Styling Navigation and Links" in Chapter 14.

Coming Soon!

Although only a few new text properties are being added to CSS3, several are under development by the CSS Work Group:

Text Outlining—**text-outline** will allow you to add a line around the character glyph and control the color and thickness of that line. Safari has already implemented a similar version of this as a Safari CSS extension called **-webkit-text-stroke**, and it's possible that this might be the final form adopted for CSS3.

Text Wrapping—Currently, text in Web pages breaks only at spaces. No hyphenation or line-breaking properties exist. The **text-wrap property** will allow you to specify how text should wrap.

Text Justification—Although text justification is possible by setting **text-align: justify**, you cannot specify how that justification is performed. This can result in awkward spacing in justified text. The **text-justify** property will include several options for spacing text, and **text-align-last** will let you specify the alignment of the last line of justified text.

Kerning—Remember that letter spacing is not kerning. The new `punctuation-trim` property will provide some rudimentary kerning capabilities.

Hanging Punctuation—One common problem in typography is what to do when alphanumeric characters are not present at the beginning of a block of text, as with quotation marks. The `hanging-punctuation` property will allow you to define how these characters are treated, either placing them in the edge of the text block or outside.

Text Line Decoration—As mentioned in my explanation of the `text-decoration` property, several new associated properties are being developed to style the text decoration, including `text-line-color`, `text-line-style`, `text-line-skip`, and `text-underline-position`.

To follow the development of these styles, visit the CSS3 Text Module at www.w3.org/TR/css3-text.

Putting It All Together

1. **Add letter, word, and line spacing to your headers.** Try out different effects, pushing the text together and moving it apart.

2. **Add line spacing to your body copy.** Specify the line height in for paragraph elements. See how increasing and decreasing the space improves or reduces readability. At what point does increasing the line height reduce readability?

3. **Set the text case of your headline text to uppercase.** You can also play with the font size to make the headlines stand out.

4. **Add a text shadow to your headlines.** Try to keep them subtle and not distracting.

5. **Fully justify your body copy.** Use the justify text alignment on the paragraph tag. Does this look better or worse than the ragged edges you get with left justification?

6. **Indent your text paragraphs.** Play around with different amounts of indentation and see what you prefer.

Color and Background Properties

Colors form the cornerstone of all design, even if they're only black and white. They create the first impression of your site. Bright, vibrant, jewel-like colors make a radically different statement than earth tones. Even if you choose to use only black and white, your design will make a statement. Beyond their decorative impact, colors can also guide the viewer's eye around the page, helping to highlight some important areas while downplaying others.

In this chapter, you will learn the primary methods used to add and control color with CSS. Keep in mind, however, you can specify color using several CSS properties. (See the sidebar "Other Ways to Add Color.") But before you learn how to code colors, let's quickly explore how to choose them.

In This Chapter

Code 7.1 The HTML5 code used for the examples in this chapter. It imports the final CSS code from Chapters 5 and 6, and imports a new file called *color-background-properties.css*, which will contain the CSS code from this chapter. For this chapter, we'll be styling Chapter 3 of Lewis Carroll's *Alice's Adventures in Wonderland*, including a navigational footer at the bottom.

```
<!-- HTML5 -->
<!DOCTYPE html>
<html lang="en">
<head>
<meta charset="utf-8">
<title>Alice's Adventure's In Wonderland | Chapter III</title>
<link href="../_css/font-properties.css" type="text/css" rel="stylesheet">
<link href="../_css/text-properties.css" type="text/css" rel="stylesheet">
<link href="../_css/color-background-properties.css" type="text/css" rel="stylesheet">

<!--[if IE ]>
  <style>@import url(_css/ie.css);</style>
  <script src="script/HTML5forIE.js" type="text/javascript"></script>
<![endif]-->

</head>
<body id="chapter3" class="book aaiw chapter">

<header class="page">
<h1>Alice&#8217;s Adventures In Wonderland</h1>
<p class="byline">by <span class="author">Lewis Carroll</span></p>
</header>

<article><!-- Article -->
<header>
<h2><strong>CHAPTER III.</strong> A Caucus-Race and a Long Tale</h2>
</header>
<p>
They were indeed a queer-looking party that assembled on the bank&mdash;the
birds with draggled feathers, the animals with their fur clinging close
to them, and all dripping wet, cross, and uncomfortable.
</p>
</article>
<footer>
  <ul>
    <li><a href="" target="_self">Table of Contents</a></li>
    <li><a href="" target="_self">About the Author</a></li>
    <li><a href="" target="_self">About the Books</a></li>
    <li><a href="" target="_self">About the Site</a></li>
  </ul>
</footer>
</body>
</html>
```

Choosing Color Values

The saying, "There is more than one way to skin a cat," is grotesque, but it is also applicable to most creative decisions, such as color values in Web designs. You can use several traditional methods to define the same Web page color, and CSS3 even introduces a few new ways.

Color keywords

Although most designers have little use for predefined colors, you have access to many predefined color values derived from lists defined in the HTML4 and SVG specifications. **Table 7.1** shows the list of keywords along with the equivalent hex and decimal values. Values in boldface indicate inclusion from HTML4.

TABLE 7.1 Color Values

Name	Form	Example	Compatibility
Keyword	<keyword>	coral	IE4, FF1, S1, C1, O3.5, CSS1
Transparent	transparent	–	IE4, FF1, S1, C1, O3.5, CSS1
Current color	currentcolor	–	FF3.6, S2, C2, O10, CSS3
RGB hex	#rrggbb, #rgb	#ff7f50, #f90	IE4, FF1, S1, C1, O3.5, CSS1
RGB decimal	rgb(rrr,ggg,bbb)	255,127,80	IE4, FF1, S1, C1, O3.5, CSS1
RGB percentage	rgb(rrr%,ggg%,bbb%)	rgb(100%, 50%,31%)	IE4, FF1, S1, C1, O3.5, CSS1
HSL	hsl(hhh,sss%,lll%)	hsl(16,65%,100%)	FF3, S2, C2, O9.5, CSS3
RGBA	rgba(rrr,ggg,bbb,d.d)	rgba(255,127,80,.86)	FF3.6, S3, C3, O9.5, CSS3
HSLA	hsl(hhh,sss%,lll%,d.d)	hsl(16,65%,100%,.23)	FF3.6, S3, C3, O9.5, CSS3

Currentcolor keyword

In addition to the color keyword list, you can use the **currentcolor** keyword. Using **currentcolor** to set any color value will use the element's current **color** value. For example, to create an aqua border color, use:

```
color: aqua;
```

```
border-color: currentcolor;
```

If you assign **currentcolor** specifically to the **color** the property, it will inherit its parent element's color value just like using **color: inherit**.

Transparent keyword

Another important keyword is **transparent**, which is the equivalent of a 0 alpha, that is, it's completely transparent. This keyword allows anything behind that element to show through.

Ⓐ RGB hex color values are represented by three couplet values, or by three single values ranging from 0–9 or A–F that indicate the levels of red, green, and blue that combine to create the color.

Ⓑ RGB decimal color values range from 0–255 to indicate the levels of red, green, and blue that combine to create the color.

RGB hex values

Hexadecimal values can range from 0–9 and a–f. Values include three couplets of hexadecimal values representing the levels of red, green, and blue (in that order) in the desired color. The color value couplets range from 00 (no color) to FF (full color) **Ⓐ**. However, if the couplets contain the same hex value, only three values are needed to define the color. For example, these two sets of values represent the same pure blue:

#0000ff

#00f

RGB decimal values

Often, simply referred to as the *RGB values*, RGB uses decimal values from 0 (no color) to 255 (full color) to represent the levels of red, green, and blue (in that order) present in the desired color **Ⓑ**.

red *green* *blue*

rgb(100%,100%,100%)

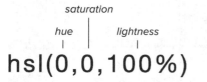 RGB percentage color values range from 0–100 to indicate the amount of red, green, and blue that is combined to create the color.

saturation

hue *lightness*

hsl(0,0,100%)

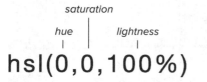 HSL color values represent hue as the angle on a standard color wheel (0–360), saturation as a percentage, and lightness as a percentage.

alpha (opacity)

rgba(255,255,255,.5)

alpha (opacity)

hsla(0,0,100%,.5)

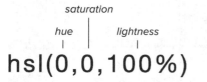 RGBA and HSLA add an alpha value as a decimal (0–1) to represent the opacity of a color with 0 completely transparent and 1 completely opaque.

Percentage values

RGB can be expressed as whole percentages from 0% (no color) to 100% (full color) to represent the levels of red, green, and blue (in that order) present in the desired color .

New in CSS3: HSL values ★

Although their notations are different, hex, decimal, and percentage values are just different ways to define the levels of red, green, and blue in a color. CSS3 adds a completely different method for defining color by its hue, saturation, and lightness (HSL) :

- **Hue**—A degree value from 0 to 360, although the degree symbol is not included. The hue is based on a color's position in the standard color wheel where red is typically at 0°, yellow at 60°, green at 120°, cyan at 180°, blue at 240°, and magenta at 300°.

- **Saturation**—A percentage from 0% (no color) to 100% (full color).

- **Lightness**—A percentage from 0% (black) to 100% (white).

New in CSS3: Color alpha values ★

Although the opacity property allows you to make elements transparent, this is applied to the entire element. CSS3 now allows you to make specific colors transparent. An alpha value is generally a fourth value in a color, but rather than representing a hue or brightness, it sets the opacity of the color—a value from 0 (transparent) to 1 (opaque). So, an alpha of .5 is the equivalent of 50% opacity .

You can set an alpha channel for either RGB decimal or HSL color values. Currently, you have no way to add alpha values to RGB hex values. The channel value is then applied only to the color used.

TIP If you specify a gradient as a background, also specify a background color to ensure that text will be legible in browsers that do not support gradients.

TIP Hex values are currently the most popular way to define color values, but they are by no means the best way to add colors. I find it much easier to imagine colors using base 10 decimal values rather than base 16 hexadecimal values.

TIP In addition to setting the color opacity, CSS includes the ability to set the opacity of an entire object and any of its content. See "Setting an Element's Opacity" in Chapter 11 for more information.

TIP Although HSL is a bit difficult to master at first, it can be easier to use when setting complementary colors. Just add 180° to the hue.

Other Ways to Add Color

Although this chapter presents the primary methods for setting colors in your design, several other CSS properties include color values:

- `text-shadow`—Although generally thought of as black or gray, you can set a text-shadow to any color. I often use this with bright colors to create a glow (see Chapter 6).

- `border`—An element's border colors can be set as part of any of the border properties or directly in the **border-color** property (see Chapter 10).

- `outline`—Like the **border** property, **outline** allows you to define a color around the edge of an element (see Chapter 10).

Hex or Decimal?

Until recently, it was assumed that colors should always be declared in RGB hexadecimal notation. In fact, I still meet designers and developers who are completely unaware that they have alternatives. RGB decimal has been around for quite awhile and will work in any browser you want to throw it at.

But which is "better"?

I personally find that it's much easier to envision a color in decimal numbers (which I've used all my life) than in hex values. I can look at the value **135, 127, 107** and know it's a reddish beige much faster than if I see **877f6b**. Additionally, since there is no alpha version for hex, if you want transparent colors, you have to use decimal values.

The only argument in favor of hex color values is that they are more compact (a smaller file size) than decimal values. But even over a large-scale Web site, you might save only a few bytes (millionths of a second in load time).

TABLE 7.2 Color Keywords

Keyword	Hex	Decimal	Keyword	Hex	Decimal
aliceblue	#F0F8FF	240,248,255	darkseagreen	#8FBC8F	143,188,143
antiquewhite	#FAEBD7	250,235,215	darkslateblue	#483D8B	72,61,139
aqua	**#00FFFF**	**0,255,255**	darkslategray	#2F4F4F	47,79,79
aquamarine	#7FFFD4	127,255,212	darkturquoise	#00CED1	0,206,209
azure	#F0FFFF	240,255,255	darkviolet	#9400D3	148,0,211
beige	#F5F5DC	245,245,220	deeppink	#FF1493	255,20,147
bisque	#FFE4C4	255,228,196	deepskyblue	#00BFFF	0,191,255
black	**#000000**	**0,0,0**	dimgray	#696969	105,105,105
blanchedalmond	#FFEBCD	255,235,205	dimgrey	#696969	105,105,105
blue	**#0000FF**	**0,0,255**	dodgerblue	#1E90FF	30,144,255
blueviolet	#8A2BE2	138,43,226	firebrick	#B22222	178,34,34
brown	#A52A2A	165,42,42	floralwhite	#FFFAF0	255,250,240
burlywood	#DEB887	222,184,135	forestgreen	#228B22	34,139,34
cadetblue	#5F9EA0	95,158,160	**fuchsia**	**#FF00FF**	**255,0,255**
chartreuse	#7FFF00	127,255,0	gainsboro	#DCDCDC	220,220,220
chocolate	#D2691E	210,105,30	ghostwhite	#F8F8FF	248,248,255
coral	#FF7F50	255,127,80	gold	#FFD700	255,215,0
cornflowerblue	#6495ED	100,149,237	goldenrod	#DAA520	218,165,32
cornsilk	#FFF8DC	255,248,220	**gray**	**#808080**	**128,128,128**
crimson	#DC143C	220,20,60	**green**	**#008000**	**0,128,0**
cyan	#00FFFF	0,255,255	greenyellow	#ADFF2F	173,255,47
darkblue	#00008B	0,0,139	gray	#808080	128,128,128
darkcyan	#008B8B	0,139,139	honeydew	#F0FFF0	240,255,240
darkgoldenrod	#B8860B	184,134,11	hotpink	#FF69B4	255,105,180
darkgray	#A9A9A9	169,169,169	indianred	#CD5C5C	205,92,92
darkgreen	#006400	0,100,0	indigo	#4B0082	75,0,130
darkgrey	#A9A9A9	169,169,169	ivory	#FFFFF0	255,255,240
darkkhaki	#BDB76B	189,183,107	khaki	#F0E68C	240,230,140
darkmagenta	#8B008B	139,0,139	lavender	#E6E6FA	230,230,250
darkolivegreen	#556B2F	85,107,47	lavenderblush	#FFF0F5	255,240,245
darkorange	#FF8C00	255,140,0	lawngreen	#7CFC00	124,252,0
darkorchid	#9932CC	153,50,204	lemonchiffon	#FFFACD	255,250,205
darkred	#8B0000	139,0,0	lightblue	#ADD8E6	173,216,230
darksalmon	#E9967A	233,150,122	lightcoral	#F08080	240,128,128

TABLE 7.2 Color Keywords *continued*

Keyword	Hex	Decimal	Keyword	Hex	Decimal
lightcyan	#E0FFFF	224,255,255	**olive**	**#808000**	**128,128,0**
lightgoldenrodyellow	#FAFAD2	250,250,210	olivedrab	#6B8E23	107,142,35
lightgray	#D3D3D3	211,211,211	orange	#FFA500	255,165,0
lightgreen	#90EE90	144,238,144	orangered	#FF4500	255,69,0
lightgrey	#D3D3D3	211,211,211	orchid	#DA70D6	218,112,214
lightpink	#FFB6C1	255,182,193	palegoldenrod	#EEE8AA	238,232,170
lightsalmon	#FFA07A	255,160,122	palegreen	#98FB98	152,251,152
lightseagreen	#20B2AA	32,178,170	paleturquoise	#AFEEEE	175,238,238
lightskyblue	#87CEFA	135,206,250	palevioletred	#DB7093	219,112,147
lightslategray	#778899	119,136,153	papayawhip	#FFEFD5	255,239,213
lightslategrey	#778899	119,136,153	peachpuff	#FFDAB9	255,218,185
lightsteelblue	#B0C4DE	176,196,222	peru	#CD853F	205,133,63
lightyellow	#FFFFE0	255,255,224	pink	#FFC0CB	255,192,203
lime	**#00FF00**	**0,255,0**	plum	#DDA0DD	221,160,221
limegreen	#32CD32	50,205,50	powderblue	#B0E0E6	176,224,230
linen	#FAF0E6	250,240,230	**purple**	**#800080**	**128,0,128**
magenta	#FF00FF	255,0,255	**red**	**#FF0000**	**255,0,0**
maroon	#800000	128,0,0	rosybrown	#BC8F8F	188,143,143
mediumaquamarine	**#66CDAA**	**102,205,170**	royalblue	#4169E1	65,105,225
mediumblue	#0000CD	0,0,205	saddlebrown	#8B4513	139,69,19
mediumorchid	#BA55D3	186,85,211	salmon	#FA8072	250,128,114
mediumpurple	#9370DB	147,112,219	sandybrown	#F4A460	244,164,96
mediumseagreen	#3CB371	60,179,113	seagreen	#2E8B57	46,139,87
mediumslateblue	#7B68EE	123,104,238	seashell	#FFF5EE	255,245,238
mediumspringgreen	#00FA9A	0,250,154	sienna	#A0522D	160,82,45
mediumturquoise	#48D1CC	72,209,204	**silver**	**#C0C0C0**	**192,192,192**
mediumvioletred	#C71585	199,21,133	skyblue	#87CEEB	135,206,235
midnightblue	#191970	25,25,112	slateblue	#6A5ACD	106,90,205
mintcream	#F5FFFA	245,255,250	slategray	#708090	112,128,144
mistyrose	#FFE4E1	255,228,225	snow	#FFFAFA	255,250,250
moccasin	#FFE4B5	255,228,181	springgreen	#00FF7F	0,255,127
navajowhite	#FFDEAD	255,222,173	steelblue	#4682B4	70,130,180
navy	**#000080**	**0,0,128**	tan	#D2B48C	210,180,140
oldlace	#FDF5E6	253,245,230	**teal**	**#008080**	**0,128,128**

TABLE 7.2 Color Keywords *continued*

Keyword	Hex	Decimal
thistle	#D8BFD8	216,191,216
tomato	#FF6347	255,99,71
turquoise	#40E0D0	64,224,208
violet	#EE82EE	238,130,238
wheat	#F5DEB3	245,222,179
white	**#FFFFFF**	**255,255,255**
whitesmoke	#F5F5F5	245,245,245
yellow	**#FFFF00**	**255,255,0**
yellowgreen	#9ACD32	154,205,50

linear   radial

Ⓐ Linear gradients can be added for Internet Explorer, Webkit browsers (including Chrome and Safari), and Mozilla-based browsers (including Firefox) Radial gradients are available only in Webkit and Mozilla browsers.

```
filter: progid:
    DXImageTransform.Microsoft.gradient
   (startColorstr='#ff000000',
    endColorstr='#77ff0000',
    gradientType='1');
          |
      Orientation

Start color
```

Ⓑ Internet Explorer uses the proprietary `filter` property to add simple linear gradients. Colors are set using a nonstandard color format that adds an alpha value to the hex code.

New in CSS3: Color Gradients in Backgrounds ★

Although not yet a part of the CSS standard, the ability to fill an element's background with a gradient has been introduced as both Webkit and Mozilla extensions, which means that you can add linear and radial gradients compatible with Safari, Chrome, and Firefox Ⓐ. Surprisingly, Internet Explorer also includes its own system for adding background linear gradients, leaving only Opera out in the cold (for now).

Although all three browsers can display gradients, the syntax has not been standardized by the W3C, so all three have a unique way to define the style.

Internet Explorer gradients

Internet Explorer uses its `filter` property, which does duty for many purposes; gradients is just one of them.

The syntax for Internet Explorer gradients is simple and clear-cut, requiring you to define only a starting color, ending color, and orientation Ⓑ. However, rather than using a straightforward RGB value, the colors are defined using a completely nonstandard ARGB color value. You guessed it: The first couplet is the alpha value from **00** (transparent) to **ff** (opaque). You can also set the orientation of the gradient (**gradientType**) as either horizontal (**1**) or vertical (**0**).

There is no radial gradient for Internet Explorer.

Mozilla gradients

In Firefox or other browsers that use **-moz** extensions, you can use the **-moz-linear-gradient** or **-moz-repeating-linear-gradient** 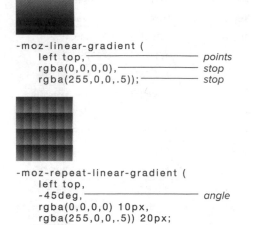 property to create a straight gradient or use **-moz-radial-gradient** or **-moz-repeating-radial-gradient** to create circular gradients **D**. The repeating gradients work just like regular gradients but will tile based on their size.

-moz gradient extensions use the following values:

- **Point**—One or two keyword values separated by a space defining the side or corner where the gradient should start. Values can include **top**, **right**, **bottom**, and/or **left**. If two values are used (separated by a space), they specify a corner, such as **top left**.

- **Position**—A background position, which is the same as setting background image positions shown later in this chapter (**Table 7.10**) for the center point of a radial gradient, such as **center**.

- **Angle**—The angle of the gradient in degrees (**deg**), grads (**grad**), or radians (**rad**), such as **45deg**.

- **Shape**—The shape of a radial gradient, either **circle** or **ellipse**.

```
-moz-linear-gradient (
    left top,————————— points
    rgba(0,0,0,0),————————— stop
    rgba(255,0,0,.5));————— stop
```

```
-moz-repeat-linear-gradient (
    left top,
    -45deg,————————————— angle
    rgba(0,0,0,0) 10px,
    rgba(255,0,0,.5)) 20px;
```

C Mozilla adds several options, allowing simple and complex gradients to be created.

```
-moz-radial-gradient(
    25px 25px -45deg,——————— point/angle
    circle cover,
    rgba(0, 0, 0, 0) 0%,————— stops
    rgba(255, 0, 0, .25) 60%,
    rgba(255, 0, 0, .5) 100%);
```

```
-moz-repeat-radial-gradient(
    25px 25px -45deg,
    circle cover,——————————— type
    rgba(0, 0, 0, 0) 0%,
    rgba(255, 0, 0, .25) 60%,
    rgba(255, 0, 0, .5) 100%);
```

D Mozilla radial gradients allow you set the size, angle, and shape.

TABLE 7.3 -moz-gradient Size Values

Value	Description
closest-side	Gradient shaped to meet closest side from its center
closest-corner	Gradient shaped to meet closest corner from its center
farthest-side	Gradient shaped to meet farthest side from its center
farthest-corner	Gradient shaped to meet farthest corner from its center
contain	Same as **closest-side**
cover	Same as **farthest-corner**

```
-webkit-gradient(
    linear,───────────── type
    left top,
    from(rgba(0,0,0,0)),
    to(rgba(255,0,0,.5)));
```

E Webkit linear gradients can be simple.

```
-webkit-gradient(
    radial,
    25 25, 100, 25 25,0── points and radius
    from(rgba(0,0,0,0)),
    to(rgba(255,0,0,.5)),
    ┌─color-stop(60%, rgba(255,0,0,.25))));
```
stops

F Webkit radial gradients get more complex, requiring you to plot several points and radii.

- **Size**—The size of a radial gradient as a keyword (**Table 7.3**).

- **Stop**—The color at a particular point along the gradient. This must include a color value (Table 7.1) and an optional percentage or length value to set where the color should be positioned along the gradient axis, such as **orange 60%**.

Webkit gradients

Safari, Chrome, and any other browsers that make use of the **-webkit** extensions use the **-webkit-gradient** property to add gradients. This property has several options, depending on whether you want to create a linear or radial gradient:

- **Type**—**linear** or **radial** **E** **F**.

- **Start point**—One or two length or keyword values separated by a space to define the location, side, or corner where the linear gradient should start. Values can include **top**, **right**, **bottom**, and/or **left**. If two values are used (separated by a space), they specify a corner, such as **top left**.

- **End point**—One or two length or keyword values separated by a space to define the location, side, or corner where the linear gradient should end. Values can include **top**, **right**, **bottom**, and/or **left**. If two values are used (separated by a space), they specify a corner, such as **bottom right**.

- **Radius**—A length value used to set the radius of a radial gradient. Associated with a start and end point, the radius of the inner and outer circles of the radial gradient are set with corresponding start and end points, such as **25 25, 100, 25 25,0** (where 100 and 0 are the radii).

continues on next page

- **From**—The value of the initial color in the gradient (Table 7.1). Same as **color-stop(0.0, <color>)**. For example, **from(rgb(255,255,255))**.

- **To**—The value of the final color in the gradient (Table 7.1). Same as **color-stop(1.0, <color>)**. For example, **to(rgb(0,0,0))**.

- **Stop**—A length, percentage (0%–100%), or decimal value (0.0–1.0) to indicate where the color should be positioned along the gradient axis, followed by a comma (,), and then the color value of a particular point along the gradient (Table 7.1). For example, **color-stop(60%, orange)**.

Gradients can be defined using the **from()** and **to()** values, **color-stops ()**, or any combination of these values separated by commas.

G A great tool for plotting gradients can be found at westciv.com/tools/gradients.

TIP Work has begun on an official W3C CSS gradient standard as a part of the new Image Module (dev.w3.org/csswg/css3-images). The bad news is that the syntax being developed does not resemble either the –moz or –webkit versions. The good news is that it looks much simpler.

TIP Gradients can be a headache to compute, especially radial gradients. I recommend using a handy online tool developed by John Allsopp that computes the code for you; browse to westciv.com/tools/gradients **G**.

TABLE 7.4 Western Color Associations

Color	Emotional Associations
Red	assertive, powerful, intense
Blue	consoling, fidelity, defense
Yellow	concern, rebirth, clarity
Green	wealth, fitness, food, nature
Brown	nature, maturity, wisdom
Orange	hospitality, exhilaration, vigor
Pink	vital, innocent, feminine
Purple	royalty, refinement, calm
Black	stark, stylish, somber
Gray	business-like, cool, detached
White	clean, pure, straightforward

Choosing Your Color Palette

Graphic designers have a saying: "No color is better than bad color." If you are not careful, color can work against you by obscuring your message and confusing your visitors. The effective use of color in design takes a lot of practice to get right.

Colors have powerful emotional meanings that cannot always be predicted, especially when used in different combinations. **Table 7.4** presents some of the most common color associations in Western culture. When you put two colors together, the meanings begin to interrelate, much like words in a sentence.

You want to make sure you don't just slap colors down on your page. If you do, they'll probably clash. The most important thing you can do to avoid this is to take time to plan your color choices. Begin by choosing the specific colors you will use and their exact RGB or HSL values. Then apply these colors consistently throughout your project.

You will need to consider the colors that you will be applying to the basic parts of your Web page (including the colors in the background images) **A**. You do not have to choose a different color hue for each part, but you should define what color will be applied to each component:

- **Body background**—Covering the entire visible area of the browser window, the background generally should provide the most contrast with the foreground text colors.

header

copy

body background

content background

A Consider which colors you will use for each component of your Web page.

- **Content background**—Often, you will use a different color for the background directly around the content of the page, allowing the body background color to absorb extra horizontal space in the browser window.

- **Border/Rule**—You may want to use contrasting colors around the borders of content areas, headers, navigation blocks, lists, and tables, or use rules to separate different chunks of content. Choose a color that contrasts with the area that the lines are meant to separate.

- **Header**—You may choose not to change the background color for section headers, but always make sure that the text color clearly contrasts with the background colors you choose.

- **Copy**—Your copy (generally sentences or paragraphs of text) should have the highest contrast with the background to maximize legibility.

- **Link/Navigation**—You may choose different colors for your site navigation and for links in the copy, but these link colors should be easily discernable from other text while still contrasting with the background.

- **List/Table**—You may choose different background colors behind lists and tables or even alternating row colors, called *zebra striping*, to improve readability.

- **Form**—You can specify the border, foreground, and background colors of many form elements to give them a more distinctive look for your site, apart from their default appearance. However, be careful not to customize them so much that the visitor does not know what they are.

Color wheel basics

A color wheel is a disc or circle that shows the spectrum of color values, providing you with a quick overview of all the possibilities from red, orange, and yellow to green, blue, indigo, and violet, and back to red again. Some color wheels also allow you to view brightness (dark to light) and saturation (full color tone to gray) levels.

You're probably familiar with color wheels, but if you want, check out the example at: *colorschemedesigner.com.*

When you get down to it, though, color is a matter of preference. Colors that I think look great together may make my wife gag (and usually result in changing my outfit). To be safe, you can count on a single color (monochrome) or one of the following color-combination schemes as (more or less) fail-safe:

- **Monochrome**—A single color with different brightnesses or saturations for contrast.

- **Complementary**—Two colors from opposite sides of the color wheel (180 degrees), providing the highest contrast.

- **Triad**—Three colors and their tones with one primary and two secondary colors that are at equal angles in the color wheel, 120 degrees to 180 degrees from the primary.

- **Tetrad**—Four colors that include one primary color, one secondary color (in direct contrast to the primary color), and two colors that are the same angle from the primary or secondary color, from 0 degrees to 90 degrees.

Color and Accessibility

Beyond attractive and compelling design, another critical consideration with color is accessibility for people who are visually impaired. The most important considerations are to provide enough contrast between foreground and background colors so that the information is readable and to make sure that color is not critical for understanding information. For example, if you are using color for links, also set off those links using some other formatting such as underlining or bold.

For more details on color and accessibility, see section 9 of the W3C's white paper "CSS Techniques for Web Content Accessibility Guidelines" at w3.org/TR/WCAG10-CSS-TECHS/#style-colors.

- **Analogic**—Three colors and their tones with one primary color and two secondary colors that are the same angle from the primary color, from 0 degrees to 60 degrees.

All of these color schemes allow you to choose the basic hue and then use various brightnesses and/or saturations of the colors to add additional shades to your palette.

Online color scheme tools

Not sure where to start planning your color scheme? Here are some excellent online tools that you can use:

- **Build a palette**—Adobe's Kuler (kuler.adobe.com) provides an excellent tool for comparing colors side by side in an interactive environment.

- **Color Wheel Selector**—Explore all of the color wheel schemes using Color-Jack's tool (colorjack.com/sphere).

- **Color palettes from photographs or other images**—If you are using graphics or photography with a particular color scheme in them, the Degrave.com Color Palette Generator (degraeve.com/color-palette) will analyze the image and then produce a color palette based on the colors in the image.

Setting Text Color

The **color** property is used to set the *text color* (sometimes called the *foreground color*) of an element (**Table 7.5**). This color will be inherited by all of the element's children (see Chapter 4), so you need only set it once in the body element and then provide overrides as needed. For example, if you set the color to gray in the **<body>**, then all text on the page will be gray. If you then set the **<p>** element to red, all paragraph text and any elements in it will be red, overriding the gray.

To define the text color:

1. **Add the text color property to your CSS declarations.** Type **color** in the CSS rule, followed by a colon (**:**) (**Code 7.2**).

   color:

2. **Specify a color value.** Type a value for the color based on color values from Table 7.1. This includes RGB, HSL, transparent, or current color.

   rgb(102,0,0);

3. **Add colors with alpha channels, as needed.** If you want the color to be partially transparent, then under the color value you can add the same again using the RGBA or HSVA value. For browsers that do not support alpha values, the first color value will be used and the second will be ignored.

   color: rgba(102,0,0,.65);

Code 7.2 *color-background-properties.css*— The header text is rendered in a variety of shades of red, the text is a dark gray, and the form button and the text that gets typed into the form field are red **A**. The brighter red text is much more prominent than the lighter red and the gray text.

```
/*** CSS3 VQS | Chapter 7 |
→ color-background-properties.css ***/

body {
  color: rgb(51,51,51); }

h1 {
  color: rgb(102,0,0);
  color: rgba(102,0,0,.65); }

article h2 strong {
  color: rgb(135,127,107); }

article header + p:first-letter {
  color: rgb(153,0,0); }

a:link {
  color: rgb(204,0,0) }

a:visited {
  color: rgb(153,0,0) }

a:hover {
  color: rgb(255,0,0) }

a:active {
  color: rgb(153,153,153) }

.byline {
  color: rgb(255,255,255);
  color: rgba(255,255,255,.5); }

.byline .author {
  color: rgb(235,235,235);
  color: rgba(255,255,255,.75)   }
```

TABLE 7.5 Color Value

Value	Compatibility
<color>	IE3, FF1, S1, C1, O3.5, CSS1
inherit	IE3, FF1, S1, C1, O3.5, CSS1

A Code 7.2 when applied to code 7.1: he contrast of the page text has been reduced by making it dark gray with titles and the drop cap rendered in shades of red. Notice that the author name seems to have disappeared. This is because it is white text on a white background. It'll be visible again when we add the background colors. Link colors in the footer are red.

TIP It's a good idea to set a default page color for the body tag, even if it's black, to ensure that colors are consistent across the page.

TIP When choosing foreground text colors, be careful to use colors that contrast with the background color or image. The lower the contrast (that is, the less difference in the brightness of the foreground and background colors), the more your readers will have to strain their eyes when reading.

TIP Color change is one important way of showing the different states of a hypertext link, but it is by no means the only style you can change. Chapter 14 will show you best practices for styling links, navigation, and controls using the anchor tag.

Setting a Background Color

The ability to set the background color on an HTML page has been around almost since the first Web browsers. However, with CSS you can define the background color, not only for the entire page, but also for individual elements using the **background-color** property **(Table 7.6)**. Unlike the color property, though, background colors are applied only to the element, and are not directly inherited by its children. That said, by the very fact they are within the parent, they will be set against that background.

To define the background color of an element:

1. **Add the background color property to your declaration list.** Start your declaration by typing **background-color** **(Code 7.3)**, followed by a colon (:).

   background-color:

2. **Specify the color value.** Type a value for the background color. This value can be the name of the color or an RGB value.

   rgb(102,0,0);

   Alternatively, you could type **transparent**, which would allow the parent element's background color to show through, or **currentcolor** to use the value of the **color** property.

Code 7.3 *color-background-properties. css*—Background colors can be set as solid, transparent, or using a gradient **Ⓐ**.

```
/*** CSS3 VQS | Chapter 7 |
→ color-background-properties.css ***/

* {
  padding: 0;
  margin: 0;
  border: none; }

body {
  color: rgb(51,51,51);
  background-color: rgb(85,85,85); }


header.page {
  display: block;
  background-color: rgh(102,0,0); }

h1 {
  color: rgb(255,225,215);
  color: rgba(255,225,225,.65); }

article {
  display: block;
  background-color: rgb(242, 237, 217); }

article h2 strong {
  color: rgb(135,127,107); }

article header + p:first-letter {
  color: rgb(153,0,0);
  background: transparent; }

footer {
  display: block;
  background: rgb(153,153,153);
  filter: progid:DXImageTransform.Microsoft.
  → gradient(startColorstr='#00000000',
  → endColorstr='#cc000000');
  background: -webkit-gradient(linear,
  → left top, left bottom, from(rgba(0,0,0,0)),
  → to(rgba(0,0,0,.5)));
```

code continues on next page

Code 7.3 *continued*

```
background: -moz-linear-gradient
↦ (top, rgba(0,0,0,0), rgba(0,0,0,.5)); }

a:link {
  color: rgb(204,0,0) }

a:visited {
  color: rgb(153,0,0) }

a:hover {
  color: rgb(255,0,0) }

a:active {
  color: rgb(153,153,153) }

.byline {
  color: rgb(255,255,255);
  color: rgba(255,255,255,.5); }

.byline .author {
  color: rgb(235,235,235);
  color: rgba(255,255,255,.75) }
```

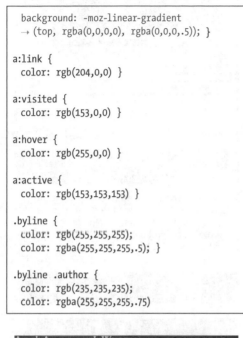

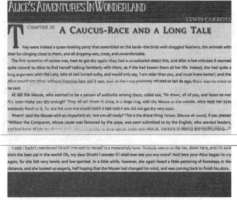

Ⓐ **Code 7.3 when applied to code 7.1:** The colors begin to define distinct areas of the page, including the page header, the article, and the footer.

3. Add background gradients as needed.
Use a separate declaration for Internet Explorer, Webkit, and Mozilla browsers.

```
filter: progid:DXImageTransform.
↦ Microsoft.gradient
↦ (startColorstr='#ff000000,
↦ endColorstr='#77000000);

background: -webkit-gradient
↦ (linear, left top, left
↦ bottom, from(rgba(0,0,0,0)),
↦ to(rgba(0,0,0,.5)));

background: -moz-linear-gradient
↦ (top, rgba(0,0,0,0),
↦ rgba(0,0,0,.5));
```

TIP The default state for an element's background color is `transparent`, so the parent element's background will show through unless the background color or image for that particular child element is set.

TIP You can also set the background color using the `background` property, as described later in this chapter in "Setting Multiple Background Values."

TIP Some older browsers had incomplete HTML5 support, so you may see variation in the displayed appearance of your code. For example, Safari 4 did not support backgrounds in HTML5-specific tags such as `<header>` unless they have `display: block` set (see Chapter 10).

TABLE 7.6 Background-Color Values

Value	Compatibility
<color>	IE4, FF1, S1, C1, O3.5, CSS1
inherit	IE4, FF1, S1, C1, O3.5, CSS1

Setting a Background Image

Beyond the ability to set an image as the background of an element, CSS includes several properties that offer you great flexibility in the exact placement of the image:

- **Repeat**—Sets whether the image tiles appear only once or repeat only horizontally or vertically.

- **Attachment**—Sets whether the image scrolls with the rest of the page or stays in one place.

- **Position**—Moves the image to the left and down (positive values) or to the right and up (negative values) from the top-left corner of the parent element.

- NEW IN CSS3 ★: **Size**—Sets the width and height of the image within the element's background as an absolute length, percentage, or the keywords **cover**, **contain**, or **auto** (which maintains the aspect ration).

- NEW IN CSS3 ★: **Clip**—Sets whether the background fits to the border or just within the content area.

- NEW IN CSS3 ★: **Origin**—Sets the position of the background relative to the border, padding, or content. This is especially useful for setting the background of inline elements that might break across multiple lines.

- NEW IN CSS3 ★: **Multiple background images**—Although not a specific property, CSS now allows you to layer multiple background images using a comma-separated list.

A **Code 7.4 when applied to code 7.1:** Adding background images makes the design come alive, giving it texture and structure. Notice the White Rabbit hiding behind the capital T. Just like Alice, he has been shrunk to best fit the area.

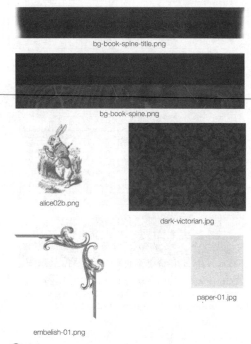

bg-book-spine-title.png

bg-book-spine.png

alice02b.png

dark-victorian.jpg

paper-01.jpg

embelish-01.png

B All of the images that go into making this design.

Code 7.4 *color-background-properties. css*—Background images are added over the background colors **A**. Notice that you can have multiple background images in a single element, and they stack on top of each other **B**.

```
/*** CSS3 VQS | Chapter 7 |
→ color-background-properties.css ***/


body {
  color: rgb(51,51,51);
  background-color: rgb(85,85,85);
  background-image: url(../_images/
  → dark-victorian.jpg);
  background-repeat: repeat;
  background-attachment: fixed;
  background-position: 0 0; }


header.page {
  display: block;
  background-color: rgb(102,0,0);
  background-image: url(../_images/
  → bg-book-spine-title.png), url(../_images/
  → bg-book-spine.jpg);
  background-repeat: no-repeat, repeat-x;
  background-position: center top, 0 0; }

h1 {
  color: rgb(255,225,215);
  color: rgba(255,225,225,.65); }

article {
  display: block;
  background-color: rgb(242, 237, 217);
  background-image: url(../_images/embelish-01
  → .png), url(../_images/paper-01.jpg);
  background-repeat: no-repeat, repeat;
  background-position: right top, 0 0; }

article h2 strong {
  color: rgb(135,127,107); }

article header + p:first-letter {
  color: rgb(153,0,0);
  background: transparent;
```

code continues on next page

To define a background image:

1. **Add the background image property to your CSS code with the image file source.** Type **background-image** , followed by a colon (**:**), **url()**, and a URL in the parenthesis for the location of the image file (GIF, JPEG, or PNG) that you want to use as the background. It can be either a complete Web address or a relative path (**Code 7.4**).

   background-image: url(alice05.gif);

   Alternatively, you could type **none** instead of **url()** along with a path to instruct the browser not to use a background image (**Table 7.7**).

continues on page 203

TABLE 7.7 Background-Image Values

Value	Compatibility
<url>	IE4, FF1, S1, C1, O3.5, CSS1
none	IE4, FF1, S1, C1, O3.5, CSS1

```
  background-image: url(../_images/alice02b.png);
  background-repeat: no-repeat;
  background-position: center center;

  -o-background-size: contain;
  -moz-background-size: contain;
  -webkit-background-size: contain;
  background-size: contain;

  -o-background-clip: padding-box;
  -moz-background-clip: padding;
  -webkit-background-clip: padding-box;
  background-size: padding-box;

  -o-background-origin: padding-box;
  -moz-background-origin: padding;
  -webkit-background-origin: padding-box;
  background-origin: padding-box; }

footer {
  display: block;
  background: rgb(153,153,153);
  filter: progid:DXImageTransform.Microsoft.gradient(startColorstr='#ffffff', endColorstr='#000000');
  background: -webkit-gradient(linear, left top, left bottom, from(rgba(0,0,0,0)), to(rgba(0,0,0,.5)));
  background: -moz-linear-gradient(top,  rgba(0,0,0,0),  rgba(0,0,0,.5)); }

a:link {
  color: rgb(204,0,0) }

a:visited {
  color: rgb(153,0,0) }

a:hover {
  color: rgb(255,0,0) }

a:active {
  color: rgb(153,153,153) }

.byline {
  color: rgba(255,255,255,.5); }

.byline .author {
  color: rgba(255,255,255,.75)  }
```

TABLE 7.8 Background-Repeat Values

Value	Compatibility
repeat	IE4, FF1, S1, C1, O3.5, CSS1
repeat-x	IE4, FF1, S1, C1, O3.5, CSS1
repeat-y	IE4, FF1, S1, C1, O3.5, CSS1
no-repeat	IE4, FF1, S1, C1, O3.5, CSS1
space	FF3.6, CSS3
round	FF3.6, CSS3

2. **Add the background repeat property and specify how the background should be tiled (or not).** Type **background-repeat**, followed by a colon (**:**)

background-repeat: no-repeat;

Then define how you want your background to repeat by typing one of the following options (**Table 7.8**):

- **repeat** instructs the browser to tile the graphic throughout the background of the element horizontally and vertically. This is the default value if the property is omitted.

- **repeat-x** instructs the browser to tile the background graphic horizontally only, so that the graphic repeats in one straight horizontal line along the top of the element.

- **repeat-y** instructs the browser to tile the background graphic vertically only, so the graphic repeats in one straight vertical line along the left side of the element.

- **no-repeat** causes the background graphic to appear only once (and not tile).

continues on next page

3. **Add the background attatchment property and specify how the background should scroll with the element.** Type **background-attachment**, followed by a colon (:).

background-attachment: fixed;

Then define how you want the background to be treated when the page scrolls by typing one of the following options (**Table 7.9**):

▸ **scroll** instructs the background graphic to scroll with the element. This is the default value if the property is omitted.

▸ **fixed** instructs the browser not to scroll the background content with the rest of the element. However, it will scroll with parent elements.

▸ **local** is similar to fixed, but the background is fixed to the content of the element, rather than the element itself.

4. **Add the background position property and specify the positioning of the background.** Type **background-position**, followed by a colon (:).

background-position: -10px 10px;

Then type one value or two values separated by a space to indicate where you want the background to appear in relation to the top-left corner of the element. If one value is entered, it is used for x, and y is centered. Use one of the following values (**Table 7.10**):

▸ **Length values,** such as **–10px**. The values can be positive or negative. The first number tells the browser the distance the element should appear from the left edge of its parent; the second value specifies the position from the top edge of the parent. See "Values and Units Used in This Book" in the Introduction for more information.

TABLE 7.9 Background-Attachment Values

Value	Compatibility
scroll	IE4, FF1, S1, C1, O3.5, CSS1
fixed	IE4, FF1, S1, C1, O3.5, CSS1
local	S2, C1, O10.5, CSS3

TABLE 7.10 Background-Position Values

Value	Compatibility
<length>	IE4, FF1, S1, C1, O3.5, CSS1
<percentage>	IE4, FF1, S1, C1, O3.5, CSS1
top	IE4, FF1, S1, C1, O3.5, CSS1
bottom	IE4, FF1, S1, C1, O3.5, CSS1
left	IE4, FF1, S1, C1, O3.5, CSS1
right	IE4, FF1, S1, C1, O3.5, CSS1
center	IE4, FF1, S1, C1, O3.5, CSS1

TABLE 7.11 Background-Size Values

Value	Compatibility
<length>	FF3.6, S3/S5, C3, O9.5, CSS3
<percentage>	FF3.6, S3/S5, C5, O9.5, CSS3
cover	FF3.6, S4/S5, C3, CSS3
contain	FF3.6, S4/S5, C3, CSS3
auto	FF3.6, S3/S5, C3, O9.5, CSS3

Firefox supports `-moz-clip-origin`

Safari 4 and Chrome 3 support `-webkit-clip-origin`

Safari 5 supports `background-size`

- **Percentage values**, such as **25%.** The first percentage indicates the horizontal position proportional to the parent element's size; the second value indicates the vertical position proportional to the parent element's size.

- **Keywords** in plain English: `top`, `bottom`, `left`, `right`, or `center`.

5. **Add the background size property and specify the exact size, percentage, or sizing method.** Type **background-size**, followed by a colon (**:**).

```
-o-background-size: contain;
→ -moz-background-size: contain;
→ -webkit-background-size:
→ contain;
→ background-size: contain;
```

Then type a value from **Table 7.11**. Two values can be included to define separate x and y sizes:

- **Length values**, such as **10px.**

- **Percentage values**, such as **25%.** The first percentage indicates the width proportionate to the parent element's width; the second value indicates the height proportionate to the parent element's height.

- **cover** fits the image to the width or height of the containing element while preserving the aspect ratio.

- **contain** scales the image to the smallest size to fit the entire image in the desired area while preserving the aspect ratio.

continues on next page

6. **Add the background clip property and specify a clipping method.** Type **background-clip**, followed by a colon (:).

```
-o-background-clip: padding-box;
→-moz-background-clip: padding;
→-webkit-background-clip:
→padding-box;
→background-size: padding-box;
```

Then type a value from **Table 7.12**. Two values can be included to define separate x and y sizes.

Mozilla and Webkit both use a slightly different syntax than what was finally implemented in the CSS3 standards.

- ▸ **border/border-box** clips the image to the outer edge of the border.
- ▸ **padding/padding-box** clips the image to the outer edge of the padding.
- ▸ **content/content-box** clips the image to the outer edge of the content.

TABLE 7.12 Background-Clip Values

Value	Compatibility
padding	FF1, S3, C3
border	FF1, S3, C3
content	S3, C3
padding-box	S3/S5, C3, O10.5, CSS3
border-box	S3/S5, C3, O10.5, CSS3

Firefox supports `-moz-clip-origin`

Safari 4 and Chrome 3 support `-webkit-clip-origin`

Safari 5 supports `background-clip`

TABLE 7.13 Background-Origin Values

Value	Compatibility
padding	FF1, S3, C3
border	FF1, S3, C3
content	FF1, S3, C3
padding-box	S3/S5, C3, O10.5, CSS3
border-box	S3/S5, C3, O10.5, CSS3
content-box	S3/S5, C3, O10.5, CSS3

Firefox supports `-moz-background-origin`

Safari 4 and Chrome 3 support `-webkit-background-origin`

Safari 5 supports `background-origin`

TIP You can mix percentage and length values in the same background position and size declarations, but you cannot mix length or percentages with plain English keywords.

TIP Several of the background images used in this example are transparent PNGs, which allow the background to show through them.

TIP Any space in the background that does not have a background graphic will be filled with the background color, so I always recommend specifying a background color with a background image.

TIP Background images are used to create CSS Sprites, discussed in Chapter 14, one of the most useful tools in your dynamic Web design arsenal.

7. **Add the background origin property and specify an origin method.** Type **background-origin** followed by a colon (:).

```
-o-background-origin: padding-box;
-moz-background-origin: padding;
-webkit-background-origin:
padding-box;
background-origin: padding-box;
```

Then type a value from **Table 7.13**. Two values can be included to define separate x and y sizes.

▸ **border/border-box** positions the image relative to the outer edge border, placing it behind the border.

▸ **padding/padding-box** positions the image relative to the inner edge of the padding.

▸ **content/content-box** positions the image relative to the outer edge of the content.

8. **Finally, specify the background image to which the above properties are applied.** To layer background images, add each value in a comma-separated list. Images will be placed *beneath* previous images in the list with background color behind all of them. Be sure to add values for all the properties, as necessary.

```
background-image: url(../_images/
embelish-01.png), url(../_images/
paper-01.jpg);
```

Using Background Shorthand

The **background** shorthand property (**Table 7.14**) allows you to define the background image and color for an entire page or individual element, rolling many of the background properties into a single quick and compressed declaration. From a coding standpoint, this method is preferable because it uses less space, but it requires that you remember the purpose of each of the values in the list.

To define the background:

1. **Add the background property to your CSS rule declerations list.** Start your declaration by typing **background**, followed by a colon (**:**). Then define a background value (**Code 7.5**).

    ```
    background:
    ```

TABLE 7.14 Background Values

Value	Compatibility
<background-color>	IE3, FF1, S1, O3.5, CSS1
<background-image>	IE3, FF1, S1, O3.5, CSS1
<background-position>	IE3, FF1, S1, O3.5, CSS1
<background-size>	CSS3
<background-repeat>	IE3, FF1, S1, O3.5, CSS1
<background-attachment>	IE4, FF1, S1, O3.5, CSS1
<background-origin>	CSS3

Code 7.5 *color-background-properties.css*— Although the results will be identical to Code 7.4, this version is much more compact, easier to scan, and cuts down on file size. If you want to see what the page looks like, look at the previous section.

```
/*** CSS3 VQS | Chapter 7 | color-background-
properties.css ***/


body {
  color: rgb(51,51,51);
  background: rgb(85,85,85)  url(../_images/
  → dark-victorian.jpg) repeat fixed 0 0; }


header.page {
  display: block;
  background: url(../_images/bg-book-spine-
  → title.png)  no-repeat center top,
  rgb(102,0,0) url(../_images/bg-book-spine.jpg)
  → repeat-x 0 0; }

h1 {
  color: rgb(255,225,215);
  color: rgba(255,225,225,.65); }

article {
  display: block;
  background: url(../_images/embelish-01.png)
  → no-repeat right top,
  rgb(242, 237, 217) url(../_images/paper-01
  → .jpg) repeat 0 0; }

article h2 strong {
  color: rgb(135,127,107); }

article p:first-of-type:first-letter {
  color: rgb(153,0,0);
  background: transparent url(../_images/
  → alice02b.png) no-repeat center center;

  -o-background-size: contain;
  -moz-background-size: contain;
  -webkit-background-size: contain;
  background-size: contain;

  -o-background-clip: padding-box;
  -moz-background-clip: padding;
```

code continues on next page

```
  -webkit-background-clip: padding-box;
  background-size: padding-box;

  -o-background-origin: padding-box;
  -moz-background-origin: padding;
  -webkit-background-origin: padding-box;
  background-origin: padding-box; }

footer {
  display: block;
  background: rgb(153,153,153);
  filter: progid:DXImageTransform.Microsoft.
   → gradient(startColorstr='#00000000',
   → endColorstr='#cc000000');
  background: -webkit-gradient(linear,
   → left top, left bottom, from(rgba(0,0,0,0)),
   → to(rgba(0,0,0,.5)));
  background: -moz-linear-gradient(top,
   → rgba(0,0,0,0),  rgba(0,0,0,.5)); }

a:link {
  color: rgb(204,0,0) }

a:visited {
  color: rgb(153,0,0) }

a:hover {
  color: rgb(255,0,0) }

a:active {
  color: rgb(153,153,153) }

.byline {
  color: rgba(255,255,255,.5); }

.byline .author {
  color: rgba(255,255,255,.75)  }
```

2. **Specify the color value.** Type a value for the background color, followed by a space. This value can be the name of the color or an RGB, HSL, or keyword value (Table 7.1) Use **transparent** if you do not want a background color to appear.

   rgb(85,85,85)

3. **Specify the URL for the background image.** Type **url()** and in the parenthesis, add an absolute or relative path to the background image (Table 7.7), followed by a space. This location is the image file (GIF, JPEG, or PNG file) that you want to use as the background and is either a complete Web address or a local filename.

   url(../_images/dark-victorian.jpg)

   Alternatively, you could type **none** instead of a URL, which would instruct the browser not to use a background image.

4. **If you included a background image, specify how it should tile.** Type a value for the way you want your background to repeat, followed by a space.

   repeat

   Use one of the following options (Table 7.8):

   ▸ **repeat** instructs the browser to tile the graphic throughout the background of the element, both horizontally and vertically.

   ▸ **repeat-x** instructs the browser to tile the background graphic horizontally only. In other words, the graphic repeats in one straight horizontal line along the top of the element.

continues on next page

- **repeat-y** instructs the browser to tile the background graphic vertically only. In other words, the graphic repeats in one straight vertical line along the left side of the element.

- **no-repeat** causes the background graphic to appear only once.

5. **If you are using a background image, specify how it should scroll.**

   `fixed`

   Type a keyword for the way you want the background attached—how it should be treated when the page scrolls—followed by a space. Use one of the following options (Table 7.9):

   - **scroll** instructs the background graphic to scroll with the element.

   - **fixed** instructs the browser not to scroll the background content with the rest of the element.

   - **local** is similar to fixed, but the background is fixed to the content of the element, rather than the element itself.

6. **If you are using a background image, specify how it should be positioned.**

   `0 0;`

   Type two values, separated by a space, to specify where you want the background positioned relative to the top-left corner of the element. Use any of the following units; you can use a mixture across the two values if you like (Table 7.10):

   - A **length value**, such as **–10px**. The values can be positive or negative. The first number tells the browser the distance the element should appear from the left edge of its parent; the second value specifies the position from the top edge of the parent.

▸ A **percentage value**, such as **25%**. The first percentage indicates the horizontal position proportional to the parent element's size; the second value indicates the vertical position proportional to the parent element's size.

▸ A position keyword, such as **top**, **bottom**, **left**, **right**, or **center**.

7. **Add multiple backgrounds to an image in a comma-separated list.**

```
background: url(../_images/bg-book-
→ spine-title.png) no-repeat
→ center top, rgb(102,0,0)
→ url(../_images/bg-book-spine.jpg)
→ repeat-x 0 0;
```

As with the stand-alone background properties, you can place multiple backgrounds in a single object. Just add the values in a comma-separated list. Place the background color value in the last value set; otherwise, it will cover everything beneath it.

TIP While it is possible to include the background image size and clip in the shorthand, the browser support for this is spotty at best. I recommend keeping these as separate declarations.

TIP The ability to place graphics behind any element on the screen is a very powerful design tool for Web pages, especially when using the CSS Sprite technique, where a single background image can be used for different dynamic states. See Chapter 14 for more information.

TIP The default state for an element's background is *none*, so the parent element's background image and/or color will show through unless the background color or background image is set for that child element.

TIP A fixed background can be particularly effective if you're using a graphic background in your layout to help define the layout grid.

Putting It All Together

1. **Using the HTML you set up in Chapter 6, set the foreground (text) color for your Web page.** Make sure the colors are readable against whatever background color you set.

2. **Add a background image to the page.** Use something with some contrast.

3. **Add a second background image, and position it over the main background.** Use a transparent PNG image and set repeating so that it's not completely covering the fist background image.

4. **Set a transparent background color behind paragraphs.** Play around with the opacity level until your text is readable against the background you chose in step 1.

5. **Combine background properties into a single declaration.** You may not be able to do this with all of your background properties, but see how many you can combine.

List and Table Properties

Most of the CSS properties discussed in this book can be applied to tables and lists. However, CSS also includes a few unique properties specifically for tables and lists. The specifications of table and list properties have not changed from CSS2 to CSS3, although Internet Explorer has improved its implementation over the standards in IE8.

Although tables should never be used for page layout, as they once were, they are still used to layout tabular data. Lists, on the other hand, are not only used to create lists (obviously), but have also become the standard way to structure Web site navigation.

Code 8.1 The HTML5 code used for examples in this chapter. It imports the final CSS from Chapters 5, 6, 7, and 8 as well as a new file, *list-table-properties.css*, which you will build in this chapter. It includes the same header and footer as in previous chapters but shows a list of characters from *Alice's Adventures in Wonderland* and a table of the attendees of the Tea Party. Initially, the page will have standard bullets and an unformatted table. You'll change all of that Ⓐ.

```
<!-- HTML5 -->
<!DOCTYPE html>
<html lang="en">
<head>
<meta charset="utf-8">
<title>Alice's Adventure's In Wonderland | Characters</title>
<link href="../_css/font-properties.css" type="text/css" rel="stylesheet">
<link href="../_css/text-properties.css" type="text/css" rel="stylesheet">
<link href="../_css/color-background-properties.css" type="text/css" rel="stylesheet">
<link href="../_css/list-table-properties.css" type="text/css" rel="stylesheet">

<!--[if IE ]>
  <style>@import url(_css/ie.css);</style>
  <script src="script/HTML5forIE.js" type="text/javascript"></script>
<![endif]-->

</head>
<body id="charachters" class="book aaiw section">
<header class="page">
<h1>Alice's Adventures in Wonderland</h1>
<p class="byline">by <span class="author">Lewis Carroll</span></p>
<nav class="global">
  <ul>
    <li><a href="" target="_self">Cover</a></li>
    <li><a href="" target="_self">About the Author</a></li>
    <li><a href="" target="_self">About the Books</a></li>
    <li><a href="" target="_self">About the Site</a></li>
  </ul>
</nav>
</header>
<article><!-- Article -->
  <h2>Characters</h2>
  <ul>
    <li><strong>Alice</strong>: The character has been said to be based on Alice Liddell, a child
    → friend of Dodgson's. Dodgson said several times that his 'little heroine' was not based on any
    → real child, but was entirely fictional.</li>
    <li><strong>The White Rabbit</strong>: In his article "Alice on the Stage," Carroll wrote "And the
    → White Rabbit, what of him? Was he framed on the "Alice" lines, or meant as a contrast?</li>
  </ul>
<table>
  <caption>The Tea Party</caption>
  <thead>
    <tr>
      <th scope="col">Name</th>
      <th scope="col">Description</th>
```

code continues on next page

Code 8.1 *continued*

```
        <th scope="col">Mad?</th>
      </tr>
    </thead>
    <tfoot>
    </tfoot>
    <tbody>
      <tr>
        <td>The Hatter </td>
        <td></td>
        <td>&otimes;</td>
      </tr>
      <tr>
        <td>The March Hare</td>
        <td>"Mad as a March hare" was a common
      → phrase in Carroll's time.</td>
        <td>&otimes;</td>
      </tr>
      <tr>
        <td>The Dormouse</td>
        <td>The Dormouse is always falling
   → asleep during the scene, waking up
   → every so often.</td>
        <td>&otimes;</td>
      </tr>
      <tr>
        <td>Alice</td>
        <td>The character has been said to be
         ↪ based on Alice Liddell, a child friend
        → of Dodgson's.</td>
        <td></td>
      </tr>
    </tbody>
  </table>
  <br>
</article>
<footer>
<nav class="global">
  <ul>
    <li><a href="" target="_self">Table of
    → Contents</a></li>
    <li><a href="" target="_self">About the
    → Author</a></li>
    <li><a href="" target="_self">About the
    → Books</a></li>
    <li><a href="" target="_self">About the
    → Site</a></li>
  </ul>
</nav>
</footer>
</body>
</html>
```

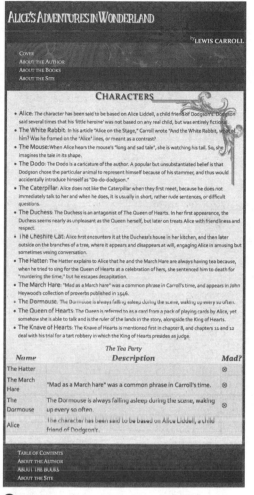

A Our Web page for this chapter before adding any list or table styles. So, the browser default styles are applied, plus a few styles added to the style the table.

Setting the Bullet Style

The `list-style-type` property (Table 8.1) controls the type of bullet to be used for list items—not just circles, discs, and squares, but also letters and numerals and dots and our own custom image bullets.

To define the bullet style:

1. Add the list style type property to your declaration list. Type **list-style-type**, followed by a colon (:) (**Code 8.2**).

   `list-style-type:`

2. Specify the bullet type. Type one of the bullet names listed in **Table 8.2**, or type **none** if you do not want a marker to appear.

   `circle;`

> **TIP** Although the list item tag `<li>` is used in this example, you can turn any element into a list item by adding the CSS list properties along with the definition `display: list-item`. See Chapter 10 for more information.

> **TIP** You can change the bullet type or image using pseudo-classes such as `:hover`, `:visited`, and `:active`.

Ⓐ Code 8.2 applied to code 8.1: Bullets are changed from discs (default) to circles.

TABLE 8.1 List-Style-Type Values

Value	Compatibility
<bullet name>*	IE4, FF1, S1, O3.5, C1, CSS1
none	IE4, FF1, S1, O3.5, C1, CSS1
inherit	IE7, FF1, S1, O7, C1, CSS1

* See Table 8.2

Code 8.2 *list-table-properties.css*—the **list-style-type** property is used to choose between the different bullet and number styles for your list.

```
/*** CSS3 VQS | Chapter 8 |
→ list-table-properties.css ***/

ul {
  list-style-type: circle; }

nav.global ul  {
  list-style: none; }
```

TABLE 8.2 List-Style Bullet Names

Name	Appearance (varies depending on system)
disc	•
circle	○
square	■
decimal	1, 2, 3
decimal-leading-zero	01, 02, 03
upper-roman	I, II, III
lower-roman	i, ii, iii
upper-alpha	A, B, C
lower-alpha	a, b, c
lower-greek	α, β, χ

TABLE 8.3 List-Style-Image Values

Value	Compatibility
<url>	IE4, FF1, S1, O3.5, C1, CSS1
none	IE4, FF1, S1, O3.5, C1, CSS1
inherit	IE7, FF1, S1, O4, C1, CSS1

Code 8.3 *list-table-properties.css*—I've created a small arrow graphic 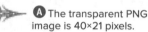 (saved as a transparent PNG) to be inserted as the bullet using **list-style-image** 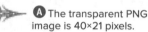.

```
/*** CSS3 VQS | Chapter 8 |
→ list-table-properties.css ***/

ul {
  list-style-type: circle;
  list-style-image: url(../_images/bullet-01.
  → png); }

nav.global ul {
  list-style: none; }
```

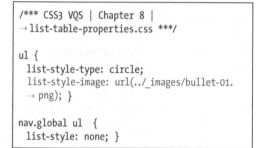

A The transparent PNG image is 40×21 pixels.

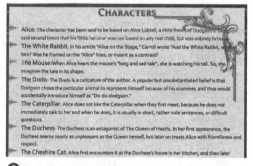

B Code 8.3 applied to code 8.1: The bullet sits to the left of the text, but because no padding is set, it actually goes off the edge of the page.

Creating Your Own Bullets

You're not limited to the preset bullet styles built into a browser. You can also use your own graphics as bullets from GIF, JPEG, and PNG files by applying the **list-style-image** property (Table 8.3).

To define your own graphic bullet:

1. Add the list-style-image property to your CSS rule. Type **list-style-image**, followed by a colon (:) (**Code 8.3**).

   `list-style-image:`

2. **Specify the location of your image bullet.** To include your own bullet, you have to tell the browser where your bullet graphic file is located.

   `url(arrow_02.png);`

   Type the complete Web address or relative path of the image. In this example, arrow_02.png is a local file.

   Alternatively, type **none** to instruct the browser to override any inherited bullet images.

> **TIP** Bullets are placed out of the layout frame by default, so they often will fall outside of the layout box if they are particularly long.

> **TIP** Keep in mind that the text being bulleted has to make space for the graphic you use. A taller graphic will force more space between bulleted items, and a wider graphic will force bulleted items farther to the right.

> **TIP** To be honest, very few developers use the list-style-image property to add image bullets to their designs. Instead most developers will use the background property with padding to get more precise styling. Want to know how to do this? Check out Chapter 17, "Navigation, Buttons, and Controls."

Setting Bullet Positions

Often, the text of a bulleted list item is longer than one line. Using the **list-style-position** property (**Table 8.4**), you can specify the position of wrapping text in relation to the bullet. Wrapped text that is indented to start below the first letter of the first line of text is called a *hanging indent* Ⓐ.

To define the line position for wrapped text in a list item:

1. Add the list-style-type property to your declarations. Type **list-style-position**, followed by a colon (:) and one of the values described in step 2 (**Code 8.4**).

   list-style-position:

2. Specify the position type.

   inside;

   Type one of the following values to set text indentation:

   ▸ **inside** aligns the left edge of the bullet with the left edge of subsequent text.

   ▸ **outside** left aligns the first line of text with subsequent text, placing the bullet as a hanging indent.

> **TIP** Generally, bulleted lists that have a hanging indent (**outside** position) stand out much better than those without a hanging indent (**inside** position).

TABLE 8.4 List-Style-Position Values

Value	Compatibility
inside	IE4, FF1, S1, O3.5, C1, CSS1
outside	IE4, FF1, S1, O3.5, C1, CSS1
inherit	IE7, FF1, S1, O4, C1, CSS1

- **Outside**...Magnus es, domine, et laudabilis valde: magna virtus tua, et sapientiae tuae non est numerus. et laudare te vult homo.

- **Inside**...Magnus es, domine, et laudabilis valde: magna virtus tua, et sapientiae tuae non est numerus. et laudare te vult homo.

Ⓐ **outside** is generally how bulleted lists are presented. You may want to override that by using **inside**.

Code 8.4 *list-table-properties*: The **list-style-position** property allows you to specify how lines of text flow under the bullet Ⓑ.

```
/*** CSS3 VQS | Chapter 8 |
→ list-table-properties.css ***/

ul {
  list-style-type: circle;
  list-style-image: url(../_images/bullet-01.
  → png);
  list-style-position: inside; }

nav.global ul {
  list-style: none;
  list-style-position: outside; }
```

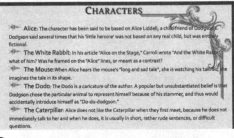

Ⓑ **Code 8.4 applied to code 8.1:** The bullet pushes into the text, so that its left edge is flush with the left edge of subsequent lines of text.

TABLE 8.5 List-Style Values

Value	Compatibility
\<list-style-type\>	IE4, FF1, S1, O3.5, C1, CSS1
\<list-style-position\>	IE4, FF1, S1, O3.5, C1, CSS1
\<list-style-image\>	IE4, FF1, S1, O3.5, C1, CSS1

Code 8.5 *list-table-properties*: The **list-style** property lets you set the type, image, and position all in one definition 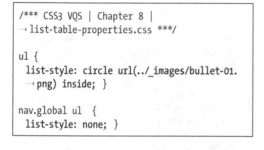.

```
/*** CSS3 VQS | Chapter 8 |
→ list-table-properties.css ***/

ul {
  list-style: circle url(../_images/bullet-01.
  →png) inside; }

nav.global ul {
  list-style: none; }
```

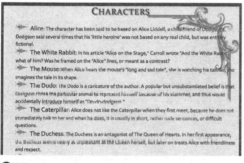

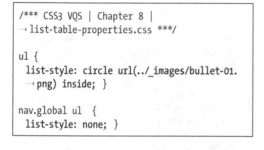 Code 8.5 applied to code 8.1: This version is identical to the previous version; only the code is different.

TIP You do not need to include all of the values to ensure that this shorthand selector will work. Omitted values are set to the default. The following example works just fine:

list-style: inside;

TIP If visitors have turned off graphics in their browsers or if a graphical bullet does not load for some reason, the browser uses the **list-style-type** that you defined in step 3.

Setting Multiple List Styles

You can use one line of code to set all list properties described in the previous three sections using the **list-style** shorthand property (**Table 8.5**), which sets the **list-style-type, list-style-position**, and **line-style-image** properties.

To define multiple list-style attributes:

1. Add the list-style property to your CSS rules. Type **list-style**, followed by a colon (:) (**Code 8.5**).

   list-style:

2. Specify the location of your bullet image (optional). Next, type a **list-style-image** value.

   url(arrow_02.png)

   To include your own bullet, you must create the bullet graphic and then tell the browser where the graphic is located using either the complete Web address or the relative path of the image. (See "Creating Your Own Bullets" in this chapter for more information.)

3. Specify the bullet type. Type a **list-style-type** value from Table 8.3, followed by a space, or type **none** if you don't want a marker to appear.

   circle

4. Specify the position type. Type a **list-style-position** value from Table 8.4.

   outside;

Setting the Table Layout

Different browsers use different methods to calculate how a particular table should be displayed. Two primary **table-layout** (**Table 8.6**) methods are favored:

- **Fixed** method bases its layout on the width of the table and the width of columns in the first row. This method is generally faster than automatic.

- **Automatic** uses the table column width along with the amount of content in the table data cell to calculate the table data cell width. This will generally render more slowly than the fixed method, but it also produces more accurate results for widths throughout the table.

To set the table layout method:

1. **Add the table layout property to a CSS rule for a table element.** Type **table-layout**, followed by a colon (:) on table elements (**Code 8.6**).

   table-layout:

TABLE 8.6 Table-Layout Values

Value	Compatibility
fixed	IE5.5, O5, S1.3, C1, CSS2
auto	IE5.5, O5, S1.3, C1, CSS2
inherit	IE5.5, O5, S1.3, C1, CSS2

Code 8.6 *list-table-properties*: The **table-layout** property lets you force the browser to use either the **fixed** Ⓐ or **auto** Ⓑ methods for rendering tables. I've also cheated a little here and set the width and margin for the table, which you will not learn until Chapter 10.

```
/*** CSS3 VQS | Chapter 8 |
→ list-table-properties.css ***/

ul {
  list-style: circle url(../_images/bullet-01.
  → png) inside; }

nav.global ul  {
  list-style: none; }

table {
  table-layout: auto;
  width: 75%;
  margin: 40px auto; }
```

A Code 8.6 applied to code 8.1 with fixed layout: The data in the second column is much longer than subsequent rows, so the table looks cramped when using `fixed`.

B Code 8.6 applied to code 8.1 with auto layout: Because all the data in the table is considered with **auto** when determining the column widths, the layout adjusts to fit all of the content.

2. Specify the layout method.

`auto;`

Type one of the following values to specify which method you want to use when displaying your table:

- ▸ **fixed** will use the first row to calculate the overall width of table data cells in that column of the table.

- ▸ **auto** will allow the browser to calculate the widths of table data cells based on their content and the overall width of the table.

TIP Although `fixed` renders faster for longer tables, `auto` generally provides better results unless the rows of data are consistent in size.

TIP I recommend `auto` because most tables since short tables will not take long to render, and long tables will need more accuracy. Either way, auto is preferred.

Setting the Space Between Table Cells

Although table data cells and table header cells can use many of the box properties we'll explore in Chapter 10, they cannot use the **margin** property. Instead, CSS has the **border-spacing** (Table 8.7) property, which sets an equal amount of space between data cells' top, bottom, left, and right sides.

To collapse the borders in a table:

1. Add the border spacing property to the CSS rule for a table element. Type **border-spacing**, followed by a colon (:) (Code 8.7).

   border-spacing:

2. Specify the spacing between table data cells.

   ~~8px;~~

   Type a length value (such as **8px**) to specify the distance between cells. (See "Values and Units Used in This Book" in the Introduction.) Alternatively, use **inherit** to use the same border spacing as a cell's parent element.

Ⓐ Code 8.7 applied to code 8.1: Spacing out data cells can make them easier for users to scan.

TABLE 8.7 Border-Spacing Values

Value	Compatibility
\<length\>	IE5.5, FF1, O5, S1.3, C1, CSS2
inherit	IE5.5, FF1, O5, S1.3, C1, CSS2

Code 8.7 *list-table-properties*: The **border-spacing** property works like a margin around the table data cell Ⓐ.

```
/*** CSS3 VQS | Chapter 8 |
→ list-table-properties.css ***/

ul {
  list-style: circle url(../_images/bullet-01.
  → png) inside; }

nav.global ul {
  list-style: none; }

table {
  table-layout: auto;
  border-spacing: 8px;
  width: 75%;
  margin: 40px auto; }

table caption, table thead {
  font: italic 1.25em Constantia, Georgia,
  → Times, "Times New Roman", Serif; }

tr {
  font-size: 1.25em; }

td {
  vertical-align: top;
  padding: .5em;
  background-color: rgba(200, 200, 180,.25);
  border: 1px solid rgb(200, 200, 180); }
```

TABLE 8.8 Border-Collapse Values

Value	Compatibility
collapse	IE5.5, FF1, O5, S1.3, C1, CSS2
separate	IE5.5, FF1, O5, S1.3, C1, CSS2
inherit	IE5.5, FF1, O5, S1.3, C1, CSS2

Code 8.8 *list-table-properties.css*—The **border-collapse** property lets you remove *all* space between the table data cells, giving each side a single border Ⓐ (on the following page), but border spacing will be ignored. Use **separate** to allow **border-spacing** to work Ⓑ (on the following page).

```
/*** CSS3 VQS | Chapter 8 |
→ list-table-properties.css ***/

ul {
  list-style: circle url(../_images/bullet-01.
  → png) inside; }

nav.global ul {
  list-style: none; }

table {
  table-layout: auto;
  border-spacing: 8px;
  border-collapse: separate;
  width: 75%;
  margin: 40px auto; }

table caption, table thead {
  font: italic 1.25em Constantia, Georgia,
  → Times, "Times New Roman", Serif; }

tr {
  font-size: 1.25em; }

td {
  vertical-align: top;
  padding: .5em;
  background-color: rgba(200, 200, 180,.25);
  border: 1px solid rgb(200, 200, 180); }
```

Collapsing Borders Between Table Cells

Every table data cell defined by the `<td>` tag has four borders: top, right, bottom, and left. The **border-collapse** property (Table 8.8) allows you to set a table so that each table data cell will share its borders with an adjacent table data cell rather than creating a separate border for each.

To collapse the borders in a table:

1. Add the border collapse property to a table element. Type **border-collapse**, followed by a colon (:) (**Code 8.8**).

   `border-collapse:`

2. Specify how borders should collapse.

   `separate;`

   Type one of the following to determine how you want to display the borders in the table:

   ▸ **collapse** will make adjacent table data cells share a common border; however, you won't be able to set **cell-spacing** if borders are collapsed.

   ▸ **separate** will maintain individual borders for each table data cell.

TIP The displayed results can vary between different browsers unless you set the border style using CSS.

TIP If the borders being collapsed do not share the same border thickness, the thicker border will be shown and its style used.

TIP If borders have the same thickness but different styles, the border style for the data cell to the left is used.

A By using **collapse**, the border between data cells has been reduced to a single, thin line.

B Code 8.8 applied to code 8.1: With **separate** set, you can set **border-spacing**.

TABLE 8.9 Empty-Cells Values

Value	Compatibility
show	FF1, O5, S1.3, C1, CSS2
hide	FF1, O5, S1.3, C1, CSS2
inherit	FF1, O5, S1.3, C1, CSS2

Code 8.9 *list-table-properties.css*—The **empty-cells** property lets you show (default) or hide empty table data cells 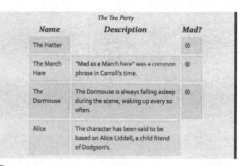.

```
/*** CSS3 VQS | Chapter 8 |
→ list-table-properties.css ***/

ul {
  list-style: circle url(../_images/bullet-01.
  → png) inside; }

nav.global ul  {
  list-style: none; }

table {
  table-layout: auto;
  border-spacing: 8px;
  border-collapse: separate;
  empty-cells: hide;
  width: 75%;
  margin: 40px auto; }

table caption, table thead {
  font: italic 1.25em Constantia, Georgia,
  → Times, "Times New Roman", Serif; }
tr {
  font-size: 1.25em; }
td {
  vertical-align: top;
  padding: .5em;
  background-color: rgba(200, 200, 180,.25);
  border: 1px solid rgb(200, 200, 180); }
```

Dealing with Empty Table Cells

If a table data cell has no data (not even spaces or nonbreaking spaces), it simply appears as a blank box at the default width and height of the column and row. The **empty-cells** property (Table 8.9) allows you to specify how that empty data cell (and, most importantly, its border) is presented.

To hide empty table data cells:

1. Add the **empty-cells** property to a table elements CSS rule. Type **empty-cells**, followed by a colon (:) (**Code 8.9**).

   empty-cells:

2. Specify how empty table cells should be treated.

   hide;

   Type one of the following to specify how the cells will be treated:

   ▸ **show** will force the empty data cell to display its background and border.

   ▸ **hide** will leave a visual gap in place of the data cell.

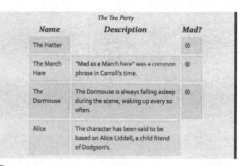

A Code 8.9 applied to code 8.1: Empty table data cells have been hidden so that their border and background colors are not displayed, leaving an empty gap in the table.

Setting the Position of a Table Caption

The **<caption>** tag lets you embed identifying text in a table. You can set the **align** attribute in the tag to define where the caption should appear in relation to the table, but this is being deprecated in favor of the CSS **caption-side** property (**Table 8.10**), which does the same thing.

To set the position of a caption in relation to its table:

1. **Add the caption side property to your CSS.** Type **caption-side**, followed by a colon (:) (**Code 8.10**).

   caption-side:

2. Type a keyword indicating which side of the table you want the caption to appear: **top** or **bottom**.

   ~~bottom;~~

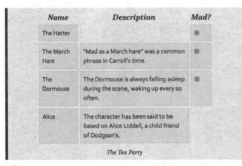

A The caption is forced to the bottom of the table rather than its natural position at the top.

TABLE 8.10 Caption-Side Values

Value	Compatibility
top	IE5.5, FF1, O7, C1, S1.3, C1, CSS2
bottom	IE5.5, FF1, O7, C1, S1.3, C1, CSS2
inherit	IE5.5, FF1, O7, C1, S1.3, C1, CSS2

Code 8.10 *list-table-properties.css*—The **caption-side** property lets you specify whether the caption should appear above (**top**) or below (**bottom**) the table **A**.

```
/*** CSS3 VQS | Chapter 8 | list-table-
properties.css ***/

ul {
  list-style: circle url(../_images/bullet-01.
png) inside; }

nav.global ul  {
  list-style: none; }

table {
  table-layout: auto;
  border-spacing: 8px;
  border-collapse: separate;
  empty-cells: hide;
  caption-side: bottom;
  width: 75%;
  margin: 40px auto; }

table caption, table thead {
  font: italic 1.25em Constantia, Georgia,
Times, "Times New Roman", Serif; }

tr {
  font-size: 1.25em; }

td {
  vertical-align: top;
  padding: .5em;
  background-color: rgba(200, 200, 180,.25);
  border: 1px solid rgb(200, 200, 180); }
```

Putting It All Together

1. **Create a list and a table to experiment with.** You can use a numbered or unnumbered list, but keep it simple. You're just playing around, so maybe 3–5 elements in the list and a 3×3 table should suffice.

2. **Set a bullet style and position it outside.** Try different bullet styles to see how they appear on your screen and then look at the code in different browsers to see if the bullets look any different.

3. **Create a bullet image using your favorite image editing software and then use it as the bullet in your list.** Make sure to save it in a Web-compatible image format: PNG, JPEG, or GIF.

4. **Combine all of your style declarations together into a single declaration.** Do you notice any difference when you view your code in a Web browser? You shouldn't.

5. **Set the table layout and border space on your table and set border collapse to separate.** See what happens when you change the collapse value to collapse and you try to increase the border space.

User Interface and Generated Content Properties

The user interface cannot, for the most part, be controlled by CSS. It is dependent on the specific operating system and browser in use. Objects such as the scroll bars are out of your control. However, CSS does provide some control over the appearance of the mouse pointer and style of quotes.

Additionally, CSS includes several properties that let you specify content to be placed on the page (generated) for specific instances. For example, you might want all chapter titles to include the word "Chapter" before them. Although you'll usually want to place all of your Web page content directly into the HTML code, on occasion you'll find it useful to have some redundant content generated for you or have it tailored to a specific language.

In This Chapter

Code 9.1 The HTML5 code used in the examples in this chapter. It imports the final CSS from Chapters 5, 6, 7, and 8 as well as a new file you will be building in this chapter, *ui-generatedcontent-properties.css*. I've set this HTML document up with the same header and footer as in previous chapters but made changes around the table of contents, turning it into a list or previous chapters above and future chapters below Ⓐ.

```
<!-- HTML5 -->
<!DOCTYPE html>
<html lang="en">
<head>
<meta charset="utf-8">
<title>Alice's Adventure's In Wonderland | Chapter 4</title>
<link href="../_css/font-properties.css" type="text/css" rel="stylesheet">
<link href="../_css/text-properties.css" type="text/css" rel="stylesheet">
<link href="../_css/color-background-properties.css" type="text/css" rel="stylesheet">
<link href="../_css/list-table-properties.css" type="text/css" rel="stylesheet">
<link href="../_css/ui-generatedcontent-properties.css" type="text/css" rel="stylesheet">

<!--[if IE ]>
  <style>@import url(_css/ie.css);</style>
  <script src="../_script/HTML5forIE.js" type="text/javascript"></script>
<![endif]-->

</head>
<body id="chapter4" class="book aaiw section">
<header class="page">
<h1>Alice's Adventures In Wonderland</h1>
<p class="byline">by <span class="author">Lewis Carroll</span></p>

<nav class="global">
  <ul>
    <li><a href="" target="_self">Cover</a></li>
    <li><a href="" target="_self">About the Author</a></li>
    <li><a href="" target="_self">About the Books</a></li>
    <li><a href="" target="_self">About the Site</a></li>
  </ul>
</nav>

</header>
<article><!-- Article -->
<br>
<div class="toc top">
  <h2>Down the Rabbit-Hole</h2>
  <h2>The Pool of Tears</h2>
  <h2>A Caucus-Race and a Long Tale</h2>
</div>
<h2><strong>CHAPTER 4.</strong> The Rabbit Sends in a Little Bill</h2>
<p>It was the White Rabbit, trotting slowly back again, and looking
anxiously about as it went, as if it had lost something; and she heard
it muttering to itself <q>The Duchess! The Duchess! Oh my dear paws! Oh
my fur and whiskers! She'll get me executed, as sure as ferrets are
ferrets! Where CAN I have dropped them, I wonder?</q> Alice guessed in a
```

Code 9.1 *continued*

```
moment that it was looking for the fan and
→ the pair of white kid gloves,
and she very good-naturedly began hunting
→ about for them, but they were
nowhere to be seen&mdash;everything seemed
→ to have changed since her swim in
the pool, and the great hall, with the glass
→ table and the little door,
had vanished completely.
</p>
<div class="toc continued">
  <h2>Advice from a Caterpillar</h2>
  <h2>Pig and Pepper</h2>
  <h2>A Mad Tea-Party</h2>
  <h2>The Queen's Croquet-Ground</h2>
  <h2>The Mock Turtle's Story</h2>
  <h2>The Lobster Quadrille</h2>
  <h2>Who Stole the Tarts?</h2>
</div>
<br>
</article>
<footer>
<nav class="global">
  <ul>
    <li><a href="" target="_self">Cover</a>
     ↵</li>
    <li><a href="" target="_self">About the
    → Author</a></li>
    <li><a href="" target="_self">About the
    → Books</a></li>
    <li><a href="" target="_self">About the
    → Site</a></li>
  </ul>
</nav>
</footer>
</body>
</html>
```

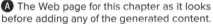 The Web page for this chapter as it looks before adding any of the generated content.

Changing the Mouse Pointer Appearance

Normally, the browser determines the appearance of the mouse pointer according to the content currently under it. If the pointer is over text, for example, the pointer becomes a text selector. Or, if the browser is working and the visitor can't do anything, the pointer becomes a timer, indicating that the visitor needs to wait.

Sometimes, it's useful to override the browser's behavior and set the appearance of the pointer yourself, using the **cursor** property (**Table 9.1**). This can be applied to any element on the screen, not just links. Also, you do not *have* to associate it with the dynamic hover state for it to work; just apply it directly to the element's CSS rule.

To set the mouse pointer's appearance:

1. **Add the cursor property to your CSS declarations.** Type **cursor** in the CSS declaration block, followed by a colon (:) (**Code 9.2**).

   `cursor:`

2. **Specify the mouse pointer.** Type one of the mouse pointer names listed in **Table 9.2** to specify the pointer's appearance.

   `crosshair;`

   Alternatively, type one of these values for **cursor:**

   ▶ **auto** to have the browser choose which mouse pointer to use.

   ▶ **none** to hide the pointer altogether.

TABLE 9.1 Cursor Values

Value	Compatibility
\<cursor type name\>	IE4, FF1, S1, O7, C1, CSS2
\<URL\>	IE6, FF1.5, S3, C3, CSS2
auto	IE4, FF1, S1, O7, C1, CSS2
none	IE4, FF1, S1, O7, C1, CSS2

Code 9.2 *ui-generatedcontent-properties.css—* I've set up different pointer types that depend on the type of object or link over which the pointer is hovering Ⓐ.

```
/*** CSS3 VQS | Chapter 9 |
 → ui-generatedcontent-properties.css ***/

.toc { margin: 0 auto; width: 90%;
 → text-align: center; font-size: .5em;}

a {
  cursor: help; }

h1 {
  cursor: url(../_images/cursor-02.png)
 → 20 20, crosshair; }
```

Ⓐ **Code 9.2 applied to code 9.1:** the pointer turns into the Cheshire Cat's head when over the book title.

TABLE 9.2 Cursor Types

Name	Appearance (varies depending on OS)
crosshair	+
e-resize	→
help	⌖?
move	✥
ne-resize	↗
n-resize	↑
nw-resize	↖
pointer	☝
progress	◉
se-resize	↘
s-resize	↓
sw-resize	↙
text	I
wait	⧗
w-resize	←

3. **Add a graphic mouse pointer.** You can also create your own pointer by adding the URL reference to an image file (generally in PNG format) to use as a custom cursor. You can specify the complete Web address or the local filename of the image.

```
cursor: url(../_images/cursor-02.
→ png) 20 20, crosshair;
```

Hotspot ★: CSS3 adds the ability to define the pointer's hotspot (the point at which the active click will happen) as determined from the upper-left corner of the image. Always include a backup pointer type.

TIP Firefox, Safari, Opera, and Chrome allow you to use CUR, ANI, GIF, PNG, or JPEG images as a custom pointer by specifying the URL for the image file. Unfortunately, Internet Explorer supports only CUR and ANI file formats for custom pointers.

TIP CUR and ANI are not standard image formats and can only be created using specialized software.

TIP Remember that the exact appearance of the pointer depends on the operating system and the Web browser in use.

TIP Although it's fun to play around with switching the mouse pointers, I've tested this feature on my own Web site and have received several emails asking me to cut it out. Most Web users have learned to recognize the common functions of specific pointers and when they should appear. Breaking these conventions tends to confuse users.

Adding Content Using CSS

For the purposes of search engine optimization and accessibility, it is usually best to keep all content within the **<body>** element of your Web page. If it is dynamically generated, then it will not be seen by web crawlers and many screen readers. However, at times you might have repetitive content that will not help (or may even hinder) your placement in a search index.

To add content, you can use the **content** property (**Table 9.3**), which allows you to specify a text string, image or sound file URL, counter, quote, or even an attribute value that should be displayed on the page.

To define generated content:

1. **Specify whether the content should go before or after the element.** Type a selector with the **:before** or **:after** pseudo-class (see "Setting the Content Before and After and Element" in Chapter 4) to define where the content will be positioned in relation to the selector (**Code 9.3**).

   .toc h2:before {...}

2. **Add the content property to your CSS.** In your declaration block, type the **content** property name, followed by a colon (**:**) and one of the values listed in step 3.

   content:

TABLE 9.3 Content Values

Value	Compatibility
normal	IE8, FF1, S1, O4, C1, CSS2
none	IE8, FF1, S1, O4, C1, CSS2
<string>	IE8, FF1, S1, O4, C1, CSS2
<url>	IE8, FF1, S1, O7, C1, CSS2
<counter>	IE8, FF1, S1, O4, C1, CSS2
attr(<selector>)	IE8, FF1, S1, O4, C1, CSS2
open-quote	IE8, FF1, S1, O4, C1, CSS2
close-quote	IE8, FF1, S1, O4, C1, CSS2
no-open-quote	IE8, FF1, S1, O4, C1, CSS2
no-close-quote	IE8, FF1, S1, O4, C1, CSS2
inherit	IE8, FF1, S1, O4, C1, CSS2

Code 9.3 *ui-generatedcontent-properties.css—* A flourish image (bullet-01), the word "Chapter," and a counter are inserted before the **h2** tag if it is in the .toc class. Another bullet is inserted afterward on the left **Ⓐ**.

```
/*** CSS3 VQS | Chapter 9 |
→ ui-generatedcontent-properties.css ***/

.toc { margin: 0 auto; width: 90%;
→ text-align: center; font-size: .5em;}

a {
  cursor: help; }

h1 {
  cursor: url(../_images/cursor-02.png)
  → 20 20, crosshair; }

.toc h2:before {
  content:  url('../_images/bullet-01.png')
  → 'Chapter ' counter(chapterNum) '. '; }

.toc h2:after {
  content: url('../_images/bullet-02.png'); }
```

A Code 9.3 applied to code 9.1: the chapter titles gain a bit more style. Notice, though, that the chapters all say 0. You have to teach the browser how to count.

TIP Because the content property is not supported until Internet Explorer 8, it is best not to rely on this property for critical information.

TIP Information rendered using the content property will not be searchable by search engine spiders, so never use it to insert information that defines your page.

TIP Content added this way is also invisible to screenreaders, so don't include anything that they will miss.

TIP One idea is to use content to add figure captions pulled from the images alt tag. Since this is visible to screenreaders and search engines, it's a good way to cut down on repetitive content.

3. **Specify the content to be added.**

```
url('../_images/bullet-01.png')
→'Chapter ' counter(chapterNum)
→'. ';
```

To define the content that is being added, type one or more of the following values, separating each value with a space:

▶ Type a string value, such as **Chapter**, within single or double quotes. Anything within the quotes will be displayed just as you typed it, including HTML code, although spaces are collapsed (that is, more than two spaces are collapsed into a single space when displayed).

▶ **url()**, with an absolute or relative url within the parentheses pointing to an external file, such as an image or sound file. For example, **url(bg_flourish.png)** will load an image.

▶ **counter()**, with a counter name in parentheses. For example, **counter(chapterNum)** adds the counter number for the **chapterNum** counter. (Counters are explained in the next section.)

▶ **open-quote** or **close-quote** to add a quotation mark using the current quotation style. (See "Specifying the Quote Style" later in this chapter.)

▶ **no-open-quote** or **no-close-quote** to increase the level of quoting by one level.

▶ **attr()**, to display the value of the indicated attribute. For example, **attr(alt)** will display the value for the alt attribute of the element being styled.

▶ **inherit**, which will use the content defined for the parent element.

▶ **normal** or **none**, which will not add any content or apply any other values.

Teaching the Browser to Count

Browsers can automatically create sequentially numbered lists, starting at 1 and counting by ones. You will explore this later in the chapter. However, what if you need to start numbering from 6 instead of 1? Or, what if you need to create two sequential lists that are nested inside each other?

CSS allows you to set up multiple counter lists to be used with the **counter** value of the **content** property (see the previous section). The **counter-reset** property (**Table 9.4**) is used to set the initial value for the count, and the **counter-increment** property (**Table 9.5**) is used to increase the counter by a specific value.

To use a counter:

1. **Set up the parent element.** Set up a CSS rule for the selector that will be the parent element for your numbered list (**Code 9.4**). This can be the **ol** (ordered list) tag.

   `.top {...}`

2. **Add the counter-reset property to your declaration block.**

   `counter-reset: chapterNum 0;`

   Type **counter-reset**, a colon (:), and then the name of the counter identifier you are defining (which can be any name you want). Then insert a space and the number you want to start the list.

TABLE 9.4 Counter-Reset Values

Value	Compatibility
<counterName>	IE8, FF1, O4, S1, C1, CSS2
<num>	IE8, FF1, O4, S1, C1, CSS2
none	IE8, FF1, O4, S1, C1, CSS2
inherit	IE8, FF1, O4, S1, C1, CSS2

TABLE 9.5 Counter-Increment Values

Value	Compatibility
<counterName>	IE8, FF1, O4, S1, C1, CSS2
<num>	IE8, FF1, O4, S1, C1, CSS2
none	IE8, FF1, O4, S1, C1, CSS2
inherit	IE8, FF1, O4, S1, C1, CSS2

Code 9.4 *ui-generatedcontent-properties. css*—The table of contents shows chapters before and after chapter 4 Ⓐ, so the continued list needs to skip to 5 Ⓑ.

```
/*** CSS3 VQS | Chapter 9 |
→ ui-generatedcontent-properties.css ***/

.toc { margin: 0 auto; width: 90%;
→ text-align: center; font-size: .5em;}

a {
  cursor: help; }

h1 {
  cursor: url(../_images/cursor-02.png)
  → 20 20, crosshair; }

.top {
  counter-reset: chapterNum 0; }

.toc h2:before {
  content:  url('../_images/bullet-01.png')
  → 'Chapter ' counter(chapterNum) '. ';
  counter-increment: chapterNum 1; }
.toc h2:after {
  content: url('../_images/bullet-02.png'); }

#chapter4 .continued {
  counter-reset: chapterNum 4; }
```

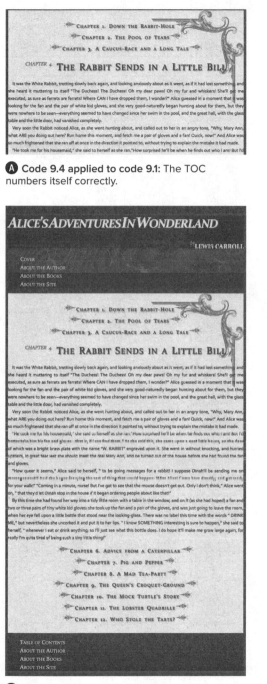

A Code 9.4 applied to code 9.1: The TOC numbers itself correctly.

B The numbering continues but skips 4 because that's the number of the current chapter.

3. **Use before or after pseudo-classes to define where the automatic numbering should be placed.** Type a selector with the `:before` or `:after` pseudo-class, which defines where the number will be positioned in relation to the selector.

   `.toc h2:before {}`

4. **Add the `counter-increment` property to the declaration block and include the name of the counter identifier.**

   `counter-increment: chapterNum 1;`

   Insert a space and then enter a value to indicate how much you want to increase the count for each instance. The default is 1, but you can increase the count by any desired value.

5. **Reset the numbering where needed.** You can now reset this counter at any-time in your page, using `counter-reset` to skip numbers as necessary.

   `counter-reset: chapterNum 4;`

   TIP Because the `counter-reset` and `counter-increment` properties are not supported in Internet Explorer until version 8, it is best not to rely on these properties for critical information.

   TIP Again, be very careful when using counter-reset because it can hamper accessibility. In fact, the example I use here is not really very good from the standpoint of universal accessibility. Shame on me!

Specifying the Quote Style

Although most writers will use the keyboard to add quotation marks to text, HTML includes the quotation tag: **<q>**...**</q>**. This tag places browser-default quotation marks around the indicated text. With CSS, you can define the exact characters to be used as quotation marks using the **quotes** property (**Table 9.6**). Although English uses single ('...') or double ("...") quotation marks, this is by no means the norm for all languages.

To define the bullet style:

1. **Add the quotes property to your declaration block.** Type **quotes**, followed by a colon (**:**) and one of the values or value pairs listed in Table 9.6 (**Code 9.5**).

   quotes:

   You can add this to any specific element, or you can key it off of a specific language as explained in "Styling for a Particular language" (Chapter 4).

TABLE 9.6 Quotes Values

Value	Compatibility
'<string>'	IE8, FF1, S1, C1, O4 CSS2
none	IE8, FF1, S1, C1, O4, CSS2
inherit	IE8, FF1, S1, C1, O4, CSS2

Code 9.5 *ui-generatedcontent-properties.css*—In this example **Ⓐ**, the quotation marks are set to use « ...», which is standard for many European languages, including French.

```
/*** CSS3 VQS | Chapter 9 |
→ ui-generatedcontent-properties.css ***/

* {
  quotes: '«' '»' '‹' ' ›; }

.toc { margin: 0 auto; width: 90%;
→ text-align: center; font-size: .5em;}

a {
  cursor: help; }

h1 {
  cursor: url(../_images/cursor-02.png)
→ 20 20, crosshair; }

.top {
  counter-reset: chapterNum 0; }

.toc h2:before {
  content:  url('../_images/bullet-01.png')
  → 'Chapter ' counter(chapterNum) '. ';
  counter-increment: chapterNum; }
.toc h2:after {
  content: url('../_images/bullet-02.png'); }

#chapter4 .continued {
  counter-reset: chapterNum 4; }
```

2. Set the value of the open and closed quotation marks within standard single or double English quotation marks ("" or "").

   '« ' ' »'

3. After a space, you can add another grouping of quotation styles for the second level quotes (quotes that occur within quotes).

   '‹ ' ' ›';

4. For the quote style to work, you will actually need to use the quote tag (<q>) to indicate quotes in your HTML document.

   <q>...</q>

TIP This property can come in handy even for English. UK and US English use the same quotes, but reversed in order. The US uses double quotes for a main quote and single for second level quotes, whereas in the UK, this is reversed.

went in without knocking, and hurried upstairs, in great fear lest she should meet the real Mary Ann, and be turned out of the house before she had found the fan and gloves.

«How queer it seems,» Alice said to herself, « to be going messages for a rabbit! I suppose Dinah'll be sending me on messages next!» And she began fancying the sort of thing that would happen: «Miss Alice! Come here directly, and get ready for your walk!» «Coming in a minute, nurse! But I've got to see that the mouse doesn't get out. Only I don't think,» Alice went on, « that they'd let Dinah stop in the house if it began ordering people about like that!»

By this time she had found her way into a tidy little room with a table in the window, and on it (as she had hoped) a fan and two or three pairs of tiny white kid gloves: she took up the fan and a pair of the gloves, and was just going to leave the room, when her eye fell upon a little bottle that stood near the looking-glass. There

Ⓐ Code 9.5 applied to code 9.1: The quotes are now set using angle quotation marks, which is standard for many European languages. I've magnified the image so that you can get a better look.

Putting It All Together

1. **Create a transparent PNG image, and use that as the pointer over your page.** You can do that by simply setting the pointer property with the image in the **<body>** element.

2. **Dynamically add a graphic at the beginning and end of a block of text.** You can use the same image from step 1.

3. **Set up a counter list that starts at 7.** If you feel really advanced, have it increment by twos.

4. **Change your quote style on the page to French style quotes.** Make sure you use the quote tag around quotations.

Box Properties

In the physical world, atoms are the building blocks of all larger objects. Every type of atom, or element, has unique properties, but when bonded with other atoms, they create molecules—larger structures with properties different from the parts.

Likewise, HTML tags are the building blocks of your Web page. Each tag, or element, has its own capabilities. Tags can be combined to create a Web page that is greater than the sum of its parts. Whether a tag is by itself or nested deep within other tags, it can be treated as a discrete element on the screen and controlled by CSS.

Web designers use the concept of the *box* as a metaphor to describe the various things that you can do to an HTML element, whether it is a single tag or several nested tags. A box can have several properties—including margins, borders, padding, width, and height—that can be influenced by CSS.

This chapter shows you how to control the box and its properties.

In This Chapter

Code 10.1 The HTML5 code used for examples in this chapter. It imports the final CSS from Chapters 5, 6, 7, 8, and 9 as well as a new file we will be building in this chapter called *box-properties.css*. For this section, I've added a figure with a caption to the HTML code and an aside to the article **A**.

```
<!-- HTML5 -->
<!DOCTYPE html>
<html lang="en">
<head>
<meta charset="utf-8">
<title>Alice's Adventure's In Wonderland | Chapter 4</title>
<link href="../_css/font-properties.css" type="text/css" rel="stylesheet">
<link href="../_css/text-properties.css" type="text/css" rel="stylesheet">
<link href="../_css/color-background-properties.css" type="text/css" rel="stylesheet">
<link href="../_css/list-table-properties.css" type="text/css" rel="stylesheet">
<link href="../_css/ui-generatedcontent-properties.css" type="text/css" rel="stylesheet">
<link href="../_css/box-properties.css" type="text/css" rel="stylesheet">
<!--[if IE ]>
  <script src="script/HTML5forIE.js" type="text/javascript"></script>
<![endif]-->
</head>
<body id="chapter5" class="book aaiw section">
<header class="page">
<h1>Alice's Adventures In Wonderland</h1>
<p class="byline">by <span class="author">Lewis Carroll</span></p>
<nav class="global">
  <ul>
    <li><a href="" target="_self">Cover</a></li>
    <li><a href="" target="_self">About the Author</a></li>
    <li><a href="" target="_self">About the Books</a></li>
    <li><a href="" target="_self">About the Site</a></li>
  </ul>
</nav>
</header>
<article><!-- Article -->
<nav>
  <ol class="toc top">
    <h2><a href="" target="_self">Down the Rabbit-Hole</a></h2>
    <h2><a href="" target="_self">The Pool of Tears</a></h2>
    <h2><a href="" target="_self">A Caucus-Race and a Long Tale</a></h2>
    <h2><a href="" target="_self">The Rabbit Sends in a Little Bill</a></h2>
  </ol>
</nav>

<h2><strong>CHAPTER 5.</strong> Advice from a Caterpillar</h2>

<figure>
<img src="../_images/AAIW-illos/alice15a.png" alt="alice15a" width="300" height="397" />
<figcaption>
In a minute or two the Caterpillar took the hookah out of its mouth
and yawned once or twice, and shook itself.
</figcaption>
```

code continues on next page

```
</figure>

<p>
The Caterpillar and Alice looked at each other for some time in silence:
at last the Caterpillar took the hookah out of its mouth, and addressed
her in a languid, sleepy voice.
</p>
<nav>
<ol class="toc continued">
  <h2><a href="" target="_self">Pig and Pepper</a></h2>
  <h2><a href="" target="_self">A Mad Tea-Party</a></h2>
  <h2><a href="" target="_self">The Queen's Croquet-Ground</a></h2>
  <h2><a href="" target="_self">The Mock Turtle's Story</a></h2>
  <h2><a href="" target="_self">The Lobster Quadrille</a></h2>
  <h2><a href="" target="_self">Who Stole the Tarts?</a></h2>
</ol>
</nav>
<br>
</article>

<aside>
<h3>About Lewis Carroll</h3>
<p>Charles Lutwidge Dodgson,...</p>
<cite>Wikipedia</cite>
</aside>

<footer class="page">
<nav class="global">
  <ul>
    <li><a href="" target="_self">Cover</a></li>
    <li><a href="" target="_self">About the Author</a></li>
    <li><a href="" target="_self">About the Books</a></li>
    <li><a href="" target="_self">About the Site</a></li>
  </ul>
</nav>
</footer>
</body>
</html>
```

CHAPTER 1. DOWN THE RABBIT-HOLE
CHAPTER 2. THE POOL OF TEARS
CHAPTER 3. A CAUCUS-RACE AND A LONG TALE
CHAPTER 4. THE RABBIT SENDS IN A LITTLE BILL

CHAPTER 5. **ADVICE FROM A CATERPILLAR**

In a minute or two the Caterpillar took the hookah out of its mouth and yawned once or twice, and shook itself.

The Caterpillar and Alice looked at each other for some time in silence: at last the Caterpillar took the hookah out of its mouth, and addressed her in a languid, sleepy voice.

'Who are YOU?' said the Caterpillar.

This was not an encouraging opening for a conversation. Alice replied, rather shyly, 'I—I hardly know, sir, just at present—at least I know who I WAS when I got up this morning, but I think I must have been changed several times since then.'

'What do you mean by that?' said the Caterpillar sternly. 'Explain yourself!'

'I can't explain MYSELF, I'm afraid, sir' said Alice, 'because I'm not myself, you see.'

'I don't see,' said the Caterpillar.

'I'm afraid I can't put it more clearly,' Alice replied very politely, 'for I can't understand it myself to begin with; and being so many different sizes in a day is very confusing.'

'It isn't,' said the Caterpillar.

'Well, perhaps you haven't found it so yet,' said Alice; 'but when you have to turn into a chrysalis—you will some day, you know—and then after that into a butterfly, I should think you'll feel it a little queer, won't you?'

'Not a bit,' said the Caterpillar.

'Well, perhaps your feelings may be different,' said Alice; 'all I know is, it would feel very queer to ME.'

'You!' said the Caterpillar contemptuously. 'Who are YOU?'

Which brought them back again to the beginning of the conversation. Alice felt a little irritated at the Caterpillar's making such VERY short remarks, and she drew herself up and said, very gravely, 'I think, you ought to tell me who YOU are, first.'

'Why?' said the Caterpillar.

Here was another puzzling question; and as Alice could not think of any good reason, and as the Caterpillar seemed to be in a VERY unpleasant state of mind, she turned away.

'Come back!' the Caterpillar called after her. 'I've something important to say!'

This sounded promising, certainly: Alice turned and came back again.

'Keep your temper,' said the Caterpillar.

'Is that all?' said Alice, swallowing down her anger as well as she could.

'No,' said the Caterpillar.

Alice thought she might as well wait, as she had nothing else to do, and perhaps after all it might tell her something worth hearing. For some minutes it puffed away without speaking, but at last it unfolded its arms, took the hookah out of its mouth again, and said, 'So you think you're changed, do you?'

'I'm afraid I am, sir,' said Alice; 'I can't remember things as I used—and I don't keep the same size for ten minutes together!'

'Can't remember WHAT things?' said the Caterpillar.

'Well, I've tried to say "HOW DOTH THE LITTLE BUSY BEE," but it all came different!' Alice replied in a very melancholy voice.

'Repeat, "YOU ARE OLD, FATHER WILLIAM,"' said the Caterpillar.

Alice folded her hands, and began—

'You are old, Father William,' the young man said,
 'And your hair has become very white;
 And yet you incessantly stand on your head—
 Do you think, at your age, it is right?'

'In my youth,' Father William replied to his son,
 'I feared it might injure the brain;
 But, now that I'm perfectly sure I have none,
 Why, I do it again and again.'

'You are old,' said the youth, 'as I mentioned before,
 And have grown most uncommonly fat;
 Yet you turned a back-somersault in at the door—
 Pray, what is the reason of that?'

'In my youth,' said the sage, as he shook his grey locks,
 'I kept all my limbs very supple
 By the use of this ointment—one shilling the box—
 Allow me to sell you a couple?'

A Code 10.1: The Web page for this chapter before adding any of the box properties. It's a scrambled mess right now, but you'll be laying down the design grid, adding margins, and adding padding to give the design some breathing room.

Understanding an Element's Box

As you learned in Chapter 2, an element is a part of an HTML document that is set off by HTML container tags. The following is an HTML element:

`<p>Alice</p>`

This is another HTML element:

```
<article><p><em>Alice
→ <img src="alice11.gif">
→ </em></p></article>
```

The first example is an element made of a single tag. The second example is a collection of nested tags, and each of those nested tags is an individual element. Remember that nested tags are called the *children* of the tags within which they are nested, which are called the *parents* (see "Inheriting Properties from a Parent" in Chapter 4).

Parts of the box

All HTML elements have four sides: top, right, bottom, and left 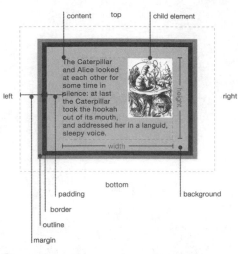. These four sides make up the element's box, to which CSS box properties can be applied. Each side of the box has the following properties:

- **Content**—At the center of the box, this is the substance of the page. The content includes all text (called copy), lists, forms, and images you use.

- **Child Elements**—Elements contained within the parent element that are set off by their own HTML tags. Child elements typically have their own box that can be controlled independently of the parent.

- **Width** and **Height**—The dimensions of the content area. If you leave width and height undefined, these dimensions are determined by the browser (see "Setting the Width and Height of an Element" in this chapter).

- **Padding**—The space between the border and the content of the element (see "Setting an Element's Padding" in this chapter). Background colors and images also fill this space. If left unset, the size of the padding is generally 0.

- **Background**—Space behind the content and padding of the element. This can be a solid color, one or more background images, or a background gradient. (See Chapter 7 for more information about backgrounds.)

- **Border**—A rule (line) that surrounds the element and can be set separately on any of the sides. The border is invisible unless you set its color, width, and style—solid, dotted, dashed, and so on. You can also set a background image. If left unset, the border size is generally 0.

A The box model in all its glory. Notice that the outline is part of the margin. If a margin is not present, the outline will appear underneath adjacent elements. Also, if two elements are stacked on each other, the margins between are not added, but collapse to the largest of the two.

- **Outline**—Similar to border, but does not occupy any space. It appears underneath the margin and any surrounding sibling elements in the background.

- **Margin**—The space between the border of the element and other elements in the window (see "Setting an Element's Margins" in this chapter). If left unset, the browser defines the margin.

It is important to remember that setting the content width and content height do not set the width and height of the space that the element occupies on the page. The overall width includes any padding and border on a side:

element width = content width + left padding + left border width + right padding + right border width

Height is a little different. If a content height is set, but overflow is not, then the height will stretch to accommodate the content plus any padding and borders:

element height = height needed to display content + top padding + top border width + bottom padding + bottom border width

If overflow is set to hidden, scroll, or auto, then height is computed:

element height = content height + top padding + top border width + bottom padding + bottom border width

Any content that does not fit within the element will either be hidden or scrollable.

TIP **Although the situation has been fixed with recent versions, Internet Explorer has a well-known and frustrating problem in the way it treats the box model. This problem exists in version 6 and partially persists in version 7. The problem is detailed in Chapter 13, "Fixing the Internet Explorer Box Model."**

Displaying an Element

In Chapter 1 you learned that all elements can be classified according to the way they're displayed—inline or block (see "Kinds of HTML Tags" in Chapter 2). By default, every tag has a display style that defines how it will fit with the surrounding tags.

You can use the `display` property to define whether an element includes line breaks above and below (block), is included with other elements without hard line breaks (inline), is treated as part of a list (list), or is displayed at all (none). Table 10.1 shows the values available for the `display` property.

To set an element's display type:

1. Start your declaration by typing the `display` property name in the CSS declaration block, followed by a colon (:), (Code 10.2).

   `display:`

2. Type one of the display types from Table 10.1.

   `block;`

   Choose a type depending on the desired result:

   ▸ `inline` flows the element horizontally and its siblings from left to right until the edge of the parent element is encountered, at which point a soft break is added wrapping the content to the next line. Hard line breaks immediately before and after the box are always suppressed Ⓐ.

   ▸ `block` places a hard line break above and below the box, flowing the elements vertically. Setting this automatically forces the width of the box to the width of the parent element's box Ⓑ.

TABLE 10.1 Display Values

Value	Compatibility
list-item	IE6, FF1, S1, C1, O3.5, CSS1
block	IE4, FF1, S1, C1, O3.5, CSS1
inline	IE4, FF1, S1, C1, O3.5, CSS1
inline-block	IE4, FF3, S1, C1, O3.5, CSS2.1
run-in	IE8, S1, C1, O3.5, CSS2
table	IE8, FF1, S1, C1, O4, CSS2
table-cell	IE8, FF1, S1, C1, O3.5, CSS2
table-footer-group	IE8, FF1, S1, C1, O3.5, CSS2
table-header-group	IE8, FF1, S1, C1, O3.5, CSS2
table-row	IE8, FF1, S1, C1, O3.5, CSS2
table-row-group	IE8, FF1, S1, C1, O3.5, CSS2
inline-table	IE8, FF3, S1, C1, O3.5, CSS2
none	IE4, FF1, S1, C1, O3.5, CSS1
inherit	IE4, FF1, S1, C1, O3.5, CSS1

element	element	element

Ⓐ Inline level elements flow horizontally.

element
element
element

Ⓑ Block level elements flow vertically.

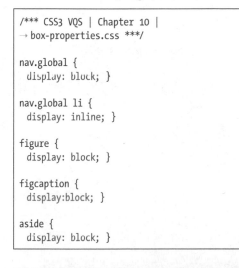

C Inline-block elements can stack vertically in the box, but the box is flowed inline.

Code 10.2 *ui-box-properties.css*—When applied to Code 10.1, adding the **display** property allows you to redefine how different elements flow within the document **D**. Defining the **figure**, **figcaption**, and **aside** as block elements will ensure that you can control their width, height, and float.

```
/*** CSS3 VQS | Chapter 10 |
→ box-properties.css ***/

nav.global {
  display: block; }

nav.global li {
  display: inline; }

figure {
  display: block; }

figcaption {
  display:block; }

aside {
  display: block; }
```

ALICE'S ADVENTURES IN WONDERLAND

*by*LEWIS CARROLL

COVER ABOUT THE AUTHOR ABOUT THE BOOKS ABOUT THE SITE

D **Code 10.2 applied to Code 10.1:** Notice that the previously block level list elements in the navigation (Cover, About the Author, About the Books, and so on) are now inline, flowing horizontally rather than vertically.

- ▸ **inline-block** defines this element as inline, but the content within it is treated as a block **C**.

- ▸ **run-in** is contextual, acting as a block element *unless* its next sibling is also a block element, in which case it will act as an inline element to its sibling. The sibling cannot be a run-in or have floating applied to it for this to work.

- ▸ **table**, or any one of the other **table** values shown in Table 10.1, allows you to turn any tag into part of a data table.

- ▸ **list-item** places a list-item marker on the first line of text, as well as a break above and below the text. This code allows the item to be used as part of a list even if you're not specifically using a list element. Using **list-item** to create lists out of non-list elements is discussed in Chapter 8.

- ▸ **inherit** uses the display value set or implicit for the element's parent.

- ▸ **none** causes this element not to display in CSS browsers. It will appear as though the content doesn't exist on the page.

TIP Although you can turn any element into a list item or table, *don't*. This is bad coding from a semantic and accessibility standpoint. Stick to HTML tags for creating lists and tables.

TIP The compact property was dropped in CSS2.1 but may make a comeback in CSS3. At present, only a placeholder exists in the CSS Work Groups Box Model documentation for CSS3.

TIP Any elements that are assigned display:none will be ignored by the browser. Be careful when using none, however. Although it is not an inherited attribute, none turns off the element display as well as the display of any children elements.

TIP display:none is useful for creating dynamic elements—such as drop-down menus—that show and hide as the user interacts with the page. However, keep in mind that this also hides the element from screen readers which can be bad for usability.

TIP Another great use for none is to use it to create a print-specific style sheet that hides elements not needed when the page is printed, such as navigation and form fields. Who needs navigation links, search forms, and low-resolution graphics in a printout?

TIP The display property should not be confused with the visibility property (see "Setting the Visibility of an Element" in Chapter 11). Unlike the visibility property, which leaves a space for the element, display:none completely removes the element from the page, although the browser still loads its content.

Code 10.3 *ui-box-properties.css*—When applied to Code 10.1, **width** and **height** are used to control element dimensions. Max **A** and min **B** values can be used to allow the design to fluidly grow or shrink to meet the user's needs.

```
/*** CSS3 VQS | Chapter 10 |
→ box-properties.css ***/

nav.global {
  display: block; }

nav.global li {
  display: inline; }

article {
  max-width: 980px;
  min-width: 660px; }

figure {
  display: block;
  width: 300px; }

figcaption {
  display:block; }

aside {
  display: block;
  width: 200px;
  height: 400px; }

footer {
  width: 100%; }
```

Setting the Width and Height of an Element

By default, the browser automatically sets the width and height of an element to 100 percent of the available width and whatever height is needed to display all the content. You can use CSS to override both the width and height of block elements. Generally, you will be setting the width of an element more often than the height unless you know the exact size of the content of a block or are willing to allow scrolling.

In addition to setting a specific width and height, you can specify a width and height range by setting a minimum and maximum width and height for an element. This can be unbelievably useful for creating flexible designs that will never stretch to unreasonable proportions on larger screens.

To define the width of an element:

1. Type the width property name in the CSS declaration block, followed by a colon (:) (Code 10.3).

   width:

continues on next page

A Code 10.3 applied to Code 10.1: Shows the example with the window open to 1280px wide.

B Code 10.3 applied to Code 10.1: Shows the example with the window open to 640px wide.

2. Type a value for the element's width.

80%;

Use one of the following values
(Table 10.2):

- ▶ A length value, generally in pixels
- ▶ A percentage, which sets the width proportional to the parent element's width
- ▶ **auto**, which uses the width calculated by the browser for the element— usually the maximum distance that the element can stretch to the right before hitting the edge of the window or the edge of a parent element

To define the height of an element:

1. Type the `height` property name in the CSS declaration block, followed by a colon (:).

   height:

2. Type a value for the element's height.

   500px;

   Use one of the following values
   (Table 10.2):

   - ▶ A length value
   - ▶ A percentage, which sets the height proportional to the parent element's height
   - ▶ **auto**, which uses a calculated height determined by the browser—whatever space the element needs to display all the content.

TABLE 10.2 Width and Height Values

Value	Compatibility
<length>	IE4, FF1, S1, C1, O3.5, CSS1
<percentage>	IE4, FF1, S1, C1, O3.5, CSS1
auto	IE4, FF1, S1, C1, O3.5, CSS1
inherit	IE4, FF1, S1, C1, O3.5, CSS1

TABLE 10.3 Max/Min-Width and Max/Min-Height Values

Value	Compatibility
<length>	IE7, FF1, S2, C1, O4, CSS2
<percentage>	IE7, FF1, S2, C1, O4, CSS2
inherit	IE7, FF1, S2, C1, O4, CSS2
none*	IE7, FF1, S2, C1, O4, CSS2

*height only

To set the maximum and minimum width:

1. Type the `min-width` and/or `max-width` property name, a colon (:), and an appropriate value from Table 10.3.

   `max-width: 980px; min-width:`
   `→ 660px;`

   The element will never grow wider or narrower than these values regardless of the browser window width.

2. Type the `min-height` and/or `min-height` property name, a colon (:), and an appropriate value from Table 10.3.

   `max-height: 300px; min-height:`
   `→ 100px;`

   The max/min-height properties work very much the same as max/min-width, but depend on the content displayed rather than the dimensions of the browser window.

TIP You don't have to include both the minimum and maximum values.

TIP If you set the width of the body tag to less than the max-width of an element, the max-width property is ignored because the body never stretches wide enough.

TIP Generally, the max-height will act like the height attribute and the min-height is ignored because, unlike the max/min width, the element will not resize with the browser window.

TIP Firefox includes several –moz CSS extensions that will more effectively fit boxes to content, but these are not yet included in the CSS3 standard.

TIP When you have too much content to display in the defined area, use the overflow property (see "Controlling Overflowing Content" in this chapter) to allow the viewer to scroll the additional material.

TIP You can resize an image (GIF, PNG, or JPEG) using the width and height properties, and override the intrinsic width and height. Doing this will more than likely create a severely distorted image, but that can sometimes be a pretty neat effect.

TIP Use width and height to keep form fields and buttons at a consistent size.

TIP If you are setting the height of an element and forcing a scrollbar, be careful not to let that element get too close to the browser window's scrollbar because it can lead to confusion and an unpleasant experience for viewers.

Controlling Overflowing Content

When an element is clipped or when the parent element's width and height are less than the area needed to display everything, some content is not displayed . The **overflow** property allows you to specify how this cropped content is treated.

NEW IN CSS3 ★: Overflow for the width or height can be controlled independently using **overflow-x** and/or **overflow-y**.

To define the overflow control:

1. Type the **overflow**, **overflow-x**, or **overflow-y** property name, followed by a colon (:) (Code 10.4).

   overflow:

A The overflow is any area (horizontally or vertically) that cannot be displayed within the given area for an element.

Code 10.4 *ui-box-properties.css*—When applied to Code 10.1, the **overflow** property automatically adds a scrollbar, but only if needed **B**. This ensures that the content will always be accessible.

```
/*** CSS3 VQS | Chapter 10 |
→ box-properties.css ***/

nav.global {
  display: block; }

nav.global li {
  display: inline; }

article {
  max-width: 980px;
  min-width: 660px; }

figure {
  display: block;
  width: 300px; }

figcaption {
  display:block; }

aside {
  display: block;
  width: 200px;
  height: 400px;
  overflow: auto; }

footer {
  width: 100%; }
```

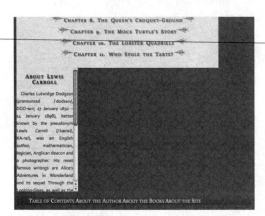

B **Code 10.4 applied to Code 10.1:** The aside area's height is restricted to 400px, but more content exists than can fit in that area, so a vertical scrollbar is added automatically.

TABLE 10.4 Overflow Values

Value	Compatibility
visible	IE4, FF1, S1, C1, O4, CSS1
hidden	IE4, FF1, S1, C1, O4, CSS1
scroll	IE4, FF1, S1, C1, O4, CSS1
auto	IE4, FF1, S1, C1, O4, CSS1

TABLE 10.5 Overflow-x and Overflow-y Values

Value	Compatibility
visible	IE5, FF1.5, S3, C2, O9.5, CSS3
hidden	IE5, FF1.5, S3, C2, O9.5, CSS3
scroll	IE5, FF1.5, S3, C2, O9.5, CSS3
auto	IE5, FF1.5, S3, C2, O9.5, CSS3

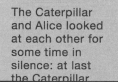

C `Visible` will override the height of the element, forcing it to display all content.

D `Hidden` will crop the element but provide no way to access the rest of the element's content.

2. Add a keyword to tell the browser how to treat overflow from the clip.

`auto;`

Use one of the following keywords (**Table 10.4** and **Table 10.5**):

▸ `visible` forces the cropped part of the element to be displayed, essentially instructing the browser to ignore the cropping, pushing the content to flow outside of the box **C**.

▸ `hidden` hides the overflow and prevents the scrollbars from appearing **D**.

continues on next page

- **scroll** sets scrollbars around the visible area to allow the visitor to scroll through the element's content. When you set this value, space will be reserved for the scrollbars, even if they are not needed 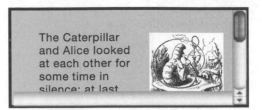.

- **auto** allows the browser to decide whether scrollbars need to be displayed .

TIP Generally, `auto` is preferred for overflow because it will show the scrollbars only as needed and hide the scrollbar chrome when there is nothing to scroll.

TIP The `overflow` property is also used to define how clipping overflow is treated.

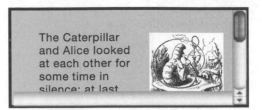

E **Scroll** places both horizontal and vertical scrollbars to access additional content in the element. However, placeholder scrollbars are added even if they're not needed.

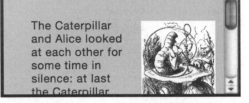

F **Auto** is generally the best option because it displays scrollbars only as needed.

Coming Soon: Text Overflow

Although being able to set box overflow is useful, often it is the text that is overflowing and needs a clear truncation. The most common way to do this is by using the three dots known as an ellipsis (...). CSS3 will soon include new properties —**text-overflow**, **text-overflow-mode**, and **text-overflow-ellipses**—that will allow you to clip or add ellipses to text that is too long to fit the space.

Code 10.5 *ui-box-properties.css*—When applied to Code 10.1, the **float** properties will cause the text to wrap around the figure and the article and aside elements to float side by side *if* the screen is wide enough to accommodate them Ⓐ.

```
/*** CSS3 VQS | Chapter 10 |
⇢ box-properties.css ***/

nav.global {
  display: block; }

nav.global li {
  display: inline; }

article {
  max-width: 980px;
  min-width: 660px;
  float: left; }

figure {
  display: block;
  width: 300px;
  float: left; }

figcaption {
  display:block; }

aside {
  display: block;
  width: 200px;
  height: 400px;
  overflow: auto;
  float: right; }

footer {
  width: 100%;
  clear: both; }
```

Floating Elements in the Window

In addition to precisely positioning elements within the document, CSS also allows you to set how an element interacts with other elements by *floating* it.

Using the CSS **float** property, you flow text around content or float block elements next to each other to create columns.

To float an element:

1. Start your definition by typing the **float** property name, followed by a colon (:) (Code 10.5).

   float:

continues on next page

Ⓐ **Code 10.5 applied to Code 10.1:** The text of the chapter is not wrapping around the figure. Notice that the aside, "About Lewis Carroll," is now a column to the right of the article. Unfortunately, the footer is also there; but don't worry, you can fix that.

2. Type a keyword to tell the browser on which side of the screen the element should float.

`right;`

Choose one of the following keywords (**Table 10.6**):

▸ **right** aligns this element to the right of other elements, causing subsequent elements to wrap horizontally to the left of this element.

▸ **left** aligns this element to the left of other elements, causing subsequent elements to wrap horizontally to the right of this element.

▸ **none** overrides floating for this element.

TABLE 10.6 Float Values

Value	Compatibility
left	IE4, FF1, S1, O3.5, CSS1
right	IE4, FF1, S1, O3.5, CSS1
none	IE4, FF1, S1, O3.5, CSS1

TABLE 10.7 Clear Values

Value	Compatibility
left	IE4, FF1, S1, O3.5, CSS1
right	IE4, FF1, S1, O3.5, CSS1
both	IE4, FF1, S1, O3.5, CSS1
none	IE4, FF1, S1, O3.5, CSS1

TIP Floating elements within other elements can often have odd consequences if both the child and parent are block elements. The child tends to ignore the height of the parent, which can have undesirable consequences. The child element will appear to begin in the parent element but will then extend beyond the bottom of the parent element. The fix for this is discussed in Chapter 13 "Fixing the Float."

TIP In Chapter 13, you'll learn how to use the `float` property to set up separate columns to replace a traditional table-based layout.

Clearing a floated element

Sometimes, you may find it necessary to override the **float** property to prevent elements that appear after a floating element from wrapping. Similar to the **clear** attribute of the HTML break tag, the CSS **clear** property allows you to specify whether you want to deny floating around the left, right, or both sides of an element (**Table 10.7**).

Code 10.6 *ui-box-properties.css*—When applied to Code 10.1, the footer is told *not* to float 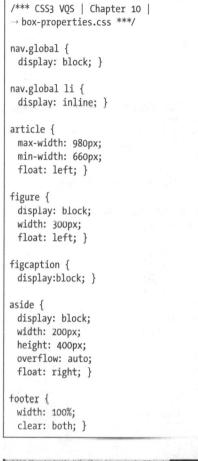 **B**.

```
/*** CSS3 VQS | Chapter 10 |
→ box-properties.css ***/

nav.global {
  display: block; }

nav.global li {
  display: inline; }

article {
  max-width: 980px;
  min-width: 660px;
  float: left; }

figure {
  display: block;
  width: 300px;
  float: left; }

figcaption {
  display:block; }

aside {
  display: block;
  width: 200px;
  height: 400px;
  overflow: auto;
  float: right; }

footer {
  width: 100%;
  clear: both; }
```

B Code 10.6 applied to Code 10.1: With the float cleared for the footer, it is now back at the bottom of the page.

To prevent an element from floating:

1. Type the `clear` property name in the CSS rule, followed by a colon (:) to start your declaration (Code 10.6).

   `clear:`

2. Type the keyword for the side that you want to prevent floating.

   `right;`

   Choose one of the following keywords:

   ▸ **left** to prevent wrapping on the left side of the element

   ▸ **right** to prevent wrapping on the right side of the element

   ▸ **both** to prevent wrapping on both sides of the element

   ▸ **none** to override a previously set **clear** property

TIP It's usually a good idea to set headers and titles to `clear:both`, so that they don't wrap around other objects.

Setting an Element's Margins

The `margin` (Table 10.8) of an element allows you to set the space between that element and other elements in the window by specifying one to four values that correspond to all four sides together, the top/bottom and left/right sides as pairs, or all four sides independently.

To define the margins of an element:

1. Start your declaration by typing the `margin` shortcut property name in the declaration block, followed by a colon (:) (Code 10.7).

   `margin:`

Setting Negative Margins

Although you can use negative margins (for example, `margin:-5em;`) to create interesting effects for overlapping pieces of text, this method is frowned upon because various browsers present different results.

Overlapping text is better achieved using CSS positioning (see Chapter 11).

Be careful when setting negative margins around a hypertext link. If one element has margins that cause it to cover the link, the link will not work as expected.

TABLE 10.8 Margin Values

Value	Compatibility
<length>	IE3, FF1, S1, C1, O3.5, CSS1
<percentage>	IE3, FF1, S1, C1, O3.5, CSS1
auto	IE6, FF1, S1, C1, O3.5, CSS1

Code 10.7 *ui-box-properties.css*—When applied to Code 10.1, `margin` is set to 0 in the body, and margins are added to help space out other elements in the screen Ⓐ.

```
/*** CSS3 VQS | Chapter 10 |
→ box-properties.css ***/

body, header.page, footer.page  {
  margin: 0; }

nav.global {
  display: block;
  margin-left: 10px; }

nav.global li {
  display: inline;
  margin-right: 10px; }

article {
  max-width: 980px;
  min-width: 660px;
  float: left;
  margin: 0 10px; }

figure {
  display: block;
  width: 300px;
  float: left;
  margin: 0 10px 10px 0; }

figcaption {
  display:block; }

aside {
  display: block;
  width: 200px;
  height: 400px;
  overflow: auto;
```

code continues on next page

```
    float: right;
    margin: 0 10px; }

footer {
    width: 100%;
    clear: both; }

h1 {
    margin: 0 20px 10px 10%; }

.byline {

    margin: 0 10% 10px 20%; }
```

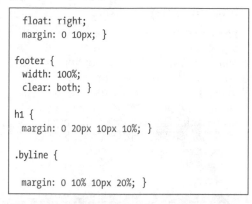

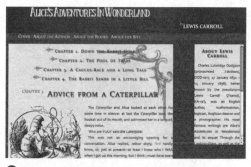

A **Code 10.7 applied to Code 10.1:** The header now fits snugly at the top of the window and stretches the entire width, and the figure has a little more room around it.

2. **Type a value for the margin.**

   `0 10px;`

   Use one of the following values:

   ▸ A length value

   ▸ A percentage, which creates a margin proportional to the parent element's width

   ▸ **auto**, which returns control of the margins to the browser's discretion

   You can enter one to four values, separated by spaces, to define the margins as follows:

   ▸ One value sets the margin for all four sides equally.

   ▸ Two values set the top/bottom margins and left/right margins.

   ▸ Three values set the top margin, the left/right margins (the same), and the bottom margin.

   ▸ Four values set each margin clockwise, starting from top: top, right, bottom, and left.

3. **You can also set the margin for just one side of the box independently without setting the other three margins.**

   `margin-right: 10px;`

   This is useful when used with an inline style to override margins set elsewhere. To do this, specify the margin side you want to define (**margin-top**, **margin-bottom**, **margin-left**, or **margin-right**) and enter a legitimate margin value from Table 10.8.

TIP You can also set margins for the <body> tag; in which case the margins define the distance that elements nested in the body should appear from the top and left sides of the browser window.

TIP The best way to center an element within its parent element is to set the margins on the left and right to auto. This is how most Web pages with the content centered in the browser window are created.

TIP When setting proportional margins, be aware that you might get very different results depending on the size of the user's window. What looks good at a resolution of 800 x 600 might be a mess at larger screen sizes.

TIP The browser has a default margin that it adds to the body of your page so the content doesn't immediately begin at the edge of the screen. However, the default is not the same on all browsers, which can be a problem when you position elements on the page (see Chapter 11). It's a good idea to set the margins in the body tag so that they remain consistent using a CSS reset, as explained in Chapter 13.

Margin Collapse

When two elements stacked vertically on top of each other determine the vertical margin between them, rather than adding the bottom and top margin together, the larger margin will be used, with the smaller margin collapsing to 0. This allows you to keep consistent margins at the top and bottom of a collection of stacked elements.

TABLE 10.9 Outline Values

Value	Compatibility
<border-width>	IE8, FF1.5, S1.2, O7, CSS2
<border-style>	IE8, FF1.5, S1.2, O7, CSS2
<border-color>	IE8, FF1.5, S1.2, O7, CSS2

Code 10.8 *ui-box-properties.css*—When applied to Code 10.1, the **outline** style can be used to highlight links being hovered over without disturbing the surrounding elements  .

```
/*** CSS3 VQS | Chapter 10 |
→ box-properties.css ***/

body, header.page, footer.page  {
  margin: 0; }

nav.global {
  display: block;
  margin-left: 10px; }

nav.global li {
  display: inline;
  margin-right: 10px; }

nav.global li a:hover {
  outline: rgba(135,127,107,.65) 10px double; }

article {
  max-width: 980px;
  min-width: 660px;
  float: left;
  margin: 0 10px; }

figure {
  display: block;
  width: 300px;
  float: left;
  margin: 0 10px 10px 0; }

figcaption {
  display:block; }

aside {
  display: block;
```

code continues on next page

Setting an Element's Outline

The outline (Table 10.9) surrounds the border and even uses the same values as the border; unlike the border, it does not increase the apparent dimensions (width or height) of the box and does not actually occupy any space on the screen. Instead, it appears under any margin and out into the page under surrounding content.

An outline can be very useful for link-rollovers, allowing you to highlight them without displacing the surrounding content.

To set a box's outline:

1. The **outline** property looks identical to the **border** property, although it behaves differently. First enter width, then style, and then color separated by spaces (Code 10.8).

   ```
   outline: rgba(135,127,107,.65)
   → 10px double;
   ```

   continues on next page

A Code 10.8 applied to Code 10.1: The link "Cover" in the global navigation is highlighted using the outline.

2. Alternatively, you can define each outline value, which is useful when you need to override one element value without changing the others.

`outline-color:`
`→ rgba(135,127,107,.65);`

`outline-width: 10px;`

`outline-style: double;`

TIP Unlike border, outline cannot be set independently for the sides.

TIP I tend to use `outline` only when I am debugging element positioning on my page, and I want to see exactly how much space each block is taking up and where they extend.

TIP Another good use of `outline` is using attribute selectors (Chapter 4) to highlight particular elements without disturbing their positioning.

Code 10.8 *continued*

```
  width: 200px;
  height: 400px;
  overflow: auto;
  float: right;
  margin: 0 10px; }

footer {
  width: 100%;
  clear: both; }

h1 {
  margin: 0 20px 10px 10%; }

.byline {

  margin: 0 10% 10px 20%; }
```

Outline Offset ★

Add the **outline-offset** property to add some distance between the outline and the border or content edge (Table 10.10). Think of this as padding for the outline:

outline-offset: 2px;

TABLE 10.10 Outline-Offset Values

Value	Compatibility
<length>	FF1.5, S1.2, C1, O7, CSS3
inherit	FF1.5, S1.2, C1, O7, CSS3

TABLE 10.11 Border Values

Value	Compatibility
<border-width>	IE4, FF1, S1, O3.5, CSS1
<border-style>	IE4, FF1, S1, O3.5, CSS1
<border-color>	IE4, FF1, S1, O3.5, CSS1

TABLE 10.12 Border-Width Values

Value	Compatibility
<length>	IE4, FF1, S1, O3.5, CSS1
thin	IE4, FF1, S1, O3.5, CSS1
medium	IE4, FF1, S1, O3.5, CSS1
thick	IE4, FF1, S1, O3.5, CSS1
inherit	IE4, FF1, S1, O3.5, CSS1

Code 10.9 *ui-box-properties.css*—When applied to Code 10.1, the border property sets a line— sometimes called a *rule* by designers—on any side of an element's box with a specific style, color, and thickness ⒶＡ.

```
/*** CSS3 VQS | Chapter 10 |
→ box-properties.css ***/

body, header.page, footer.page  {
  margin: 0; }

nav.global {
  display: block; }

nav.global li {
  display: inline;
  margin-right: 10px; }

nav.global li a:hover {
  outline: rgba(135,127,107,.65) 10px double; }

article {
  max-width: 980px;
```

code continues on next page

Setting an Element's Border

The **border** property allows you to set a rule (line) around all four sides of your box in any color and thickness using a variety of line styles (**Table 10.11**). Also, using additional **border** properties, you can independently set the borders on any of the four sides, giving you amazing design versatility.

To set the border:

1. To set the border on all four sides, type the **border** property name in the CSS declaration block, followed by a colon (:) (Code 10.9).

   border:

2. Type a **border-width** value, followed by a space.

   6px

   This value can be one of the following (**Table 10.11**):

   ▸ A length value; a value of **0** prevents the border from appearing, even if the style and color are set.

   ▸ A relative-size keyword, such as **thin**, **medium**, or **thick** (Table 10.12).

   ▸ **inherit** will cause the element to use the same border styles as its parent element.

continues on next page

3. Type the name of the style you want to assign to your border.

double

Table 10.13 shows a complete list of available border styles.

Alternatively, you can type **none**, which prevents the border from appearing.

4. Type a color value, which is the color you want the border to be as defined in Table 10.14.

rgb(142, 137, 129);

This can be the name of the color or an RGB value.

5. You aren't stuck using the same border on all four sides. You can set each side (**border-top, border-bottom, border-left**, and/or **border-right**).

border-top: 2px solid
→rgb(142, 137, 129);

If those options aren't enough, see the sidebar "Other Ways to Set a Border."

TIP You do not have to include all the individual border attributes in your definition list, but if you don't, the default value will be used.

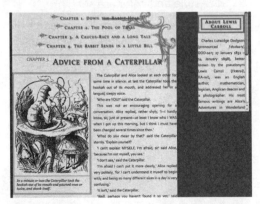

A Code 10.9 applied to Code 10.1: The figure is now surrounded by a double-lined border with the caption adding a border at the top to set it off from the image above. The chapter title also receives a border, as does the aside header.

Code 10.9 *continued*

```
 min-width: 660px;
 float: left;
 margin: 0 10px; }

figure {
 display: block;
 width: 300px;
 float: left;
 margin: 0 10px 10px 0;
 border: 6px double rgb(142, 137, 129); }

figcaption {
 display:block;
 padding: 10px;
 border-top: 2px solid rgb(142, 137, 129); }

aside {
 display: block;
 width: 200px;
 height: 400px;
 overflow: auto;
 float: right;
 margin: 0 10px; }

footer {
 width: 100%;
 clear: both; }

h1 {
 margin: 0 20px 10px 10%; }

article h2 {
 border-top: 2px solid rgb(142, 137, 129); }

article nav h2 {
 border-top: none; }

aside h3 {
 border: 1em double rgb(142, 137, 129); }

.byline {

 margin: 0 10% 10px 20%; }
```

TABLE 10.13 Border-Style Values

Value	Appearance	Compatibility
dotted	• • • • • • • • •	IE5.5, FF1, S1, C1, O3.5, CSS1
dashed	▬ ▬ ▬ ▬ ▬ ▬ ▬	IE5.5, FF1, S1, C1, O3.5, CSS1
solid	▬▬▬▬▬▬	IE4, FF1, S1, C1, O3.5, CSS1
double	════════	IE4, FF1, S1, C1, O3.5, CSS1
groove	▬▬▬▬▬▬	IE4, FF1, S1, C1, O3.5, CSS1
ridge	▬▬▬▬▬▬	IE4, FF1, S1, C1, O3.5, CSS1
inset	▬▬▬▬▬▬	IE4, FF1, S1, C1, O3.5, CSS1
outset	▬▬▬▬▬▬	IE4, FF1, S1, C1, O3.5, CSS1
none		IE4, FF1, S1, C1, O3.5, CSS1
inherit		IE4, FF1, S1, C1, O3.5, CSS1

TABLE 10.14 Border-Color Values

Value	Compatibility
<color>	IE4, FF1, S1, O3.5, CSS1
transparent	IE4, FF1, S1, O3.5, CSS1
inherit	IE4, FF1, S1, O3.5, CSS1

Other Ways to Set a Border

CSS gives you the freedom to define aspects of the border's appearance one side at a time, as follows:

`border-style: solid dashed → double ridge;`

`border-width: 1px 2px 4px 8px ;`

`border-color: red green blue → purple;`

The values for these are shown in Tables 10.4 through 10.6.

As with margins, you can include one to four values for each of these properties to set each border side independently, as follows:

- One value sets the property for all four sides.

- Two values set the property for the top/bottom and left/right sides.

- Three values set the top property, the left/right properties (the same), and the bottom property.

- Four values set the property for each side in this order: top, right, bottom, and left.

This method is useful for overriding the values set by the single **border** property.

Your final option for setting a border on a single side (as if you really needed another option!) is to set the individual properties for a specific side (top, bottom, left, right):

`border-top-width: 3px;`

`border-top-style: solid;`

`border-top-color: #f00;`

NEW IN CSS3: Rounding Border Corners ★

Rounded corners can help soften an otherwise sharp design, but they have been difficult to achieve using images. CSS3 includes a simple method for rounding off one or all of the corners of an element's box: **border-radius**.

Both Mozilla and Webkit have implemented their own versions of **border-radius** in advance of the final W3C pronouncement, and you need to take these browser extensions into account for the widest interoperability (**Table 10.15**).

To set rounded corners:

1. Add the Webkit, Mozilla, and standard CSS3 border-radius properties (Code 10.10).

   `-webkit-border-radius:`

   `-moz-border-radius:`

   `border-radius:`

   Although the order doesn't matter, it's generally preferred to have the CSS3 version last because it's the version that *should* be used.

TABLE 10.15 Border-Radius Values

Value	Compatibility
<length>	FF1, S3, C1 O10.5, CSS3
<percentage>	FF1, O10.5, CSS3

Code 10.10 *ui-box-properties.css*—When applied to Code 10.1, the **border-radius** property is used to round the corners of different elements **A**.

```
/*** CSS3 VQS | Chapter 10 |
→ box-properties.css ***/

body, header.page, footer.page  {
  margin: 0; }

nav.global {
  display: block; }

nav.global li {
  display: inline;
  margin-right: 10px; }

article {
  max-width: 980px;
  min-width: 660px;
  float: left;
  margin: 0 10px;
  -webkit-border-top-right-radius: 20px;
  -moz-border-radius-topright: 20px;
  border-top-right-radius: 20px; }

figure {
  display: block;
  width: 300px;
  float: left;
  margin: 0 10px 10px 0;
  border: 6px double rgb(142, 137, 129);
  -webkit-border-radius: 5px;
  -moz-border-radius: 5px;
  border-radius: 5px; }

figcaption {
  display:block;
  padding: 10px;
```

code continues on next page

```
  border-top: 2px solid rgb(142, 137, 129); }

aside {
  display: block;
  width: 200px;
  height: 400px;
  overflow: auto;
  float: right;
  margin: 0 10px;
  -webkit-border-top-left-radius: 20px;
  -webkit-border-bottom-left-radius: 20px;
  -moz-border-radius: 20px 0 0 20px;
  border-radius: 20px 0 0 20px; }

footer {
  width: 100%;
  clear: both; }

h1 {
  margin: 0 20px 10px 10%; }

aside h3 {
  border: 1em double rgb(142, 137, 129); }

article nav h2 {
  border-top: none; }

.byline {

  margin: 0 10% 10px 20%; }
```

A Code 10.10 applied to Code 10.1: The main article and aside have been rounded off, giving them the look of a notebook. The figure area border also has slightly rounded corners but only on the outer line of the double line border.

2. Type a `border-radius` value, followed by a semicolon, using the same value for all three instances.

   5px;

   This value can be one of the following depending on browser compatibility (Table 10.15):

   ▸ A length value, which sets the radius of an imaginary circle at the corner, which is used to round it off. The larger the value, the rounder the edge.

   ▸ A percentage (**0%** to **50%**), which uses the size of the element to set the corner radius. Higher values produce rounder corners, with **50%** joining corners into a semicircle. Percentage is *not* supported in Webkit.

continues on next page

Setting Elliptical Corners

One final option is to create elliptical rather than circular corners by defining two radius points. For Webkit, the values are separated by a space, whereas Mozilla and CSS3 use a slash (/):

```
-webkit-border-radius: 20px 10px;
-moz-border-radius: 20px/10px;
border-radius: 20px/10px;
```

I find, however, that the anti-aliasing distortion becomes even more exaggerated in some browsers when an elliptical corner is used, so I avoid these for now.

3. Each corner's border radius can be set independently without specifying the other corner radii.

```
-webkit-border-top-right-radius:
→20px;
```

```
-moz-border-radius-topright:
→20px;
```

```
border-top-right-radius: 20px;
```

Mozilla has a slightly different syntax from Webkit and W3C (used by Opera), but the equivalents are shown in **Table 10.16**.

4. For -moz and standard CSS3 instances (but *not* -webkit), you can include up to four values.

```
-webkit-border-top-left-radius:
→20px;
```

```
-webkit-border-bottom-left-
→radius: 20px;
```

```
-moz-border-radius: 20px
→0 0 20px;
```

```
border-radius: 20px 0 0 20px;
```

Separate each value by a space as a shortcut for setting the border radius:

- ▸ One value sets all four-corner radii the same.

- ▸ Two values set the radius for the top-left/bottom-right and bottom-left/top-right corners.

- ▸ Three values set the corner radius for the top left, bottom left/top right (the same), and the bottom right corners.

- ▸ Four values set the radius for each corner in this order: top left, top right, bottom right, and bottom left.

With Webkit you must set corners separately because it treats a second value as the second point in the radius to create elliptical (rather than circular) corners.

TABLE 10.16 Border-Radius Equivalents

CSS3	Mozilla	Webkit
border-radius	-moz-border-radius	-webkit-border-radius
border-top-right-radius	-moz-border-radius-topright	-webkit-border-top-right-radius
border-bottom-right-radius	-moz-border-radius-bottomright	-webkit-border-bottom-right-radius
border-bottom-left-radius	-moz-border-radius-bottomleft	-webkit-border-bottom-left-radius
border-top-left-radius	-moz-border-radius-topleft	-webkit-border-top-left-radius

TIP Although `border-radius` does anti-alias the curves to make them appear smooth, the results can be hit or miss. I recommend keeping the contrast between your lines and background low to improve the curve appearance.

TIP Curved borders will *not* clip the content in the box. So, an image that might normally be in the corner of the box will still be there, sticking out into the curve.

TABLE 10.17 Border-Image Values

Value	Compatibility
<url>	FF3.5, S3, C2, O10.5, CSS3
<offsetnumber>	FF3.5, S3, C2, O10.5, CSS3
round	FF3.5, S3, C2, O10.5, CSS3
repeat	FF3.5, S3, C2, O10.5, CSS3
stretch	FF3.5, S3, C2, O10.5, CSS3

Ⓐ *border-02.png*—The border image is used to fill in the corners and sides of the border. I've constructed this one using a grid with each square 27px on a side.

NEW IN CSS3: Setting a Border Image ★

A new feature in CSS3 is the ability to use a rectangular image that can be applied to the box's border, overriding the line style. Mozilla and Webkit have implemented almost identical systems, and CSS3 has (thankfully) followed their lead. Although some differences exist, setting a basic image border background is identical among the three systems.

The background image system (The **border-image** takes a rectangular image and slices it into nine parts. The eight parts around the edges are used as the side and corner images, and the center is hidden to allow the content within the element to show through. The corners are applied to the corners of the element box with a size based on the offset you set. Then the middle of the sides of the image are *stretched* or *tiled* to fill the width and height.

To set the border background image:

1. Create your background image and save it, preferably as a transparent PNG, although any format will work For this example **Ⓐ**, I've divided the image into a grid of 27px squares, fitting the corners and edges of my background into each of these. This will make the math easier.

continues on next page

2. Add the Webkit, Mozilla, and standard CSS3 border-image properties.

`-webkit-border-image:`

`-moz-border-image:`

`border-image:`

Although the order doesn't matter, it's generally preferred to have the CSS3 version last because it's the version that *should* be used (**Code 10.11**).

3. Add the URL that indicates the path to the image file you created in step 1.

`url(../_images/border-02.png)`

4. You can include up to four values that specify the border image offset—basically how far into the image the background should extend (how wide the border slices should be)—separated by a space.

27

If you set up your image as a grid, this will be the size of a square in your grid:

▸ One value sets all four sides.

▸ Two values set the offset for the top/ bottom and left/right, respectively.

▸ Three values set the offset for the top, left/right, and bottom, respectively.

▸ Four values set the offset for each side in this order: top, right, bottom, and left.

Code 10.11 *ui-box-properties.css*—When applied to Code 10.1, the header in the aside column uses the file border-02.png as its source for adding a border **B**.

```
/*** CSS3 VQS | Chapter 10 |
→ box-properties.css ***/

body, header.page, footer.page  {
  margin: 0; }

nav.global {
  display: block; }

nav.global li {
  display: inline;
  margin-right: 10px; }

article {
  max-width: 980px;
  min-width: 660px;
  float: left;
  margin: 0 10px;
  -webkit-border-top-right-radius: 20px;
  -moz-border-radius-topright: 20px;
  border-top-right-radius: 20px; }

figure {
  display: block;
  width: 300px;
  float: left;
  margin: 0 10px 10px 0;
  border: 6px double rgb(142, 137, 129);
  -webkit-border-radius: 5px;
  -moz-border-radius: 5px;
  border-radius: 5px; }

figcaption {
  display:block;
  padding: 10px;
  border-top: 2px solid rgb(142, 137, 129); }

aside {
  display: block;
  width: 200px;
  height: 400px;
  overflow: auto;
```

Code 10.11 *continued*

```
   float: right;
   margin: 0 10px;
   -webkit-border-top-left-radius: 20px;
   -webkit-border-bottom-left-radius: 20px;
   -moz-border-radius: 20px 0 0 20px;
   border-radius: 20px 0 0 20px; }

footer {
   width: 100%;
   clear: both; }

h1 {
   margin: 0 20px 10px 10%; }

aside h3 {
   border: 1em double rgb(142, 137, 129);
   -webkit-border-image: url(../_images/
→ border-02.png) 27 round;
   -moz-border-image: url(../_images/border-02
→ .png) 27 round;
   border-image: url(../_images/border-02.png)
→ 27 round; }

article nav h2 {
   border-top: none; }

.byline {

   margin: 0 10% 10px 20%; }
```

5. Set one or two values to dictate how the images in the middle of a side should be tiled or stretched.

round;

Choose from the following values:

▸ **stretch** (default value) scales images to fit the width or height of the box.

▸ **repeat** tiles the images to the width and height of the element.

▸ **round** is similar to **repeat.** It tiles the images but scales them so they fit exactly within the width or height.

TIP More properties and values for setting the border image are in the CSS2 specification, but they are not yet supported in most browsers.

TIP Opera 10.5 supports the CSS3 version of the **border** image property.

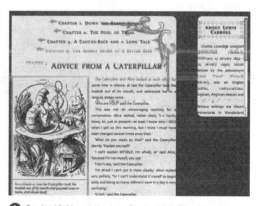

B Code 10.11 applied to Code 10.1: The border tiles on the sides as needed to surround the element.

Setting an Element's Padding

At first glance, **padding** (Table 10.18) seems to have an effect identical to **margins**: It adds space around the element's content. The difference is that **padding** sets the space between the border of the element and its content rather than between the element and the other elements in the window. Padding is useful when you're using borders and background colors and don't want the content butting right up to the edges.

To set padding:

1. Start your declaration by typing the **padding** property name, followed by a colon (:) (Code 10.12).

   padding:

2. Type a value for the element's padding.

   10px;

   Use one of the following values:

   ▸ Length values, which create padding of the exact size you specify

   ▸ A percentage, which creates padding proportional to the parent element's width

   ▸ **inherit** to use the parent's **padding** value

TABLE 10.18 Padding Values

Value	Compatibility
<length>	IE4, FF1, S1, C1, O3.5, CSS1
<percentage>	IE4, FF1, S1, C1, O3.5, CSS1
inherit	IE8, FF1, S1, C1, O7, CSS2

Code 10.12 *ui-box-properties.css*—When applied to Code 10.1, the padding property allows you to add space between the border of an element and its content **Ⓐ**.

```
/*** CSS3 VQS | Chapter 10 |
→ box-properties.css ***/

body, header.page, footer.page {
  margin: 0;
  padding: 0; }

nav.global {
  display: block; }

nav.global li {
  display: inline;
  margin-right: 10px;
  padding-right: 10px; }

article {
  max-width: 980px;
  min-width: 660px;
  float: left;
  margin: 0 10px;
  -webkit-border-top-right-radius: 20px;
  -moz-border-radius-topright: 20px;
  border-top-right-radius: 20px;
  border-top: 10px transparent solid;
  border-right: 10px transparent solid;
  padding: 80px 50px; }

figure {
  display: block;
  width: 300px;
  float: left;
  margin: 0 10px 10px 0;
  border: 6px double rgba(142, 137, 129,.5);
  -webkit-border-radius: 5px;
```

code continues on next page

Code 10.12 *continued*

```
  -moz-border-radius: 5px;
  border-radius: 5px; }

figcaption {
  display:block;
  padding: 10px;
  border-top: 2px solid rgba(142, 137, 129,.5);
  padding: 10px; }

aside {
  display: block;
  width: 200px;
  height: 400px;
  overflow: auto;
  float: right;
  margin: 0 10px;
  -webkit-border-top-left-radius: 20px;
  -webkit-border-bottom-left-radius: 20px;
  -moz-border-radius: 20px 0 0 20px;
  border-radius: 20px 0 0 20px;
  padding: 25px; }

footer {
  width: 100%;
  clear: both; }

h1 {
  margin: 0 20px 10px 10%;
  padding-top: 10px; }

article h2 {
  border-top: 2px solid rgba(142, 137, 129,.5);
  padding: 20px 0, }

article nav h2 {
  border-top: none;
  padding: 0; }

aside h3 {
  border: 1em double rgb(142, 137, 129);
  -webkit-border-image: url(../_images/
  → border-02.png) 27 round;
  -moz-border-image: url(../_images/border-02
  → .png) 27 round;
  border-image: url(../_images/border-02.png)
  → 27 round; }

.byline {
  margin: 0 10% 10px 20%; }
```

To set each side's padding value separately, you can type from one to four values.

- ▸ One value sets the padding for all four sides.
- ▸ Two values set the padding for the top/bottom and left/right sides.
- ▸ Three values set the top padding, the padding for the left/right sides (the same), and the bottom padding.
- ▸ Four values set the padding for each side in this order: top, right, bottom, and left.

3. As with margins, padding can also be set independently on all four sides of the box (top, right, bottom, and left).

   `padding-right: 10px;`

TIP If there is no border around or background-color behind the element, setting the margin will have the same visual effect as padding, and you won't run into the issues surrounding box model measurements (see Chapter 13, "Fixing the Internet Explorer Box Model Problem").

Ⓐ **Code 10.12 applied to Code 10.1:** With padding added, the whole design finally comes alive, opening up the page and making it easier to scan and navigate.

Coming Soon!

Watch for a number of new properties and features that are planned for CSS in the future. These include:

Text Overflow. The `overflow` property (this chapter) defines how content (text or otherwise) is treated when there is not enough space in the element to display it all. `text-overflow` will allow you to control how text that can not fit within its given area will be treated, allowing you to use ellipses to indicate continued text.

Box Sizing. The actual space a box takes up is calculated based on the width/height, plus the padding, plus the border. The box-sizing property let's you change how the box size is calculated, such that the size is calculated from border to border.

Resize. Allows you to set a box as being resizable by the user. This is especially useful in text for fields where someone may have a lot to say.

Multi-column Layout. One of the most exciting coming soon features, multi-column layout should replace the float method, finally allowing designers to create more versatile layout grids.

Animation. In addition to transitions and transformations, true animation that will rival Adobe Flash will soon be coming to a web browser near you. Already implemented in Safari, Firefox, and Opera.

Putting it All Together

1. **Create three block level elements.** Use `<div>` tags and give each one a unique ID but the same class.

2. **Set a width and height of 300px for each block.** The blocks will still be invisible, though, because they don't have any content, border, or background.

3. **Add a border to each element.** Use the class to define the border style and width, and then the ID to add a different color for each box.

4. **Add a margin to the boxes.** The boxes should separate slightly, but notice that the margin is not cumulative; instead it collapses to whichever margin is largest (top or bottom).

5. **Add floating to all three boxes.** They should no be arranged vertically, as long as your browser window is open wide enough.

6. **Add text to the three boxes.** Notice that it overflows if you add too much.

7. **Specify how the overflow should be treated for each box.** Try a different method for each.

8. **Add padding to the boxes.** Notice that the boxes grow to fit the padding, but the text stays the same width and height.

Visual Formatting Properties

Whether your designs are meant to be pixel perfect or fluid, element positioning is the key to any good design. You've already learned how to use CSS to control margins and padding in your composition (Chapter 10). With CSS, you can also position elements in the window, either exactly (absolutely or fixed) or in relation to other elements in the document (relatively). You can also set the visibility of any element in the window, making it visible, hidden, transparent, or even clipped on its sides.

This chapter introduces you to the methods you can use to position HTML elements using CSS, including how to stack elements on top of one another and float elements next to each other.

In This Chapter

Code 11.1 The HTML5 code for Chapter 11 is similar to the previous chapter but includes a new "gallery" element at the bottom of the article. It imports the final CSS from Chapters 5, 6, 7, 8, 9, and 10, as well as a new file you will build in this chapter, *visualformatting-properties.css*.

```
<!-- HTML5 -->
<!DOCTYPE html>
<html lang="en">
<head>
<meta charset="utf-8">
<title>Alice's Adventure's In Wonderland | Chapter 4</title>
<link href="../_css/font-properties.css" type="text/css" rel="stylesheet">
<link href="../_css/text-properties.css" type="text/css" rel="stylesheet">
<link href="../_css/color-background-properties.css" type="text/css" rel="stylesheet">
<link href="../_css/list-table-properties.css" type="text/css" rel="stylesheet">
<link href="../_css/ui-generatedcontent-properties.css" type="text/css" rel="stylesheet">
<link href="../_css/box-properties.css" type="text/css" rel="stylesheet">
<link href="../_css/visualformatting-properties.css" type="text/css" rel="stylesheet">
<!--[if IE ]>
  <script src="script/HTML5forIE.js" type="text/javascript"></script>
<![endif]-->
</head>
<body id="chapter6" class="book aaiw section">
<header class="page">
<h1>Alice's Adventures In Wonderland</h1>
<p class="byline">by <span class="author">Lewis Carroll</span></p>
<nav class="global">
  <ul>
    <li><a href="" target="self">Cover</a></li>
    <li><a href="" target="self">About the Author</a></li>
    <li><a href="" target="self">About the Books</a></li>
    <li><a href="" target="self">About the Site</a></li>
  </ul>
</nav>
</header><article><!-- Article -->
<nav>
  <ol class="toc top">
    <h2><a href="" target="self">Down the Rabbit-Hole</a></h2>
    <h2><a href="" target="self">The Pool of Tears</a></h2>
    <h2><a href="" target="self">A Caucus-Race and a Long Tale</a></h2>
    <h2><a href="" target="self">The Rabbit Sends in a Little Bill</a></h2>
    <h2><a href="" target="self">Advice from a Caterpillar</a></h2>
  </ol>
</nav>

<h2><strong>CHAPTER 6.</strong> Pig and Pepper</h2>

<figure>
<img src="../_images/AAIW-illos/alice22a.png" alt="alice15a" width="300" height="440">
<figcaption>
Alice was just beginning to think to herself, 'Now, what am I to do with
this creature when I get it home?'
```

code continues on next page

```
</figcaption>
</figure>

<p>
For a minute or two she stood <strong>looking at the house</strong>, and wondering what
to do next, when suddenly a footman in livery came running out of the
wood&mdash;(she considered him to be a footman because he was in livery:
otherwise, judging by his face only, she would have called him a
fish)&mdash;and rapped loudly at the door with his knuckles. It was opened
by another footman in livery, with a round face, and large eyes like a
frog; and both footmen, Alice noticed, had powdered hair that curled all
over their heads. She felt very curious to know what it was all about,
and crept a little way out of the wood to listen.
</p>
<div class="gallery">
<figure id="f1">
  <img src="../_images/AAIW-illos/alice20a.png" alt="alice15a">
</figure>
<figure id="f2">
  <img src="../_images/AAIW-illos/alice21a.png" alt="alice15a">
</figure>
<figure id="f3">
  <img src="../_images/AAIW-illos/alice22a.png" alt="alice15a">
</figure>
</div>

<nav>
<ol class="toc continued">
  <h2><a href="" target="_self">A Mad Tea-Party</a></h2>
  <h2><a href="" target="_self">The Queen's Croquet-Ground</a></h2>
  <h2><a href="" target="_self">The Mock Turtle's Story</a></h2>
  <h2><a href="" target="_self">The Lobster Quadrille</a></h2>
  <h2><a href="" target="_self">Who Stole the Tarts?</a></h2>
</ol>
</nav>
<br>
</article>

<aside>
<h3>About Lewis Carroll</h3>
<h4>From <cite>Wikipedia</cite></h4>
<p>Charles Lutwidge Dodgson...</p>
</aside>

<footer class="page">
<nav class="global">
  <ul>
```

code continues on next page

Code 11.1 *continued*

```
    <li><a href="" target="_self">Cover</a></li>
    <li><a href="" target="_self">About the
→ Author</a></li>
    <li><a href="" target="_self">About the
→ Books</a></li>
    <li><a href="" target="_self">About the
→ Site</a></li>
  </ul>
</nav>
</footer>
</body>
</html>
```

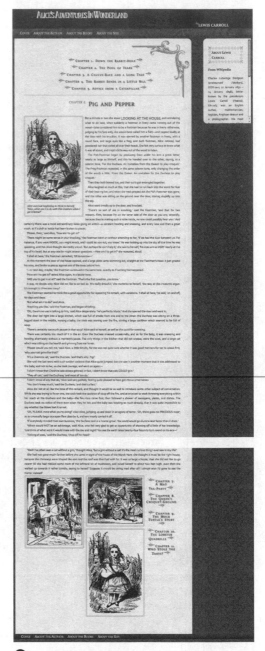

A How the page looks before the CSS file *visualformatting-properties.css* is applied. Notice the rather awkward gallery of images at the bottom. You'll have this fixed by the end of the chapter.

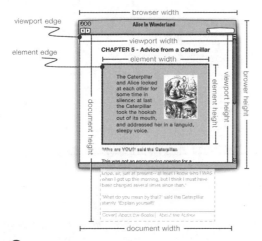

The following labels appear on the diagram:

- browser width
- viewport edge
- element edge
- 600
- Alice In Wonderland
- viewport width
- CHAPTER 5 - Advice from a Caterpillar
- element width
- browser height
- viewport height
- element height
- document height

The Caterpillar and Alice looked at each other for some time in silence: at last the Caterpillar took the hookah out of its mouth, and addressed her in a languid, sleepy voice.

'Who are YOU?' said the Caterpillar.

This was not an encouraging opening for a

know, sir, just at present—at least I know who I WAS when I got up this morning, but I think I must have been changed several times since then.'

'What do you mean by that?' said the Caterpillar sternly. 'Explain yourself!'

Cover | About the Books | About the Author

- document width

A The browser window displaying a document that will require some vertical scrolling to reveal the rest of its content.

Understanding the Window and Document

A Web page (also referred to as the *document*) is displayed within a browser window's *viewport*. Everything that you can present to the viewer is displayed in that area, although the document will require scrolling if it is larger than the viewport.

You can open multiple windows (each displaying its own documents in its own viewport), resize and position windows on the screen, or insert smaller viewports called *iframes*. Everything that you present, however, is displayed within a browser window as part of a document.

Like the elements contained within it (see "Understanding an Element's Box" in Chapter 10), the window has a width and height, as well as a top, bottom, left, and right. In fact, you can think of the browser window as the ultimate element in your Web design—the parent of all other elements **A**. Browser windows and the documents they contain have several distinct parts:

- **Browser width and height** refers to the dimensions of the entire window, including any browser controls and other interface items.

- **Viewport** is the area of the display area. All fixed-position elements will be placed in relation to the viewport edges.

continues on next page

- **Viewport width and height** refers to the live *display area* of the browser window's viewport. The live dimensions, obviously, are always less than the full window dimensions. Generally, when I refer to "the window," I'm referring to the viewport.

- **Document width and height**, sometimes called the *rendered* width and height, refers to the overall dimensions of the Web page contained within the body tag. If the document's width and/or height are larger than the viewport width and/or height, you'll see scroll bars that let you view the rest of the document.

- The **element edge** is the edge of an element *within* the border. Elements are positioned relative to their parent element's edges *if* the parent element has also been positioned. Otherwise, the element is positioned relative to the document edge.

- **Element width and height** should not be confused with *content* width and height (defined in Chapter 10); this is the total space occupied when border and padding are added to the content width and height.

TIP The document width is most often the same as the viewport width since horizontal scrolling is generally not preferred.

TIP Normal flow refers to where an element will appear in the Web page if no positioning is applied to it.

TABLE 11.1 Position Values

Value	Compatibility
static	IE4, FF1, S1, C1, O4, CSS2
relative	IE4, FF1, S1, C1, O4, CSS2
absolute	IE4, FF1, S1, C1, O4, CSS2
fixed	IE7, FF1, S1, C1, O4, CSS2
inherit	IE7, FF1, S1, C1, O5, CSS2

element	element	element

Ⓐ A statically positioned element stays right where it is.

Setting the Positioning Type

CSS positioning allows you to set several properties associated with the HTML element's position not only in 2D but also in 3D, clipping, and visibility. But first, you have to declare *how* the element's positing should be treated.

An element can have one of four position values—`static`, `relative`, `absolute`, or `fixed` (Table 11.1). The position value tells the browser how to treat the element when placing it into the document.

In addition to setting the position of an element, other position-dependent properties include:

- **Stacking order** is available for absolutely and fixed-position elements, allowing you to move elements in 3D.

- **Visibility** hides an element's content but not the element itself, effectively setting its opacity to 0.

- **Clipping** is used to hide parts of the content, "clipping" its sides.

Static positioning

By default, elements are positioned as static in the document unless you define them as positioned absolutely, relatively, or fixed. Static elements, like the relatively positioned elements explained in the following section, flow into a document one after the next. Static positioning differs, however, in that a static element cannot be explicitly positioned or repositioned, cannot be clipped, and cannot have its visibility changed Ⓐ.

Relative positioning

A relative element is positioned in context to where it would have been positioned if left alone. A relatively positioned element will be offset based on its position in the normal flow of the document. However, the space it occupied will remain but appear empty 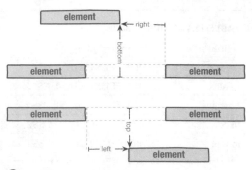.

Absolute positioning

Absolute positioning takes an element out of the normal flow of the document, leaving no space behind. An element that is defined in this way is placed at an exact point in the window by means of x and y coordinates relative to its most recently positioned parent element's edges or the body if none of its parents are positioned **C**.

B A relatively positioned element is moved relative to the indicated side—top, right, bottom, and/or left—where it would have appeared if untouched. Negative values move the element in the opposite direction but still relative to the same side.

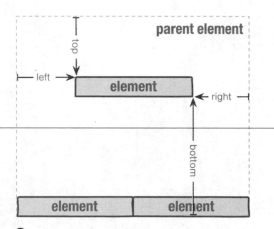

C An absolutely positioned element is removed from the normal flow and positioned from a positioned parent element's sides (or the document sides if it has no positioned parents).

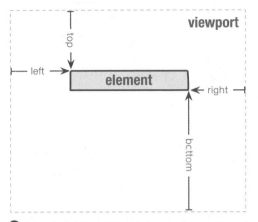

D A fixed-positioned element is always positioned relative to the viewport's edge.

Code 11.2 *visualformatting-properties.css—* When applied to Code 11.1, this CSS adds absolute positioning to the aside and gallery figures positioned relative to the gallery itself and with fixed positioning to the footer **E**. I've also set position-relative positioning for the strong tag to fix a spacing problem that's been bugging me since Chapter 5.

```
/*** CSS3 VQS | Chapter 11 |
→ visualformatting-properties.css ***/

aside {
  position: absolute; }

strong {
  position: relative; }

footer {
  position: fixed; }

footer ul {
  position: relative; }

div.gallery {
  position: relative; }

div.gallery figure {
  position: absolute; }
```

Fixed positioning

Fixing an element's position in the window is similar to absolute positioning except that it is always in a locked position relative to the viewport edge (rather than its parent). When a document scrolls in the viewport, fixed elements stay in their initial positions and do not scroll with the rest of document. This allows you to establish constant elements in the screen that do not scroll with the rest of the content **D**.

To set an element's position type:

1. Add the position property to your declaration list. Type **position** in a rule's declaration block or in the **style** attribute of an HTML tag, followed by a colon (:) (**Code 11.2**).

   position:

continues on next page

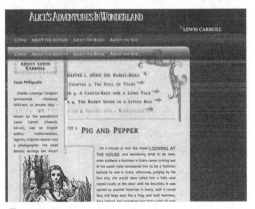

E Code 11.2 applied to code 11.1. Position types have been set, but—without actually setting positions—the elements look to be a jumble. The footer, which is fixed, is now at the top of the page! Also, note how low the text marked with the strong tag is. This was caused by increasing its font size relative to the surrounding text. You will fix that in the next section.

2. **Specify the positioning.**

`relative;`

Type a position-type value, which can be one of the following:

- ▸ **static** flows the content normally; however, none of the position properties can be set for this element.

- ▸ **relative** also flows the element normally, but allows the position to be set relative to its normal position using the values set on the **top**, **left**, **right**, and **bottom** properties.

- ▸ **absolute** places the element relative to the edge of its most recently positioned parent element. This element will be the body of the document or the element within which it is nested if that element's positioning has been set.

- ▸ **fixed** places the element relative to the edges of the viewport, independent of any other content on the page and ignoring its parent elements. Unlike an absolutely positioned element, when the window is scrolled, the fixed element stays where it is in the viewport as the rest of the content moves.

- ▸ **inherit** uses the position type of the element's immediate parent. If no position is set, this will default to static (see the sidebar "Inheriting Position Types").

Inheriting Position Types

inherit is another value for positioning. It tells the element to use the same positioning type as its parent, overriding the default static value. This can be tricky to use, though, because tying the child's position type to its parent can radically alter the layout if you change the parent's position type.

TIP Absolutely positioned and fixed-positioned elements take up no space within the parent element. So if you have an element—such as an image—that is absolutely positioned, its width and height are *not* included as part of the width and height of the parent content.

TIP You can position elements within other positioned elements. For example, you can set the relative position of a child element that is within an absolutely positioned parent or set the absolute position of an element within an absolutely positioned parent.

TIP Remember that the browser adds a default margin to the body of your Web page, but the default value is not consistent across all browsers. To correct this, you should always set your own margin in the body tag, which allows you to position elements consistently. See Chapter 12 for details on using a browser reset.

TIP Positioning can also vary from browser to browser due to rounding errors. It's generally best to use "clean" numbers, rounded to the nearest even number.

TIP When an element's position type has been set to anything other than static, you can use JavaScript or other scripting languages to move the element, change the clip, change the stacking order, hide it, or display it.

TIP Browsers that do not understand the fixed position type default to static for the position type.

Setting an Element's Position

All positioned elements can have a top value, a right value, a bottom value, and a left value to position the element from those four sides (**Tables 11.2** and **11.3**). A relative element will be offset relative to its own edges. An absolute element will be offset relative to its parent's edges. A fixed element will be offset relative to the viewport's edges.

To define an element's position:

1. **Specify a position type.** For details, see "Setting the Positioning Type" earlier in this chapter.

2. **Add a position side property to your CSS declaration list.** Type **left, right**, **top**, or **bottom** in the CSS rule, followed by a colon (**:**) (**Code 11.3**).

    top:

3. **Specify the position.**

    120px;

    Type a value for the element's offset. You can enter any of the following:

    ▸ A length value such as **120px**, **2.3em**, or **1.25cm**.

    ▸ A percentage value, such as **1%,** which creates a fluid offset.

    ▸ **auto**, which allows the browser to calculate the value if the position is set to absolute; otherwise, the default value will be **0.**

TIP You don't have to include the top, right, bottom and left declarations, but if they are not included, they are treated as auto.

TABLE 11.2 Top and Left Values

Value	Compatibility
<length>	IE4, FF1, S1, C1, O4, CSS2
<percentage>	IE4, FF1, S1, C1, O5, CSS2
auto	IE4, FF1, S1, C1, O5, CSS2
inherit	IE4, FF1, S1, C1, O5, CSS2

TABLE 11.3 Bottom and Right Values

Value	Compatibility
<length>	IE5, FF1, S1, C1, O4, CSS2
<percentage>	IE5, FF1, S1, C1, O4, CSS2
auto	IE5, FF1, S1.3, C1, O4, CSS2
inherit	IE4, FF1, S1, C1, O5, CSS2

Code 11.3 *visualformatting-properties.css—* When applied to Code 11.1, this CSS positions the footer at the bottom of the viewport (and keeps it there); positions the aside in a convenient location in the top-right corner of the screen; and offsets our gallery images slightly. It also pulls up the strong text, so that its baseline matches the surrounding text. It looks *much* better Ⓐ.

```
/*** CSS3 VQS | Chapter 11 |
→ visualformatting-properties.css ***/

aside {
  position: absolute;
  right: 1%;
  top: 120px; }

strong {
  position: relative;
  top: -.15em; }

footer {
  position: fixed;
  bottom: 0;
  left: 0; }

footer ul {
  position: relative;
  top: 10px; }

div.gallery {
  position: relative; }

div.gallery figure {
  position: absolute; }

div.gallery figure.f1 {
  left: 0;
  top: 0; }

div.gallery figure.f2 {
  left: 150px;
  top:50px; }

div.gallery figure.f3 {
  left: 300px;
  top: 100px; }
```

TIP You can use negative values to move the content up and to the left instead of down and to the right.

TIP Child elements that are not absolutely positioned always move with their parent element.

TIP What happens if you set the `top`/`left` and `bottom`/`right` positions for the same element? The answer depends on the browser. Internet Explorer always defaults to the `top` and `left` positions. But most others will stretch elements that do not have a definite width or height to accommodate the values that are set.

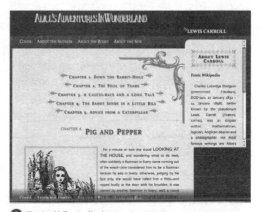

Ⓐ **Code 11.3 applied to code 11.1.** The page is starting to come together. Notice that the strong text is now aligned with the rest of the paragraph Ⓑ.

Ⓑ Even when scrolling, the footer still stays at the bottom of the screen.

Stacking Objects in 3D

Although the screen is a two-dimensional area, positioned elements can be given a third dimension: a relative stacking order.

Positioned elements are assigned stacking numbers automatically, starting with 0 and continuing incrementally—1, 2, 3, and so on—in the order in which the elements appear in the HTML and relative to their parents and siblings. Elements with higher numbers appear above those with lower numbers. This system is called the *z-index* (**Table 11.4**). An element's z-index number establishes its 3D relationship to other elements in its parent element.

When the content of elements overlap, the element with a higher z-index number will appear on top of the element with a lower number 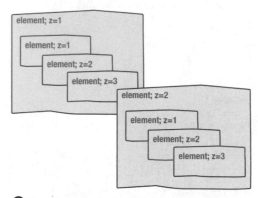. The z-index is always relative to an element's siblings, *not* to its parents.

You can override the natural order of the z-index by setting a value for the **z-index** property.

To define an element's z-index:

1. **Specify a position type.** For details, see "Setting the Positioning Type" earlier in this chapter (**Code 11.4**).

2. **Add the z-index property to your CSS rule.** Type **z-index** in the same declaration block, followed by a colon (**:**).

   `z-index:`

TABLE 11.4 Z-Index Values

Value	Compatibility
\<number\>	IE4, FF1, S1, C1, O3.5, CSS2
auto	IE4, FF1, S1, C1, O3.5, CSS2
inherit	IE4, FF1, S1, C1, O3.5, CSS2

A The z-index order is relative to an element's siblings.

Code 11.4 *visualformatting-properties.css—* When applied to Code 11.1, this CSS will reverse the stacking order of the images in the gallery and set the footer to a sufficiently high number to ensure that it will be placed on top of most elements in the viewport **B**.

```
/*** CSS3 VQS | Chapter 11 |
 → visualformatting-properties.css ***/

aside {
  position: absolute,
  right: 1%;
  top: 120px; }

strong {
  position: relative;
  top: -.15em; }

footer {
  position: fixed;
  bottom: 0;
  left: 0;
  z-index: 99; }

footer ul {
  position: relative;
  top: 10px; }

div.gallery {
  position: relative; }

div.gallery figure {
  position: absolute; }

div.gallery figure.f1 {
  left: 0;
  top: 0;
  z-index: 3; }

div.gallery figure.f2 {
  left: 150px;
  top:50px;
  z-index: 2; }

div.gallery figure.f3 {
  left: 300px;
  top: 100px;
  z-index: 1; }
```

3. **Specify the position number.** Type a positive or negative number (no decimals allowed), or **0**.

3;

This step sets the element's z-index in relation to its siblings, where **0** is on the same level.

Alternatively, you can use **auto** to allow the browser to determine the element's z-index order.

Using a negative number for the z-index causes an element to be stacked that many levels below its parent.

B Before the z-index is changed **C**.

C Code 11.4 applied to code 11.1. The order of the images in the gallery is reversed by changing the z-index value.

Setting the Visibility of an Element

The **visibility** property designates whether an element is visible in the window. If visibility is set to **hidden** (Table 11.5), the element is invisible but still occupies space in the document, and an empty rectangle appears where the element is located Ⓐ.

To set an element's visibility:

1. **Specify a position type.** For details, see "Setting the positioning Type" earlier in this chapter.

2. **Add the visibility property to your CSS.** Type **visibility** in the element's CSS declaration block, followed by a colon (**:**) (**Code 11.5**).

   visibility:

3. **Specify how the element's visibility should be treated.**

   hidden;

   Type one of the following keywords to specify how you want this element to be treated:

   ▸ **hidden** makes the element invisible when the document is initially rendered on the screen.

   ▸ **visible** makes the element visible.

   ▸ **inherit** causes the element to inherit the visibility of its parent element.

TABLE 11.5 Visibility Values

Value	Compatibility
hidden	IE4, FF1, S1, C1, O4, CSS2
visible	IE4, FF1, S1, C1, O4, CSS2
inherit	FF1, S1, C1, O3.5, CSS2

Ⓐ The hidden element no longer appears, although its location is shown as an empty space indicated by the dotted line in this figure (no, there will not actually be a dotted line).

Code 11.5 *visualformatting-properties.css*—When applied to Code 11.1, this CSS hides the navigation in the header, since it's now always available in our fixed footer. Don't worry; the top navigation will return later in the book **B**.

```
/*** CSS3 VQS | Chapter 11 |
→ visualformatting-properties.css ***/

header navigation {
  visibility: hidden; }

aside {
  position: absolute;
  right: 1%;
  top: 120px; }

strong {
  position: relative;
  top: -.15em; }

footer {
  position: fixed;
  bottom: 0;
  left: 0;
  z-index: 99; }

footer ul {
  position: relative;
  top: 10px; }

div.gallery {
  position: relative; }

div.gallery figure {
  position: absolute; }

div.gallery figure.f1 {
  left: 0;
  top: 0;
  z-index: 3; }

div.gallery figure.f2 {
  left: 150px;
  top:50px;
  z-index: 2; }

div.gallery figure.f3 {
  left: 300px;
  top: 100px;
  z-index: 1; }
```

TIP Although the properties seem similar, `visibility` differs radically from `display` (Chapter 10). When `display is set to none`, the element is scrubbed from the document, and no space is reserved for it. `Visibility` reserves and displays the empty space like the invisible man in his bandages.

TIP Generally, `display:none` is used for JavaScript effects, such as drop-down menus and pop-up text, in which elements are alternately hidden and shown. Because this property will remove the element, it prevents the element from interfering with the layout of the page when not needed.

TIP I recommend using display none to hide elements, such as navigation, when creating a Print styling sheet.

TIP One downside to hidden elements is that Web search engines will not see them nor will screen readers used by the vision impaired. If you do hide content, make sure it's not something that is not vital for SEO.

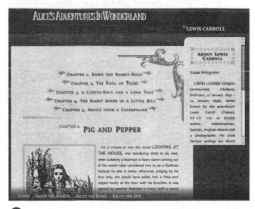

B Code 11.5 applied to code 11.1. The header navigation is now gone, but not forgotten.

Clipping an Element's Visible Area

Unlike setting the width and the height of an element, which controls the element's dimensions (see Chapter 10), clipping an absolute- or fixed-position element designates how much of that element's content will be visible (**Table 11.6**). The part that is not designated as visible will still be present, but viewers won't be able to see it, and the browser will treat it as empty space **A**.

To define the clip area of an element:

1. **Specify a position type.** For details, see "Setting the positioning Type" earlier in this chapter.

2. **Add the clip property to your declaration list.** Type the `clip` property name, followed by a colon (:) as shown in Code 11.6.

   `clip:`

3. **Specify the rectangular clipping region.** Type `rect` to define the shape of the clip as a rectangle, an opening parenthesis ((), four values separated by spaces, a closing parenthesis ()), and a semicolon (;).

   `rect(50px 250px 250px 50px);`

   The numbers define the *top*, *right*, *bottom*, and *left* lengths of the clip area, respectively. All these values are distances from the element's origin (top-left corner), not from the indicated side.

   Each value can be a length value or **auto**, which allows the browser to determine the clip size (usually, 100 percent).

TABLE 11.6 Clip Values

Value	Compatibility
rect (<top> <right> <bottom> <left>)	IE5.5, FF1, S1, C1, O7, CSS2
auto	IE5.5, FF1, S1, C1, O7, CSS2
inherit	IE5.5, FF1, S1, C1, O7, CSS2

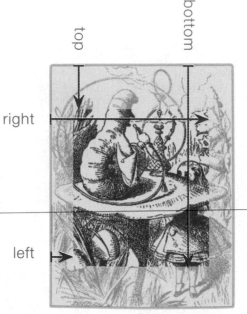

A The center area is clipped based on the top, right, bottom, and left values provided to the clip property. The transparent area will not be visible.

Code 11.6 *visualformatting-properties.css—*
When applied to Code 11.1, this CSS hides the edges of the figures in the gallery, creating consistently sized thumbnails **B**.

```
/*** CSS3 VQS | Chapter 11 |
→ visualformatting-properties.css ***/

header navigation {
  visibility: hidden; }

aside {
  position: absolute;
  right: 1%;
  top: 120px; }

strong {
  position: relative;
  top: -.15em; }

footer {
  position: fixed;
  bottom: 0;
  left: 0;
  z-index: 99; }

footer ul {
  position: relative;
  top: 10px; }

div.gallery {
  position: relative; }

div.gallery figure {
  position: absolute;
  clip: rect(50px 250px 250px 50px); }

div.gallery figure.f1 {
  left: 0;
  top: 0;
  z-index: 3; }

div.gallery figure.f2 {
  left: 150px;
  top:50px;
  z-index: 2; }

div.gallery figure.f3 {
  left: 300px;
  top: 100px;
  z-index: 1; }
```

TIP The element's borders and padding, but not its margin, are clipped along with the content of the element.

TIP Currently, clips can only be rectangular.

TIP Auto should restore an element to its unclipped original state. However, Safari and Chrome will only restore the clip to the outer edges of the border while still slipping the outline or box shadow.

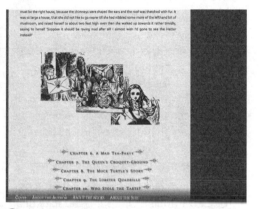

B **Code 11.6 applied to code 11.1.** Your gallery is now made up of consistently sized thumbnails. Later in the book, you'll learn how to make these pop back open to full size.

NEW IN CSS3: Setting an Element's Opacity ★

One of the earliest, widely implemented CSS3 features was the ability to set element opacity, which let you transform an element from opaque to transparent and any translucency in between 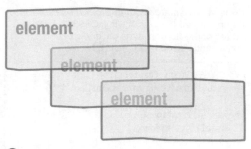. However, different browsers implement opacity in different ways.

A Changing opacity allows you to see through to the element underneath.

For example, rather than implementing the W3C CSS syntax, Internet Explorer builds on its existing **filter** functionality, whereas other W3C-compliant browsers simply add the **opacity** property (Table 11.7). Because Internet Explorer ignores the other browsers' code, you can place both declarations in the rule list for an element to control its opacity.

TABLE 11.7 Opacity Values

Value	Compatibility
<alphavalue>	FF1, S1.3, C1, O9, CSS2
inherit	FF1, S1.3, C1, O9, CSS2

To set the opacity of an element:

1. **Add the IE filter property to your CSS declaration list.** To control opacity of an element displayed in Internet Explorer for Windows, type the **filter** property name in the declaration block, followed by a colon (**:**) (**Code 11.7**).

   `filter:`

2. **Specify the opacity for Internet Explorer.**

   `alpha(opacity=75);`

   Add the **alpha()** code to define the filter and value used. You do not want to change this code except for the alpha value after **opacity**, which can range between **0** (completely transparent) and **100** (completely opaque). End the declaration with a semicolon (;).

3. **Add the opacity property to your CSS.** To control the opacity of an element, type **opacity** followed by a colon (:).

   `opacity:`

Code 11.7 *visualformatting-properties.*
css—When applied to Code 11.1, this CSS allows the overlapping thumbnails to show what is underneath **B**.

```
/*** CSS3 VQS | Chapter 11 |
→ visualformatting-properties.css ***/

header navigation {
  visibility: hidden; }

aside {
  position: absolute;
  right: 1%;
  top: 120px; }

strong {
  position: relative;
  top: -.15em; }

footer {
  position: fixed;
  bottom: 0;
  left: 0;
  z-index: 99; }

footer ul {
  position: relative;
  top: 10px; }

div.gallery {
  position: relative; }

div.gallery figure {
  position: absolute;
  clip: rect(50px 250px 250px 50px);
  filter: alpha(opacity=0.75);
  opacity: .5; }

div.gallery figure.f1 {
  left: 0;
  top: 0;
  z-index: 3; }

div.gallery figure.f2 {
  left: 150px;
  top:50px;
  z-index: 2; }

div.gallery figure.f3 {
  left: 300px;
  top: 100px;
  z-index: 1; }
```

4. Specify the opacity. Enter an alpha value for the opacity of the element, which can range between **0.0** (completely transparent) and **1.0** (completely opaque).

0.75;

You could also use **inherit**, which will set the element's opacity to the same value as its parent. So, if the parent has an opacity of 0.75, **inherit** will cause the child element to reduce its opacity 75 percent *in addition to* the 75 percent already set for the parent.

TIP Opacity is applied to the entire element and to all of its children, with no way to override it in child elements. However, you can independently set the opacity of two sibling elements and then position one on top of the other.

TIP Opacities are cumulative, so if an element with .5 opacity is within an element with .5 opacity, it will have a cumulative opacity of .25.

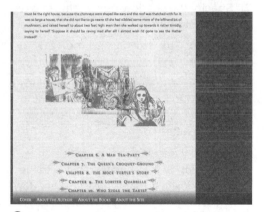

B Code 11.7 applied to code 11.1. The thumbnails are now semitransparent. This can be a useful effect, especially when combined with a hover effect that turns the element back to opaque to indicate user interaction.

NEW IN CSS3: Setting an Element's Shadows ★

Just as with text shadows (Chapter 6), you can add one or more drop shadows to the box of any element on the screen—positioned or not **A**. The term "shadow" is a bit misleading, though, since you can make the color anything you like—including light colors—to great a glow effect.

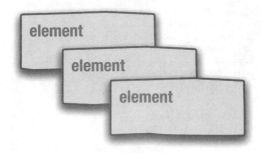

A Shadows provide a sense of depth and texture.

To set an element shadow:

1. **Add the box shadow property to your CSS rule.** Type the **box-shadow** property names, including Mozilla and Webkit browser extension versions, followed by a colon (:), (**Code 11.8**).

   -webkit-box-shadow:

   -moz-box-shadow:

   box-shadow:

2. **Specify the shadow offset, blur, choke, color, and inset.**

   1px 1px 5px 1px rgba(0,0,0,.25)
   → inset

   Type the following keywords or values (**Table 11.8**) to specify how you want this element's shadow to be treated (from right to left):

   ▸ **x** and **y** offset length values set the position of the shadow relative to the box. Positive values offset the shadow down and to the right, whereas negative values move the shadow up and to the left. These are required.

   ▸ A **blur** length value is a positive value that increases the fuzziness of the shadow and spreads it out. The higher the value, the bigger and lighter the shadow. This is optional but defaults to **0** when left unset.

TABLE 11.8 Box-Shadow Values

Value	Compatibility
inset	FF3.5, S3, C2, O10.5, CSS3
<x-offset>	FF3.5, S3, C2, O10.5, CSS3
<y-offset>	FF3.5, S3, C2, O10.5, CSS3
<blur>	FF3.5, S3, C2, O10.5, CSS3
<spread>	FF3.5, S3, C2, O10.5, CSS3
<color>	FF3.5, S3, C2, O10.5, CSS3

Code 11.8 *visualformatting-properties.css*— When applied to Code 11.1, this CSS adds a drop shadow to the article and both a drop and interior shadow to the aside. It also adds shadows to the gallery images, but because they are clipped, they don't show up **B**.

```
/*** CSS3 VQS | Chapter 11 |
→ visualformatting-properties.css ***/

header nav {
  visibility: hidden; }

article {
  -webkit-box-shadow: rgba(0,0,0,.7) 5px 5px
  → 15px;
  -moz-box-shadow: 5px 5px 10px rgba(0,0,0,.7);
  box-shadow: 5px 5px 10px rgba(0,0,0,.7); }

aside {
  position: absolute;
  right: 1%;
  top: 120px;
```

code continues on next page

```
  -webkit-box-shadow: 1px 1px 5px 1px
→ rgba(0,0,0,.25) inset, 3px 3px 15px
→ rgba(0,0,0,.5);
  -moz-box-shadow: 1px 1px 5px 1px
→ rgba(0,0,0,.25) inset, 3px 3px 15px
→ rgba(0,0,0,.5);
  box-shadow: 1px 1px 5px 1px rgba(0,0,0,.25)
→ inset, 3px 3px 15px rgba(0,0,0,.5); }

strong {
  position: relative;
  top: -.15em; }

footer {
  position: fixed;
  bottom: 0;
  left: 0;
  z-index: 99; }

footer ul {
  position: relative;
  top: 10px; }

figure {
  -webkit-box-shadow: rgba(0,0,0,.7) 5px 5px
→ 10px;
  -moz-box-shadow: 5px 5px 10px rgba(0,0,0,.7);
  box-shadow: 5px 5px 10px rgba(0,0,0,.7); }

div.gallery {
  position: relative; }

div.gallery figure {
  position: absolute;
  clip: rect(50px 250px 250px 50px);
  filter: alpha(opacity=0.75);
  opacity: .5; }

div.gallery figure.f1 {
  left: 0;
  top: 0;
  z-index: 3; }
div.gallery figure.f2 {
  left: 150px;
  top:50px;
  z-index: 2; }

div.gallery figure.f3 {
  left: 300px;
  top: 100px;
  z-index: 1; }
```

▸ A **spread** length value—sometimes called the *choke*—is a positive value used to specify the break point for the shadows fade. It has the affect of increasing the darker area of the shadow before it begins to fade. This is optional but defaults to **0** when left unset.

▸ A **color** value is any of the standard color values outlined in Chapter 7. This is optional but defaults to **transparent** when left unset, rendering the shadow invisible.

▸ **inset** causes the shadow to appear within the element's edges, creating an inner shadow. This is optional.

3. **Add more shadows as desired.**

   `, 3px 3px 15px rgba(0,0,0,.5);`

   You can repeat the shadow code as many times as desired to create multiple shadows under or within the element, separating each value list by a comma (,) and always remembering to end your CSS rule with a semicolon (;).

TIP If only one length value is included after the x/y offset length values, it will be assumed to be the blur, not the spread.

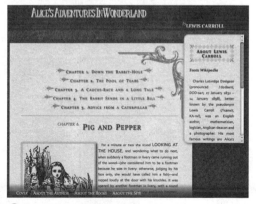

B Code 11.8 applied to code 11.1. The shadows add to the illusion of pages in a book, giving them a sense of weight and thickness.

Putting It All Together

1. **Using the three boxes you built in Chapter 10, set their position types.** Set the first to absolute, the second to relative, and the third to fixed.

2. **Set the position of each box.** Use the same values on each and note how the different position types affect how the values are used.

3. **Set the z-index.** Set up the boxes to overlap each other, and then set the z-index to change which box is on top.

4. **Set the opacity of each box.** Notice how the colors combine.

5. **Add a box shadow to each box.** Try multiple shadows and continue out and inset shadows. Can you create a glow effect?

Transformation and Transition Properties

Although the use of transform and transition properties is still somewhat controversial, the ability to apply these changes to elements without using JavaScript will be a boon for Web designers and developers. Think of these as temporal styles that not only change the appearance of an element—as do other styles—but also change that element's appearance over time and space.

The styles presented in this chapter are extremely new, at least by Web standards. Although Webkit has had them in one form or another for a while and FireFox and Opera have started adapting them, it is only in the last year or so that work has started on making them part of the standard CSS3 canon. Approach these with some caution making sure they degrade gracefully in older browsers, but I can't wait to see how you use them.

Code 12.1 The HTML5 code for Chapter 12 is similar to the previous chapter **Ⓐ**. It imports the final CSS from Chapters 5, 6, 7, 8, 9, 10, and 11 as well as a new file we will be building in this chapter called *transformation-transition-properties.css*.

```html
<!-- HTML5 -->
<!DOCTYPE html>
<html lang="en">
<head>
<meta charset="utf-8">
<title>Alice's Adventure's In Wonderland | Chapter 7</title>
<link href="../_css/font-properties.css" type="text/css" rel="stylesheet">
<link href="../_css/text-properties.css" type="text/css" rel="stylesheet">
<link href="../_css/color-background-properties.css" type="text/css" rel="stylesheet">
<link href="../_css/list-table-properties.css" type="text/css" rel="stylesheet">
<link href="../_css/ui-generatedcontent-properties.css" type="text/css" rel="stylesheet">
<link href="../_css/box-properties.css" type="text/css" rel="stylesheet">
<link href="../_css/visualformatting-properties.css" type="text/css" rel="stylesheet">
<link href="../_css/transformation-transition-properties.css" type="text/css" rel="stylesheet">
<!--[if IE ]>
  <script src="script/HTML5forIE.js" type="text/javascript"></script>
<![endif]-->
</head>
<body id="chapter7" class="book aaiw section">
<header class="page">
<h1>Alice's Adventures In Wonderland</h1>
<p class="byline">by <span class="author">Lewis Carroll</span></p>
<nav class="global">
  <ul>
    <li><a href="" target="_self">Cover</a></li>
    <li><a href="" target="_self">About the Author</a></li>
    <li><a href="" target="_self">About the Books</a></li>
    <li><a href="" target="_self">About the Site</a></li>
  </ul>
</nav>
</header>
<article><!-- Article -->
<nav>
  <ol class="toc top">
    <h2><a href="" target="_self">Down the Rabbit-Hole</a></h2>
    <h2><a href="" target="_self">The Pool of Tears</a></h2>
    <h2><a href="" target="_self">A Caucus-Race and a Long Tale</a></h2>
    <h2><a href="" target="_self">The Rabbit Sends in a Little Bill</a></h2>
    <h2><a href="" target="_self">Advice from a Caterpillar</a></h2>
    <h2><a href="" target="_self">Pig and Pepper</a></h2>
  </ol>
</nav>
<h2><strong>CHAPTER 7.</strong> A Mad Tea-Party</h2>
<figure>
<img src="../_images/AAIW-illos/alice26a.png" alt="alice15a">
<figcaption>
"Twinkle, twinkle, little bat!<br/>
```

code continues on next page

```
How I wonder what you're at!"
</figcaption>
</figure>
<p>
There was a table set out under a tree in front of the house, and the
March Hare and the Hatter were having tea at it: a Dormouse was sitting
between them, fast asleep, and the other two were using it as a
cushion, resting their elbows on it, and talking over its head. 'Very
uncomfortable for the Dormouse,' thought Alice; 'only, as it's asleep, I
suppose it doesn't mind.'
</p>
<div class="gallery">
<figure id="f1">
  <img src="../_images/AAIW-illos/alice24a.png" alt="alice15a">
</figure>
<figure id="f2">
  <img src="../_images/AAIW-illos/alice25a.png" alt="alice15a">
</figure>
<figure id="f3">
  <img src="../_images/AAIW-illos/alice27a.png" alt="alice15a">
</figure>
</div>
<nav>
<ol class="toc continued">
  <h2><a href="" target="_self">The Queen's Croquet-Ground</a></h2>
  <h2><a href="" target="_self">The Mock Turtle's Story</a></h2>
  <h2><a href="" target="_self">The Lobster Quadrille</a></h2>
  <h2><a href="" target="_self">Who Stole the Tarts?</a></h2>
</ol>
</nav>
</article>
<aside>
<h3>About Lewis Carroll</h3>
<h4>From <cite>Wikipedia</cite></h4>
<p>Charles Lutwidge Dodgson,...</p>
</aside>
<footer class="page">
<nav class="global">
  <ul>
    <li><a href="" target="_self">Cover</a></li>
    <li><a href="" target="_self">About the Author</a></li>
    <li><a href="" target="_self">About the Books</a></li>
    <li><a href="" target="_self">About the Site</a></li>
  </ul>
</nav>
</footer>
</body>
</html>
```

A The page appearance before the CSS file *transformation-transition-properties.css* is applied. Notice that the gallery of images is still very grid-like in its appearance.

TABLE 12.1 2D Transform Values

Value	Compatibility
rotate(<angle>)	FF3.5, S3.1, C5, O10.5, CSS3
rotateX(<angle>)	FF3.5, S3.1, C5, O10.5, CSS3
rotateY(<angle>)	FF3.5, S3.1, C5, O10.5, CSS3
scale(<num×2>,)	FF3.5, S3.1, C5, O10.5, CSS3
scaleX(<number>)	FF3.5, S3.1, C5, O10.5, CSS3
scaleY(<number>)	FF3.5, S3.1, C5, O10.5, CSS3
skew(<angle×2>,)	FF3.5, S3.1, C5, O10.5, CSS3
skewX(<angle>)	FF3.5, S3.1, C5, O10.5, CSS3
skewY(<angle>)	FF3.5, S3.1, C5, O10.5, CSS3
translate(<length×2>,)	FF3.5, S3.1, C5, O10.5, CSS3
translateX(<length>)	FF3.5, S3.1, C5, O10.5, CSS3
translateY(<length>)	FF3.5, S3.1, C5, O10.5, CSS3
matrix(<various×6>,)	FF3.5, S3.1, C5, O10.5, CSS3

TABLE 12.2 Transform-Origin Values

Value	Compatibility
<percentage>	FF3.5, S3.1, C5, O10.5, CSS3
<length>	FF3.5, S3.1, C5, O10.5, CSS3
<keyword>	FF3.5, S3.1, C5, O10.5, CSS3

NEW IN CSS3: Transforming an Element ★

Transformations are a bit of a cheat. Yes, they enable you to create incredibly cool designs that finally break out of the rectangular layout grid, allowing you to rotate, scale, skew, and move elements. However, each transform "value" shown in **Table 12.1** (for 2D) and **Table 12.2** (for 3D) could actually be a property in and of itself because each takes its own parenthetical values. But, instead, they are all associated with the **transform** property, and we'll have to live with that.

Tansform values, in turn, have three basic value types we might use:

- **Angle** can be defined in degrees (**90deg**), grads (**100grad**), or radians (**1.683rad**). Negative values and values greater that **360deg** are allowed but are translated into positive values.

- **Number** can be any integer or decimal value, positive or negative. Numbers are generally used as a multiplier.

- **Length** is a length value as defined in the introduction of this book. This can include relative values (em, px, %) or absolute values (in, mm, cm).

Many transform values can take multiple parenthetical values, separated by a comma:

scale(2,1.65)

Generally, two or three values will represent the X, Y, and Z axes. If only one value is included, it is assumed to be used for both or all three.

As with many advanced CSS3 properties, transformations are currently implemented using extensions to browsers, including Mozilla, Webkit, and Opera.

2D transformations

Currently, the most stable and widely available transformations are in two dimensions, but this is a good starting point 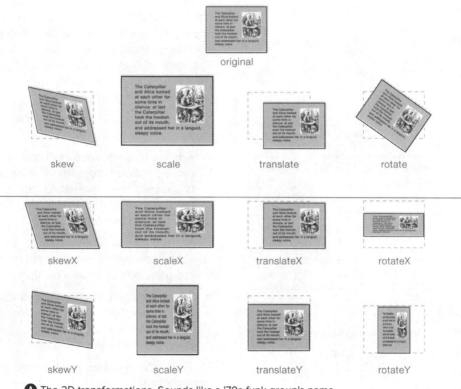.

A The 2D transformations. Sounds like a '70s funk group's name.

Code 12.2 *transformation-transition-properties. css*—When applied to Code 12.1, several transformations are applied to give the aside a jaunty angle and break up the grid the images are in **B C**. Notice that four lines of code are required for maximum cross-browser compatibility.

```
/*** CSS3 VQS | Chapter 12 | transformation-
→ transition-properties.css ***/

aside {
  -webkit-transform: rotate(-2deg);
  -moz-transform: rotate(-2deg);
  -o-transform: rotate(-2deg);
  transform: rotate(-2deg); }

div.gallery figure {
  width: auto;
  -webkit-transform-origin: left 25%;
  -moz-transform-origin: left 25%;
  -o-transform-origin: left 25%;
  transform-origin: left 25%; }

#f1 {
  -webkit-transform: scale(.75) rotate(10deg);
  -moz-transform: scale(.75) rotate(10deg);
  -o-transform: scale(.75) rotate(10deg);
  transform: scale(.75) rotate(10deg); }

#f2 {
  -webkit-transform: scale(.75) rotate(-8deg);
  -moz-transform: scale(.75) rotate(-8deg);
  -o-transform: scale(.75) rotate(-8deg);
  transform: scale(.75) rotate(-8deg); }

#f3 {
  -webkit-transform: scale(.75)rotate(3deg);
  -moz-transform: scale(.75)rotate(3deg);
  -o-transform: scale(.75) rotate(3deg);
  transform: scale(.75) rotate(3deg); }
```

To add a 2D transformation to an element:

1. Add the **transform** property for Webkit, Mozilla, Opera, and standard CSS.

   -webkit-transform:

   → **-moz-transform:**

   → **-o-transform:**

   → **transform:**

   The exact order is not important, although standard CSS should always come last (**Code 12.2**).

   continues on next page

B At the top of the page, the aside is at a light angle that adds to the notebook-like appearance.

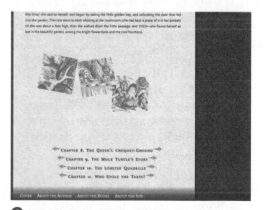

C At the bottom of the page, our photo gallery is now a little more jumbled looking.

2. **Specify the transition type and value.**

   `rotate(-2deg);`

   For each property, add the same transform value (Table 12.1) with its relevant parenthetical value:

   ▸ **rotate()** with an angle value to rotate the element. Positive values turn the element clockwise, whereas negative values turn the element counterclockwise.

   ▸ **rotateX()** or **rotateY()** with an angle value to turn the element around the X or Y axis. Positive values turn the element clockwise, whereas negative values turn the element counterclockwise.

   ▸ **scale()**, **scaleX()**, or **scaleY()** with numeric values that act as multipliers to the width (X) and/or height (Y) of the element. Positive numbers increase element size. Negative values will still increase size *but also* reflect the element along its axis. Decimal numbers decrease scale.

   ▸ **skew()**, **skewX()**, or **skewY()** with angle values that skew the element along the X and/or Y axis of the element. Positive values skew up and to the left, whereas negative values skew down and to the right.

   ▸ **translate()**, **translateX()**, or **translateY()** with length values that offset the element along the X axis and/or Y axis of the element. Positive values offset down and to the right, whereas negative values offset up and to the left.

   ▸ **matrix()** is a 3×3 matrix of values that can be used as a shorthand to represent any of the preceding transformations alone or in combination.

TABLE 12.3 Transform-Origin Keywords

Value
left
right
top
bottom
center

Do Browser Extensions Ever Go Away?

Yes, browser extensions eventually go away. After a browser implements the standard W3C syntax of a property, the browsers generally support the extension for the next two versions of the browser, although this is by no means a hard and fast rule. This is why—if standard CSS syntax has been defined—it's best to include it at the bottom of the list of browser extension properties to ensure that it's the version that is used, if supported.

3. Add more transformations as needed.

   `transform: scale(.75) rotate(3deg);`

   You can include multiple transformation values separated by a space.

4. Specify the transformation origin, if it is not the center of the element.

   `-webkit-transform-origin: 0, 25%;`

   `-moz-transform-origin: 0, 25%;`

   `-o-transform-origin: 0, 25%;`

   `transform-origin: 0, 25%;`

   By default, all transformations use the center of the element as the point of origin. Thus, a rotate transform will rotate around the middle of the element.

   To change this, add the `transform()` property with one or two values for the X and Y location of the origin (Table 12.2) as a percentage, length, or a keyword (**Table 12.3**). If you specify only a single value, it will be used for both X and Y. Positive values move the origin up and to the left of the element, whereas negative values move the origin down and to the right of the center of the element.

3D transformations

As of this writing, 3D transitions are supported only in Safari and Chrome, although that can rapidly change as new versions of Firefox are released. As a result, I don't advocate the use of 3D transitions except in cases where you know the only browser being used is one that supports these properties—for example, in iOS applications or pages created for iPhone, iPod touch, or iPad display. That said, because this is a standard under development by the W3C, you should also include the standard CSS3 syntax for future compatibility.

To transform an element in three dimensions

1. Add the transform style property to your CSS declarations and specify the style.

   `-webkit-transform-style: flat;`

   `transform-style: flat;`

   Add **transform-style** to the elements being transformed (**Code 12.3**), which allows you to specify whether child elements should be set flat against the parent element or treated separately in their own 3D spaces (**Table 12.4**).

2. Add the perspective style property to your CSS declarations and specify the perspective value.

   `-webkit-perspective: 500;`

   `perspective: 500;`

   Perspective works like the transform **perspective()** value described later in this chapter but is used to apply a perspective to an element's positioned children, not the element itself (**Table 12.5**).

Code 12.3 *transformation-transition-properties. css*—When applied to Code 12.1, this replaces the transform styles from Code 12.2 with Webkit-only 3D transforms. Other browsers will still look like **C**, and Webkit browsers will look like **D**.

```
/*** CSS3 VQS | Chapter 12 | transformation-
→ transition-properties.css ***/

aside {
  -webkit-transform: rotate(-2deg);
  -moz-transform: rotate(-2deg);
  -o-transform: rotate(-2deg);
  transform: rotate(-2deg); }

div.gallery figure {
  width: auto;
  -webkit-transform-origin: left 25%;
  -moz-transform-origin: left 25%;
  -o-transform-origin: left 25%;
  transform-origin: left 25%;
  -webkit-transform-style: flat;
  transform-style: flat;
  -webkit-perspective: 5000;
  perspective: 5000;
  -webkit-perspective-origin: 25% 25%;
  perspective-origin: 25% 25%;
  -webkit-backface-visibility: visible;
  backface-visibility: visible; }

#f1 {
  -webkit-transform: perspective(250)
  → scale3d(.75,.5,1) rotate3d(5,4,2,-10deg);
  -moz-transform: scale(.75) rotate(10deg);
  -o-transform: scale(.75) rotate(10deg);
  transform: scale(.75) rotate(10deg); }

#f2 {
  -webkit-transform: perspective(250)
  → scale3d(.5,.75,1.5) rotate3d(-3,10,-8,18deg);
  -moz-transform:scale(.75) rotate(-8deg);
```

code continues on next page

TABLE 12.4 Transform-Style Values

Value	Compatibility
flat	S3.1, C5, CSS3
preserve-3d	S3.1, C5, CSS3

TABLE 12.5 Perspective Values

Value	Compatibility
<number>	S3.1, C5, CSS3
none	S3.1, C5, CSS3

Code 12.3 *continued*

```
  -o-transform: scale(.75) rotate(-8deg);
  transform: scale(.75) rotate(-8deg); }

#f3 {
  -webkit-transform: perspective(250)
  → scale3d(1,.5,.75) rotate3d(3,6,10,20deg);
  -moz-transform: scale(.75)rotate(3deg);
  -o-transform: scale(.75) rotate(3deg);
  transform: scale(.75) rotate(3deg); }

#f1:hover, #f2:hover, #f3:hover {
  opacity: 1;
  -webkit-transform: rotate(0);
  -moz-transform: rotate(0);
  -o-transform: rotate(0);
  transform: rotate(0);
  cursor: pointer;
  clip: auto;
  z-index: 9999; }
```

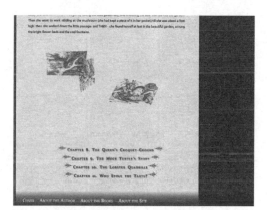

D In Webkit browsers, the thumbnails now appear to be rotated in a 3D space.

3. Add the transform style property to your CSS declarations and one or two values.

   ```
   -webkit-perspective-origin:
   → 25% 25%;
   → perspective-origin: 25% 25%;
   ```

   Add **perspective-origin** with one or two values that specify an origin point for the perspective property (not the transform value), defining the X and Y position at which the viewer appears to be viewing an element's children (**Table 12.6**). **Perspective-origin** keywords are the same as **transform-origin** keywords (Table12. 3).

4. Add the backface visibility property to your CSS declarations and one value.

   ```
   -webkit-backface-visibility:
   → visible;
   ```

   ```
   backface-visibility: visible;
   ```

   Add **backface-visibility** for the special case in which two elements are placed back to back (like a playing card) and need to be flipped together. This property will hide the back of flipped elements using **rotateZ** or **rotatate3D** (**Table 12.7**).

continues on next page

TABLE 12.6 Perspective-Origin Values

Value	Compatibility
\<percentage\>	S3.1, C5, CSS3
\<length\>	S3.1, C5, CSS3
\<keyword\>	S3.1, C5, CSS3

TABLE 12.7 Backface-Visibility Values

Value	Compatibility
visible	S3.1, C5, CSS3
hidden	S3.1, C5, CSS3

5. Add the transform property to your CSS declarations for the different browser extensions.

`-webkit-transform:`

`-moz-transform:`

`-o-transform:`

`transform:`

3D transformations use the same properties as 2D transformations, only the values are different.

6. Establish the perspective.

`perspective(250)`

To create a three-dimensional transformation, a three-dimensional **perspective** property should be established in the element to define a depth. Values start at 0 with lower values giving a more pronounced perspective and higher values creating less three-dimensional foreshortening.

7. Add the transform values.

`scale3d(.75,.5,1)`
`→rotate3d(5,4,2,-10deg);`

For each browser-specific property, add the same transform value (**Table 12.8**) with its relevant parenthetical value:

▸ **rotate3d()** requires three numbers to define the X, Y, Z axes and an angle value to turn the element around those axes. Positive values turn the element clockwise, whereas negative values turn the element counterclockwise.

▸ **rotateZ()** uses an angle value to turn the element around the Z axis. Positive values turn the element clockwise, whereas negative values turn the element counterclockwise.

TABLE 12.8 3D Transform-Style Values

Value	Compatibility
perspective(<number>)	S3.1, C5, CSS3
rotate3d(<number×3>,<angle>)	S3.1, C5, CSS3
rotateZ(<angle>)	S3.1, C5, CSS3
translate3d(<length×3>,)	S3.1, C5, CSS3
translateZ(<length>)	S3.1, C5, CSS3
scale3d(<number×3>,)	S3.1, C5, CSS3
scaleZ(<length>)	S3.1, C5, CSS3
matrix3d(<various×16>)	S3.1, C5, CSS3

- **scale3d()** requires three numeric values that act as a multiplier to the width (X) and/or height (Y) and depth (Z) of the element. Positive numbers increase element size. Negative values will increase size *and* reflect the element along that axis. Decimal numbers decrease scale.

- **scaleZ()** adds numeric values that act as a multiplier to the depth (Z) of the element. Positive numbers increase element size. Negative values will increase size *and* reflect the element along that axis. Decimal numbers decrease scale.

- **translate3d()** requires three length values that offset the element along the X axis, Y axis, and/or Z axis of the element. Positive values offset down, to the right, and forward (larger), whereas negative values offset up, to the left, and backward (smaller).

- **translateZ()** adds a length value that offsets the element along the Z axis of the element. Positive values offset forward, whereas negative values offset backwards. Unlike the X and Y values, a percentage is not allowed with Z.

- **matrix3d()** is a 4×4 matrix of 16 values that can be used as shorthand to represent any of the preceding transformations alone or in combination.

TIP I find the 3D transformations to be a bit of a mindblower when it comes to trying to figure out what does what. Don't worry if this doesn't seem intuitive at first. Experimentation is the best remedy for confusion.

NEW IN CSS3: Adding Transitions Between Element States ★

Despite people's expectations to see change and movement on the screen, CSS and HTML have few controls that allow you to design interactivity, and those that do exist have been binary up to this point:

- A link is one color *or* another.
- A text field is one size *or* another.
- A photo is transparent *or* opaque.

No in-betweens have existed in the past from one state to the next. No transitions.

This has led to most Web pages feeling abrupt, with elements shifting and changing ungracefully.

What we need is a quick and easy way to add simple transitions to a page, and that's where CSS transitions come into the picture.

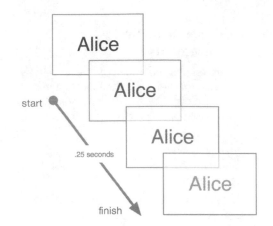

A A transition is like several frames in a movie, changing gradually over time rather than instantly.

What can be transitioned?

Almost any CSS property that has a color, length, or position component—including many of the new CSS3 properties—can be given a transition, changing it from one style to another style over time.

Table 12.9 shows a list of the CSS properties available and the values that can be transitioned. One exception is **box-shadows**.

For a transition to occur, there has to be a state change in the element, using one of the link or dynamic pseudo classes discussed in Chapter 3. Transitions work by changing a style between different element states over a period of time. For example, the color value of the default state of an element will pass through intermediate colors in the spectrum before appearing as the color value for the hover state **A**.

TABLE 12.9 CSS Properties with Transitions

CSS Property	Which Transitions	CSS Property	Which Transitions
background-color	Color	margin-right	Length
background-image	Only gradients	margin-top	Length
background-position	Percentage, length	max-height	Length, percentage
border-bottom-color	Color	max-width	Length, percentage
border-bottom-width	Length	min-height	Length, percentage
border-color	Color	min-width	Length, percentage
border-left-color	Color	opacity	Number
border-left-width	Length	outline-color	Color
border-right-color	Color	outline-offset	Integer
border-right-width	Length	outline-width	Length
border-spacing	Length	padding-bottom	Length
border-top-color	Color	padding-left	Length
border-top-width	Length	padding-right	Length
border-width	Length	padding-top	Length
bottom	Length, percentage	right	Length, percentage
color	Color	text-indent	Length, percentage
crop	Rectangle	text-shadow	Shadow
font-size	Length, percentage	top	Length, percentage
font-weight	Number	transform	Number, angle, width
grid-*	Various	vertical-align	Keywords, length, percentage
height	Length, percentage	visibility	Visibility
left	Length, percentage	width	Length, percentage
letter-spacing	Length	word-spacing	Length, percentage
line-height	Number, length, percentage	z-index	Integer
margin-bottom	Length	zoom	Number
margin-left	Length		

To add a transition effect between states:

1. Add the **transition** property.

   -webkit-transition:

   -moz-transition:

   -o-transition:

   transition:

   Include versions for the browser extensions including Webkit, Mozilla, Opera, and standard CSS3, including the standard property at the bottom of the list (**Code 12.4**).

2. Add values for each transition.

   color .25s ease-in transform
   → .25s ease-in-out 0

   Choose from the following values (**Table 12.10**):

   ▸ A **Transition Property** from **Table 12.11** indicates which specific CSS property is affected.

TABLE 12.10 Transition-Shorthand Values

Value	Compatibility
\<transition-property>	FF4, S3.1, C5, O10.5, CSS3
\<transition-duration>	FF4, S3.1, C5, O10.5, CSS3
\<transition-delay>	FF4, S3.1, C5, O10.5, CSS3

TABLE 12.11 Transition-Property Values

Value	Compatibility
\<CSSPropertytransition>*	FF4, S3.1, C5, O10.5, CSS3
none	FF4, S3.1, C5, O10.5, CSS3
all	FF4, S3.1, C5, O10.5, CSS3

*Table 12.9

Code 12.4 *transformation-transition-properties. css*—When applied to Code 12.1, transitions are now applied to the color, opacity, and transformations, resulting in a gradual rather than instant change **Ⓑ**.

```
/*** CSS3 VQS | Chapter 12 | transformation-
→ transition-properties.css ***/

* {
  -webkit-transition: color .25s ease-in,
  → opacity .5s ease, -webkit-transform
  → .25s ease-in-out 0;
  -moz-transition: color .25s ease-in,
  → opacity .5s ease, -moz-transform .
  → 25s ease-in-out 0;
  -o-transition: color .25s ease-in,
  → opacity .5s ease, -o-transform .25s
  → ease-in-out 0;
  transition: color .25s ease-in, opacity
  → .5s ease, transform .25 ease-in-out 0;  }

aside {
  -webkit-transform: rotate(-2deg);
  -moz-transform: rotate(-2deg);
  -o-transform: rotate(-2deg);
  transform: rotate(-2deg); }

div.gallery figure {
  width: auto;
  -webkit-transform-origin: left 25%;
  -moz-transform-origin: left 25%;
  -o-transform-origin: left 25%;
  transform-origin: left 25%;
  -webkit-transform-style: flat;
  transform-style: flat;
  -webkit-perspective: 5000;
  perspective: 5000;
  -webkit-perspective-origin: 25% 25%;
  perspective-origin: 25% 25%;
  -webkit-backface-visibility: visible;
  backface-visibility: visible; }

#f1 {
  -webkit-transform: perspective(250)
  → scale3d(.75,.5,1) rotate3d(5,4,2,-10deg);
  -moz-transform: scale(.75) rotate(10deg);
```

code continues on next page

Code 12.4 *continued*

```
  -o-transform: scale(.75) rotate(10deg);
  transform: scale(.75) rotate(10deg); }

#f2 {
  -webkit-transform: perspective(250)
  → scale3d(.5,.75,1.5) rotate3d(-3,10,-8,18deg);
  -moz-transform:scale(.75) rotate(-8deg);
  -o-transform: scale(.75) rotate(-8deg);
  transform: scale(.75) rotate(-8deg); }

#f3 {
  -webkit-transform: perspective(250)
  → scale3d(1,.5,.75) rotate3d(3,6,10,20deg);
  -moz-transform: scale(.75)rotate(3deg);
  -o-transform: scale(.75) rotate(3deg);
  transform: scale(.75) rotate(3deg); }

#f1:hover, #f2:hover, #f3:hover {
  opacity: 1;
  -webkit-transform: rotate(0);
  -moz-transform: rotate(0);
  -o-transform: rotate(0);
  transform: rotate(0);
  cursor: pointer;
  clip: auto;
  z-index: 9999; }
```

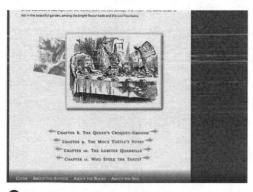

B When the user hovers a pointer over the image, it transitions over time and animates from its thumbnail position to the full-frame presentation. This includes any rotation, color, and opacity changes.

▶ **Duration** sets how long the transition should take from beginning to end, generally in seconds (**Table 12.12**). This is optional, and the default will be **0**.

▶ **Timing Function** defines the behavior of the transition's speed as it progresses (**Table 12.13**). This value is not required, and defaults to `linear` when not set.

▶ **Delay** specifies how long the duration should pause before starting (**Table 12.14**). This is optional and defaults to **0** if not set.

continues on next page

TABLE 12.12 Transition-Duration Values

Value	Compatibility
<time>	FF4, S3.1, C5, O10.5, CSS3

TABLE 12.13 Transition-Timing-Function Values

Value	How It Works
cubic-bezier (<number×4>,)	X and Y values are between 0 and 1 to define the shape of a bezier curve used for the timing function.
linear	Constant speed
ease	Gradual slowdown
ease-in	Speed up
ease-out	Slow down
ease-in-out	Speed up and then slow down

TABLE 12.14 Transition-Delay Values

Value	Compatibility
<time>	FF4, S3.1, C5, O10.5, CSS3

3. Add more transitions as needed.

```
, opacity .5s ease, transform
→.25 ease-in-out 0;
```

You can add as many transitions as you want, separated by commas. If you are setting a transition for the **transform** value, be sure to use the browser extension version with the right transition browser extension as shown here.

TIP This example uses the transition shorthand, but each of these properties can be set separately, using the **transition-property**, **transition-duration**, **transition-timing-function**, and **transition-delay** properties. Of course, you will need to set all of this independently for all three browser extensions as well as the standard CSS version, which can lead to a lot of code. Still, using these can be useful to override a particular value.

A Universal Transition

I added default transitions to the universal selector, applying these styles to *every* element on the screen. This ensures a consistent transition across my design and cuts down on the amount of code needed, since I apply it only once. You can then override the transitions, as necessary.

The concern with using the universal selector in this way is that applying a style like this to every element on the page might slow down rendering, but my own experiments have shown that it has little or no impact, even on large and complex pages.

Putting It All Together

1. **Building on your code from Chapter 11, add 2D transformations to your 3 elements.** Play around with the different transformations and values to see what their effect is.

2. **Add 3D transformations to the mix.** Your elements should not begin to look as if they are lifting off the page.

3. **Add a color transition to each element.** The transition should be between two contrasting colors and last for at least a second or more.

Fixing CSS

I won't sugar coat it: CSS has bugs, inconstancies, and some downright stupid features that you could spend hours trying to figure out and overcome. But you are not without tools. In this chapter, we'll review the most common problems, the most important fixes, and how to level the playing field to achieve more consistent default styles across all browsers.

Adjusting CSS for Internet Explorer

Without a doubt, the most issues and limitations you face when coding Web pages, especially if you are using CSS3, are in Internet Explorer. Sometimes called the *IE factor*, these limitations are the bane of Web designers who want to stay standards compliant but refuse to ignore the large portion of the Web public who use Firefox, Safari, Opera, and other browsers (see the sidebar "Designing with Progressive Enhancements."

The current versions of Internet Explorer are behind the times, with the most recent version (IE8) barely supporting CSS2, and older versions still in common use with far less CSS support. However, you will face the biggest problems when you have to support IE6, IE7, and IE8 in quirks mode (see the sidebar "What Is Quirks Mode?" in this chapter).

IE9, which may be available by the time you read this, promises to change all of that (see "CSS3 and the Promise of Internet Explorer 9" in Chapter 1), by adding full CSS3 and HTML5 compatibility, but no one knows for sure how long it will take for IE9 to replace its predecessors. The reality is you will need to include code to tailor your design to Internet Explorer for some time to come.

Fortunately, the solutions are provided—intentionally and unintentionally—by Internet Explorer itself.

What Is Quirks Mode?

CSS implementations in early versions of Internet Explorer were full of bugs, non-standard behaviors, and outright misinterpretations of the W3C standards. Internet Explorer 6 and later versions corrected most of these "quirks," but if Web browsers had instantly switched to standards compliance, older Web sites would have started breaking left and right.

The answer was doctype switching (see Chapter 2), which allowed designers to specify whether to support the old quirks, the standards, or a hybrid of the two.

In theory, to set a mode, all you have to do is set a doctype:

- **Quirks mode**—Used by the browser if it detects that the page is not standards compliant or if it uses the transitional doctype. This basically renders the page as if it were IE6.

- **Strict mode**—Uses the standards as defined by the particular browser and uses the strict doctype.

- **Almost Standards mode**—Firefox, Safari, and Opera (version 7.5 and later) have a third mode that uses all of the CSS2 standards except for table cell vertical sizing.

The underscore hack

A *hack* is code that is used because it is *not* supposed to work but does work under certain circumstances and can be exploited to fix a specific problem. Although several hacks allow us to include CSS code that will work *only* in Internet Explorer, the hack I find easiest to use and most reliable is the underscore hack.

Designing with Progressive Enhancements

It's clear that not all browsers are created equal, so why should we expect all Web sites to treat them that way? For years Web designers have tried to design to the lowest common denominator (IE), ignoring the great new features available to them in the belief that they had to create the exact same experience in all browsers.

Why?

As long as the site functions effectively and is as good as it can be *for that browser*, why not take advantage of the new features? Why not design with *progressive enhancements* that improve the experience for those who can see them without penalizing those who cannot? This is a question that has been debated back and forth by Web designers for several years.

The best reason for *not* using progressive enhancement comes down to your client's expectations: Most clients—who may not be schooled on the ways of Web design—have a hard time understanding why the Web site they paid good money for does not look as good on Internet Explorer as on other browsers.

However, I find that all it takes is a little education to get clients past this. Show them that working with progressive enhancements is:

1. *faster* to develop—Rather than spending time kludging together a bunch of images for rounded corners, drop shadows, and other effects, a few lines of code takes care of it all.

2. *cheaper* to maintain—Changing code is much more cost effective than reworking, re-cutting, and redeploying images.

3. *better* looking—Since the styles are native to the browser, they will display more precisely than images that are being shoehorned in.

If these arguments don't sway your client, then show them the budget for cost of designing with progressive enhancements compared to without. Usually this is enough to convince even the most stubborn client.

The underscore hack is the simplest way to include CSS code specifically for Internet Explorer browsers in quirks mode, exploiting a mistake in the way the underscore at the beginning of a CSS declaration should be treated. According to CSS standards, any declaration that starts with an underscore should be ignored, as if commented out. However, when Microsoft created earlier versions of Internet Explorer, it apparently didn't get that memo, and any version of Internet Explorer in quirks mode *will* pay attention to this declaration **Ⓐ**. We can use this error to hide CSS overrides meant for quirks mode from other browsers.

To use the IE underscore hack:

1. **Add your standards-compliant declarations to the CSS rule.** This is the code you want browsers to use for your design (**Code 13.1**).

   ```
   max-width: 980px;
   →min-width: 640px;
   →width: 100%
   ```

2. **Add the IE-specific declaration with an underscore (_) in front.** This value will override previous values for that property for any browsers using the IE quirks mode.

   ```
   _width: 800px;
   ```

TIP The underscore hack is a quick and easy way to set and test styles in IE, but it is not very good coding. I recommend using this only during development and then moving the hacked code into IE conditional CSS.

IE-specific CSS

_width: 800px;

Underscore

Ⓐ General syntax for the underscore hack. Any CSS placed on the same line as the underscore is ignored by browsers other than Internet Explorer in quirks mode.

Code 13.1 Standards-compliant browsers will use the range from 640px to 980px depending on browser width **Ⓑ**, whereas due to cascade, IE6 will always use 800px because it does not support max/min width **Ⓒ**. This can be applied in *any* situation where you need a different property or value applied.

```html
<!DOCTYPE html>
<html dir="ltr" lang="en-US">
  <head>
    <meta charset="utf-8">
    <title>Alice's Adventures in Wonderland</title>
    <style type="text/css">
      p {
        padding: 10px;
        margin: 10px auto;
        max-width: 980px;
        min-width: 640px;
        width: 100%
        _width: 800px;
        outline: 1px solid red;
        _border: 1px solid red; }
    </style>
  </head>
  <body>
    <p>Suddenly she came,...</p>
    <p>Alice opened the,....</p>
    <p>There seemed to,...</p>
  </body>
</html>
```

Suddenly she came upon a little three-legged table, all made of solid glass; there was nothing on it except a tiny golden key, and Alice's first thought was that it might belong to one of the doors of the hall; but, alas! either the locks were too large, or the key was too small, but at any rate it would not open any of them. However, on the second time round, she came upon a low curtain she had not noticed before, and behind it was a little door about fifteen inches high: she tried the little golden key in the lock, and to her great delight it fitted!

Alice opened the door and found that it led into a small passage, not much larger than a rat-hole: she knelt down and looked along the passage into the loveliest garden you ever saw. How she longed to get out of that dark hall, and wander about among those beds of bright flowers and those cool fountains, but she could not even get her head though the doorway; 'and even if my head would go through,' thought poor Alice, 'it would be of very little use without my shoulders. Oh, how I wish I could shut up like a telescope! I think I could, if I only know how to begin.' For, you see, so many out-of-the-way things had happened lately, that Alice had begun to think that very few things indeed were really impossible.

There seemed to be no use in waiting by the little door, so she went back to the table, half hoping she might find another key on it, or at any rate a book of rules for shutting people up like telescopes: this time she found a little bottle on it, ('which certainly was not here before,' said Alice,) and round the neck of the bottle was a paper label, with the words 'DRINK ME' beautifully printed on it in large letters.

B Code 13.1 in Firefox. The width will expand and contract with the window width.

Suddenly she came upon a little three-legged table, all made of solid glass; there was nothing on it except a tiny golden key, and Alice's first thought was that it might belong to one of the doors of the hall; but, alas! either the locks were too large, or the key was too small, but at any rate it would not open any of them. However, on the second time round, she came upon a low curtain she had not noticed before, and behind it was a little door about fifteen inches high: she tried the little golden key in the lock, and to her great delight it fitted!

Alice opened the door and found that it led into a small passage, not much larger than a rat-hole: she knelt down and looked along the passage into the loveliest garden you ever saw. How she longed to get out of that dark hall, and wander about among those beds of bright flowers and those cool fountains, but she could not even get her head though the doorway, 'and even if my head would go through,' thought poor Alice, 'it would be of very little use without my shoulders. Oh, how I wish I could shut up like a telescope! I think I could, if I only know how to begin.' For, you see, so many out-of-the-way things had happened lately, that Alice had begun to think that very few things indeed were really impossible.

There seemed to be no use in waiting by the little door, so she went back to the table, half hoping she might find another key on it, or at any rate a book of rules for shutting people up like telescopes: this time she found a little bottle on it, ('which certainly was not here before,' said Alice,) and round the neck of the bottle was a paper label, with the words 'DRINK ME' beautifully printed on it in large letters.

C Code 13.1 in Internet Explorer 6. Although the page looks much the same, it is actually using **border** rather than **outline** and will not dynamically resize with the window.

IE conditional CSS

Internet Explorer (and *only* Internet Explorer) has the ability to interpret conditional statements (if this...then do that) that are ignored by other browsers 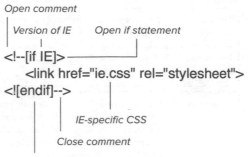. This allows you to insert links to style sheets that can tailor your CSS for any version of Internet Explorer.

To set up conditional styles for Internet Explorer:

1. **Add your standards-compliant CSS.** This can be embedded in the head of your document in a `<style>` tag or imported using the `<link>` tag or `@import` rule (Code 13.2):

   `<style type="text/css">...</style>`

2. **Add a conditional comment, specifying the version of IE you want to target.** Within an HTML comment, use an **if** statement within square brackets and specify which version of Internet Explorer the CSS overrides should be used with:

   `<!--[if lte IE 8]>`

   Table 13.1 shows the possible logical operators you can include for targeting specific browsers or a range of browser versions.

   Using just **IE** will cause the CSS to be used in any version of Internet Explorer. Adding a space followed by a number will specify the version number. For example, **IE 6** allows CSS to be used only in Internet Explorer 6 regardless of the doctype.

Open comment

Version of IE   *Open if statement*

`<!--[if IE]>`
　　`<link href="ie.css" rel="stylesheet">`
`<![endif]-->`

IE-specific CSS

Close comment

End if statement

 General syntax for conditional statements. Anything placed between the comments will be used only by the specified versions of Internet Explorer.

TABLE 13.1 IE Conditionals

IE	Any version of IE
lt IE <version>	Versions less than version
lte IE <version>	Versions less than or equal to version
IE <version>	Specific version
gte IE <version>	Versions greater than or equal to version
gt IE <version>	Versions greater than version

TIP Because IE9 is promising HTML5 and CSS3 compatibility, I recommend setting your IE conditional to "let IE 8," which will apply the overrides only to versions of Internet Explorer *less than or equal to* 8.

TIP Although you can add specific code for different versions of Internet Explorer, try to keep the number of links and imports to a minimum. The more external files you bring in, the longer it will take your Web page to load.

3. **Add the IE-specific CSS for the browser version(s).** This value will override previous values for that property for standard CSS. This can be embedded in the head of your document using the **<style>** tag or imported using the **<link>** tag or **@import** rule:

   @import url(ie-fix.css);

4. **Close the conditional comment.** Close your conditional comment with an **endif** in brackets:

   <![endif]-->

Code 13.2 The final HTML from Chapter 12 ⓔ, now includes a link to a special CSS file tailored to Internet Explorer (**Code 13.3**) that will be added only if the browser version is IE8 or lower ⓕ ⓖ. The *library.css* file (not shown) combines all of the CSS from Chapters 5–12 in one file.

```
<!-- HTML5 -->
<!DOCTYPE html>
<html dir="ltr" lang="en">
<head>
<meta http-equiv="Content-Type" content="text/html; charset=UTF-8" />
<title>Alice's Adventures in Wonderland</title>
<link href="../_css/library.css" type="text/css" media="all" rel="stylesheet">
  <!--[if lte IE 8 ]>
    <script src="../_script/HTML5forIE.js" type="text/javascript"></script>
    <link href="../_css/ie-fix.css" type="text/css" media="all" rel="stylesheet">
  <![endif]-->
</head>
<body id="chapter07" class="book aaiw chapter">
<header class="page">
<h1>Alice's Adventures In Wonderland</h1>
<p class="byline">by <span class="author">Lewis Carroll</span></p>

<nav class="global">
  <ul>
    <li><a href="" target="_self">Cover</a></li>
    <li><a href="" target="_self">About the Author</a></li>
    <li><a href="" target="_self">About the Books</a></li>
    <li><a href="" target="_self">About the Site</a></li>
  </ul>
</nav>
```

code continues on next page

Code 13.2 *continued*

```
</header>
<article><!-- Article -->
<nav>
  <ol class="toc top">
    <h2><a href="" target="_self">Down the Rabbit-Hole</a></h2>
    <h2><a href="" target="_self">The Pool of Tears</a></h2>
    <h2><a href="" target="_self">A Caucus-Race and a Long Tale</a></h2>
    <h2><a href="" target="_self">The Rabbit Sends in a Little Bill</a></h2>
    <h2><a href="" target="_self">Advice from a Caterpillar</a></h2>
    <h2><a href="" target="_self">Pig and Pepper</a></h2>
  </ol>
</nav>
<h2><strong>CHAPTER 7.</strong> A Mad Tea-Party</h2>
<figure>
<img src="../_images/AAIW-illos/alice26a.png" alt="alice15a">
<figcaption>
"Twinkle, twinkle, little bat!<br/>
How I wonder what you're at!"
</figcaption>
</figure>
<p>
There was a table set out under a tree in front of the house, and the
March Hare and the Hatter were having tea at it: a Dormouse was sitting
between them, fast asleep, and the other two were using it as a
cushion, resting their elbows on it, and talking over its head. 'Very
uncomfortable for the Dormouse,' thought Alice; 'only, as it's asleep, I
suppose it doesn't mind.'
</p>
<div class="gallery">
<figure id="f1">
  <img src="../_images/AAIW-illos/alice24a.png" alt="alice15a">
</figure>
<figure id="f2">
  <img src="../_images/AAIW-illos/alice25a.png" alt="alice15a">
</figure>
<figure id="f3">
  <img src="../_images/AAIW-illos/alice27a.png" alt="alice15a">
</figure>
</div>
<nav>
<ol class="toc continued">
  <h2><a href="" target="_self">The Queen's Croquet-Ground</a></h2>
  <h2><a href="" target="_self">The Mock Turtle's Story</a></h2>
  <h2><a href="" target="_self">The Lobster Quadrille</a></h2>
  <h2><a href="" target="_self">Who Stole the Tarts?</a></h2>
```

code continues on next page

Code 13.2 *continued*

```
</ol>
</nav>
<br>
</article>
<aside>
<h3>About Lewis Carroll</h3>
<h4>From <cite>Wikipedia</cite></h4>
<p>Charles Lutwidge Dodgson,...</p>
</aside>
<footer class="page">
<nav class="global">
  <ul>
    <li><a href="" target="_self">Cover</a></li>
    <li><a href="" target="_self">About the
    → Author</a></li>
    <li><a href="" target="_self">About the
    → Books</a></li>
    <li><a href="" target="_self">About the
    → Site</a></li>
  </ul>
</nav>
</footer>
</body>
</html>
```

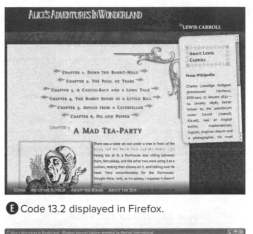

E Code 13.2 displayed in Firefox.

F Code 13.2 displayed in Internet Explorer 7 *without* adding the IE fix CSS.

G Code 13.2 displayed in Internet Explorer 7, and using the IE fix (Code 13.3) to shape the page for Internet Explorer.

Code 13.3 *ie-fix.css*—Styles are used to override styles from library.css to display the page as well as possible in Internet Explorer. This includes increasing the font size a little; replacing multiple backgrounds with a single background; changing colors to nonalpha values; setting appropriate widths and heights for the IE box mode; and, most important, setting all the new HTML5 elements to be block level.

```css
/*** CSS3 VQS | Chapter 13 | ie-fix.css ***/

/*** font properties ***/

body { font-size: 110%; }

/*** color & background properties ***/

header.page {
  background: rgb(102,0,0)
  → url(../_images/bg-book-spine-title.png)
  → no-repeat center top;
  height: 130px; }

article {
  background: rgb(242, 237, 217)
  → url(../_images/paper-01.jpg) repeat 0 0; }

article h2 strong {
  color: rgb(135,127,107); }

td {
  background-color: rgb(235,235,235); }

.byline {
  color: rgb(248, 240, 227); }

.byline .author {
  color: rgb(248, 240, 227); }

/*** list & table properties ***/

td {
  background-color: rgb(235,235,235); }

/*** box properties ***/

article,aside,canvas,details,dialog,
→ eventsource,figure,footer,header,hgroup,
→ mark,menu,meter,nav,output,progress,section,
→ time,video { display: block; }
```

code continues on next page

Code 13.3 *continued*

```css
header li {
  visibility: visible;
  float: left; }

figure {
  border: 6px double rgb(142, 137, 129); }

figcaption {
  border-top: 2px solid rgb(142, 137, 129);
  width: 100%; }

aside {
  width: 300px;
  height: 450px; }

aside h3 {
  padding: 5px;
  border: 6px double rgb(142, 137, 129); }

/*** visual formatting properties ***/

aside {
  position: relative;
  top: 10px; }

/*** transforamtion & transition properties
→ ***/
```

Fixing the Internet Explorer Box Model

All elements are rectangular "boxes" with a margin, border, padding, and content that has a width and height. But remember that this is Web design—it can never be that simple, right?

Right. The problems begin when you realize that not all browsers define boxes in the same way, the main culprit being IE6.

The W3C definition of a box created using CSS specifies that the width and height define the width and height of only the content area, the area where images and other objects are displayed. However, the *total* area that the element occupies includes the content area *plus* the padding and border sizes. So, the apparent width would be calculated in the following way:

width(content) + left padding + right padding + left border + right border = width (total)

Unfortunately, Internet Explorer through version 5.5 defined width and height values as the apparent width and height including padding and borders. This effectively subtracted the padding and border sizes to determine the content width and height:

width(total) − left padding − right padding − left border − right border = width (content)

So, given the following CSS code:

```
#object1 {
border: 5px solid #000;
padding: 10px;
width: 100px;
}
```

browsers using the W3C standard (Firefox, Safari, Opera) would set the content area to 100 pixels wide but have a total width of 130 pixels Ⓐ:

100 + 5 + 5 + 10 + 10 = 130

On the other hand, Internet Explorer 5.5 and earlier would set the total width of the element (from border to border) as 100 pixels, shrinking the width of the content to 70 pixels Ⓑ:

100 - 5 - 5 - 10 - 10 = 70

This is a problem, and it only gets worse.

Versions 6 and later of Internet Explorer fix this problem by following the W3C standards. However, if you are using the transitional document type definition (DTD) for your page—which is still very common—or a DTD that the browsers do not recognize—such as HTML5—IE6 and IE7 revert to the "quirky" version of the box model. Unfortunately, more often than not, your site will probably trigger IE's quirks mode.

So what's a good Web designer to do? You have a few options:

- Do not use a border and/or padding with any element that has a set dimension. If you do, don't expect pixel-precise layouts. Generally, this solution isn't practical, but for simple pages it might do the trick.

- Code for the strict DTD so that the browser uses the standards-compliant box model. Generally, this approach is not practical because the slightest error can return the browser to quirks mode and destroy the whole design.

- Use one of the IE techniques (most likely the conditional comments) to code separate "equalizing" widths and/or heights for Internet Explorer.

Ⓐ The box using the CSS box model. The content area is 100 pixels across with padding and border added for a total width of 130 pixels.

Ⓑ Internet Explorer box model has its own way of dealing with the width, making the total width 100 pixels and shrinking the content area to 70 pixels.

TIP Interestingly, a new CSS3 property (box-sizing) that's still under development will allow you to choose which of these box models you want to use.

Resetting CSS

In Chapter 2, you learned about browser default styles. Recall that the browser developers set the default styles applied by HTML tags. Far too many Web sites are designed by default. The designers and developers allow the browser manufacturer to have the final word on how the content is displayed. Additionally, all browser default styles are not the same from browser to browser. CSS resets were developed to level the playing field and help prevent "vanilla" designs.

The exact CSS reset you choose will depend on your design needs. I like to keep my reset simple, adding styles to specific tags only as needed. However, several styles are inconsistent or (in my opinion) poorly set in most browsers.

Redefining important CSS properties (generally to none or 0) provides a few benefits:

- **Reduces bad styles.** Undoes some of the questionable and downright annoying styles added by browser manufacturers, and eliminates the styles that simply do not work. One example is using an outline to highlight items that are in focus, such as form fields. Although highlighting is useful for keyboard navigation, you should design this yourself.

- **Eliminates design by default.** Sets a level playing field from which to begin a design. Rather than allowing the browser manufacturers to dictate your page appearance, you take control.

continues on next page

- **Makes browser styles consistent.**
Ensures values across all browser types and versions are the same. Because browsers slightly vary their default style values, a good reset will allow your designs to appear with greater consistency regardless of how your visitor is viewing it.

To use a CSS reset, simply add the desired code at the very top of your CSS code. That's it. The code does the rest.

A simple CSS reset

The easiest way to reset styles is to use the universal selector and set the default styles you want applied to all tags, as shown in **Code 13.4**. Remember that you want to keep your CSS reset compact. **Code 13.5** does the same thing but removes all spaces and returns.

This is a quick way to reset the most important styles, but it has one drawback: IE6 does not recognize the universal selector. If you are concerned about supporting IE6, you will want to include all the HTML tags in the selector list. The advantage of using the universal selector, other than compactness, is that it will always apply itself to new HTML tags as they become available.

Code 13.4 *cssreset-simple.css*—This version of the CSS uses the universal selector to reset the browser default values of several key properties including margin, padding, border, outline, line-height, vertical-align, and text-decoration.

```
/*** CSS3 VQS | Chapter 13 |
→ cssreset-simple.css ***/

* {margin: 0;
   padding: 0;
   border: 0;
   outline: 0;
   line-height: 1.4em;
   vertical-align: baseline;
   text-decoration: none; }
```

Code 13.5 *cssreset-simple.css*—The same code as 13.4, but it's compressed by removing all line breaks and spaces.

```
/*** CSS3 VQS | Chapter 13 |
→ cssreset-simple.css ***/

*{margin:0;padding:0;border:0;outline:0;
→ line-height:1.4em;vertical-align:
→ baseline;text-decoration:none;}
```

YUI2: Reset CSS

Yahoo! developed the YUI2: Reset CSS to remove and neutralize inconsistencies in the default styling of HTML elements, to create a level playing field across browsers, and according to their documentation, to provide a sound foundation upon which you can explicitly declare your intentions.

This CSS Reset (Code 13.6) addresses the styles of many specific HTML tags, zeroing them out, as well as resolving some problems with font sizes, weights, and the use of quotation marks.

developer.yahoo.com/yui/reset/

Code 13.6 *cssreset-YUI2.css*—Developed by Yahoo!, the YUI2 reset does a more thorough job of overriding specific browser default styles.

```
/*** CSS3 VQS | Chapter 13 | cssreset-YUI2.css ***/

body,div,dl,dt,dd,ul,ol,li,h1,h2,h3,h4,h5,h6,pre,form,fieldset,input,textarea,p,blockquote,th,td {
  margin:0;
  padding:0; }
table {
  border-collapse:collapse;
  border-spacing:0; }
fieldset,img {
  border:0; }
address,caption,cite,code,dfn,em,strong,th,var {
  font-style:normal;
  font-weight:normal; }
ol,ul {
  list-style:none; }
caption,th {
  text-align:left; }
h1,h2,h3,h4,h5,h6 {
  font-size:100%;
  font-weight:normal; }
q:before,q:after {
  content:''; }
abbr,acronym {
  border:0; }
```

Eric Meyer's reset

Partially in response to Yahoo!, noted Web pundit Eric Meyer developed his own CSS reset script. According to his blog, he felt that the Yahoo! code went too far in some areas and not far enough in others. This script (**Code 13.7**) is useful for resetting typographic styles.

meyerweb.com/eric/tools/css/reset/

TIP Applying styles globally to every tag puts a burden on the browser's rendering engine. This is mostly an argument against using the universal selector (*), which applies the styles to every tag. However, I have not seen any data showing exactly what this lag is and haven't found any noticeable degradation in my own tests, even on complex pages.

Code 13.7 *cssreset-ericmeyer.css*—Developed by Eric Meyer, this reset is simpler than the Yahoo! Reset.

```
/*** CSS3 VQS | Chapter 13 |
→ cssreset-ericmeyer.css ***/

/* v1.0 | 20080212 */
html, body, div, span, applet, object, iframe,
h1, h2, h3, h4, h5, h6, p, blockquote, pre,
a, abbr, acronym, address, big, cite, code,
del, dfn, em, font, img, ins, kbd, q, s, samp,
small, strike, strong, sub, sup, tt, var,
b, u, i, center,
dl, dt, dd, ol, ul, li,
fieldset, form, label, legend,
table, caption, tbody, tfoot, thead, tr, th,
→ td {
  margin: 0;
  padding: 0;
  border: 0;
  outline: 0;
  font-size: 100%;
  vertical-align: baseline;
  background: transparent;
}
body {
  line-height: 1;
}
ol, ul {
  list-style: none;
}
blockquote, q {
  quotes: none;
}
blockquote:before, blockquote:after,
q:before, q:after {
  content: '';
  content: none;
}
/* remember to define focus styles! */
:focus {
  outline: 0;
}
/* remember to highlight inserts somehow! */
ins {
  text-decoration: none;
}
del {
  text-decoration: line-through;
}
/* tables still need 'cellspacing="0"' in the
→ markup */
table {
  border-collapse: collapse;
  border-spacing: 0;
}
```

What Should You Reset?

As a designer, I recommend resetting many of the typographic and box styles and then setting your own defaults. In addition to not allowing the browser to set the direction, another good argument for resetting styles is that different browsers have slightly different values.

- **Padding, borders, and margins77**—These are the main styles that designers like to reset, especially because they vary so much from browser to browser.

- **Text underlining**—Never use the **text-decoration** property to underline text. I have never seen a design in which underlining did anything other than add visual noise, even for links. Instead of using **underline**, applying **border-bottom** gives a similar effect with more precise control, allowing you to specify the thickness, color, and line style of the underline.

- **Line height**—The default value for line height on text is 1 em, which means the text has little or no breathing room. All text can benefit by bumping this up to at least 1.4 em.

- **Outline**—Outlines are applied by some browsers to highlight elements, such as form fields, when they come into focus. Although this is a good idea, the nature of this highlight should be up to you, not the browser.

- **Vertical alignment**—Vertical alignment is tricky to deal with and rarely works the way you expect. The best procedure is to set the vertical alignment to the baseline and then use relative positioning to move elements up or down manually.

- **Other**—These are the basics, but most CSS resets will go beyond this, cleaning up other perceived problems, generally with specific tag implementation.

Fixing the Float

CSS has one nasty little bug that was apparently meant to be a feature: When you float block-level elements within a block-level element, the child elements do not take up any space in their parent **A**. Make no mistake, the child elements are still on the Web page where you expect them to be, but if you add a background or border to their parent, the box collapses to a size as if they were not present! This can be incredibly annoying if you are trying to set up columns.

Several solutions have been developed to combat this little "feature" and force the parent element to acknowledge all of its prodigal children **B**, but I find two solutions to be most reliable. The first is structural in the HTML; the other is pure and simple CSS.

Break tag clear all fix

The problem with floating elements is that they are taken out of the normal flow of the document so, in effect, nothing anchors the bottom of the element and identifies where the bottom is. To fix this, you have to clear floating at the bottom of the element (after all of its floating children) so it will open to its natural height.

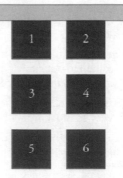

A Without a fix, the parent element (article) rolls up like a cheap newspaper, leaving its child elements high and dry.

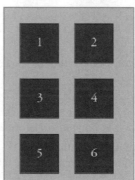

B With the fix in place, the parent is there to protect its children.

Code 13.8 The break tag clear fix involves adding a new structural element (the break tag) to the bottom of the parent element to clear the floating and snap the parent back open.

```
<!DOCTYPE html>
<html dir="ltr" lang="en-US">
  <head>
    <meta charset="utf-8">
    <title>Alice's Adventures in Wonderland</title>
    <style type="text/css">
      article {
        padding: 10px;
        background-color: rgb(204,204,204);
        border: 1px solid rgb(153,153,153);
        display: block;
        width: 150px; }
      .object {
        float: left;
        display: block;
        text-align: center;
        line-height: 50px;
        color: rgb(255,255,255);
        background-color: rgb(255,0,0);
        border: 1px solid rgb(153,0,0);
        margin: 10px;
        width: 50px;
        height: 50px; }
      .clearfix {
        clear: both; }
    </style>
    <!--[if lte IE 8 ]>
      <script src="../_script/HTML5forIE.js"
type="text/javascript"></script>
    <![endif]-->
  </head>
  <body>
    <article>
      <div class="object">1</div>
      <div class="object">2</div>
      <div class="object">3</div>
      <div class="object">4</div>
      <div class="object">5</div>
      <div class="object">6</div>
      <br class="clearfix">
    </article>
  </body>
</html>
```

To add the clearfix:

1. **Create a class in your CSS called clearfix.** This class will include the single declaration to clear all floating (Code 13.8):

   `.clearfix { clear: both; }`

2. **Add the clearfix class to a break tag at the bottom of every parent element that contains floating elements.** This class will clear floating, and the element will snap to its natural height:

   `<br class="clearfix">`

TIP Although I've used clearfix here for the specific purpose of fixing the floating box problem, this class can be applied anywhere you want to clear floating.

TIP A much more complex kludge of the clearfix class exists, but it has been replaced with a better method as explained below.

Overflow fix

The second method for preventing a parent element from collapsing is so simple that if it weren't so important, it would hardly be worth mentioning: To restore the element's height, just set its **overflow**. That's it. You can even just set the element overflow to the default of **auto**, apparently reminding the element to accommodate its children.

To add the overflow fix:

1. **For any element that is collapsing, add the overflow property.** You can set the value to anything, including the default value **auto**, to restore the parent to its proper height (**Code 13.9**):

   overflow: auto;

2. **Set up your parent element with floating children.** As long as the parent element includes the **overflow** declaration, you are safe.

   <aside>...</aside>

TIP You may notice a little trick I used to center the numbers in the blocks horizontally (easy) and also vertically. Horizontal is achieved by adding text align center. Vertical is done by setting the line-weight to be the same value as the height of the box. As long as only a single line of text is present, it will stay vertically centered in the element.

Code 13.9 The overflow fix requires you to add the overflow property to the parents' styles, and everything is as it should be.

```
<!DOCTYPE html>
<html dir="ltr" lang="en-US">
  <head>
    <meta charset="utf-8">
    <title>Alice's Adventures in Wonderland</
title>
    <style type="text/css">
      article {
        padding: 10px;
        background-color: rgb(204,204,204);
        border: 1px solid rgb(153,153,153);
        width: 150px;
        display: block;
        overflow: auto; }
      .object {
        float: left;
        text-align: center;
        line-height: 50px;
        color: rgb(255,255,255);
        background-color: rgb(255,0,0);
        border: 1px solid rgb(153,0,0);
        margin: 10px;
        width: 50px;
        height: 50px; }
    </style>
    <!--[if lte IE 8 ]>
      <script src="../_script/HTML5forIE.js"
type="text/javascript"></script>
    <![endif]-->
  </head>
  <body>
    <article>
      <div class="object">1</div>
      <div class="object">2</div>
      <div class="object">3</div>
      <div class="object">4</div>
      <div class="object">5</div>
      <div class="object">6</div>
    </article>
  </body>
</html>
```

Essential CSS Techniques

There are a few critical recipes that every Web designer needs to know to begin putting their CSS skills to work. These applications of CSS have become so standard that they form the core of the vast majority of Web designs you will see.

Let's look at these core applications of CSS to create columns, style menus, and drop-down menus; and use CSS sprites.

In This Chapter

Code 14.1 The HTML5 code you'll be playing with in this chapter **Ⓐ**. It's a little different from the code used in Chapters 5–12 so that you can better play with columns and menus.

```html
<!DOCTYPE html>
<html dir="ltr" lang="en-US">
  <head>
    <meta charset="utf-8">
    <title>Alice's Adventures in Wonderland</title>
  </head>
  <link href="code14_02.css" rel="stylesheet" media="all">
  <link href="code14_03.css" rel="stylesheet" media="screen">
  <link href="code14_04.css" rel="stylesheet" media="screen">
  <link href="code14_05.css" rel="stylesheet" media="screen">
  <link href="code14_06.css" rel="stylesheet" media="print">
  <body id="chapter01" class="book aaiw chapter">
    <header class="site">
      <h1>Alice's Adventures In Wonderland</h1>
      <p class="byline">by <span class="author">Lewis Carroll</span></p>
    </header>
    <section>
    <nav class="toc">
      <ul class="menu" >
        <li>Table of Contents</li>
        <ol class="drop">
         <li><a href="ch01.html">Down the Rabbit-Hole</a></li>
         <li><a href="ch02.html">The Pool of Tears</a></li>
         <li><a href="ch03.html">A Caucus-Race and a Long Tale</a></li>
         <li><a href="ch04.html">The Rabbit Sends in a Little Bill</a></li>
         <li><a href="ch05.html">Advice from a Caterpillar</a></li>
         <li><a href="ch06.html">Pig and Pepper</a></li>
         <li><a href="ch07.html">A Mad Tea Party</a></li>
         <li><a href="ch08.html">The Queen's Croquet-Ground</a></li>
         <li><a href="ch09.html">The Mock Turtle's Story</a></li>
         <li><a href="ch10.html">The Lobster Quadrille</a></li>
         <li><a href="ch11.html">Who Stole the Tarts?</a></li>
         <li><a href="ch12.html">Alice's Evidence</a></li>
        </ol>
      </ul>
    </nav>
      <article>
      <header class="page"><h2>Chapter 1. <strong>Down The Rabbit-Hole</strong></h2></header>
      <p>
      Alice was beginning <a href="" target="_self">to get very tired</a> of sitting by her sister
      → on the
      bank, and of having nothing to do: once or twice she had peeped into the
      book her sister was reading, but it <a href="" target="_self">had no pictures or
      → conversations</a> in
      it, 'and what is the use of a book,' <a href="" target="_self">thought Alice</a> 'without
      → pictures or
```

code continues on next page

Code 14.1 *continued*

```
      conversation?'
      </p>
    </article>
    <aside>
      <h3>About Lewis Carroll</h3>
      <h4>From <cite>Wikipedia</cite></h4>
      <p>Charles Lutwidge Dodgson,...</p>
    </aside>
  </section>
  <footer class="site">
  <h4>
    THE MILLENNIUM FULCRUM EDITION 3.0
  </h4>
  </footer>
</body>
</html>
```

Alice's Adventures In Wonderland

by Lewis Carroll

- Table of Contents
  1. Down the Rabbit-Hole
  2. The Pool of Tears
  3. A Caucus-Race and a Long Tale
  4. The Rabbit Sends in a Little Bill
  5. Advice from a Caterpillar
  6. Pig and Pepper
  7. A Mad Tea Party
  8. The Queen's Croquet-Ground
  9. The Mock Turtle's Story
  10. The Lobster Quadrille
  11. Who Stole the Tarts?
  12. Alice's Evidence

Chapter 1. Down The Rabbit-Hole

Alice was beginning to get very tired of sitting by her sister on the bank, and of having nothing to do: once or twice she had peeped into the book her sister was reading, but it had no pictures or conversations in it, 'and what is the use of a book,' thought Alice 'without pictures or conversation?'

So she was considering in her own mind (as well as she could, for the hot day made her feel very sleepy and stupid), whether the pleasure of making a daisy-chain would be worth the trouble of getting up and picking the daisies, when suddenly a White Rabbit with pink eyes ran close by her.

However, this bottle was NOT marked 'poison,' so Alice ventured to taste it, and finding it very nice, (it had, in fact, a sort of mixed flavour of cherry-tart, custard, pine-apple, roast turkey, toffee, and hot buttered toast,) she very soon finished it off.

'What a curious feeling!' said Alice; 'I must be shutting up like a telescope.'

And so it was indeed: she was now only ten inches high, and her face brightened up at the thought that she was now the right size for going through the little door into that lovely garden. First, however, she waited for a few minutes to see if she was going to shrink any further: she felt a little nervous about this; 'for it might end, you know,' said Alice to herself, 'in my going out altogether, like a candle. I wonder what I should be like then?' And she tried to fancy what the flame of a candle is like after the candle is blown out, for she could not remember ever having seen such a thing.

After a while, finding that nothing more happened, she decided on going into the garden at once; but, alas for poor Alice! when she got to the door, she found she had forgotten the little golden key, and when she went back to the table for it, she found she could not possibly reach it: she could see it quite plainly through the glass, and she tried her best to climb up one of the legs of the table, but it was too slippery; and when she had tired herself out with trying, the poor little thing sat down and cried.

'Come, there's no use in crying like that!' said Alice to herself, rather sharply; 'I advise you to leave off this minute!' She generally gave herself very good advice, (though she very seldom followed it), and sometimes she scolded herself so severely as to bring tears into her eyes; and once she remembered trying to box her own ears for having cheated herself in a game of croquet she was playing against herself, for this curious child was very fond of pretending to be two people. 'But it's no use now,' thought poor Alice, 'to pretend to be two people! Why, there's hardly enough of me left to make ONE respectable person!'

Soon her eye fell on a little glass box that was lying under the table: she opened it, and found in it a very small cake, on which the words 'EAT ME' were beautifully marked in currants. 'Well, I'll eat it,' said Alice, 'and if it makes me grow larger, I can reach the key; and if it makes me grow smaller, I can creep under the door; so either way I'll get into the garden, and I don't care which happens!'

She ate a little bit, and said anxiously to herself, 'Which way? Which way?', holding her hand on the top of her head to feel which way it was growing, and she was quite surprised to find that she remained the same size: to be sure, this generally happens when one eats cake, but Alice had got so much into the way of expecting nothing but out-of-the-way things to happen, that it seemed quite dull and stupid for life to go on in the common way.

So she set to work, and very soon finished off the cake.

About Lewis Carroll

From *Wikipedia*

Charles Lutwidge Dodgson (pronounced /ˈdɒdsən/, DOD-sən; 27 January 1832 – 14 January 1898), better known by the pseudonym Lewis Carroll (/ˈkærəl/), R.A.H., was an English author, mathematician, logician, Anglican deacon and a photographer. His most famous writings are Alice's Adventures in Wonderland and its sequel Through the Looking-Glass, as well as the poems "The Hunting of the Snark" and "Jabberwocky", all examples of the genre of literary nonsense. He is noted for his facility at word play, logic, and fantasy, and there are societies dedicated to the enjoyment and promotion of his works and the investigation of his life in many parts of the world, including the United Kingdom, Japan, the United States, and New Zealand.

THE MILLENNIUM FULCRUM EDITION 3.0

Ⓐ The Web page (Code 14.1) without any styles applied to it. The content is all stacked vertically on top of each other.

Creating Multicolumn Layouts with Float

The most common way to lay out a page is by establishing a grid, which is generally made up of two or more columns **A**. This allows the designer to present multiple sources of information and functionality in the same horizontal plane, making better use of the screen and reducing the need to scroll.

Although not explicitly intended to perform this duty, the **float** property (discussed in Chapter 10) is now the standard method for creating a grid structure of columns in most modern Web designs. This is done by taking block level elements that would normally stack vertically and horizontally and "floating" them next to each other **B**.

To set up a multicolumn layout using CSS:

1. Create an external CSS file called *layout.css* (Code 14.2).

   `layout.css`

   This file contains the CSS needed to create your grid and is linked to your HTML in **Code 14.1**.

2. **Add rules to define the width of your content.** This generally involves defining a width for the site's header and footer, as well as the section into which you will add the articles. The width depends on your design needs, but 980 pixels is a typical width for many Web pages:

   ```
   header.site, section,
   → footer.site {...}
   ```

continues on page 349

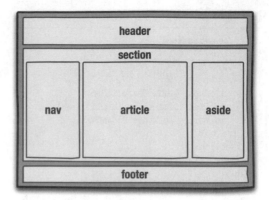

A The basic wireframe for your page, showing the three columns within the surrounding section element.

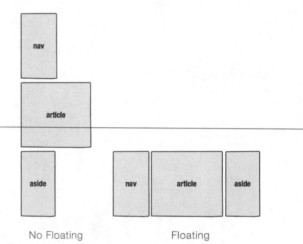

No Floating   Floating

B When floating is applied, the columns flow horizontally next to each other.

Code 14.2 *layout.css*—Creates columns when applied to Code 14.1 **C**. In addition to a simple CSS reset, the layout code sets the width of the total page, along with the width and padding of each column (for a fixed width page this must equal the overall width of the page), and then floats the three columns so that they horizontally flow next to each other rather than stacking.

```css
/*** CSS3 VQS | Chapter 14 | layout.css ***/

/* CSS Simple Reset
------------------------------------------------------------- */

*{margin:0;padding:0;border:0;outline:0;line-height:1.4em;vertical-align:baseline;text-
decoration:none;}


/* Layout
------------------------------------------------------------- */
header, nav, section, article, aside, footer {
  display: block; /* Sets HTML5 elements to block */
  overflow: hidden; /* Fixes Child Float Problem */ }
body {
  background-color: rgb(153,153,153);
  font: normal 1em/1.4em Perpetua, Constantia, times, "times new roman", serif; }

header.site, section, footer.site {
  width: 980px;
  clear: both;
  margin: 0 auto; }

section {
  background: rgb(204,204,204); }

nav, article, aside {
  float: left; }

nav {
  width: 235px;
  _width: 205px;     }

article {
  padding: 0 20px;
  background: rgb(255,255,255);
  width: 470px;
  _width: 430px;   }

aside {
  padding: 0 20px;
  width: 135px;
  _width: 95px;    }

ul {
  list-style: none;
  margin: 1em; }
```

Alice's Adventures In Wonderland

by Lewis Carroll

Chapter 1. Down The Rabbit-Hole

Alice was beginning to get very tired of sitting by her sister on the bank, and of having nothing to do: once or twice she had peeped into the book her sister was reading, but it had no pictures or conversations in it, 'and what is the use of a book,' thought Alice 'without pictures or conversation?'

So she was considering in her own mind (as well as she could, for the hot day made her feel very sleepy and stupid), whether the pleasure of making a daisy-chain would be worth the trouble of getting up and picking the daisies, when suddenly a White Rabbit with pink eyes ran close by her.

There was nothing so VERY remarkable in that; nor did Alice think it so VERY much out of the way to hear the Rabbit say to itself, 'Oh dear! Oh dear! I shall be late!' (when she thought it over afterwards, it occurred to her that she ought to have wondered at this, but at the time it all seemed quite natural); but when the Rabbit actually TOOK A WATCH OUT OF ITS WAISTCOAT-POCKET, and looked at it, and then hurried on, Alice started to her feet, for it flashed across her mind that she had never before seen a rabbit with either a waistcoat-pocket, or a watch to take out of it, and burning with curiosity, she ran across the field after it, and fortunately was just in time to see it pop down a large rabbit-hole under the hedge.

In another moment down went Alice after it, never once considering how in the world she was to get out again.

The rabbit-hole went straight on like a tunnel for some way, and then dipped suddenly down, so suddenly that Alice had not a moment to think about stopping herself before she found herself falling down a very deep well.

Either the well was very deep, or she fell very slowly, for she had plenty of time as she went down to look about her and to wonder what was going to happen next. First, she tried to look down and make out what she was coming to, but it was too dark to see anything; then she looked at the sides of the well, and noticed that they were filled with cupboards and book-shelves; here and there she saw maps and pictures hung upon pegs. She took down a jar from one of the shelves as she passed; it was labelled 'ORANGE MARMALADE', but to her great disappointment it was empty: she did not like to drop the jar for fear of killing

About Lewis Carroll

From *Wikipedia*

Charles Lutwidge Dodgson (pronounced /ˈdɒdsən/, DOD-sən; 27 January 1832 – 14 January 1898), better known by the pseudonym Lewis Carroll (/ˈkærəl/, KA-rəl), was an English author, mathematician, logician, Anglican deacon and a photographer. His most famous writings are Alice's Adventures in Wonderland and its sequel Through the Looking-Glass, as well as the poems "The Hunting of the Snark" and "Jabberwocky", all examples of the genre of literary nonsense. He is noted for his facility at word play, logic, and fantasy, and there are societies dedicated to the

C Code 14.2 applied to code 14.1. The columns now all line up horizontally and we can see all three columns at once.

3. **Set the `float` property for your columns.** Most columns use a **`float:left`** but **`float:right`** or a combination will work, depending on your needs.

```
nav, article, aside {...}
```

4. **Set the column widths.** Until these widths are set, the columns will stretch the full width of the parent element (**`section`**) and not actually float next to each other. Additionally, you will want to set margins and any padding. Of course, if you are using padding, you will run afoul of the box model problem in Internet Explorer (see Chapter 12). So you will also want to set a separate width using either the underscore hack (as I did here) or more preferably, conditional styles as explained in Chapter 12:

```
nav {...}, article {...}, aside {...}
```

TIP My general rule of thumb is to leave one to five pixels or 1 to 2% (for fluid columns) as a "fudge factor" between floated elements. The difference between columns that float and rows stacked on each other can literally come down to a single pixel. However, you will need to test your design on multiple browsers at multiple window sizes to find the exact fudge factor for your design.

TIP Although I used three columns here, you can add as many columns as you want. Just add more `<aside>` or `<div>` elements with the `float` property and adjust your column.

Styling Links Versus Navigation

The Web is nothing without links. Many designers are content to rely on default browser styles applied to their links, but this is not only boring, it also makes all the links on your page look exactly the same, whether they are global navigation or content links.

Styling links using pseudo-classes was covered in Chapter 4, but to bring your navigation to life, you need to style your links depending on the context.

To style navigation and links:

1. **Create an external CSS file called** *links.css* **(Code 14.3).** This file contains the CSS needed to style the link types for Code 14.1.

2. **Style the default link styles.** In the links.css file, add rules for the anchor tag and its :link, :visited, :hover, and :active states.

   a {...}

   a:link {...}

   a:visited {...}

   a:hover {...}

   a:active {...}

   I recommend setting text decoration to "none" to eliminate the unattractive underlining. You can then add link underlining using the **border-bottom** property as needed.

   continues on page 352

Code 14.3 *links.css*—Styles the links in Code 14.1, with a default link style applied to all link (**a**) elements, and applies special styles for links in paragraphs and links used for navigation Ⓐ.

```
/*** CSS3 VQS | Chapter 14 | links.css ***/

/* Default Link Styles
----------------------------------------------------------------- */

a {
  text-decoration: none; }
a:link {
  color: rgb(204,0,0); }
a:visited {
  color: rgb(153,0,0); }
a:hover {
  color: rgb(255,0,0); }
a:active {
  color: rgb(0,255,255); }

/* Contextual Link Styles
----------------------------------------------------------------- */

p a {
  font-style: italic;
  font-size: 1.2em;}

p a:link, p a:visited {
  border-bottom: 1px dotted rgb(255,153,153); }

p a:hover, p a:active {
  background-color: rgb(255,235,235);
  border-bottom: 1px solid rgb(255,102,102); }

/* Navigation Link Styles
----------------------------------------------------------------- */
nav.toc .menu a {
  display: block;
  text-decoration: none;
  padding: 10px;
  width: 100%;
  height:100%; }

nav.toc .menu a:link, nav.toc .menu a:visted {
  color: rgb(153,0,0); }

nav.toc .menu a:hover {
  color: rgb(255,255,255);
  -webkit-transition: color .25s ease;
  -moz-transition: color .25s ease;
```

code continues on next page

3. **Style specific hypertext link styles such as paragraphs, lists, and tables.** Links in paragraphs need a little extra attention because they are surrounded by other text.

`p a {...}`

`p a:link {...}`

`p a:visited {...}`

`p a:hover {...}`

`p a:active {...}`

In addition to color, some options to differentiate hypertext from text include:

▸ **Underline** using **border-bottom** to control the style, thickness, and color of the underline.

▸ **Italics or bold** to give the linked text extra style or weight.

▸ **A background color or image** to create a highlight effect. (See "Using CSS Sprites" in this chapter.)

▸ **Increase size** slightly.

4. **Style the navigation links.** Navigation links are most commonly set up as a list to allow the links to appear in a list even if CSS is present. (Remember progressive enhancements in Chapter 13?)

`nav ol {...}`

These are the basic styles applied to the navigation links, but you are not quite done styling the menu itself. You'll get to that in the next two sections.

Code 14.3 *continued*

```
  -o-transition: color .25s ease;
  transition: color .25s ease; }

nav.toc .menu a:active {
  color: rgb(153,0,0); }

nav.toc ul {
  list-style: none;
  margin: 0;
  padding: 0; }

nav.toc .menu {
  display: block;
  position: relative;
  height: auto;
  width: 230px;
  background-color: rgb(235,235,235);
  cursor: pointer; }

nav.toc .menu:hover {
  background: rgb(0,0,0);
  color: rgb(255,255,255);
}

nav.toc .menu li {
  font-weight: bold;
  padding: 5px;
  margin: 5px 0; }

nav.toc .menu .drop {
  display: block;
  background-color: rgb(235,235,235);
  position: relative;
  width: auto; }
```

Alice's Adventures In Wonderland

by Lewis Carroll

Chapter 1. Down The Rabbit-Hole

Alice was beginning *to get very tired* of sitting by her sister on the bank, and of having nothing to do: once or twice she had peeped into the book her sister was reading, but it *had no pictures or conversations* in it, 'and what is the use of a book,' *thought Alice* 'without pictures or conversation?'

So she was considering in her own mind (as well as she could, for the hot day made her *feel very sleepy and stupid*), whether the pleasure of making a daisy-chain would be worth the trouble of getting up and picking the daisies, when suddenly a *White Rabbit* with pink eyes ran close by her.

There was nothing so VERY remarkable in that; nor did Alice think it so VERY much out of the way to hear the Rabbit say to itself, 'Oh dear! Oh dear! I shall be late!' (when she thought it over afterwards, it occurred to her that she ought to have wondered at this, but at the time it all seemed quite natural); but when the Rabbit actually TOOK A WATCH OUT OF ITS WAISTCOAT-POCKET, and looked at it, and then hurried on, Alice started to her feet, for it flashed across her mind that she had never before seen a rabbit with either a waistcoat-pocket, or a watch to take out of it, and burning with curiosity, she ran across the field after it, and fortunately was just in time to see it pop down a large rabbit-hole under the hedge.

In another moment down went Alice after it, never once considering how in the world she was to get out again.

The rabbit-hole went straight on like a tunnel for some way, and then dipped suddenly down, so suddenly that Alice had not a moment to think about stopping herself before she found herself falling down a very deep well.

Either the well was very deep, or she fell very slowly, for she had plenty of time as she went down to look about her and to wonder what was going to happen next. First, she tried to look down and make out what she was coming to, but it was too dark to see anything; then she looked at the sides of the well, and noticed that they were filled with cupboards and book-shelves; here and there she saw maps and pictures hung upon pegs. She took down a jar from one of the shelves as she passed; it was labelled 'ORANGE MARMALADE', but to her great

About Lewis Carroll

From *Wikipedia*

Charles Lutwidge Dodgson (pronounced / ˈdɒdsən /, DOD-sən; 27 January 1832 – 14 January 1898), better known by the pseudonym Lewis Carroll (/ ˈkærəl /, KA-rəl), was an English author, mathematician, logician, Anglican deacon and a photographer. His most famous writings are Alice's Adventures in Wonderland and its sequel Through the Looking-Glass, as well as the poems "The Hunting of the Snark" and "Jabberwocky", all examples of the genre of literary nonsense. He is noted for his facility at word play, logic, and fantasy, and there are societies dedicated to the

A Shows the Web page (Code 14.1) when the *links.css* (Code 14.3) styles are added. The difference between hypertext links in paragraphs and navigation links in the menu are now clear.

Using CSS Sprites

The *CSS sprite* technique lets you create a single image that contains the different states used for buttons, menus, or interface controls using dynamic pseudo-classes. In that file, you place all of the individual sprites that make up your button, separated by enough space so that they don't run into each other. You then call this image as the background for an element, and set the background position property (using negative values to move the background up and/or left) to position the correct sprite. Because only one image must load, the browser needs to make only one server call, which speeds up your site.

For example, in your menu from the previous section, it might be nice to place a pointer icon to the right of the options to show that you will be loading a new page. The sprite includes all three versions of the icon for all three dynamic states.

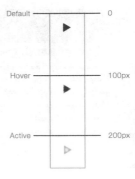

A *sprite-pointer.png*— The image used to create the multiple states used for the arrow. They are arranged at regular intervals to help you more quickly and accurately switch them.

To add CSS image rollovers to a Web page:

1. **Create an image with the different dynamic states for your icon.** You will create icons for each of the dynamic states you need (default, hover, and active, in this example) all in the same image file, separated by a small amount of space **A** and name it *sprite-pointer. png*. Generally, you will want to regularly space the states' positions, making them easy to remember. For example, I set the top of each graphic at intervals of 100 pixels.

B Shows your Web page (Code 14.1) when the *sprites.css* (Code 14.4) styles are included.

Default
Hover
Active

2. **Create an external CSS file called *sprites.css* (Code 14.4).** This file contains the CSS needed to style the menu in Code 14.1.

3. **Add the sprite to the element you are using as a control.**

```
nav.toc .menu .drop li {...}
```

4. **Set the background image to not repeat.** You will need to set the horizontal position to left or right and then adjust the vertical position up (negative values) or down (positive values) as needed for appearance.

```
background: transparent
→ url('../_images/sprite-pointer.
→ png') no-repeat right 8px;
```

Although this is a link, you are using the list element to add your sprite because this provides better control over positioning. However, sprites work just as well on links, lists, or any other element.

continues on next page

Code 14.4 *sprites.css*—When applied to your Web page (Code 14.1), this code adds a graphic arrow to the menu, providing visual interaction as the visitor uses the menu and further differentiating that link style **B**.

```
/*** CSS3 VQS | Chapter 14 | sprites.css ***/

/* CSS Sprites
------------------------------------------------------------ */

nav.toc .menu .drop li {
  font-weight: normal;
  margin: 0;
  padding: 0;
  border-top: 1px solid rgb(204,204,204);
  background: transparent url('../_images/sprite-pointer.png') no-repeat right 0;  }

nav.toc .menu .drop li:hover {
  background-color: rgb(102,0,0);
  background-position: right -100px;  }

nav.toc .menu .drop li:active {
  background-color: rgb(255,255,255);
  background-position: right -200px;  }
```

5. **Move the background image up or down, depending on the state.** Add rules for all the link states (**:link**, **:visited**, **:hover**, **:active,** and **:focus**), setting the **background-position** property with the correct vertical offset values to display the relevant rollover state.

```
nav.toc .menu .drop li:hover {...},
→nav.toc .menu .drop li:active
→{...}
```

For example, the visited state would use:

```
background-position: right -100px;
```

So only the visited button state is shown **C**.

You can, of course, include whatever other style changes you want. In this example, I'm also changing the background color.

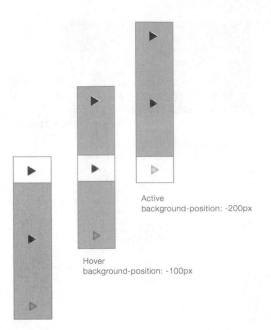

Active
background-position: -200px

Hover
background-position: -100px

Default
background-position: 0

C With the height of the element set, only a part of the background image is revealed, hiding the rest. By changing the background position within the element, it appears as if the image has changed.

TIP The idea (and the last part of the name) for CSS sprites originated in the early days of video games, when memory and speed were at a premium. To overcome system limitations, video game producers would lay out the thousands of small graphics used to create the game into a grid and then display each sprite as needed, masking out all but the needed part of the larger image.

TIP The example here is a simple one, but it's possible to place dozens, hundreds, or more images on a single sprite to cut down on server requests and speed up your site.

Creating a CSS Drop-down Menu

Drop-down menus are a standard way to reduce navigation noise, allowing you to present a lot of links in a little space. Although generally thought of as the domain of JavaScript, drop-down menus can also be achieved using only a little bit of CSS.

To make a pure CSS drop-down menu:

1. Create an external CSS file called drop-menu.css **(Code 14.5)**. This file contains the CSS needed to style the menu in Code 14.1.

continues on page 359

Code 14.5 *menu.css*—When applied to your Web page (Code14.1), this collapses the menu, leaving only a menu label **A**, which when the pointer hovers over it, expands the menu to full height **B**.

```
/*** CSS3 VQS | Chapter 14 | dropmenu.css ***/

/* Drop Menu
----------------------------------------------------------- */

nav.toc .menu .drop {
  overflow: hidden;
  height: 0;
  opacity: 0; }

nav.toc .menu:hover>.drop {
  height: auto;
  opacity: 1;
  -webkit-transition: opacity .25s linear;
  -moz-transition: opacity .25s linear;
  -o-transition: opacity .25s linear;
  transition: opacity .25s linear;  }
```

Alice's Adventures In Wonderland

by Lewis Carroll

Table of Contents

Chapter 1. Down The Rabbit-Hole

Alice was beginning *to get very tired* of sitting by her sister on the bank, and of having nothing to do: once or twice she had peeped into the book her sister was reading, but it *had no pictures or conversations* in it, 'and what is the use of a book,' *thought Alice* 'without pictures or conversation?'

So she was considering in her own mind (as well as she could, for the hot day made her *feel very sleepy and stupid*), whether the pleasure of making a daisy-chain would be worth the trouble of getting up and picking the daisies, when suddenly a *White Rabbit* with pink eyes ran close by her.

There was nothing so VERY remarkable in that; nor did Alice think it so VERY much out of the way to hear the Rabbit say to itself, 'Oh dear! Oh dear! I shall be late!' (when she thought it over afterwards, it occurred to her that she ought to have wondered at this, but at the time it all seemed quite natural); but when the Rabbit actually TOOK A WATCH OUT OF ITS WAISTCOAT-POCKET, and looked at it, and then hurried on, Alice started to her feet, for it flashed across her mind that she had never before seen a rabbit with either a waistcoat-pocket, or a watch to take out of it, and burning with curiosity, she ran across the field after it, and fortunately was just in time to see it pop down a large rabbit-hole under the hedge.

In another moment down went Alice after it, never once considering how in the world she was to get out again.

The rabbit-hole went straight on like a tunnel for some way, and then dipped suddenly down, so suddenly that Alice had not a moment to think about stopping herself before she found herself falling down a very deep well.

Either the well was very deep, or she fell very slowly, for she had plenty of time as she went down to look about her and to wonder what was going to happen next. First, she tried to look down and make out what she was coming to, but it was too dark to see anything; then she looked at the sides of the well, and noticed that they were filled with cupboards and book-shelves; here and there she saw maps and pictures hung upon pegs. She took down a jar from one of the shelves as she passed; it was labelled 'ORANGE MARMALADE', but to her great

About Lewis Carroll

From *Wikipedia*

Charles Lutwidge Dodgson (pronounced /ˈdɒdsən/, DOD-sən; 27 January 1832 – 14 January 1898), better known by the pseudonym Lewis Carroll (/ˈkærəl/, KA-rəl), was an English author, mathematician, logician, Anglican deacon and a photographer. His most famous writings are Alice's Adventures in Wonderland and its sequel Through the Looking-Glass, as well as the poems "The Hunting of the Snark" and "Jabberwocky", all examples of the genre of literary nonsense. He is noted for his facility at word play, logic, and fantasy, and there are societies dedicated to the

A Code 14.5 applied to code 14.1. Initially, the menu is hidden **B**.

Alice's Adventures In Wonderland

by Lewis Carroll

Table of Contents

Down the Rabbit-Hole ▶

The Pool of Tears ▶

A Caucus-Race and a Long Tale ▶

The Rabbit Sends in a Little Bill ▶

Advise from a Caterpillar ▶

Pig and Pepper ▶

A Mad Tea Party ▶

The Queen's Croquet-Ground ▶

The Mock Turtle's Story ▶

The Lobster Quadrille ▶

Who Stole the Tarts? ▶

Alice's Evidence ▶

Chapter 1. Down The Rabbit-Hole

Alice was beginning *to get very tired* of sitting by her sister on the bank, and of having nothing to do: once or twice she had peeped into the book her sister was reading, but it *had no pictures or conversations* in it, 'and what is the use of a book,' *thought Alice* 'without pictures or conversation?'

So she was considering in her own mind (as well as she could, for the hot day made her *feel very sleepy and stupid*), whether the pleasure of making a daisy-chain would be worth the trouble of getting up and picking the daisies, when suddenly a *White Rabbit* with pink eyes ran close by her.

There was nothing so VERY remarkable in that; nor did Alice think it so VERY much out of the way to hear the Rabbit say to itself, 'Oh dear! Oh dear! I shall be late!' (when she thought it over afterwards, it occurred to her that she ought to have wondered at this, but at the time it all seemed quite natural); but when the Rabbit actually TOOK A WATCH OUT OF ITS WAISTCOAT-POCKET, and looked at it, and then hurried on, Alice started to her feet, for it flashed across her mind that she had never before seen a rabbit with either a waistcoat-pocket, or a watch to take out of it, and burning with curiosity, she ran across the field after it, and fortunately was just in time to see it pop down a large rabbit-hole under the hedge.

In another moment down went Alice after it, never once considering how in the world she was to get out again.

The rabbit-hole went straight on like a tunnel for some way, and then dipped suddenly down, so suddenly that Alice had not a moment to think about stopping herself before she found herself falling down a very deep well.

Either the well was very deep, or she fell very slowly, for she had plenty of time as she went down to look about her and to wonder what was going to happen next. First, she tried to look down and make out what she was coming to, but it was too dark to see anything; then she looked at the sides of the well, and noticed that they were filled with cupboards and book-shelves; here and there she saw maps and pictures hung upon pegs. She took down a jar from one of the shelves as she passed; it was labelled 'ORANGE MARMALADE', but to her great

About Lewis Carroll

From *Wikipedia*

Charles Lutwidge Dodgson (pronounced /ˈdɒdsən/, DOD-sən; 27 January 1832 – 14 January 1898), better known by the pseudonym Lewis Carroll (/ˈkærəl/, KA-rəl), was an English author, mathematician, logician, Anglican deacon and a photographer. His most famous writings are Alice's Adventures in Wonderland and its sequel Through the Looking-Glass, as well as the poems "The Hunting of the Snark" and "Jabberwocky", all examples of the genre of literary nonsense. He is noted for his facility at word play, logic, and fantasy, and there are societies dedicated to the

B When the user hovers a pointer over the menu header, the menu drops down and is ready for the user to select a menu option.

Preventing Navigation Noise

One of my chief gripes about most Web sites is the overabundance of unorganized links. You've probably seen sites with long lists of links that stretch off the window. These links add visual noise to the design and waste precious screen space without assisting navigation.

Web surfers rarely take the time to read an entire Web page. Instead, they scan for relevant information. But human beings can process only so much information at a time. If a Web page is cluttered, visitors must wade through dozens or hundreds of links to find the one path to the information they desire.

Anything designers can do to aid visitors' abilities to scan a page, such as organizing links in lists and hiding sublinks until they're needed, will improve the Web site's usability. Drop-down, sliding, and collapsible menus are a great way to organize your page and prevent navigation noise.

2. **Hide the drop menu.** To show the menu—"dropping" it down—you first need to hide it. Give it a triple whammy by setting its height to 0, overflow to hidden, and opacity to completely transparent.

```
nav.toc .menu .drop {...}
```

3. **Set the drop menu to appear when the user's pointer hovers over it.** When the pointer hovers over any part of the menu—including the title at the top—set the height to auto and opacity to opaque. You can also couple this with a transition to create a more subtle opening effect.

```
nav.toc .menu:hover>.drop {...}
```

TIP It would be cool if the menu could unroll by using a transition to go from 0 to the menu's full height. You could do this if you knew the exact height of the menu, but this is rarely the case, especially in a dynamic Web site.

TIP Because this trick relies on the child selector, it will not work in IE6, so you will need to either show the menu (using conditional CSS to set display and opacity) or make other navigational arrangements.

Managing Style Sheets

It's not enough to write CSS that makes your pages look pretty. To create the best Web pages, you must also write clean code that's easy to read, easy to maintain, and loads quickly.

To manage your style sheets you need to know how to create well-organized code, work with CSS libraries and Frameworks, optimize the linking of style sheets, validate your CSS, and compress the code by *minifying* it.

This chapter will help you realize all these goals and finish with a review of the best practices I've presented throughout the book.

In This Chapter

Creating Readable Style Sheets

Although the computer interprets the CSS code to render a Web page, you and other humans have to create and edit it. During development, your code will probably get pretty messy, which makes it hard to track down rule interactions, determine the cascade order, or even locate rules that need changing.

Keeping your code organized *while* you work can actually save you time. Follow these simple suggestions to keep your code as readable as possible during development, and then double-check and clean up your code before you deploy.

Include an introduction and TOC

Place an introduction at the top of your CSS that includes basic information such as the title, site name, version, change date, usage, and other notes (**Code 15.1**). Additionally, some developers like to insert a rough table of contents, outlining the organizational structure of the style sheets.

Define colors, fonts, and other constants

It's sometimes difficult to keep track of all the values that you are using in your design. It's unlikely that CSS will ever include constants, so it will help to keep notes in an easy-to-reference location in your document. Creating a glossary of colors and types leads to more consistent and attractive designs (**Code 15.2**).

Code 15.1 An example of an introduction and TOC for an external CSS file. Notice that the hierarchy of the file shown in the TOC is based on page structure.

```
/*----------------------------------------------------------------

# Default Stylesheet

Filename:    default.css
Site:        speakinginstyles.com
Version:     1.1
Last change: 09/11/10 [added gallery view, jct]
Author:      Jason Cranford Teague (jct)
Desciption:  Default styles to be applied to all pages in the site

## TOC

* HTML Selectors (Defaults)
  ** Headers
  ** Body
  ** Lists
  ** Forms
  ** Tables
* Navigation
  ** Menu
  ** Breadcrumb
  ** Footer
* Content
  ** Aside
    *** Right
    *** Left
  ** Article
    *** Blockquotes
    *** Paragraphs
    *** Lists
    *** Tables
  ** Comments
* Footer

-----------------------------------------------------------*/
```

Code 15.2 Constant values such as colors and font stacks can be defined at the top of the page as a handy reference.

```
/*----------------------------------------------------------------

## Color Glossary

dark gray: rgb(51, 51, 85)
red:   rgb(255, 15, 34)
white:   rgb(235,235,355)
blue:    rgb(0, 0, 102)

## Font Glossary

header:   diavlo, "gill sans", helvetica, arial, sans-serif
body:   baskerville, georgia, times, "times new roman", serif
aside:   "gill sans", helvetica, arial, sans-serif

-----------------------------------------------------------*/
```

Use section headers

Although section headers and dividers really aren't anything more than CSS comments, they do help organize your CSS and allow you to quickly scan your code to locate particular CSS rule groups. If you have established a TOC, I recommend reflecting that organization here. In this example (**Code 15.3**), I'm using asterisks to indicate a section level.

The @ rules go at the top

All of the CSS rules starting with @ (@media, @font-face, @import) need to be placed above any other CSS in the external style or embedded style sheet. In addition to making these rules easier to find, many of them won't work unless they're placed at the top.

Code 15.3 Section dividers used to organize the CSS file. Notice that they mimic the TOC.

```
/* HTML Selectors
----------------------------------------------------------------*/

/**  HTML Selectors | Headers
----------------------------------------------------------------*/

/* Content
----------------------------------------------------------------*/

/** Content | Aside
----------------------------------------------------------------*/

/*** Content | Aside | Right
----------------------------------------------------------------*/

/*** Content | Aside | Left
----------------------------------------------------------------*/

/** Content | Article
----------------------------------------------------------------*/
```

Choose an organization scheme

You should choose a consistent organization pattern and stick to it. I'm not going to tell you *how* to organize your style sheets—that depends on what works for you—but here are a few ideas to consider:

- **Organize by selector type.** Start with HTML selectors, then IDs, and then classes.

- **Organize based on page structure.** Group rules based on their parent tags. This works even better with HTML5 because page structure is stronger. The downside occurs when the same rules need to be applied at different places in the page. You don't want redundant code, so it's best to separate those rules out into their own section.

- **Organize based on purpose.** Group rules based on which element a style is being applied to. Instead of being grouped according to where the element is in the page, the styles are grouped based on their content, module, functionality, or other specific use (such as headings, typography, ads, article, asides, layout grid, and so on.)

- **Organize alphabetically.** Literally list the selectors in alphabetical order. No, really. I've never used this method, but I've heard several developers swear by it. To me, it seems like a lot of work to maintain this organization scheme. Plus, what if you need to override a style later in the cascade, but it doesn't fit alphabetically?

You can use one of these methods, a combination of these methods, or a method you make up yourself. The key is to be consistent.

Use specificity for hierarchy

Regardless of the overall organization scheme you choose, specificity (explained in Chapter 4) provides a natural organizational hierarchy for CSS rules (**Code 15.4**). Simply organizing your CSS rules using the selector specificity can make it a lot easier to find rules and track down problems.

Code 15.4 CSS rules ordered by specificity hierarchy. This makes them easier to follow.

```
article {,...}
article .intro {,...}
article .intro figure {,...}
article .intro figure figcaption {,...}
article .intro p {,...}
article .intro p em {,...}
article .intro p:firstline {,...}
```

A The home page of Blueprint, one of the more popular CSS Frameworks.

CSS Libraries and Frameworks

A *CSS library* is simply a collection of common styles that you use throughout one Web site and potentially multiple Web sites. The library can include your CSS reset, general typography, general transition styles, or any other style that requires consistency.

CSS Frameworks are ready-built CSS libraries that allow you to quickly deploy well-tested and finely crafted CSS code to your own Web site. Generally, CSS frameworks are free, community-based efforts maintained by interested volunteers.

For simple Web sites, Frameworks can be overkill, adding a lot of code that will never be used. However, even for medium-sized sites, Frameworks can be a real time-saver.

Some of the more popular CSS Frameworks include:

- **Blueprint**—Provides a solid layout grid, typographic styles, and a style sheet for printing pages **A**.

  Visit www.blueprintcss.org.

- **Emastic**—Uses ems to create elastic layouts.

  Visit code.google.com/p/emastic.

- **Typogridphy**—Uses 12 and 16 column grids at 960px wide and typographic style rules to create a strong vertical rhythm.

  Visit csswizardry.com/typogridphy.

- **YUI Grids**—Yahoo!'s CSS Grids framework provides fixed and fluid layouts.

  Visit developer.yahoo.com/yui/grids.

Style Sheet Strategies

Once your libraries, frameworks, and site-wide CSS are ready to go live, you need to pick the best strategy for deployment. It is always recommended that you place all your styles in one or more external style sheets, and then use either the **<link>** or **@import** code to apply them to a Web document.

At this juncture, you have two competing priorities:

- **Keep the file size as small as possible.** The larger the file size, the longer it takes to download. Of course, because it's text, your files have to be pretty large for this to be a problem, but it happens.

- **Keep the number of links and imports as low as possible.** The more links and imports you have to external CSS files, the more server calls you make, and the slower the page will load.

You can reduce file size by splitting style sheets into multiple external files and then linking only to the ones you need, but this means more links. You can have a single, all-inclusive CSS file, but such a file can grow quite large. Your job will be to balance these two issues. Here are a few methods for doing so.

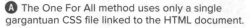

A The One For All method uses only a single gargantuan CSS file linked to the HTML document.

The One For All method

The One For All method includes all your styles in a single master style sheet. With this method, creating well-organized and readable style sheets with a TOC is critical because you may be poring through hundreds or even thousands of lines of code **A**.

Pros—One download is faster than multiple downloads, and the file is then cached for use on other pages. In addition, with all of your code in one place, you don't have to worry about whether a page has access to the right styles.

Cons—This method may lead to large file sizes that can slow down the page loading time and take longer to render. Additionally, these files are harder to manage and edit.

The Divide and Conquer method

The Divide and Conquer method uses multiple links to multiple style sheets on an as-needed basis per page. Start with a link to a file with global styles used by all pages, and then add links to styles used for that page only. For example, if you use a special carousel module only on the main page, it would not go into the global file, but would exist as a separate CSS file for the home page or as part of a CSS file of general components **B**.

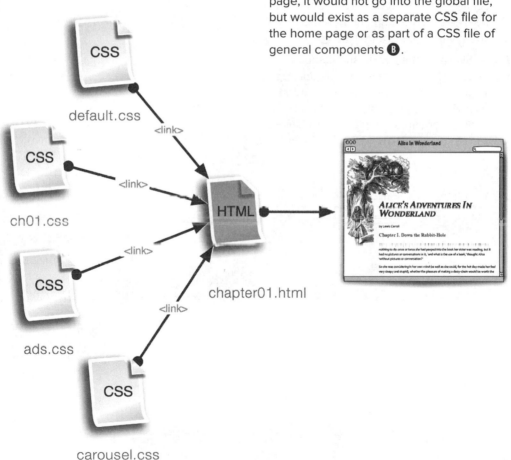

B The Divide and Conquer method splits the CSS into multiple files, which are then applied only if they are relevant to the page.

Pros—Mix and match style sheets from your library to load only the styles you need and reduce bloated file sizes. Plus, as long as you keep your files organized, these are generally easier to edit.

Cons—Multiple files mean multiple server calls, which slows downloads. Plus, multiple files can be hard to keep up with, and their cascade order can conflict in unpredictable ways.

The Aggregate method

The Aggregate method uses `@import` to collect all the relevant CSS files from your library. The HTML document then has to link to only a single external file **C**.

Pros—Similar to the Divide and Conquer method, but by using only a single link, it's easier to add or remove styles as needed because they are in a single CSS file rather than spread out across multiple HTML files.

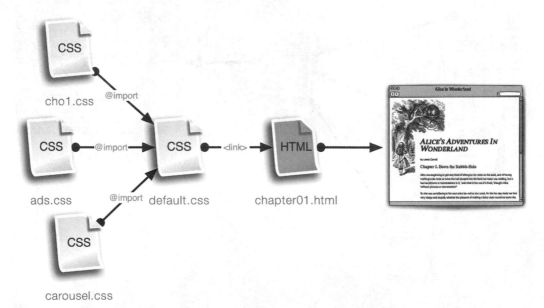

C The Aggregate method uses the @import rule to bundle the style sheets into a single file that is linked to the HTML document.

Cons—Similar to the Divide and Conquer method but worse. This used to be a very popular CSS strategy until someone discovered that using **@import** often prevents external style sheets from loading simultaneously. Instead, they must load one after another, which slows things down. Additionally, since the linked parent style sheet has to load before the imported style sheets are seen by the browser, this method can lead to the page rerendering as new styles become available.

The Dynamic method

The Dynamic method relies not on your skills as a CSS coder, but on your skills writing server-side code. It is possible to write server scripts that take an aggregated CSS file full of **@imports** and combine them on the server into a single file for deployment **D**.

Pros—Combines the ease of use and lean file size of the Aggregate method with the speed of the One For All method.

Cons—Requires knowledge of server-side coding that is beyond the scope of this book. Talk to your server admin or developer for more details.

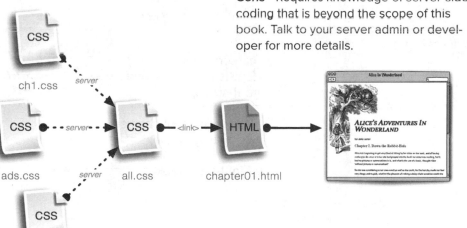

D The Dynamic method relies on the server to dynamically bundle the relevant CSS for an HTML document into a single CSS file.

Troubleshooting CSS Code

All too often, you carefully set up your style sheet rules, go to your browser, and see... *nothing*. Or the page is displayed as an ugly mishmash of content. Don't worry; this happens to everyone. Before you panic and throw your expensive laptop out the window, read through these suggestions.

Ask these questions

Many things could be preventing your style sheet rules from working properly; most of them are easily spotted. Ⓐ points out some common problems you may encounter:

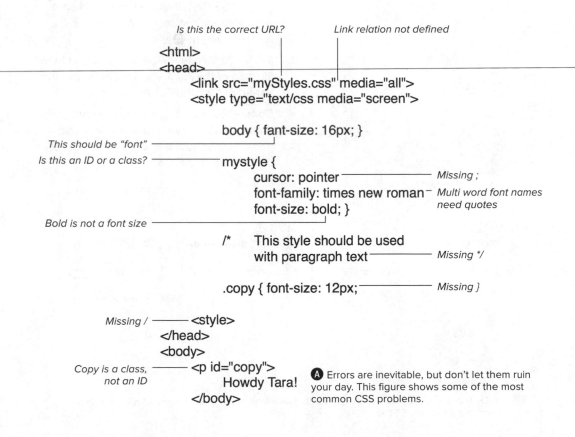

Is this the correct URL?   Link relation not defined

```
<html>
<head>
    <link src="myStyles.css" media="all">
    <style type="text/css media="screen">

            body { fant-size: 16px; }
```

This should be "font" ——————— body { fant-size: 16px; }
Is this an ID or a class? ——————— mystyle {

```
            cursor: pointer                 ———— Missing ;
            font-family: times new roman ~   Multi word font names
            font-size: bold; }                need quotes
```

Bold is not a font size ————————— font-size: bold; }

```
        /*    This style should be used
              with paragraph text ———— Missing */

        .copy { font-size: 12px; ———— Missing }
```

Missing / ———— <style>
```
            </head>
            <body>
```
Copy is a class, ———— <p id="copy">
not an ID   Howdy Tara!
            </body>

Ⓐ Errors are inevitable, but don't let them ruin your day. This figure shows some of the most common CSS problems.

- **Are you missing any semicolons?** A missing semicolon at the end of a declaration will cause the entire rule to fail.

- **Did you remember to set the link relation?** If you leave out the `rel` property, many browsers will not load the external style sheet.

- **Did you open and close the declaration block with curly brackets?** If not, there's no telling what will happen.

- **Did you remember to close all your multiline comment tags?** If not, the rest of the CSS is treated as a comment. (See "Adding Comments to CSS" in Chapter 3.)

- **Does your selector contain typos?** If you forget the opening period or number sign (#) for classes and IDs, they won't work.

- **Did you mix up a class with an ID or vice versa?** I often think I've set up a selector as an ID, but it was actually a class.

- **Do the properties contain typos?** Typos in one property can cause the entire rule to fall.

- **Are the values you're using permitted for that property?** Using improper values may cause a definition to fail or behave unpredictably.

- **Does this property work on the browser you are testing on?** This is especially a problem if you are using new CSS3 properties. See Appendix A to make sure a property works on the browser you are using.

continues on next page

- **If your rules are in the head, did you use the `<style>` tag correctly?** Typos in the `<style>` tag mean that none of the definitions are used. In addition, if you set the media type, the styles will affect only the output to that medium. So setting the media type to print will prevent those styles from affecting content displayed on the screen. (See "Adding Styles to a Web Page" in Chapter 3.)

- **If you are linking or importing style sheets, are you retrieving the correct file?** Check the exact path for the file. Also, remember that you should not include the `<style>` tag or any other non-CSS code in an external CSS file. (See "Adding Styles to a Web Site" in Chapter 3.)

- **Do you have multiple, conflicting rules for the same tag?** Check your cascade order. (See "Determining the Cascade Order" in Chapter 4.)

If all else fails, try these ideas

If you've looked for the preceding errors and still can't get your code to work, here are a few more things to try:

- **Make the declaration `!important`.** Often, your declarations will conflict with each other, and it may be hard to track down where the conflict is. Adding `!important` to the declaration (see "Making a Declaration Important" in Chapter 4 will ensure that if it is working, it is applied to the page.

- **Delete the rules and retype them.** When you can't see what's wrong, retyping code from scratch sometimes fixes the problem.

- **Test the same code on another browser and/or operating system.** It's possible that a property is buggy and doesn't work correctly in your browser. It's even possible that the browser doesn't allow that property to work with that tag.

- **Give up and walk away.** Just joking—although you might want to take a 15-minute break before looking at the problem again.

- **If nothing else works...** Try a different solution for your design.

Debugging CSS in Firebug and Web Inspector

Most Web designers work in Firefox, Safari, or Chrome while they are developing because all three have excellent add-ons and built-in tools for analyzing and editing code. For Firefox, this functionality is provided by the Firebug add on, while both Safari and Chrome use the Web Inspector provided with Webkit.

Both tools allow on-the-fly editing of the CSS and HTML of the Web page you are viewing, which allows you to modify and debug your code on your local computer without affecting the live version. Although each tool has many unique features, both share several key capabilities for working with CSS:

- **Highlight elements.** As you roll over elements in the screen, they are highlighted in the HTML code or vice-versa.

- **View all rules applied to an element.** As elements are selected, the applied CSS code is displayed, showing declarations that have been overridden or crossed out.

- **Turn declarations on and off.** You can selectively enable and disable declarations to see how they affect the design.

- **Edit declaration properties and values.** In addition to switching declarations on and off, you can directly edit or add them to a rule.

- **View errors.** Display any HTML or CSS errors encountered.

Firebug for Firefox

The Firebug plug-in tool for Firefox has become the de facto standard for Web designers everywhere 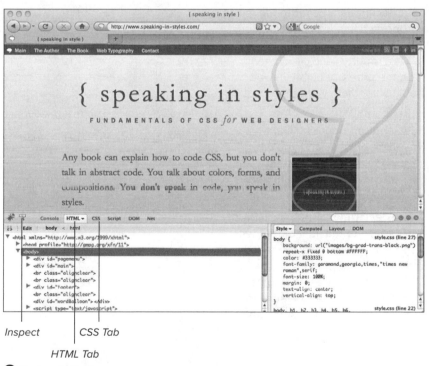. You can get it from the Firefox add-ons Web site or directly from the Firebug Web site, getfirebug.com (Win/Mac).

Getting started with Firebug

1. **Open the Firebug panel.** Navigate to the Web page you want to look at and then click the Firebug icon in the lower right of the browser window or choose View>Firebug.

continues on next page

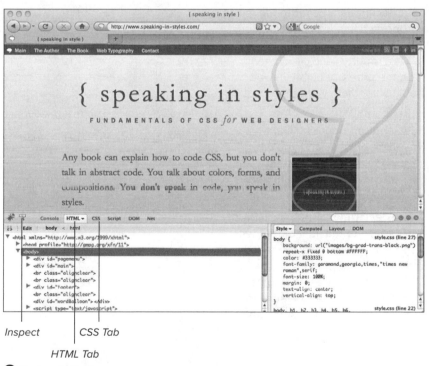

Inspect

CSS Tab

HTML Tab

Ⓐ Firebug in Firefox.

2. **View the CSS.** You can view the CSS by itself by clicking the CSS tab, or view it side by side with the HTML by clicking the HTML tab. I generally work in side-by-side mode.

3. Inspect an element. Click the Inspect button and then click the element in the screen you want to inspect. As you hover over an element, its box will be outlined with color-coded margins and padding. Firebug also highlights the element in the HTML code and displays all of the CSS being applied. Declarations are crossed out if they have been overridden by other declarations and are not being applied. Click to select an element for editing.

4. **Turn off a declaration.** Hover to the left of the property name in the declaration, and a *not* symbol (⊘) appears. Click it to turn off the property , and click it again to turn on the property. In the viewport, you should immediately see the effect of turning the property on and off.

5. **Edit a declaration.** Double-click the property name or value and you can type a new one. The effects of any changes will be visible almost immediately as you type.

6. **Add a new declaration.** Double-click the empty space to the right of the declaration you want to precede your new declaration, type the property name, press Tab, and then type the property value. Do *not* type the closing semicolon (;). Changes should appear instantly as you type.

Web Inspector in Safari and Chrome

Both Safari and Chrome have this built-in Web developer tool, which allows you to quickly analyze and edit your CSS and HTML **B**. Both Safari and Chrome are available for Windows and Mac OS X:

www.apple.com/safari (Win/Mac)

www. google.com/chrome (Win/Mac)

Getting Started with Web Inspector

1. **Turn on the Developer menu in Safari.** Open the Preferences panel for the browser (Safari>Preferences...), choose the Advanced tab, and select "Developer Menu in Menu Bar".

continues on next page

Insepect   Elements Tab

B The Web Inspector in Safari. It looks pretty much the same in Chrome.

2. **Open the Web Inspector panel.** Navigate to the Web page you want to look at and in Safari choose Develop>Show Web Inspector, or in Chrome choose View>Developer>Developer Tools.

3. **View the CSS.** You can view the CSS side by side with the HTML by clicking the Elements tab.

4. **Inspect an element.** Click the Inspect icon (magnifying class) and then click the element in the screen you want to inspect. As you hover over an element, its box will be outlined, along with color-coded margins and padding. Firebug also highlights the element in the HTML code and displays all of the CSS being applied. Declarations are crossed out to indicate that they have been overridden by other declarations and are not being applied. Click to select an element for editing.

5. **Turn off a declaration.** Hover over the declarations in the CSS, and a check box will appear next to each on the right side. Deselect the check box to turn off the declaration. Select the check box to turn it on. In the viewport, you should immediately see the effect of turning the declaration on and off.

6. **Edit a declaration.** Double-click the declaration you want to change and edit it as necessary. The effects of any changes will be visible almost immediately as you type.

7. **Add a new declaration.** Double-click the empty space to the right of the declaration you want to precede your new declaration, type the property name, and then type the property value. Do *not* type the closing semicolon (;). Press Return to make the changes appear.

TIP Keep in mind that if you reload the page at any point, any changes you have made will be lost.

A The W3C's Validator.

Validating Your CSS Code

The W3C provides a Web site called the CSS Validator **A** that lets you check your CSS code to confirm that it meets the requirements set in the W3C standards.

To use the W3C's CSS Validator:

1. To go to the W3C validator Web site, point your Web browser to jigsaw.w3.org/css-validator.

2. Choose the method to validate your CSS. You can enter a URL (by URI), enter the CSS code directly in a form (with a text area), or upload your files (by file upload). In this example, you'll submit a URL.

3. Enter the URL of your Web site or style sheet. I recommend entering the exact URL of the style sheet.

4. Wait. The validation takes only a few seconds. You're given a report of errors and other possible problems with your CSS.

TIP Although you don't need valid CSS for a browser to display your code, the validation process often helps locate code errors.

Minifying Your CSS

Although creating readable CSS is great for editing and maintaining your code, all of those comments, spaces, and returns end up adding a lot of overhead to your file size. Additionally, although I'm sure you are a fine coder, there is always more room to sort and merge selectors for optimization.

If you want to cut down on your file size, before you deploy your site to the Web, create a *minified* version of your CSS code. Depending on the size of your CSS file, this can go far to reduce file size.

Don't delete the readable version. You need to keep that version around to make changes.

Minifying your own code is possible but can lead to numerous errors. Fortunately, several online tools are available to help you. My favorite is Minify CSS's CSS Compressor & Minifier 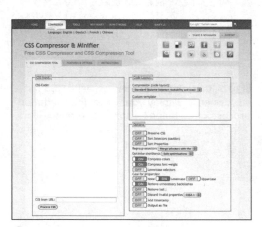.

A The Minify CSS Compressor page at www.minifycss.com/css-compressor.

Code 15.5 My CSS code before being minified.

```
/*** CSS3 VQS | Chapter 10 |
→ box-properties.css ***/

body, header.page, footer.page  {
  margin: 0;
  padding: 0;
}

navigation.global {
  display: block;
}

navigation.global li {
  display: inline;
  margin-right: 10px;
  padding-right: 10px;
}

article {
  width: 65%;
  min-width: 560px;
  max-width: 980px;
  float: left;
  margin: 0 10px;
  -webkit-border-top-right-radius: 20px;
  -moz-border-radius-topright: 20px;
  border-top-right-radius: 20px;
  border-top: 10px transparent solid;
  border-right: 10px transparent solid;
  padding: 80px 50px;
}

figure {
  display: block;
  width: 300px;
  float: left;
  margin: 0 10px 10px 0;
  border: 6px double rgba(142, 137, 129,.5);
  -webkit-border-radius: 5px;
  -moz-border-radius: 5px;
  border-radius: 5px;
}

figcaption {
  display:block;
  padding: 10px;
  border-top: 2px solid rgba(142, 137, 129,.5);
```

code continues on next page

```
  padding: 10px;
}

aside {
  display: block;
  width: 200px;
  height: 400px;
  overflow: auto;
  float: right;
  margin: 0 10px;
  -webkit-border-top-left-radius: 20px;
  -webkit-border-bottom-left-radius: 20px;
  -moz-border-radius: 20px 0 0 20px;
  border-radius: 20px 0 0 20px;
  padding: 25px;
}

footer {
  clear: both;
}

h1 {
  margin: 0 20px 10px 10%;
  padding-top: 10px;
}


article h2 {
  border-top: 2px solid rgba(142, 137, 129,.5);
  padding: 20px 0;
}

article navigation h2 {
  border top: none;
  padding: 0;
}

aside h3 {
  border: 1em double rgb(142, 137, 129);
  -webkit-border-image: url(../_images/
  → border-02.png) 27 round;
  -moz-border-image: url(../_images/border-02
  → .png) 27 round;
  border-image: url(../_images/border-02.png)
  → 27 round;
}

.byline {
  margin: 0 10% 10px 20%;
}
```

To minify your CSS:

1. **Visit Minify CSS.** Once you have finished your CSS code and are ready to go live on the Web, point your browser to www.minifycss.com/css-compressor.

2. **Load your CSS code.** You can either paste it directly into the form field or enter a URL from which to grab the CSS (**Code 15.5**). I pulled this code from Chapter 10.

3. **Choose your options.** Experiment to get the desired effect, but remember that your goal is to reduce your code file size as much as possible. You can also choose whether to output the code for you to copy or as a separate CSS file.

continues on next page

4. Process CSS. Click the Process CSS button under the field where you added your code. After a few seconds, a list of messages will appear showing the invalid properties discovered. Under that is your code to download or copy (**Code 15.6**).

If you are using CSS3, you can expect to see several invalid properties, since the Minifier does not include those yet.

5. TEST, TEST, TEST! Depending on how much you compressed your code, it may have changed a little or a lot. Regardless, it's different and may behave differently. If you encounter problems with the new CSS code, try minifying it again using different settings.

Code 15.6 The same CSS code after being minified.

```
/* CSSTidy 1.3: Wed, 11 Aug 2010 22:03:32
-0500 */.byline{margin:0 10% 10px 20%}
article{-moz-border-radius-topright:20px;-
webkit-border-top-right-radius:20px;border-
right:10px transparent solid;border-top:10px
transparent solid;border-top-right-
radius:20px;float:left;margin:0 10px;max-
width:980px;min-width:560px;padding:80px
50px;width:65%}article h2{border-top:2px solid
rgba(142,137,129,.5);padding:20px 0}article
navigation h2{border-top:none;padding:0}
aside{-moz-border-radius:20px 0 0 20px;-
webkit-border-bottom-left-radius:20px;-webkit-
border-top-left-radius:20px;border-radius:20px
0 0 20px;display:block;float:right;height
:400px;margin:0 10px;overflow:auto;paddi
ng:25px;width:200px}aside h3{-moz-border-
image:url(../_images/border-02.png) 27
round;-webkit-border-image:url(../_images/
border-02.png) 27 round;border:1em double
#8e8981;border-image:url(../_images/border-02.
png) 27 round}body,header.page,footer.
page{margin:0;padding:0}figcaption{border-
top:2px solid rgba(142,137,129,.5);display:bloc
k;padding:10px}figure{-moz-border-radius:5px;-
webkit-border-radius:5px;border:6px double
rgba(142,137,129,.5);border-radius:5px;dis
play:block;float:left;margin:0 10px 10px
0;width:300px}footer{clear:both}h1{margin:0
20px 10px 10%;padding-top:10px}navigation.
global{display:block}navigation.global
li{display:inline;margin-right:10px;padding-
right:10px}
```

32 CSS Best Practices

Throughout the pages of this book, I've offered numerous tips, recommendations, and suggestions. I've tried to follow my own advice in all of the code I'm presenting, but the necessities of creating useful examples had to be balanced against the needs of best practices for coding. So, to clear up any confusion, here are the 32 most important best practices for CSS, along with cross-references showing where you can find additional information.

1. **Always specify units for values except when the value is 0.** It's a simple equation:

   ```
   0px = 0in = 0em = 0cm = 0% =
   → 0mm = 0
   ```

   Zero is always zero, and you don't need to define what kind of 0 it is.

   See "Units Used in This Book" in the Introduction.

2. **Structure first, then presentation.** Some designers want to start designing pages without first placing the HTML structure, but this is like trying to put siding on a house that hasn't been framed yet.

   See "How Does HTML5 Structure Work?" in Chapter 2.

3. **Specify a doctype.** These days, using a DTD should go without saying, but an HTML document without a doctype is like a book without a cover. Not only do you not know what's in it, but the whole thing tends to fall apart.

   See "How Does HTML5 Structure Work?" in Chapter 2.

continues on next page

4. **All styles should be external.** To keep the Web site as easy to change as possible, the final styles should *always* be located in external files and *never* be embedded in the head or inline. Embed or inline styles are acceptable during development but should all be moved into an external style sheet before deployment.

   See "External: Adding Styles to a Web Site" in Chapter 3.

5. **Keep the number of external style sheets to a minimum.** This may seem to contradict the previous statement, but every external style sheet is a call to the Web server, and every call slows down Web page loading. This is true whether you are using `<link>` or `@import`.

   See "External: Adding Styles to a Web Site" in Chapter 3.

6. **Place style links in the `<head>`, never in the `<body>`.** Styles placed in the `<body>` of an HTML document will not be applied to the page until *after* the Web page has displayed, causing the entire document to briefly flash as it rerenders the page with the styles. This is annoying and unattractive.

   See "External: Adding Styles to a Web Site" in Chapter 3.

7. **Use link to add styles to an HTML document and `@import` to add styles to other style sheets.** Older versions of Internet Explorer will load styles in the `<head>` as if they were in the `<body>,` causing the annoying flash as the page rerenders.

   See "External: Adding Styles to a Web Site" in Chapter 3.

8. **Include default styles for HTML elements.** Don't design by default. Use a CSS override to reset some values, but always define the default style for as many HTML elements as you will be using in your designs.

   See "(Re)defining HTML Tags" in Chapter 3.

9. **Use generic class names.** Classes are reused throughout a page, often combined with different elements, and are subject to change. If the name is based on a value, changing the value can make the class name confusing.

   See "Defining Reusable Classes" in Chapter 3.

10. **Use specific ID names.** IDs should be used only once per HTML document, so the name needs to specify what it is or what it's for.

    See "Defining Unique IDs" in Chapter 3.

11. **Add a unique class name or ID to the body tag of every page.** This gives every page its own unique identification, which you can then leverage to style the page separately from other pages.

    You can also add classes for the page's section or other designations that distinguish it in the site. This can help you reduce the number of external style sheets because it allows you to add styles for selective pages all in the same external file.

    See "Defining Reusable Classes" and "Defining Unique IDs" in Chapter 3.

continues on next page

12. Mix and match classes. You can apply multiple classes to a single element simply by placing the class names in the same class property in the tag, separated by spaces. This allows you to combine classes rather than creating new ones to meet a specific need.

See "Defining Reusable Classes" in Chapter 3.

13. Combine rules into selector lists. Elements that have the same CSS properties and values can be combined into a single CSS rule.

See "Defining Elements with the Same Styles" in Chapter 3.

14. Use dynamic styles for form elements, buttons, and other interface elements. Many elements, such as form fields and form buttons, can have multiple dynamic states that can provide visual feedback for hover and also when a button is clicked or a form field is selected. Don't forget to style these too.

See "Working with Pseudo-classes" in Chapter 4.

15. Use @media rules and media queries to tailor the page to the device. Although not available to all browsers, media quarries allow you to distinguish many mobile browsers, such as the iPhone, so that you can deliver a custom experience.

See "Querying the Media" in Chapter 4.

16. Favor specificity over classes and IDs, but only be as specific as necessary. Specificity allows you to selectively style an element *without* explicitly identifying it with a class or ID. Although classes and IDs can be useful, they will often limit the versatility of the page structure. Before adding a new class or ID to an element, see if you can use contextual styles.

On the other hand, don't make styles so specific that they apply only to very specific cases, when they may need to apply more broadly.

See "Getting Specific with Selectors" in Chapter 4.

17. **Avoid !important.** The **!important** value is a blunt weapon. It turns styles on and overrides the cascade order. This also means that it can be very tricky to override. If you do use **!important** during development, try to take it out before your site goes live.

    See "Making a Declaration !important" in Chapter 4.

18. **Avoid unnecessary and repetitive repetition.** Style sheets can quickly become cluttered with redundant properties and values that do not actually change the value of whatever is already set. Remember that once a property value is set, It will cascade down to child elements.

    For example, if you set the font size for the body, you will *never need to set it again* unless a specific element uses a different size. All too often I see the same font size set for element after element. Remember to check whether a style has already been set for a parent element before you set it.

    See "Determining the Cascade Order" in Chapter 4.

19. **Use Relative sizes for font size.** Although it is sometimes easier to use sizes such as pixels, using relative sizes such as ems allows you to scale text sizes on the page uniformly and keep better typographic rhythm.

    See "Setting the Font Size" in Chapter 5.

continues on next page

20. **Prefer shorthand properties.** The shorthand properties, such as **font,** allow you to set multiple values with a single property. This not only cuts down on the amount of code, it also keeps similar property values together, making editing easier.

See "Setting Multiple Font Values" in Chapter 5.

21. **Use RGB for color.** You may see hex color values more often than RGB, but there is no really good reason to use one over the other from a code standpoint. Because RGB values are easier for mere mortals to understand *and* you can now set transparent colors using RGBA, I recommend always using RGB.

See "Choosing Color Values" in Chapter 7.

22. **Use background images or other styles for interface chrome.** The **<img>** tag should be used for images that are content: photographs, figures, or illustrations. Chrome constitutes the visual elements of the interface such as backgrounds, buttons, and other controls.

Instead of using the **<img>** tag to add these, interface chrome should be added using background images. This makes it easier to make changes or to completely rework the design without touching the HTML code.

See "Setting Background Images" in Chapter 7.

23. **Use CSS sprites.** CSS sprites can be used to add images to different dynamic states with only a single file that changes position to reveal each state. CSS sprites are faster to load than multiple images and do not flash as the states change.

See "Using CSS Sprites" in Chapter 14.

24. **Use CSS for simple for background gradients.** Simple gradients are supported in most browsers now and can be used in backgrounds. Rather than slowing things down with images, use CSS gradients.

See "Color Gradients in Backgrounds" in Chapter 7.

25. **Start with a clean slate.** CSS resets allow you to set a level playing field, making it easier to design across multiple browsers.

See "Using CSS Reset" in Chapter 13.

26. **Favor margin over padding.** Due to problems with Internet Explorer and the box model, padding can cause problems with elements that have a defined width or height. If you have a choice, use margin.

See "Adjusting CSS for Internet Explorer" in Chapter 13.

27. **Test your code in Firefox, Chrome, and/or Safari while building, and then fix it for Internet Explorer.** Although IE still has the lion's share of the browser market, it's easiest to build a site to Web standards, and then accommodate for IE's idiosyncrasies rather than the other way around.

See "Adjusting CSS for Internet Explorer" in Chapter 13.

28. **Style all link states.** Many designers will style only the default link state and maybe the hover state. However, you can also style visited and active states, which provide visual feedback to the user when clicking a link.

See "Styling Links Versus Navigation" in Chapter 14.

continues on next page

29. Use comments to keep notes and organize your code, especially for constant values. Notes are helpful for recording notes about your design, especially in color or font values that you will be using consistently throughout your design. Notes can also be used to create section dividers in your code to help organize and make scanning for particular parts easier.

See "Creating Readable Style Sheets" earlier in this chapter.

30. Use specificity to organize your code. Specificity is not just a great idea for styling; you can use it to create an outline-like format for your code, making it easier to scan and find related elements.

See "Creating Readable Style Sheets" earlier in this chapter.

31. Favor `<link>` over `@import`. Although both can be used to bring style sheets into Web documents, tests have shown that most browsers will download linked style sheets faster than imported ones. This is even true if the `@import` is in an external style sheet because the parent external style sheet has to be loaded before its children are considered.

See "Style Sheet Strategies" earlier in this chapter.

32. Minify your CSS before you launch. Mean and lean code leads to faster download speeds, which always make for a better user experience. While you are developing your site, your code should be as readable as possible. But when you launch the site, you can remove all spaces, returns, and notes from your code.

See "Minifying Your CSS" earlier in this chapter.

CSS Quick Reference

Throughout this book, wherever new properties were introduced, I included a table showing the values for that property and the specific browser version in which support first appeared. But for quick reference, all you really care about is "does it work *now*?" or at least "does it work in browsers with major market share?" You also need to know in a hurry what the default value is, which types of elements the property applies to, and whether its child elements will inherit the values. Well, look no further.

The following tables include all of the CSS properties included in this book. However, to make it easier to scan for just those properties that will work, symbols indicate if a value is available for use (or not) by a particular browser:

- ■ **Available**—Supported. Supported in all versions of the browser in common usage.

- ◆ **Recently Available**—Versions of the browser may still be in common use that do not support this value.

- ❍ **Not available**—Not currently supported in any version of this browser.

Browsers legend

IE   Internet Explorer

FF   Firefox

S   Safari

C   Chrome

O   Opera

Table value legend

Applies to All—Property can be applied to any HTML tag.

Applies to Block—Property can be applied only to block-level tags.

Applies to Inline—Property can be applied only to inline tags.

Inherited- Yes—Styles are also applied to descendent elements.

Inherited- No—Styles are also not applied to descendent elements.

Default Value:value—Values in bold are the default values for that property.

What about IE9?

At the time of this writing, IE9 had not yet been released to the public, but was in beta. IE9 promises much wider support of CSS3, but until it is released, it's impossible to know how complete that final support will be. I will publish an update to this table on the book's support Web site (www.speaking-in-styles.com/css3vqs) when it becomes available (**Table A.1**).

TABLE A.1 Basic Selectors

Type	Name	IE	FF	S	C	O
a	HTML	■	■	■	■	■
.class	Class	■	■	■	■	■
#id	ID	■	■	■	■	■
a b	Contextual	■	■	■	■	■
a * b	Universal	◆	■	■	■	■
a > b	Child	◆	■	■	■	■
a + b	Adjacent Sibling	◆	■	■	■	■
a ~ b	General Sibling	◆	■	■	■	■
[ATTR]	Attribute	◆	■	■	■	■

TABLE A.2 Pseudo-Classes

Name	IE	FF	S	C	O
:active	◆	■	■	■	■
:hover	■	■	■	■	■
:focus	◆	■	■	■	■
:link	■	■	■	■	■
:target	○	■	■	■	■
:visited	■	■	■	■	■
:root	○	■	■	■	■
:empty	○	■	■	■	■
:only-child	○	■	■	■	■
:only-of-type	○	■	■	■	■
:first-child	○	■	■	■	■
:nth-child(n)	○	■	■	■	■
:nth-of-type(n)	○	■	■	■	■
:nth-last-of-type(n)	○	■	■	■	■
:last-child	○	■	■	■	■
:first-of-type	○	■	■	■	■
:last-of-type	○	■	■	■	■
:lang()	◆	■	■	■	■
:not(s)	○	■	■	■	■

TABLE A.3 Pseudo-Elements

Name	IE	FF	S	C	O
:first-letter, ::first-letter	■	■	■	■	■
:first-line, ::first-line	■	■	■	■	■
:after, ::after	◆	■	■	■	■
:before, ::before	◆	■	■	■	■

TABLE A.5 Text Properties

Name	Values	Applies To	Inherited	IE	FF	S	C	O
letter-spacing	**normal**	All	Yes	■	■	■	■	■
	<length>			■	■	■	■	■
line-height	**normal**	Block	Yes	■	■	■	■	■
	<length>			■	■	■	■	■
	<percentage>			■	■	■	■	■
	<number>			■	■	■	■	■
text-align	**auto**	Block	Yes	■	■	■	■	■
	left			■	■	■	■	■
	right			■	■	■	■	■
	center			■	■	■	■	■
	justify			■	■	■	■	■
	inherit			■	■	■	■	■
text-decoration	**none**	All	Yes	■	■	■	■	■
	underline			■	■	■	■	■
	overline			■	■	■	■	■
	line-through			■	■	■	■	■
text-indent	**<length>**	Block	Yes	■	■	■	■	■
	<percentage>			■	■	■	■	■
text-shadow	**none**	All	Yes	○	■	■	■	◆
	<color>			○	■	■	■	◆
	<x–offset>			○	■	■	■	◆
	<y–offset>			○	■	■	■	◆
	<blur>			○	■	■	■	◆
text-transform	**none**	All	Yes	■	■	■	■	■
	capitalize			■	■	■	■	■
	uppercase			■	■	■	■	■
	lowercase			■	■	■	■	■
vertical-align	**baseline**	Inline	No	■	■	■	■	■
	super			■	■	■	■	■
	sub			■	■	■	■	■
	<relative>			■	■	■	■	■
	<length>			■	■	■	■	■
	<percentage>			◆	■	■	■	■
white-space	**normal**	All	Yes	■	■	■	■	■
	pre			■	■	■	■	■
	nowrap			■	■	■	■	■
word-spacing	**normal**	All	Yes	■	■	■	■	■
	<length>			■	■	■	■	■

TABLE A.4 Font Properties

Name	Values	Applies To	Inherited	IE	FF	S	C	O
font	<font-style>	All	Yes	■	■	■	■	■
	<font-variant>			■	■	■	■	■
	<font-weight>			■	■	■	■	■
	<font-size>			■	■	■	■	■
	<font-height>			■	■	■	■	■
	<font-family>			■	■	■	■	■
	<visitor styles>			■	■	■	■	■
font-family	<family-name>	All	Yes	■	■	■	■	■
	serif			■	■	■	■	■
	sans-serif			■	■	■	■	■
	cursive			■	■	■	■	■
	fantasy			■	■	■	■	■
	monospace			■	■	■	■	■
font-size	<length>	All	Yes	■	■	■	■	■
	<percentage>			■	■	■	■	■
	smaller			■	■	■	■	■
	larger			■	■	■	■	■
	xx-small			■	■	■	■	■
	x-small			■	■	■	■	■
	small			■	■	■	■	■
	medium			■	■	■	■	■
	large			■	■	■	■	■
	x-large			■	■	■	■	■
	xx-large			■	■	■	■	■
font-size-adjust	none	All	No	○	■	○	○	○
	<number>			○	■	○	○	○
font-style	normal	All	Yes	■	■	■	■	■
	italic			■	■	■	■	■
	oblique			■	■	■	■	■
font-variant	normal	All	Yes	■	■	■	■	■
	small-caps			■	■	■	■	■
font-weight	normal	All	Yes	■	■	■	■	■
	bold			■	■	■	■	■
	lighter			■	■	■	■	■
	bolder			■	■	■	■	■
	100–900			■	■	■	■	■

TABLE A.6 Color and Background Properties

Name	Values	Applies To	Inherited	IE	FF	S	C	O
background-attachment	**scroll**	Block	No	■	■	■	■	■
	fixed			■	■	■	■	■
	local			○	■	■	■	○
background-color	**inherit**	All	No	■	■	■	■	■
	<color>			■	■	■	■	■
background-image	**none**	All	No	■	■	■	■	■
	<url>			■	■	■	■	■
background-position	**top**	All	No	■	■	■	■	■
	left			■	■	■	■	■
	bottom			■	■	■	■	■
	Right			■	■	■	■	■
	<length>			■	■	■	■	■
	<percentage>			■	■	■	■	■
background-repeat	**repeat**	All	No	■	■	■	■	■
	repeat-x			■	■	■	■	■
	repeat-y			■	■	■	■	■
	no-repeat			■	■	■	■	■
	space			○	◆	◆	◆	◆
	round			○	◆	◆	◆	◆
background-size	**auto**	All	No	○	◆	◆	◆	◆
-moz-background-size	<length>			○	◆	◆	◆	◆
-webkit-background-size	<percentage>			○	◆	◆	◆	◆
	cover			○	◆	◆	◆	◆
	contain			○	◆	◆	◆	◆
background-clip	**border-box**	All	No	○	◆	◆	◆	◆
-moz-background-clip	padding-box			○	◆	◆	◆	◆
-webkit-background-clip	padding			○	■	■	■	◆
	border			○	■	■	■	◆
	content			○	◆	◆	◆	◆
background-origin	**border-box**	All	No	○	◆	◆	◆	◆
-moz-background-origin	padding-box			○	◆	◆	◆	◆
-webkit-background-origin	content-box			○	◆	◆	◆	◆
	padding			○	■	◆	◆	◆
	border			○	■	◆	◆	◆
	content			○	◆	◆	◆	◆
color	**inherit**	All	Yes	■	■	■	■	■
	<color>			■	■	■	■	■

TABLE A.7 List Properties

Name	Values	Applies To	Inherited	IE	FF	S	C	O
list-style	<list-style-type>	List	No	■	■	■	■	■
	<list-style-position>			■	■	■	■	■
	<list-style-image>			■	■	■	■	■
list-stye-Image	**none**	List	Yes	■	■	■	■	■
	inherit			◆	■	■	■	■
	<url>			■	■	■	■	■
list-stye-position	**inside**	List	Yes	■	■	■	■	■
	outside			■	■	■	■	■
	inherit			◆	■	■	■	■
list-stye-type	**none**	List	Yes	■	■	■	■	■
	inherit			◆	■	■	■	■
	<bullet-name>			■	■	■	■	■

TABLE A.8 Table Properties

Name	Values	Applies To	Inherited	IE	FF	S	C	O
border-spacing	**<length>**	Table	Yes	■	■	■	■	■
	inherit			■	■	■	■	■
border-collapse	**separate**	Table	Yes	■	■	■	■	■
	collapse			■	■	■	■	■
	inherit			■	■	■	■	■
captlon-side	**top**	Table	Yes	■	■	■	■	■
	bottom			■	■	■	■	■
	inherit			■	■	■	■	■
empty-cells	**show**	Table	Yes	○	■	■	■	■
	hide			○	■	■	■	■
	inherit			○	■	■	■	■
table-layout	**auto**	Table	No	■	■	■	■	■
	fixed			■	■	■	■	■
	inherit			■	■	■	■	■

TABLE A.9 User Interface and Generated Content Properties

Name	Values	Applies To	Inherited	IE	FF	S	C	O
content	**normal**	All	No	◆	■	■	■	■
	none			◆	■	■	■	■
	\<string\>			◆	■	■	■	■
	\<url\>			◆	■	■	■	■
	\<counter\>			◆	■	■	■	■
	attr(\<selector\>)			◆	■	■	■	■
	open-quote			◆	■	■	■	■
	close-quote			◆	■	■	■	■
	no-open-quote			◆	■	■	■	■
	no-close-quote			◆	■	■	■	■
	inherit			◆	■	■	■	■
counter-increment	**none**	All	No	◆	■	■	■	■
	\<counter-name\>			◆	■	■	■	■
	\<num\>			◆	■	■	■	■
	inherit			◆	■	■	■	■
counter-reset	**none**	All	No	◆	■	■	■	■
	\<counter-name\>			◆	■	■	■	■
	\<num\>			◆	■	■	■	■
	inherit			◆	■	■	■	■
cursor	**auto**	All	Yes	■	■	■	■	■
	\<url\>			■	■	■	■	○
	\<cursor-type-name\>			■	■	■	■	■
	none			■	■	■	■	■
quotes	none	All	Yes	◆	■	■	■	■
	\<string\>			◆	■	■	■	■
	inherit			◆	■	■	■	■

TABLE A.10 Box Properties

Name	Values	Applies To	Inherited	IE	FF	S	C	O
border	<border-width>	All	No	■	■	■	■	■
	<border-style>			■	■	■	■	■
	<border-color>			■	■	■	■	■
border-color	**transparent**	All	No	■	■	■	■	■
	<color>			■	■	■	■	■
	inherit			■	■	■	■	■
border-image	**none**	All	No	○	■	■	■	♦
-moz-border-image	<url>			○	■	■	■	♦
-webkit-border-radius<offsetnumber>			○	■	■	■	♦	
	round			○	■	■	■	♦
	repeat			○	■	■	■	♦
	stretch			○	■	■	■	♦
border-radius	<length>	All	No	○	■	■	■	♦
-moz-border-radius *-webkit-border-radius*	<percentage>			○	■	■	■	♦
border-style	**none**	All	No	■	■	■	■	■
	dotted			■	■	■	■	■
	dashed			■	■	■	■	■
	solid			■	■	■	■	■
	double			■	■	■	■	■
	groove			■	■	■	■	■
	ridge			■	■	■	■	■
	inset			■	■	■	■	■
	outset			■	■	■	■	■
	inherit			■	■	■	■	■
border-width	<length>	All	No	■	■	■	■	■
	thin			■	■	■	■	■
	medium			■	■	■	■	■
	thick			■	■	■	■	■
	inherit			■	■	■	■	■
clear	**none**	All	No	■	■	■	■	■
	left			■	■	■	■	■
	right			■	■	■	■	■
	both			■	■	■	■	■
	none			■	■	■	■	■

table continues on next page

TABLE A.10 Box Properties *continued*

Name	Values	Applies To	Inherited	IE	FF	S	C	O
display	**normal**	All	No	■	■	■	■	■
	block			■	■	■	■	■
	inline			■	■	■	■	■
	inline-block			■	■	■	■	■
	run-in			◆	■	■	■	■
	table			◆	■	■	■	■
	table-cell			◆	■	■	■	■
	table-footer-group			◆	■	■	■	■
	table-header-group			◆	■	■	■	■
	table-row			◆	■	■	■	■
	table-row-group			◆	■	■	■	■
	inline-table			◆	■	■	■	■
	none			■	■	■	■	■
	inherit			■	■	■	■	■
float	**none**	All	No	■	■	■	■	■
	left			■	■	■	■	■
	right			■	■	■	■	■
height	**auto**	Block	No	■	■	■	■	■
	<length>			■	■	■	■	■
	<percentage>			■	■	■	■	■
	inherit			■	■	■	■	■
margin	**<length>**	All	No	■	■	■	■	■
	auto			■	■	■	■	■
	<percentage>			■	■	■	■	■
max/min-height	**none**	Block	No	◆	■	■	■	■
	<length>			◆	■	■	■	■
	<percentage>			◆	■	■	■	■
	inherit			◆	■	■	■	■
max/min-width	**none**	Block	No	◆	■	■	■	■
	<length>			◆	■	■	■	■
	<percentage>			◆	■	■	■	■
	inherit			◆	■	■	■	■
outline	**<outline-width>**	All	No	◆	■	■	■	■
	<outline-style>			◆	■	■	■	■
	<outline-color>			◆	■	■	■	■
outline-color	**transparent**	All	No	◆	■	■	■	■
	<color>			◆	■	■	■	■
	inherit			◆	■	■	■	■

table continues on next page

TABLE A.10 Box Properties *continued*

Name	Values	Applies To	Inherited	IE	FF	S	C	O
outline-offset	<length>	All	No	○	■	■	■	■
	inherit			○	■	■	■	■
outline-style	**none**	All	No	◆	■	■	■	■
	dotted			◆	■	■	■	■
	dashed			◆	■	■	■	■
	solid			◆	■	■	■	■
	double			◆	■	■	■	■
	groove			◆	■	■	■	■
	ridge			◆	■	■	■	■
	inset			◆	■	■	■	■
	outset			◆	■	■	■	■
	inherit			◆	■	■	■	■
outline-width	**<length>**	All	No	◆	■	■	■	■
	thin			◆	■	■	■	■
	medium			◆	■	■	■	■
	thick			◆	■	■	■	■
	inherit			◆	■	■	■	■
overflow	**visible**	Block	No	■	■	■	■	■
	hidden			■	■	■	■	■
	scroll			■	■	■	■	■
	auto			■	■	■	■	■
overflow-x/y	**visible**	Block	No	■	■	■	■	■
	hidden			■	■	■	■	■
	scroll			■	■	■	■	■
	auto			■	■	■	■	■
padding	**<length>**	All	No	■	■	■	■	■
	<percentage>			■	■	■	■	■
width	**auto**	Block	No	■	■	■	■	■
	<length>			■	■	■	■	■
	<percentage>			■	■	■	■	■
	inherit			■	■	■	■	■

Name	Values	Applies To	Inherited	IE	FF	S	C	O
bottom	auto	All	No	■	■	■	■	■
	\<percentage\>			■	■	■	■	■
	\<length\>			■	■	■	■	■
	inherit			◆	■	■	■	■
box-shadow	none	All	No	○	◆	◆	◆	◆
-moz-box-shadow	inset			○	◆	◆	◆	◆
-webkit-box-shadow	\<x-offset\>			○	◆	◆	◆	◆
	\<y-offset\>			○	◆	◆	◆	◆
	\<blur\>			○	◆	◆	◆	◆
	\<spread\>			○	◆	◆	◆	◆
	\<color\>			○	◆	◆	◆	◆
clip	auto	Positioned	No	■	■	■	■	■
	rect(\<top\> \<right\> \<bottom\> \<left\>)			■	■	■	■	■
	inherit			■	■	■	■	■
left	auto	Positioned	No	■	■	■	■	■
	\<percentage\>			■	■	■	■	■
	\<length\>			■	■	■	■	■
	inherit			◆	■	■	■	■
opacity	\<alphavalue\>	All	No	○	■	■	■	■
	inherit			○	■	■	■	■
position	static	Positioned	No	■	■	■	■	■
	relative			■	■	■	■	■
	absolute			■	■	■	■	■
	fixed			◆	■	■	■	■
	inherit			◆	■	■	■	■
right	auto	Positioned	No	■	■	■	■	■
	\<percentage\>			■	■	■	■	■
	\<length\>			■	■	■	■	■
	inherit			◆	■	■	■	■
top	auto	Positioned	No	■	■	■	■	■
	\<percentage\>			■	■	■	■	■
	\<length\>			■	■	■	■	■
	inherit			◆	■	■	■	■
visibility	visible	Positioned	Yes	■	■	■	■	■
	hidden			■	■	■	■	■
	collapse			○	■	■	■	■
z-index	auto	Positioned	No	■	■	■	■	■
	\<number\>			■	■	■	■	■
	inherit			■	■	■	■	■

TABLE A.12 Transform Properties (-webkit-, -moz-, -o-)

Name	Values	Applies To	Inherited	IE	FF	S	C	O
backface-visibility	visible	All	No	○	○	◆	◆	○
	hidden			○	○	◆	◆	○
perspective	none	All	No	○	○	◆	◆	○
	<number>			○	○	◆	◆	○
perspective-origin	<percentage>	All.	No	○	○	◆	◆	○
	<length>			○	○	◆	◆	○
	<keyword>			○	○	◆	◆	○
transform	matrix(<angle>)	All	No	○	◆	◆	◆	◆
	matrix3d(<variations×16>)			○	○	◆	◆	○
	perspective(<num>			○	○	◆	◆	○
	rotate(<angle>)			○	◆	◆	◆	◆
	rotateX(<angle>)			○	◆	◆	◆	◆
	rotateY(<angle>)			○	◆	◆	◆	◆
	rotateZ(<angle>)			○	○	◆	◆	○
	rotate3d(<number×3>)			○	○	◆	◆	○
	scale(<num×2>)			○	◆	◆	◆	◆
	scaleX(<num>)			○	◆	◆	◆	◆
	scaleY(<num>)			○	◆	◆	◆	◆
	scaleZ(<length>)			○	○	◆	◆	○
	scale3d(num×3)			○	○	◆	◆	○
	skew(<angle×2>)			○	◆	◆	◆	◆
	skewX(<angle>)			○	◆	◆	◆	◆
	skewY(<angle>)			○	◆	◆	◆	◆
	translate(<length×2>)			○	◆	◆	◆	◆
	translateX(<angle>)			○	◆	◆	◆	◆
	translateY(<angle>)			○	◆	◆	◆	◆
	translateZ(<angle>)			○	○	◆	◆	○
	translate3d(<number×3>)			○	○	◆	◆	○
transform-origin	<percentage>	All	No	○	◆	◆	◆	◆
	<length>			○	◆	◆	◆	◆
	<keyword>			○	◆	◆	◆	◆
transform-style	flat	All	No	○	○	◆	◆	○
	preserve-3d			○	○	◆	◆	○

TABLE A.13 Transition Properties (-webkit-, -moz-, -o-)

Name	Values	Applies To	Inherited	IE	FF	S	C	O
transition	<transition-property>	All	No	○	◆	◆	◆	◆
	<transition-duration>			○	◆	◆	◆	◆
	<transition-delay>			○	◆	◆	◆	◆
transition-delay	**<time>**	All	No	○	◆	◆	◆	◆
transition-duration	**<time>**	All	No	○	◆	◆	◆	◆
transition-property	**none**	All	No	○	◆	◆	◆	◆
	<CSSProperty>			○	◆	◆	◆	◆
	all			○	◆	◆	◆	◆
transition-timing-function	**linear**	All	No	○	◆	◆	◆	◆
	ease			○	◆	◆	◆	◆
	ease-in			○	◆	◆	◆	◆
	ease-out			○	◆	◆	◆	◆
	ease-in-out			○	◆	◆	◆	◆
	cubic-bezier(<number×4>,)			○	◆	◆	◆	◆

HTML and UTF Character Encoding

In Chapter 5, you explored using special HTML- and UTF-encoded characters. These are generally harder to find on your keyboard or may not be included in a particular font you are using. To ensure that they are properly represented, you should use the code presented in this appendix when adding the characters to your Web document.

TABLE A.1 HTML and UTF Character Encoding

HTML	Unicode	Glyph	Description
‘		'	left single quote
’		'	right single quote
&sbquo		,	single low-9 quote
“		"	left double quote
”		"	right double quote
„		„	double low-9 quote
†		†	dagger
‡		‡	double dagger
‰		‰	per mill sign
‹		‹	single left-pointing angle quote
›		›	single right-pointing angle quote
♠		♠	black spade suit
♣		♣	black club suit
♥		♥	black heart suit
♦		♦	black diamond suit
‾		‾	overline
←		←	left arrow
↑		↑	up arrow
→		→	right arrow
↓		↓	down arrow
™		™	trademark sign
				horizontal tab

	
		line feed

	 		space
	!	!	exclamation mark
"	"	"	double quotation mark
	#	#	number sign
	$	$	dollar sign
	%	%	percent sign
&	&	&	ampersand
	'	'	apostrophe
	(	(	left parenthesis
	)	)	right parenthesis

table continues on next page

HTML	Unicode	Glyph	Description
	&#42;	*	asterisk
	&#43;	+	plus sign
	&#44;	,	comma
	&#45;	-	hyphen
	&#46;	.	period
&frasl;	&#47;	/	slash
	0 – 9	0–9	digits 0–9
	&#58;	:	colon
	&#59;	;	semicolon
&lt;	&#60;	<	less-than sign
	&#61;	=	equals sign
&gt;	&#62;	>	greater-than sign
	&#63;	?	question mark
	&#64;	@	at sign
	A – Z	A–Z	uppercase letters A–Z
	&#91;	[	left bracket
	&#92;	\	backslash
	&#93;	]	right bracket
	&#94;	^	caret
	&#95;	_	underscore
	&#96;	`	grave accent
	a – z	a-z	lowercase letters a–z
	&#123;	{	left curly bracket
	|			vertical bar
	&#125;	}	right curly bracket
	&#126;	~	tilde
&ndash;	&#150;	–	en dash
&mdash;	&#151;	—	em dash
			nonbreaking space
&iexcl;	&#161;	¡	inverted exclamation
&cent;	&#162;	¢	cent sign
&pound;	&#163;	£	pound sterling
&curren;	&#164;	¤	general currency sign

table continues on next page

TABLE A.1 HTML and UTF Character Encoding *continued*

HTML	Unicode	Glyph	Description
&yen;	&#165;	¥	yen sign
&brkbar;	&#166;	¦	broken vertical bar
&sect;	&#167;	§	section sign
&uml;	&#168;	¨	umlaut
&copy;	&#169;	©	copyright
&ordf;	&#170;	ª	feminine ordinal
&laquo;	&#171;	«	left angle quote
&not;	&#172;	¬	not sign
&shy;	&#173;		soft hyphen
&reg;	&#174;	®	registered trademark
&macr;	&#175;	¯	macron accent
&deg;	&#176;	°	degree sign
&plusmn;	&#177;	±	plus or minus
&sup2;	&#178;	²	superscript two
&sup3;	&#179;	³	superscript three
&acute;	&#180;	´	acute accent
&micro;	&#181;	µ	micro sign
&para;	&#182;	¶	paragraph sign
&middot;	&#183;	·	middle dot
&cedil;	&#184;	¸	cedilla
&sup1;	&#185;	¹	superscript one
&ordm;	&#186;	º	masculine ordinal
&raquo;	&#187;	»	right angle quote
&frac14;	&#188;	¼	one-fourth
&frac12;	&#189;	½	one-half
&frac34;	&#190;	¾	three-fourths
&iquest;	&#191;	¿	inverted question mark
&Agrave;	&#192;	À	uppercase A, grave accent
&Aacute;	&#193;	Á	uppercase A, acute accent
&Acirc;	&#194;	Â	uppercase A, circumflex accent
&Atilde;	&#195;	Ã	uppercase A, tilde
&Auml;	&#196;	Ä	uppercase A, umlaut
&Aring;	&#197;	Å	uppercase A, ring

table continues on next page

HTML	Unicode	Glyph	Description
&AElig;	&#198;	Æ	uppercase AE
&Ccedil;	&#199;	Ç	uppercase C, cedilla
&Egrave;	&#200;	È	uppercase E, grave accent
&Eacute;	&#201;	É	uppercase E, acute accent
&Ecirc;	&#202;	Ê	uppercase E, circumflex accent
&Euml;	&#203;	Ë	uppercase E, umlaut
&Igrave;	&#204;	Ì	uppercase I, grave accent
&Iacute;	&#205;	Í	uppercase I, acute accent
&Icirc;	&#206;	Î	uppercase I, circumflex accent
&Iuml;	&#207;	Ï	uppercase I, umlaut
&ETH;	&#208;	Ð	uppercase Eth, Icelandic
&Ntilde;	&#209;	Ñ	uppercase N, tilde
&Ograve;	&#210;	Ò	uppercase O, grave accent
&Oacute;	&#211;	Ó	uppercase O, acute accent
&Ocirc;	&#212;	Ô	uppercase O, circumflex accent
&Otilde;	&#213;	Õ	uppercase O, tilde
&Ouml;	&#214;	Ö	uppercase O, umlaut
&times;	&#215;	×	multiplication sign
&Oslash;	&#216;	Ø	uppercase O, slash
&Ugrave;	&#217;	Ù	uppercase U, grave accent
&Uacute;	&#218;	Ú	uppercase U, acute accent
&Ucirc;	&#219;	Û	uppercase U, circumflex accent
&Uuml;	&#220;	Ü	uppercase U, umlaut
&Yacute;	&#221;	Ý	uppercase Y, acute accent
&THORN;	&#222;	Þ	uppercase THORN, Icelandic
&szlig;	&#223;	ß	lowercase sharps, German
&agrave;	&#224;	à	lowercase a, grave accent
&aacute;	&#225;	á	lowercase a, acute accent
&acirc;	&#226;	â	lowercase a, circumflex accent
&atilde;	&#227;	ã	lowercase a, tilde
&auml;	&#228;	ä	lowercase a, umlaut
&aring;	&#229;	å	lowercase a, ring
&aelig;	&#230;	æ	lowercase ae

table continues on next page

HTML	Unicode	Glyph	Description
ç	ç	ç	lowercase c, cedilla
è	è	è	lowercase e, grave accent
é	é	é	lowercase e, acute accent
ê	ê	ê	lowercase e, circumflex accent
ë	ë	ë	lowercase e, umlaut
ì	ì	ì	lowercase i, grave accent
í	í	í	lowercase i, acute accent
î	î	î	lowercase i, circumflex accent
ï	ï	ï	lowercase i, umlaut
ð	ð	ð	lowercase eth, Icelandic
ñ	ñ	ñ	lowercase n, tilde
ò	ò	ò	lowercase o, grave accent
ó	ó	ó	lowercase o, acute accent
ô	ô	ô	lowercase o, circumflex accent
õ	õ	õ	lowercase o, tilde
ö	ö	ö	lowercase o, umlaut
÷	÷	÷	division sign
ø	ø	ø	lowercase o, slash
ù	ù	ù	lowercase u, grave accent
ú	ú	ú	lowercase u, acute accent
û	û	û	lowercase u, circumflex accent
ü	ü	ü	lowercase u, umlaut
ý	ý	ý	lowercase y, acute accent
þ	þ	þ	lowercase thorn, Icelandic
ÿ	ÿ	ÿ	lowercase y, umlaut

Index

Symbols

: (colon)
    CSS tips, 37
    pseudo-element syntax, 95
. (period), defining classes, 51, 54
; (semicolon)
    character entities and, 123
    troubleshooting CSS code, 373
'...' (single quotes)
    CSS tips, 37
    specifying style, 238–239
/ (slash), adding comments to CSS, 66–67
, (comma), for grouping selectors, 62
"..." (double quotes)
    adding generated content, 235
    CSS tips, 37
    specifying style, 238–240
:: (double colon), pseudo-element syntax, 95
= (equals sign), CSS tips, 37
(pound), defining ID selectors, 55
& (ampersand), as character entity, 123
* (asterisk)
    adding comments to CSS, 66–67
    defining universal selectors, 59
    styling descendants, 71
[ ] (square brackets), in attribute selector
    syntax, 96
{ } (curly brackets)
    in declarations, 48
    troubleshooting CSS code, 373
~ (tilde sign), defining general sibling selectors,
    78
> (close angle bracket), styling children, 74

Numbers

2D transformations, 308–311
3D
    stacking objects in, 292–293
    transformations, 311–315

A

absolute font sizes, 135
absolute positioning
    defined, 286
    setting, 288
    tip, 289
accessibility
    access keys for, 350
    color and, 195
    counter-reset and, 237
accesskey attribute, 350
:active
    defined, 82
    setting contrasting appearances with,
        84–85
    styling for interaction, 86–87
adjacent sibling elements
    defined, 70
    styling based on context, 76–77
:after
    counters, 237
    defined, 94
    defining generated content, 234
Aggregate method, as style sheet strategy,
    370–371
alignment
    floating elements and, 258–259
    horizontal text, 162–163
    vertical text, 164–166, 339

external CSS
adding to Web site, 41–47
always locating final styles in external files, 386
keeping number of external style sheets to minimum, 386

F

fantasy fonts, 122
figures (`<figure>`), 26
file formats, downloadable Webfonts and, 127–128
file size, style sheet strategies and, 368
files, creating external CSS, 41–47
filter
opacity, 298
radial gradient, 187
Firebug
debugging CSS code in Firefox, 377–378
tools for analyzing/editing code, 376
Firefox
color gradients, 188
CSS extension, 12
CSS support, 324
sizing elements, 253
testing code in, 391
tools for analyzing/editing code, 376
using Firebug add-on, 377
W3C box standard, 334
:first-child, 88–89
:first-letter, 92–93
:first-line, 92–93
:first-of-type, 88–89
fixed, table layout, 220–221
fixed backgrounds, 211
fixed positioning
defined, 287
setting, 288
tip, 289
floating elements (**float**)
box properties and, 257–259
break tag clear fix, 340–341
creating multicolumn layout, 346–349
CSS fixes for, 340

overflow fix, 342
overview, 257–259
:focus, styling for interaction, 86–87
font families
defining fonts for Web, 129
defining multiple font values, 147
generic, 120–122
overview, 119
setting font stack, 124–125
font properties
adjusting size for understudy fonts, 136–138
bolding, 142–143
finding fonts, 126–130
Font Squirrel, 131
italicizing, 139–141
multiple values, 146–149
overview, 117–118
putting it all together, 150
setting font stack, 124–125
setting size, 133–135
small caps, 144–145
typography on Web, 119–123
Webfont, 132
Font Squirrel, 131
@font-face, 128, 364
fonts
creating glossary of fonts used, 362–363
new in CSS3, 14
quoting names, 37
relative sizing, 389
font-size
defining multiple font values, 148
scientific notation, 166
setting, 133–135
font-size-adjust, 136–138
font-stretch, 139
font-style, 139–141, 146, 148
font-variant, 144–146, 148
font-weight, 142–143, 146, 148
footers (`<footer>`)
overview, 26
using HTML5 structure, 29

formats
  custom pointer, 233
  font difficulties, 131
  font file, 127–128
  pseudo-classes, 81
  visual properties. *See* visual formatting
    properties
forms
  color palette options for, 193
  dynamic styles for, 388
frame tags, in HTML5, 25
frameworks, CSS Frameworks, 367
from, Webkit gradient value, 190

G

generated content
  CSS for, 234–235
  putting it all together, 240
generic font families
  overview, 120–122
  setting font stack, 125
glyph, 119
gradients
  in backgrounds, 187–190, 391
  color values, 184
graphics
  adding mouse pointer, 233
  as bullets, 217
  styling for print, 108
grids, multicolumn layout, 346
grouping, elements using same styles, 62–65

H

hacks, 325
hanging-punctuation, 176
head (**<head>**)
  overview of, 17
  placing style links in, 386
  using HTML5 structure, 28
header (**<header>**)
  choosing color palette, 193
  defined, 17
  overview of, 26
  using HTML5 structure, 28

height
  adjusting line, 156–157
  box properties, 246–247
  height property, 100
  setting element, 251–253
  window and document, 283–284
hex color values
  color keywords, 185–187
  defined, 181–182
  vs. decimal color values, 184
hiding
  cursor, 232
  elements, 250–251, 294–295
  empty table cells, 225
  overflow, 255
hierarchy, organizing based on CSS rules, 366
horizontal alignment, of text, 162–163
:hover
  overview of, 82
  setting contrasting appearances with, 84–87
HSL values, 183–184
HTML (HyperText Markup Language)
  box properties. *See* box properties
  character entities, 123
  class attributes added to, 54
  CSS and, 8
  defined, 16–18
  id added to, 56
  inline styles added to, 35–37
  redefining tags, 48–50
  text control, 119
HTML selectors
  basics, 34
  defining, 48–50
  overview of, 9
HTML5
  applying structure, 27–31
  basic HTML defined, 16–18
  elements, 19–21
  evolution of, 22–24
  new in, 25
  overview, 15
  putting it all together, 32
  structure, 26

hue, 183
hypertext links. *See* links

I

icon:, mimicking visitor styles, 149
ID selectors
  basics, 34
  defining, 55–56
  overview of, 10
  styling with pseudo-classes, 85
  troubleshooting CSS code, 373
IDs
  defining unique, 55–58, 387
  rules, 10
iframes, 283
image rollovers, added to Web pages,
    354–356
images
  custom pointer, 233
  resizing, 253
  setting background, 200–207, 209–210
  setting border, 271–273
  using as bullets, 217
@import
  Aggregate method and, 370
  Dynamic method and, 371
  favoring **<link>** over, 392
  importing external CSS files, 46
  placing at top of CSS, 364
!important
  adding to declarations, 375
  cascade order of, 114
  making declarations, 111–112
  removing before site goes live, 389
importing
  CSS files, 42
  external CSS files, 46
  external CSS to Web pages, 43
  style sheet strategies and, 368
indentation, text paragraphs, 167–168
inheritance
  anchor link styles, 85
  bullet positioning, 218
  cascade order and, 115

element display, 250
element opacity, 299
element visibility, 294
generated content and, 235
position type, 288–289
of properties from parent, 109–110
setting space between table cells, 222
inline elements
  displaying, 248
  HTML selectors for, 19–20
inline styles
  adding to HTML tag, 35–37
  cascade order of, 114
inline-block, 250
insetting element shadow, 301
inside, bullet positioning, 218
interface chrome, background images or styles
    for, 390
interface elements, dynamic styles for, 388
Internet Explorer (IE)
  box model and, 247
  child sibling support, 78
  color gradients, 187
  CSS extensions, 12
  CSS3 support in IE 9, 14, 324
  element opacity settings, 298–299
  fixing code in, after testing in other
      browsers, 391
  HTML5 in, 30–31
  pseudo-element syntax support, 95
  universal selector support, 59
Internet Explorer (IE), CSS fixes for
  correcting box model in IE6, 333–334
  overview, 324
  setting up conditional styles in IE, 328–332
  underscore hack, 325–327
introduction section, adding at top of CSS, 362
iPhone, styles tailored for, 103–105
ISO 8859-1 character set, 120
italics
  fonts, 139–141
  link styles and, 352

opacity
color, 184
element settings, 298–299
new in CSS3, 14
OpenType fonts (OTF), 127, 130
Opera
CSS extension, 12
CSS support, 324
W3C box standard, 334
operating system, troubleshooting code on different, 375
order, determining cascade, 113–115
organization scheme, choosing consistent pattern for CSS, 365
orientation, 102
origin, setting background image, 200, 207
OTF (OpenType fonts), 127, 130
outline-offset, 264
outlines
adding color with, 184
box properties, 247
CSS resets for, 339
setting element, 263–264
text, 175
outside, bullet positioning, 218
overflow
controlling element, 254–256
fix for floating elements, 342
tip, 253
overlapping text, 260
overline, 172

P

padding
box properties, 246, 274–275
clipping element, 297
CSS resets for, 339
favoring margins over, 391
setting **background-clip**, 206
setting **background-origin**, 207
page breaks, styling for print, 108
page structure, organization based on, 365

palette, color, 190–195
Color Palette Generator, 195
overview of, 190–192
selecting, 192–194
paragraphs
indentation, 167–168
links, 352
parent elements
box properties, 245
defining styles based on context, 71–79
determining cascade order, 115
floating, 258
inheriting properties from, 109–110
overview of, 70
pasting, converting quotes when, 37
percentage values
background position settings, 205
color settings, 183
period (.), defining classes, 51, 54
perspective, 3D transformations, 312, 314
perspective-origin, 3D transformations, 313
point
Mozilla gradient, 188
overview of, 135
position
Mozilla gradient value, 188
setting background image, 200, 204–205
positioning
background images, 200, 204–205, 210–211
bullets, 218
captions in table, 226
elements, 290–291
objects in 3D, 292–293
type, 285–289
pound (#), defining ID selectors, 55
pre white-space, 169–170
preceding sibling elements, 70
prefixes, browser, 12
presentation, focusing on structure prior to presentation, 385
presentation tags, in HTML5, 25
Presto, CSS extension, 12
primary fonts, 124

SGML (Standard Generalized Markup Language), 17

shadows
    adding to text, 160–161
    visual formatting properties, 300–301

shape, Mozilla gradient value, 188

shorthand
    background, 208–211
    properties, 390
    setting multiple list styles, 219

sibling elements
    defined, 70
    opacity of, 299
    styling based on context, 76–79

single quotes (' ')
    CSS tips, 37
    specifying style, 238–239

size
    Mozilla gradient value, 189
    setting background image, 200, 205

sizing
    adjusting understudy fonts, 136–138
    background images, 200, 205
    boxes, 276
    choosing fonts with similar size, 125
    defining multiple font values, 147–148
    setting elements, 252–253
    setting fonts, 133–135

skew(), 2D transformations, 310

slash (/), adding comments to CSS, 66–67

small caps, 144–145

small-caption:, mimicking visitor styles, 149

spacing
    between cells, 222
    text, 153–157

<span> tags, creating HTML tags, 54

specificity
    best practices for, 388–389
    determining cascade order, 115
    organization of code and, 392

spread, setting element shadow, 301

sprite technique
    best practices for, 390
    overview of, 354

square brackets ([ ]), in attribute selector syntax, 96

stack, font, 124–125

stacking objects in 3D, 292–293

stacking order, setting positioning type, 285

Standard Generalized Markup Language (SGML), 17

standards, evolution of CSS and, 6–7

Standards mode, CSS support and, 324

start point, Webkit gradient value, 189

states
    pseudo-class, 80
    transitions between element, 316–320

static positioning, 285, 288

status-bar:, mimicking visitor styles, 149

stop
    Mozilla gradient value, 189
    Webkit gradient value, 190

strategies, style sheet
    Aggregate method, 370–371
    Divide and Conquer method, 369–370
    Dynamic method, 371
    One For All method, 368–369
    overview, 368

stretch, to fill borders, 273

stretching fonts, 139

stretching images, 271–273

Strict mode, CSS support and, 324

strings, defining styles based on attributes, 97–99

structural pseudo-classes, 80–81

structure
    applying HTML5 now, 27–31
    focusing on structure prior to presentation, 385
    HTML, 16–17
    HTML5, 25–26

style sheets
    Aggregate method, 370–371
    best practices, 385–392
    comments in, 66–67
    creating minified version of CSS code, 382–384
    creating readable, 362–366
    CSS Libraries and Frameworks and, 367